Law and Liability in Athletics, Physical Education, and Recreation

Law and Liability in Athletics, Physical Education, and Recreation

James A. Baley

Jersey City State College

David L. Matthews

Matthews-Petsche-Zych & Associates

Allyn and Bacon, Inc.

Boston   London   Sydney   Toronto

Library of Congress Cataloging in Publication Data

Baley, James A.
  Law and liability in athletics, physical education, and
recreation.

  Includes index.
  1. Liability for sports accidents—United States.
I. Matthews, David L.   II. Title.
KF1290.S66B36   1984   346.7303'22   83-22492
ISBN 0-205-08115-0   347.306322

Printed in the United States of America.

10 9 8 7 6 5 4 3 2 1   89 88 87 86 85 84

Contents

/ 3 /   **Limitations on Liability Immunity   41**

/ 4 / Legal Duties and Responsibilities 53

/ 5 / Administrative Procedures for Avoiding Lawsuits 77

/ 12 / Alternatives to Litigation   295

Foreword

The legal profession has become deeply involved with the entire world of the physical educator, athletic coach, supervisor, and sports administrator. Sports have experienced a litigation explosion very much in keeping with what has happened to society in general, and major sports have seen significant rule changes as a result of successful litigation. At every level of competition from the youngest Pee Wee leagues to the most sophisticated professional sports, boys and girls, men and women, are deeply absorbed in sports. The potential is ever present for bodily injury and perhaps death. Physical educators, coaches and administrators must be aware of their legal responsibilities and immunities.

Law and Liability in Athletics, Physical Education, and Recreation is one of the most comprehensive, most explicit, most understandable books on this subject available. It should be placed on the bookshelf of every professional in the fields related to physical activity.

Sports medicine has been instrumental in addressing sports injuries and pressing for new methods of treatments. New machines such as the PERT scans, CAT scans, ultrasound, arthroscopy, centesis methods and imaging techniques are now able to obtain specific information and definite locations of injuries. Many attorneys will take a sports medicine course at a nearby university when retained for a large lawsuit or will retain a personal medical adviser in that particular area of expertise. Physical educators and coaches need to be well versed in backgrounds related to their profession, such as electromyographical analysis, computer printouts, and drugs. As attorneys become more involved with expertise in sports and athletics, the juries they select also will be better educated.

Although the defendant's lawyer has presented a good defense and has been thorough in background evidence, the jury members are bound to be empathetic when the plaintiff appears in the courtroom with an obvious permanent injury. The best defense is preventive in nature.

This book has been carefully prepared so that there is a balance of physical education background, coaching techniques, supervision suggestions, safety rules and guidelines, and necessary skill development along with a discussion of the ethical aspects of play. The content is written from a philosophical viewpoint completely congruent with a wholistic foundation with which we are all familiar. The content is followed by a thorough citing of relevant legal cases that further explain and present the legal issues and judgments rendered.

The section on how violence violates the very essence of play and how it is related to the value systems of today's society is extremely well done. Chapter 8 could stand alone as a separate text, for it reviews every sport from a legal preventive viewpoint as safety features are presented. Testing programs are reviewed to illustrate "proximate cause" procedures. The use of anabolic steroids is examined, and the most recent research data are listed. Special issues and problems deal with sensitive areas related to deviant sexual behaviors, shoplifting, and drug involvement and are treated with the experienced understanding of a caring physical educator with full collaboration of a competent attorney. The authors present context from a well-documented history of research.

Today, all segments of society are demanding their rights. Consumerism as a trend is here to stay, and with the expanded interpretation of the 14th Amendment of the Constitution, all persons are more aware of the legal rights they can employ. Student rights and the rights of athletes will be protected via the courts when there is evidence of negligence on the part of supervisors. With the pressure to win and with technology in the field of coaching improving, there may be even more areas for negligence to be charged. As older people remain physically active and leisure becomes more abundant, we need to become more knowledgeable about responsible supervision and guidelines that will help all physical activity to become safe and free of legal liability. Hopefully the knowledge gained from this very well-documented text will prepare more careful, caring, protected professionals.

Dr. Fay R. Biles
Professor, Kent State University
Former President, American
Alliance for Health, Physical
Education, Recreation and
Dance and USOC Education Council

Preface

This book was necessary for two reasons. The first is the increased incidence of lawsuits to compensate students and others injured as a result of the negligence of those working in athletics, physical education, and recreation. This situation has made it mandatory that workers in these areas fully understand their responsibilities for the prevention of injuries, and that they understand how to protect themselves from charges of negligence.

The second reason for writing this book is that attorneys for both the plaintiff and the defendant need a concise and ready reference to determine whether liability is present in a case, as well as to determine the degree of liability.

One of the coauthors is a practicing attorney, with many years of experience in tort law, and a past president of the Indiana Tort Lawyers Association. His writing will be most helpful to those involved in the teaching, coaching, and administration of sports programs, as well as to owners/operators of ski resorts, health clubs, camps, or related enterprises. The experience he brings to this text will, of course, also be helpful to other attorneys.

The other coauthor has had almost forty years of experience in teaching, coaching, and administering a great variety of sports programs and teacher preparation courses, including courses in sports safety and injury prevention. His writing will be most helpful to attorneys, who will gain a ready reference to determine whether safety standards have been met for a variety of activities. This will save many hours of research, making it unnecessary to peruse textbooks on specific sports or recreational activities.

Safety standards for a large number of sports and other activities, from the standpoints of equipment, facilities, teaching and coaching methods, and administration, are presented. This information will be helpful to those involved in such teaching, coaching, and administration because if there are no injuries, tort liability cannot result.

In addition to covering tort law and procedures to decrease the incidence of injuries, the authors discuss other topics of concern, such as student and faculty rights, mainstreaming of special students, Title IX and women's rights, sports violence, product liability, and transportation of students and athletic teams. The authors feel that the book thus covers the field of law and liability in athletics, physical education, and recreation in a practical and thorough manner.

The guiding purpose behind the book was neither to entertain nor to recite a litany of relevant cases. Rather, the authors have endeavored to present practical and useful information in order to decrease the probability of lawsuits. Rather than proceeding from cases to vague principles, the authors present cases to illustrate principles and legal procedures.

The book was written primarily for the layman and is therefore presented in layman's language. Consequently, it should be an appropriate text for undergraduate and graduate courses in law and liability in athletics, physical education, and recreation. Colleges and universities offering a major in physical education and recreation must now offer such courses, in view of the rising incidence of lawsuits brought against coaches, physical educators, and administrators of these programs.

ACKNOWLEDGMENTS

Jim Baley

First I must acknowledge the efforts of my wife of thirty-eight years, who not only typed several drafts of the manuscript, but who also served as a sounding board and who provided many helpful ideas and suggestions. Without her help, this book would never have been completed.

I must also acknowledge the research efforts and other work of the AAHPERD, the ACSM, and the NATA, who do much of the hard "spade work" to make books like this one possible.

Both Dave and I are also greatly indebted to Catherine Matthews Rohrs, Dave's daughter, who is also an attorney now, for her untiring research efforts and insightful suggestions.

Dave Matthews

I wish to acknowledge and express appreciation for the assistance of the editorial staff of the Association of Trial Lawyers of America, especially Mary Frances Edwards, Esq., Manager, Educational Resources.

Further debts are owed to the publishing staffs of various sources that proved to be of special value, including:

The Association of Trial Lawyers of America, publishers of *Trial Magazine*, vol. 14, no. 6 (1978); vol. 16, nos. 3 and 8 (1980); and a transcript of proceedings entitled "How to Recognize and Handle Recreational Liability Cases: Sports-Torts."

The Practicing Law Institute, publishers of the *Sports Injury Litigation, Litigation, and Administrative Practice Series.*

The Defense Research Institute, publishers of *For the Defense,* vol. 22, no. 3 (1980).

The authors wish to express special appreciation to John Murphy of the Murphy Insurance Agency, Orland Park, Illinois, for his contributions to the chapter on insurance.

/ 1 /

The Incidence and Rationale for Lawsuits

The probability that a coach, physical educator, recreation director or athletic director will be the defendant in a sports-related lawsuit has increased manyfold in the last ten years. The same is also true for the operator of a camp, ski resort, racquet club, health spa or swimming pool. There are a number of reasons for this increase in lawsuits. Interest in sports participation has been stimulated through televising sports contests. Increased leisure time has allowed more people to participate in sports. There has been a phenomenal increase in participation in sports by females. Also, the promotional efforts of the President's Physical Fitness Council and the teaching of lifetime sports in schools and colleges has resulted in more people, male and female, continuing their participation in sports after graduation. Given this increased participation in sports, it is not surprising that there is also an increased number of lawsuits. There would be an inevitable increase even if the injury rate remained the same and the same percentage of injured persons initiated a lawsuit.

In fact, the percentage of injured persons who initiate lawsuits has increased for several reasons. Small claims courts have improved the availability of legal services to people with median incomes. There is a greater number of attorneys who will take cases on a contingency basis, where the attorney is only paid for expenses until after he/she wins the case. Also, the switch from contributory to comparative negligence in most states has increased the probability of a plaintiff receiving an award in court.

There are still other reasons for the increased incidence of sports-related lawsuits. The growth of consumerism and changed laws permitting individuals to sue the state or its employees has resulted in more cases. Lawsuits by one player against another in which there is a charge of use of excessive violence are beginning to be initiated. This is related to the greater value now put on individual rights. Manufacturers today are being sued for defects in cars, helmets, home appliances, skis, and trampolines when these defects contribute to injuries.

None of these trends is likely to be reversed. Therefore, the best way to reduce the incidence of lawsuits is to decrease the incidence of injuries. Where there is no injury there is unlikely to be reason for a lawsuit.

The incidence and rationale for sports-related lawsuits, and the way such lawsuits may be decreased, is the subject of this chapter.

THE INCREASE IN LAWSUITS

A chubby, fourteen-year old girl with blond hair attempts a rope climb as part of her gym class. Suddenly she falls to the floor. All activities stop; all eyes are upon her. As a result of this accident, a lawsuit is filed against the teacher for negligent supervision.

Such lawsuits are becoming all too commonplace in schools and courts today. In 1976, there were an estimated 16,767 trampoline-related accidents, 384,502 football-related accidents, 355,898 baseball-related accidents, 343,973 basketball-related accidents, and 447,279 bicycle-related accidents. Not all of these accidents resulted in lawsuits. But if there were not so many sports-related accidents, there would be far fewer lawsuits. What is the rationale for sports-related lawsuits? Why is the number of such lawsuits increasing? There are a number of reasons to consider.

Increased Leisure

With the advent of the four-day work week and an increased amount of leisure time, the number of people and the frequency of their participation in sports are increasing. With this greater exposure, the possibility of injury, and an ensuing lawsuit, also increases. Moreover, leisure time activities are taught to children at an earlier age than ever before. This creates special hazards, of which coaches, teachers, and operators are expected to be aware. It is their job to foresee these hazards, to minimize them, and to prevent thoughtless children and adults from exposing themselves to danger. Still, with more people participating in sports, the number injured is almost certain to grow. And the more people injured, the greater the number of lawsuits, assuming the proportion of those injured who initiate suits remains constant.

The Female Sports Boom

Girls and women are becoming more and more involved in athletic activities. With greater numbers of females present on the fields and in the gymnasiums, new situations arise that coaches, teachers, owners, or operators may be unprepared to meet. Consider, for example, the different teaching techniques employed in men's versus women's gymnastics. Since there are anatomic and physiologic differences between men and women, not only are new techniques required, but new equipment must be utilized.

Television

With television exposure to the Olympics and other athletic events, more and more people are encouraged to participate in sports such as soccer, track, gymnastics, etc. There is a much greater awareness on the part of teachers and operators, as well as on the part of the consuming public (students, parents, and users) of the safe and proper way for these sports to be played.

Lifetime Sports

Teachers are being asked to teach "lifetime" sports, such as tennis, bowling, backpacking, skiing, mountain climbing, and horseback riding, in place of the usual calisthenics and basketball of years past. As a result, teachers must instruct and supervise athletic activities in which they are not prepared, or of which they have a limited knowledge.

With sports fast becoming a key feature of our leisure society, there will be a greater demand for the services of trained professionals. Physical education has finally become an accepted discipline. With highly educated athletic personnel, we will see an increased amount of research in the field of physical education. This will result in a greater awareness of the causes of injury and of their long-term effects.

Legal Negligence

Legal negligence is based upon foreseeability. With increased awareness, there is greater foreseeability of possible injury, which will result in a greater duty on the part of the professional to prevent injury. With greater awareness, what was once regarded as reasonable is no longer adequate and may now be termed negligent by a court of law.

As an example, consider swimming and its related activities. No longer are these activities limited to the summer months. All sorts of new facilities, heaters, solar blankets, etc., now make water sports year-round activities. With regard to these sports, cases involving infection have been few and far between. The tenuous causal relationship between a lack of disinfection and the transmittal of disease rarely is shown successfully. With increased research, however, it will be easier to show the necessary causal relationship.

The increase in the volume of athletics and the variety of new athletic activities have created greater exposure to the risk of injury and, therefore, to the risk of being sued.

The consuming public is more sophisticated today than during our parents' time. Whereas children used to play in the sandlot with no supervision, they are now playing in neighborhood playgrounds and are involved in organized contests. Little League and Pop Warner baseball have replaced the vacant lot game. In other words, we have institutionalized sports. Further, we have developed health spas, indoor tennis and handball courts, ski areas, etc.

With this sophistication has come a greater awareness of the activities conducted around us. Today people are much better atuned to their individual rights, and they are not afraid to sue for an injury or a wrong done to them, whereas their parents would never have thought of consulting a lawyer. They are, for example, more aware of the permanent effects of knee and other injuries than were past generations and, as a result, feel they should be compensated for an injury that handicaps them for the rest of their lives.

Increased Accessibility of Legal Services

We also see more lawsuits today because the court system is being restructured to provide greater accessibility. For example, there are now more small claims courts, wherein an individual can bring a suit without the aid or expense of an attorney.

There are more lawyers in the world today than ever before, and their number includes more members of minority races. Also, lawyers have broader contacts with various groups of "laymen." Since there are more attorneys, more people will have contact with an attorney socially. Increased social contact means that people probably will be less intimidated by lawyers and the law.

Increased Transportation of Athletes

The increased use of transportation in connection with athletic events, such as transporting collegiate teams by air or having parents and teachers drive students to functions, has opened new fields for lawsuits. The abolition of governmental immunity (whereby the government, including schools, could not be sued) and popular awareness that school corporations and most individuals are insured, also have fostered more litigation.

Comparative Negligence

At one time, contributory negligence was widely accepted as a complete defense against an action alleging wrongdoing. If the negligence of the injured party contributed to his injury, the party would be barred from recovering anything from the other person. To date, however, some form of comparative negligence has been adopted by about thirty-five of the fifty states. Comparative negligence means that the negligence of the plaintiff (the injured party) is compared to the negligence of the defendant (the party being sued), and the damages are prorated between the two parties. Thus, as a replacement for contributory negligence, comparative negligence is a factor in increasing the number of lawsuits pursued.

Increased Valuing of Individual Rights

In general, there is greater consumer acceptance of claims and lawsuits when someone suffers injury. This is evidenced by the increasing frequency of medical and other professional malpractice lawsuits. The courts have recently expanded their interpretation of the Fourteenth Amendment to the U.S. Constitution, which provides equal protection for the individual citizen. Today we can find cases in which children are bringing actions against their teachers and even against their parents, say, for child abuse.

Consumerism

More and more lawsuits are being filed due to the wave of consumerism. Legally speaking, this means that when someone pays money for a commodity, such as an automobile, there is an implied warranty that the automobile is fit for the use for which it was purchased. By the same token, when someone purchases an education for his child with tax dollars, our system of social justice is advancing to the point that there is an implied warranty that the child will receive the education that is reasonably anticipated.

For a breach of this warranty, a lawsuit and liability could follow. The damages in such a case would run high, since the allegation would certainly be that the child was permanently damaged. If a child who has been socially promoted through graduation cannot read or write well enough to fill out a job application, or to qualify for a position appropriate to a high school graduate, the child has been permanently injured. ("Social promotion" means passing a student to the next grade even if he has not mastered the previous grade.)

While education today is treated like any other commodity, athletics is "big business." Eighty billion dollars per year — ten percent of the gross national product — is spent annually on leisure and recreational activities. Consider all the product liability suits for defective football helmets and other sports equipment. Inevitably, we think of large awards. And the more frequently we hear of large awards, the more apt we are to vote, when jurors, to award a large sum. Claims for damages for sports injuries are usually based on one of the following:

1. Permitting injured or unfit persons to play.
2. Permitting unequal players to compete.

3. Failing to provide safe facilities.
4. Failing to provide safe equipment, including defective, damaged, mismatched, or misfitting equipment.
5. Failing to employ a competent coach or teacher.
6. Failing to provide proper training or instruction.
7. Failing to provide proper supervision during the contest.

Further, there is a growing number of lawsuits for negligently moving an injured player, thereby worsening his condition.

Rights of Officials

Another area in which we will see more lawsuits involves sports officials, including coaches and volunteer officials as well as referees. These suits will include not only failure to supervise or control an athletic contest, but also actions brought by officials for defamation. A referee is responsible to himself and to the participants to protect his reputation. Like the judge in the courtroom, his success rests upon his reputation for being able to judge activities fairly. (Line referees in football are now called line judges.)

It is not uncommon to read a newspaper article claiming "lousy officiating" at the previous night's game, or about a coach who cries "Conspiracy! They're trying to get rid of me." Referees and other sports officials have a right to bring suit for defamation when a fan or critic damages their good name or reputation through a false statement. Such a cause of action arises when a publication exposes an official to distrust, hatred, contempt, ridicule, or shame, or when the comments tend to be injurious to the person's office, occupation, business, or employment, as seen in the minds of a substantial segment of the community.

Libel and Slander

The distinction between libel and slander is an important one in the courtroom. The referee or umpire will have a much harder time recovering for the wrong done to him if he only alleges slander. In such a case, the party alleging injury must prove monetary loss as a result of the false statement.

In short, oral, temporary defamation is slander; written, relatively permanent defamation is libel. The courts have reasoned that radio and television fall within the latter category, due to their broad dissemination.

There are a few specific types of slander that are treated as slander per se due to their serious nature. Slander is presumed in actions based on the following types of statements:

1. Accusations of participation in a crime of moral turpitude.
2. Accusations of carrying a venereal disease.
3. Accusations of serious sexual misconduct.
4. Statements that cause harm to the victim in his trade or profession.

This last category includes nonprofessional officials, if they are in some way compensated for their services.

At this point, some are likely to think, "Hmmm, I'll soon be rich if this is all I need to show." But it is not quite that easy; there is a considerable catch. Before a "public" official can recover for loss as a result of a defamatory statement, it must be proven that the person who made the statement did so maliciously, with knowledge or with reckless disregard of the consequences to the defamed individual.

The next question is, "Will I, an official and a public figure, have a more difficult case to prove than does the private individual?" The law does not provide any easy answer. Generally, a public figure is one who, through his office or activities, commands a substantial amount of public attention. One could be a "limited public figure" for a limited range of activities, say, when one interjects oneself into the limelight to influence the outcome of an issue.

The following factors should be weighed by the individual and his attorney in order to gauge the chances of success in a courtroom contest:

1. Determine where on the following continuum the individual (victim) stands:

Private Individual	Limited Public Figure	Public Official
Little League coaches, officials, etc.	High school or college coaches, officials, etc.	Professional referees, umpires, coaches, players, etc.

2. Determine the burden upon the individual to prove, for example, specific malice or monetary loss.
3. Consider the media coverage given to the particular event and the general notoriety of the individual in his field or community.
4. Consider the number of years the individual has been officiating and at what level.

If a defamatory statement is directed against an entire class of people ("All lawyers are shysters"), an individual member of that class (one attorney) would not be able to bring suit against the proclaimer. Likewise, there could be no recovery if the statement was truthful or made without the intention of defaming.

A statement is conditionally privileged when it is fairly made in the discharge of a public or private duty, whether legal or moral, and in the conduct of one's own affairs in matters where his interest is concerned.

If you make a statement that carries a tinge of defamation, it is better to retract it. Though the damage has already occurred, retraction of a statement by the same source that disseminated it does much to mitigate the extent of those damages.

Player Suits Charging Excessive Violence

Another reason for the increased number of lawsuits today is the trend among players to bring an action for injuries stemming from excessive violence. One need not be a sports fan to have several names come to mind. Consider the following examples from the professional arenas.

Cleveland Denny was driven to the mat by Gaeten Hart in a boxing match in Montreal; seventeen days later, Denny died. Darryl Stingley's football career was terminated by a smashing blow from Jack Tatum. In New York's Madison Square Garden, nine Boston Bruins hockey players wreaked havoc in the stands, injuring several people.

Whether or not violence has actually increased in sports is a topic left for debate elsewhere. It should be noted, however, that professional sports organizations have recognized the influence of the coach on the behavior and values of youths.

Question: If a coach encourages greater violence on the part of players against the other team, resulting in injury to a player on the other team, can the coach be held legally responsible? Will he be liable to respond in damages for the injury that results?

During a basketball game played on December 9, 1977, between the Los Angeles Lakers and the Houston Rockets, Laker player Kermit Washington and Rocket player Kevin Kunnert got into a scuffle. When Rocket player Rudy Tomjanovich stepped forward, supposedly to break up the bout, Kermit Washington struck him. Tomjanovich was left with a broken jaw, a broken nose, a fractured skull, and other serious complications. Testimony at the trial included the following descriptions of the event: "like a baseball bat smashing a wall"; "like a watermelon being dropped on a cement floor"; "the most violent act the referee had ever seen on the basketball court."

Washington had been thrown out of the game before this incident took place. The National Basketball Association levied a fine of $10,000 and suspended Washington for sixty days. Not finding this to be sufficient compensation for his injuries, Tomjanovich brought a civil action against the Los Angeles Lakers. The jury found that Washington's malicious act went far beyond mere self-defense, and they found that the blow delivered by Washington went far beyond the normal conduct allowed by the rules or customs of the game. The jury found that the defendant, the owner of the Lakers, failed in his duty to properly supervise, train, and discipline his players against the use of violence. One and one-half million dollars in punitive damages was assessed against the Lakers management for this failure to properly instruct the players and for their retention of the violence-prone player even after the club had knowledge of his tendencies.

The jury's total award for Tomjanovich's personal injuries came to $3,246,376. In addition to this sum, the Houston Rockets Basketball Association settled an action against the Los Angeles Lakers for about $750,000 for their losses as a result of Tomjanovich's absence.[1]

---

[1]*Tomjanovich* v. *California Sports, Inc., D/B/A Los Angeles Lakers,* F. Supp. S.D. No. H-78-243 (August 17, 1977), 23 Atla L. Rep. 107.

Excessive violence will continue as long as it is not penalized. Too often the coach attempts to incite his players to overly aggressive behavior in the belief that it will enhance the chances of victory. But when this tactic does not work, the players will be discouraged and their reflexes will not be as sharp as those of the opponents, leading to an increased chance of injury.

An increase in violence results in an increase in injuries. Traditional calisthenics simply do not prepare the muscles for the hits and blocks received on the field. In high school alone, more than a million boys and girls will be injured while playing football this fall. About half of all high school players will receive some type of injury during their four-year term. While some injuries will be so minor that the students may continue playing the game, other students will die.

A coach may work hard all week to teach his players to participate in a sportsmanlike manner. However, his work is undone during the weekend, when the players see their "heroes" in the professional leagues spear tackling (using a rigid-shell helmet as a battering ram to smash a player who is already downed), stick blocking (grabbing the facemask), spiking, and hitting late. Indeed, college and professional players incur the most serious injuries. The National Football League official injury rate is no less than 100%.

Violence is a necessary element of any contact sport, but excessive violence is unnecessary. There is presently much discussion regarding the ability of the leagues and the participants, administrators, coaches, and players to police themselves. The courts cannot resolve this problem until it is determined where legitimate, aggressive play ends and illegal conduct begins. This can only be accomplished through a case-by-case examination.

It is clear, however, that if a coach encourages excessive violence, he may be held legally responsible. Individual negligence, arising from a duty personally owed to a player, will not be lost even under the guise of governmental immunity. Such a coach would not be acting as an employee within the scope of employment. One need not murder the opponent to win the contest.

Product Liability

Another area of increased lawsuits is that of product liability. As technology increases, so do the number of lawsuits brought for improper or defective equipment. Distributing defective equipment is distinguishable in the courts from mere faulty supervision.

The trampoline has been nicknamed the "paraplegic machine." Artificial surfaces such as Astroturf have been known to crack, develop holes or air pockets, or heat up to over 120° F. About one-third of all football injuries are attributable to helmet-inflicted blows. The leather harness worn by rugby players to protect their ears seems to yield fewer serious head injuries than the helmet-facemask combination used by football players, although dental injuries might increase with the former. The plastic-nubbed shoes used in soccer are taking the place of football's metal-cleated shoes.

As an example of product liability suits, a Florida jury ordered Riddell, Inc., manufacturers of football helmets, to pay $4,000,000 to Greg Stead, who was paralyzed after being struck in the spine with the back of Riddell's TK2 helmet.

As another example, a major manufacturer of gymnastic equipment, who was quoted a $300,000 annual premium for liability coverage, decided to self-insure. Shortly afterward, the company faced lawsuits totaling $67,000,000. Another major gymnastic equipment manufacturer was informed by its insurer that its policy will likely be cancelled.

A girl who broke her arm while vaulting over a side horse sued the manufacturer of one of the mats in the gym, even though (a) it was not the mat she landed on, (b) the company did not manufacture the mats on which she landed, and (c) there was no record of mats having been sold to the school by that company.

Richard T. Ball, special counsel to Riddell, Inc. and American Baseball Cap Company, cites verdicts in Dade County, Florida, for $5,300,000 and in Philadelphia for $600,000.[2] He points out that the expense of preparing a case and taking it to trial usually exceeds $100,000, and that it may be two to three times this amount. Further, at any one time there are usually fifty to sixty lawsuits pending against manufacturers of football helmets alone. As a result, insurance premiums charged to manufacturers of athletic equipment are from fifty to one hundred times the amounts of a few years ago.

Jeffrey O'Connel, Professor of Law at the University of Illinois, during a speech at the Twenty-Third Annual Alumni Institute at the University of Minnesota, stated that sixty-three cents of the product liability insurance dollar goes to insurance overhead and to the plaintiffs' and defendants' lawyers.[3]

The prohibitive insurance premiums charged to manufacturers of sports equipment have forced many smaller companies to disband. Other manufacturers have coped by increasing the price of their product. This increased cost of sports equipment, the increased liability insurance costs to schools, the rapid growth of women's sports and Title IX requirements, and decreasing financial support of schools, are making it virtually impossible to finance all the sports programs at the level deemed necessary by participants. Further, the schools must employ consulting attorneys and invest increased funds in injury prevention measures. Costs are further increased because schools wishing to avoid legal damages must purchase the most expensive equipment, employ equipment managers and athletic trainers, hire consulting physicians, and use the best (and usually the most expensive) forms of transportation. In addition, the schools must employ a greater number of coaches and faculty to ensure complete supervision of the athletic activities.

---

[2]Richard T. Ball, "Litigation: Will It Destroy Athletics?" *Trial,* July 1980.

[3]"Senate to Consider Product Liability Act," *Athletic Purchasing and Facilities,* April/May 1977, pp. 28–30.

With the budget cuts common during recessions and times of inflation, as well as cuts due to decreasing enrollments, something has to give. In view of the greatly increasing number of suits against educational institutions and the six- or seven-digit dollar amounts of these suits, school officials will elect to increase expenditures for participant safety, rather than adding to the number and variety of sports offered. Indeed, they may even be forced to drop some sports teams, unless the taxpayers are willing to approve greater expenditures for athletics, physical education, and extracurricular clubs.

In recent years, there has been a growing interest in high-risk activities such as mountain climbing, spelunking, white water canoeing, parachute jumping, sky diving, and hang gliding. Interest in other activities such as gymnastics, the martial arts, skiing, and wilderness camping has also grown.

Although a few high schools and colleges offer physical education courses and/or have organized extracurricular clubs for these activities, others have avoided them due to the fear of student injuries and debilitating lawsuits. Most of the expense of these suits comes out of the taxpayer's pocket, rather than directly from the school budget; nevertheless, the suits consume the time of school administrators and are embarrassing and harmful to the reputation of the school.

DECREASING THE PROBABILITY OF LAWSUITS

Some attorneys and most administrators of athletic programs feel that litigation arising out of athletic injuries is accelerating to the point of being out of control and that, if the trend continues, athletic programs may not survive. The first line of defense must lie in efforts to educate the general public regarding the hazards to worthwhile sports programs of litigation gone wild. These efforts should take the form of letters to the editor, articles in professional journals, and letters to Congressmen written by defense attorneys, institutional administrators, coaches, and physical educators. Research regarding the increased cost of athletic programs should be promulgated by associations of coaches, physical educators, and defense attorneys. Research grants in this area should be made available.

The second line of defense is to decrease the incidence of injuries, particularly incapacitating or fatal injuries. This can be accomplished, in part, by following the suggestions in this book. Of much greater significance will be the ongoing efforts of professional associations of physical educators, coaches, and school administrators, through revisions of rules, articles in professional journals, clinics, convention topics, pamphlets and books designed to improve safety in sports. Manufacturers of sports equipment and facilities are part of this second line of defense. They can devote a greater proportion of funds to research efforts in product safety. They can give a higher priority to the safety of their product in comparison to its marketability. They can help to educate the general public and the users of their product in the principles of sports safety.

A third line of defense involves the keeping of complete records of athletic injuries, demonstrating genuine concern for injured players, and retaining skilled defense attorneys.

In the case of an athlete in his physical prime and about to embark upon his income-producing years, loss of life must, in justice, be compensated if the injury was caused by an unsafe product or the negligence of a coach or instructor.

In most legal suits, attorneys for the plaintiff list several parties as defendants. In sports injury cases, this list will include the coach or physical educator, the athletic director or chairperson of the physical education department, probably the principal, dean, or college president, and, almost certainly, the manufacturer of any sports equipment in use at the time of the injury.

Manufacturers of sports equipment generally carry large liability insurance policies. Since manufacturers and school personnel are almost always codefendants, it would seem mutually beneficial for the two groups to join in sponsoring clinics, seminars, and research dealing with the prevention of injury in sports and athletic training, as well as research dealing with litigation procedures.

The National Product Liability Act

In January of 1977, Senator Pearson of Kansas introduced bill S 403, which would establish "programs, standards, and procedures for determining responsibilities and liabilities arising out of product-related injuries. . . ." This bill provides insurance for risks, hazards, or liabilities through federally chartered insurance companies when suitable insurance markets do not exist, or when needed coverage is only available at excessive rates or with unreasonable deductibles. Additionally, the National Product Liability Act, as it is called, includes an arbitration program to reduce the number of claims going to court. If the product is not used for the purpose for which it was designed, if the product has been altered or modified in any way, or if any changes in the warning, labeling, or instructions for use of the product (except those made or authorized by the seller) are made, manufacturers would not be held responsible.

The act also provides for a ten-year limitation on claims and allows manufacturers to establish a "useful life" of the product that would preclude claims for injuries sustained after the useful life had run out. Products such as mouthpieces, mats, trampoline beds, chest protectors, and other padded material obviously wear out with use, and the amount of protection they provide decreases.

The bill reads as follows:

> It shall be a defense to any action seeking legal or equitable relief which alleges a product defect or failure resulting in injury, death, or proper damage that the manufacturer or seller thereof complied with all federal or state laws, including administrative regulations which prescribe standards for

design, testing, labeling, inspection, performance or manufacture of any such product at the time of its design and manufacture, except upon proper proof that such injury, death, or property damage was caused by the failure of such manufacturer or seller to comply with such federal or state or administrative laws and regulations.

Duty to Warn and Adequacy of Warning in Product Liability Cases

People have been injured through improper use of helmets, trampolines, skis, whirlpools, sunlamps, heat lamps, and pharmaceuticals used in athletic training. To what degree can the manufacturer be held liable in the event of dangerous, improper, or inappropriate use of the product? This was discussed in an article by Donald J. Hirsch and Jerry D. Zimmerman.[4] An abstract of the points made in this article, as they apply to manufacturers of sports equipment, is offered in the following.

A manufacturer has a duty to warn of dangerous propensities of his product, but he is not required to warn of open and obvious dangers. For example, if a college student jumps from a balcony onto a mat or trampoline, the manufacturer would probably be declared not liable, since the potential danger of this act is obvious. However, whether a danger is open and obvious should be determined by the facts in each case. The status, intelligence, and training of the particular user should all be considered.

In *Suchomajcz* v. *Hummel Chemical Company* (524 F. 2d 19 [3d Cir. 1975]), the court stated: "In the absence of special reason to expect otherwise, the maker is entitled to assume that his product will be put to a normal use for which the product is intended or appropriate; and he is not subject to liability when it is safe for all such uses and harm results only because it is mishandled in a way which he has no reason to expect or is used in some unusual and unforeseeable manner."

To be considered adequate, a warning must catch the attention of the reasonably prudent man in the circumstances of its use, and it must be comprehensible to the average user and convey a fair indication of the nature and extent of the danger to a reasonably prudent person. Implicit is the duty to warn with a degree of intensity that would cause a reasonable man to exercise caution commensurate with the potential danger. Vague or "fudging" words should be avoided. Also, the warning should be conspicuous and prominent, with print large enough to be easily read.

Football Helmets

According to the projections of the National Electronic Injury Surveillance System, of the 318,000 football injuries treated each year in hospital emer-

---

[4]Material paraphrased with permission from Donald J. Hirsch and Jerry D. Zimmerman, "Duty to Warn and Adequacy of Warning in Product Liability Cases," *For the Defense*, vol. 20, no. 6 (June 1976), pp. 135–41. Copyright 1976, The Defense Research Institute. All rights reserved.

gency rooms, 30,000 involve the head and neck. Classed as head and neck injuries are subdural hematomas, spinal cord injuries, pinched nerves, vascular injuries, severe concussions, fractured cervical vertebrae, and fracture dislocations. Comparison of the incidence of these types of injuries in recent years shows reductions in subdural hematomas, contusions of the brain, and concussions. However, there has been a great increase in spinal cord injuries and the pinched nerve syndrome.

This decrease in injuries to the brain and increase in injuries to the spinal cord coincided with a switch in the type of helmet being used. The change was made from helmets made of acrylonitrile, butadiene, and styrene (ABS), which is more brittle and which, consequently, cracks upon impact to the face guard attached to the helmet, to helmets made of the less brittle polycarbonate. The polycarbonate helmet shells, being tougher, distribute the force of the impact more effectively. The problem is that the force is transmitted to the neck, increasing the incidence of neck injuries. When the ABS helmet cracked, some of the kinetic energy of the blow was absorbed. With the newer polycarbonate helmets, the kinetic energy of the blow is distributed over a greater area of the skull, but it is not absorbed to a significant degree, and the force is transmitted to the cervical vertebrae as the head is moved at its articulation with the neck.

An analogy could be made to the act of trying to hammer a rusty nail into cement versus hammering a strong, rigid nail into the same cement. When the rusty nail bends or breaks, it absorbs some of the kinetic energy transmitted by the hammer, and the cement is barely penetrated. However, the new, strong, rigid nail transmits almost all of the kinetic energy of the hammer to the cement, and the cement is penetrated. Similarly, with a rigid helmet, almost all the kinetic energy of the blow is transmitted to the cervical vertebrae which, incidentally, are the smallest and weakest vertebrae of the entire spinal column. The higher cervical vertebrae are smaller and weaker because they support less weight than the vertebrae lower on the spinal column.

The human vertebral column differs from those of rams and billy goats. It is not designed for "spearing" or for use as a battering ram. Players who persist in using their heads (and vertebral columns) as battering rams can be likened to an elephant who wishes to swing through the trees like a monkey. Coaches who teach or permit spearing are either stupid or sadistic.

Kinesiologic Principles for Prevention of Injuries

Soft tissues such as fat, muscle, tendons, and ligaments have considerable elasticity and, consequently, will return to their original size and shape after a force, impact, or stress is removed.[5] Bone, however, has little elasticity and

---

[5]John Piscopo and James A. Baley, *Kinesiology: The Science of Movement* (New York: John Wiley & Sons, 1981).

will fracture. If a player strikes an opponent on the rigid shin bone, he will inflict more damage to the opponent than if he struck him on the soft tissue of the buttocks.

When a sky diver's chute fails to open, the diver does not sustain injuries until the kinetic energy generated during the fall is suddenly absorbed upon striking the ground. He is not hurt by the fall; it is the sudden stop at the end that does harm. This is true even if the diver falls five miles, unless he dies of heart failure during the fall. If the diver falls into water in a streamlined position, he has a fair chance of surviving because his momentum is absorbed over a greater period of time. Parachutists have fallen into trees and bushes and survived. People have fallen several stories and survived when they fell through a canopy or landed on top of a car whose roof caved in, allowing the kinetic energy to be absorbed over a greater period.

Survival in such falls is due to the application of two principles for prevention of injury: (1) the kinetic energy must be absorbed over a greater period of time; and (2) the impact must be disbursed over a greater surface area by landing flat on the back.

If 1,000 pounds of force is distributed over the 100 square inches of the back, the force per square inch equals ten pounds. If the 1,000 pounds of force is distributed over ten square inches of the head, the force per square inch is 100 pounds. If the same force is distributed over the approximately 2.25 square inches of a cervical vertebra, the force is over 444 pounds per square inch.

The heavier the football player and the greater his speed, the greater his momentum, since momentum equals mass times velocity. The greater the momentum of an object, the greater must be the force and time over which the force acts to decelerate the object. This is why, when catching a ball, one extends the arm toward the oncoming ball and then allows the hand to be carried backward with the ball. We all learned as children that if you don't do this, your hand will sting; and if the ball has a great deal of momentum by virtue of its speed, bones in the hand can be broken. The momentum developed by a 250-pound tackler moving at a speed of ten yards per second is considerable. To this must be added the momentum of the opposing player as they collide.

The product of force and the time over which it acts is called impulse. The greater the momentum of an object, the greater the impulse required to accelerate, decelerate, or change the direction of the object. This is illustrated by the formula: $Ft = m(VI - Vf)$ where F = force, t = the time over which the force acts, m = mass, VI = initial velocity, and Vf = final velocity. At the moment of head contact, there is considerable mass, and its initial velocity comes to zero in a very short time. This means that the force must be very great.

The formula demonstrates why a football player must develop very powerful neck muscles. These muscles must apply the force necessary to quickly decelerate the forward- or backward-moving head before it traverses to the cervical vertebra, shattering it and possibly severing the spinal cord. Football players should be required to develop powerful neck muscles through isometric and weight-training exercises.

There is considerable doubt as to whether it is possible to design a football helmet that will eliminate neck injuries. The time over which momentum is absorbed is considerable on the trampoline, since the bed and shock cord stretch and the impact is absorbed over a distance of some two feet before the bed begins to carry the trampolinist upward again. Can a football helmet with two-foot-thick padding be designed? Even this would probably not accomplish the purpose, since trampolinists sometimes break their necks when they land on the bed head first.

Design of Helmets

The face guard should be banned. If it were, the incidence of dental and facial injuries would likely increase, but the much more disabling neck injuries and subsequent paralysis would decrease.

Several studies indicate the scope of the problem of head and neck injuries. One study reports that one out of every three college freshmen football players shows radiographical evidence of neck injuries received prior to playing college football.[6] No helmet manufacturer has incorporated spring-release mechanisms into face guards to minimize spinal cord injuries. In 1975, Dr. Joseph Torg of the Temple Institute of Sports Medicine presented a report on spinal cord injuries in the states surrounding Philadelphia. A national projection of these data indicates that there may have been forty to fifty spinal cord injuries in football in the U.S. in 1975.

Now consider the difficulties facing football equipment manufacturers, at least as represented by Richard T. Ball, an attorney who serves as Special Counsel to Riddell, Inc. on helmet product liability, and who also represents the Baseball Cap Company. Ball points out that designers of equipment must consider a number of factors, among which are the cost of the product, its comfort, its durability, and user acceptance.[7] He further notes that, for many years, most baseball players refused to wear any protective helmet, and even today players refuse to wear a helmet that they do not consider light, comfortable, attractive, and convenient. It is difficult to design a helmet that incorporates these characteristics and yet protects against a pitched ball that may be traveling at speeds exceeding 100 mph.

Ball goes on to discuss the problems faced by manufacturers of football helmets. He notes that the same type of helmet will be worn by ninth-grade students and by adult professionals. It will be worn two to three hours per

---

[6]Harry M. Philo and Gregory Stine, "The Liability Path to Safer Helmets," *Trial,* January 1977, pp. 38–40.

[7]Richard T. Ball, "Capabilities and Limitations of Protective Equipment," *The First Aider* (Gardner, Kansas: Cramer Products, Inc., 1978), pp. 19–23.

day, five or six days per week, over a period of three to four months; and it may be used in both blistering heat and freezing cold, in conditions of high and low humidity, in rain and snow, in mud and dust, and on grass, on hard-packed dirt, or on concrete covered with Astroturf.

The helmet must be strong enough to resist the impacts, must be light enough to be comfortable, and must cover as much of the head as possible without restricting vision or impairing hearing. It is obvious that players of different ages and skill levels could wear different types of helmets, and manufacturers could design them to meet the special needs of each age group and skill level.

Ball states that "statistically it has been proven that the protection given by all the helmets on the market today is the same . . . regardless of the protective system. Since all helmets give the same high level of protection, a coach or athletic director must decide which is the most practical and functional and what trade-offs are involved."[8]

Ball contends that, to his knowledge, "there is not a single lawsuit alleging massive brain injury or neck and spinal cord injury in which the helmet is said to have failed. The serious cases all involve claims that the design of the product is inadequate to give the required protection, or that the design contributes to the injury."[9] He contends that the attacks upon athletic equipment are based upon laboratory experiments, rather than actual experience in play. He condemns the practice of comparing the safety of one helmet to another on the basis of laboratory experiments.

WHAT IS TO COME?

In this chapter we have explained why the number of lawsuits in athletics, physical education and recreation has increased to the point where the fear of being sued has produced genuine concern among workers in this area. This concern and anxiety could cause leaders in sports, fitness, and recreation programs to limit the quantity and quality of their offerings with the result that inherent benefits of these programs would be limited. Activities with some hazard could be eliminated. The variety of offerings could be restricted. The number of people served could be diminished.

Rather than withdraw in fear, it is better to continue the advance in scope and difficulty of athletic skills taught while instituting those methods, progressions, safety procedures, equipment improvements, administrative procedures, and improvements in facilities which will decrease the incidence of injuries. When the number of injuries decreases, the number of lawsuits decreases. Additionally, when workers in the area of human movement understand the relevant laws, court procedures, and kinesiologic

---

[8]Ibid.
[9]Ibid.

principles for prevention of injury they are less likely to find themselves as the defendant in court.

Readers of this book who implement the precepts presented are unlikely to find themselves in the unpleasant position of being a defendant in a liability suit. In the chapters that follow, readers will learn about the steps in a lawsuit, their legal duties, administrative procedures for avoiding lawsuits, student and faculty rights, procedures for reducing the incidence of injury in twenty-eight sports and recreational activities, record keeping (which can be useful in defending against a lawsuit), requirements of Title IX, Public Law 94-142 requirements, current laws affecting transportation of students and athletes, and alternatives to litigation.

Some physical educators, coaches, and administrators may regard the increased incidence of lawsuits as harassment. But the fact that workers in this area are now being held to a higher degree of responsibility can also be viewed as a complement. Workers in sports and athletics are increasingly being regarded as professionals who must pass through a rigorous period of preparation and must continue to study and keep abreast of the constantly growing body of knowledge in the field of human movement.

/ 2 /

The Nature of a Lawsuit

A *tort* is defined as a wrongful act against another person, resulting in injury to that person. A tort obligation arises through operation of law, where the law imposes a duty.

A wrongful act can result in either a criminal or civil action, or both. A criminal action in turn results in a fine or imprisonment due to violation of a criminal law, i.e., it is an action brought by the state, or in the name of the state, against a person. For example: Mary Jones drives her car down the street and stops at a red light. John Brown crashes into the rear of her car. In this case, the criminal action occurs when John Brown receives a ticket and pays a fine. The tort action occurs when Mary Jones files a civil suit against John Brown for damages to her car and to herself.

A tort action or a civil action of the type discussed in this book is a damage suit brought by one citizen against another citizen or corporate entity. The result of such a civil action is not a jail sentence or a fine, but rather a money judgment.

WHO CAN SUE? WHO CAN BE SUED?

The *plaintiff* is the party who brings a civil action. In tort, anyone who has sustained a loss due to another's negligence may bring action as a plaintiff. If the injured person is a minor, both he and his parents have a claim, the latter as a result of the injury to their child.

The *defendant* is the party against whom the action is brought. Today there really is no limitation on who can be sued in tort. The defendant might be the immediately supervising coach or teacher, together with some or all of the following: referees, umpires, the coach of the other team, the department head, the principal, school board members (both individually and as a group), the school corporation, the city, the state, and whoever owned or had control of the facility. The test to determine responsibility for an injury is to ask, "Who should have anticipated the harm, and could he have acted, before the harm occurred, to prevent it?"

If you receive a letter from an attorney, or some kind of legal notice of a claim, immediately take it to your attorney or insurance carrier so that they may handle it.

THE ARENA

As we enter the courtroom, immediately we are inspired by the majestic height of the ceiling, the ominous portraits, the rich earth tones of the woodwork. The doors playing hide-and-seek in the paneling tug at our curiosity. We are intrigued by the age-old traditions and the judge's robe. No matter what reason brings us to court, anxiety overcomes us as we think, "What if the judge calls on me?" Inevitably, fear pounds on our heart like a tom-tom. What will the outcome of this contest bring?

The surroundings may be foreign to the newcomer, but if we take a moment to contemplate them, we realize that it is much like a basketball contest, complete with uniforms. Relish each moment in this new arena as you watch the coaches/attorneys arrive in their three-piece uniforms/suits. The judge, too, has a uniform — the robe. In sports, different rules apply and different equipment is necessary. In England, judges still wear powdered wigs.

Compare the courtroom to the gymnasium. As we enter the courtroom from the rear, we walk past the spectators' benches, the front one functioning as a boundary, much as it would in basketball. On the far right is the jury box; liken it to the scorekeeper's box. Straight ahead is the judge's bench; consider him the rules keeper or referee. Between the judge/referee and the jury/scorekeeper is the witness stand; imagine this as the free throw line, safe from harrassment by either side. Usually found in front of the judge's bench is the court reporter, who takes down everything that is said. He keeps the record of the "game." In front of the spectators and to one side, at their bench, is the team of the plaintiff. On the bench to the other side is the defending team, the defense attorney and the defendants.

The formal rules of play are set out in the trial procedure manuals, much as with a sporting activity. Indeed, it is competition and in a splendid arena! (No betting on the game, though, please!)

WHEN SHOULD I CONSULT A LAWYER?

Many people fail to consult a lawyer when they should because they don't know how to select a lawyer who is competent to handle their case. Further, people are reluctant to consult a lawyer to determine whether they have a legal case, when it is the lawyer who is capable of making the determination.

Such problems have plagued many people in many fields, including coaches and teachers, as well as the parents of injured students. The purpose of this chapter is to explain when to inquire, where to inquire, and when to consult an attorney.

First of all, don't be afraid of attorneys because they might charge a fee. Ask the attorney, before you consult with him, what his fee schedule is, or what his fee is for the first consultation. Frequently there is no charge for the initial consultation, especially in the case of injuries where a contingent fee might be involved.

A *contingent fee* refers to an agreement whereby the lawyer will accept a case on the basis of receiving a percentage of the settlement (usually one-third, but sometimes slightly higher in the event of a full trial and final judgment).

There are many more lawyers available in the marketplace today than ever before. This increased competition has resulted in reduced, or more competitive, fees. Don't hesitate to discuss fees with the attorney at the first contact with him. You would not hesitate to ask a price in a department store or at an automobile dealer. You should be no less hesitant with the attorney. You are purchasing a service. An attorney's time and advice are his stock-in-trade.

When searching for an attorney, it is appropriate to consult friends and neighbors, the same as when selecting a physician. It is especially prudent to consult with someone in the field. For example, if you have a business, real estate, or tax matter, you might consult your banker for referral of an attorney. If you have an injury accident, it might be appropriate to consult with the liability insurance man who sold you your automobile insurance.

Though lawyers are not allowed to advertise that they specialize in a particular field, most lawyers do concentrate on one field of law. Attorneys may specialize in corporation law, taxes, real estate, or personal injury. The best, most competent professional help you can get, whether it be in the field of medicine or law, is the cheapest in the long run.

Fees are usually charged either on the basis of time spent or on a contingent fee basis. A retainer fee is sometimes charged, though not usually when contingent fees are involved. Out-of-pocket expenses are usually required in advance. These include court filing fees, which range from $25 to $100, and out-of-pocket expenses for such items as the cost incurred for medical reports, hospital records, and deposition fees. If you are unable to advance these expenses, the attorney may agree to deduct them from the final settlement, or he may delay their payment until final judgment. An initial conference of some fifteen minutes will usually cost in the neighborhood of $25.

An attorney's overhead is high due to office rent, taxes, insurance, utility bills, secretarial help, and other salaries. Legal secretaries are among the best and highest paid in the profession, since the courts require high standards. Libraries are expensive to maintain, as are other expenses necessary to keep current in the legal profession. Such expenses include attendance at legal institutes and subscriptions to periodicals.

If an attorney charges $40 to $50 per hour, he is doing well to take home $15 or $20 per hour. It is sometimes difficult for the client to realize that, while the attorney spends only thirty minutes with the client, he spends hours in the preparation and handling of the case. This is particularly true in litigation that may last for years. A great deal of time is spent on the telephone talking to doctors, insurance adjusters, investigators, engineers, and other professionals. Further, time is spent waiting in the courtroom and preparing and filing motions, briefs, and other material, as well as handling correspondence. And a great deal of time is spent in legal research, since every case is unique in its facts and in the legal issues presented. The most recent cases in the jurisdiction must be researched to support a position.

Attorneys are held to a high standard of ethics, designed for the protection of the client. While a lawyer cannot guarantee results, if you are dissatisfied you can dismiss your attorney and employ another. If you feel that you have been wronged by your attorney, you have recourse to another attorney and to the local bar association.

The high standards of today's law schools serve to protect the client. Their screening processes ensure that you will be working with a highly intelligent person. The client is further protected by having recourse to complain to the judge handling the case or to the board of bar overseers or bar association, whose job it is to govern and police attorneys.

Attorneys are in a fiduciary relationship. This is a position of trust that requires the highest standards. Most bar associations also have a client security fund, which compensates clients if attorneys do, in fact, wrong them. There is also recourse to malpractice suits against attorneys.

All too frequently, people put off going to a lawyer just as they put off going to a doctor. Most of us have a tendency to put things off for as long as possible, in hopes that the problem will resolve itself. If a legal problem exists, there is a juris doctor to handle it. Avail yourself of this. You are sure to feel more at ease if you consult an attorney and place the matter in his hands.

Preventive law, like preventive medicine, is a good thing. The peace of mind it gives is worth the trip and any cost involved. Only a doctor can tell you when you need medical care and what it should be; so it is also that only an attorney can tell you if you really need a lawyer and make recommendations for a solution to your problem.

Generally speaking, if you *think* you need a lawyer, you probably do. If the matter involves a threat of serious damage to you, if it involves a lot of money, if it might affect your future, or if it is complicated and worrying to you, you should consult a lawyer. And if the other party has engaged an attorney, you should immediately consult with an attorney of your own.

It is not recommended that you act as your own doctor when you have a medical problem; likewise, you should not act as your own attorney if you think you have a legal problem. There is an old legal bromide that states: "He who acts as his own attorney has a fool for a client."

Often there are periods of limitation for legal notices. These notices must be served before any action can be brought, and they must be served within a very short period of time. Therefore, an attorney should be consulted quickly.

Legal matters take time. Clients become very impatient with the delays, and attorneys become very frustrated also. The old adage holds true: "Justice delayed is justice denied." But sometimes delays are beneficial to your side of the case, and patience is required.

Preparation prior to seeing the attorney can cut down the amount of time spent with him and can prove very helpful to both you and the attorney. It is often helpful to write out a statement of the facts in chronological order. This should be done in an informal way, much as you would in writing a letter to someone, telling them what happened.

In your initial telephone call, state briefly what the matter concerns and ask the attorney if he handles that type of case, or if he could recommend someone who does. Inquire as to the amount of the initial fee or what the fee will be. It is often difficult for the attorney to give a specific total fee, since he does not know the amount of his time that will be involved, or what all the facts are, until he has a chance to interview you in his office.

While attorneys are not allowed to specialize or list themselves as specialists in most states, most attorneys do concentrate their work in a specific field or fields. When you consult an attorney, it is important that a rapport be established and that you have confidence in him and his competence to handle your case. Nothing can replace such a rapport. While advertising is now permitted, many older, competent lawyers will not advertise and are worth seeking out.

When you engage an attorney, you are usually engaging everyone in his office, including other lawyers who work with him on cases, investigators, and secretaries. If the attorney's partner or associate handles your case, it is usually under the supervision of the attorney whom you engaged, and you should not feel that you are being given second-class or lesser treatment because your attorney does not personally handle every facet of the case. If you have engaged a competent attorney, he will no doubt have engaged competent help to assist him.

If you have any papers pertaining to the matter, such as medical bills, a medical report, insurance papers, letters, contracts, or any other papers that are pertinent, you can save yourself time and money by taking them with you on the initial visit.

On your initial visit, you should be aware that this is the time for you to decide whether or not you want this attorney to represent you. Exercise your judgment, just as you would if you were a juror. Evaluate your attorney's speech, appearance, dress, manner, and how he impresses you in general. Pay attention to the surroundings in which he works. Does he impress you as being up-to-date and knowledgeable about the current state of the law in the relevant areas? Does he have a library readily accessible? Does he return calls? Is he courteous? If you are not favorably impressed, the jury and the other side will probably feel likewise. In this event, thank him for his time and leave. If he has given you his advice, you may owe him a small fee for the consultation.

You are paying the lawyer for his knowledge, skills, and time. Not all of his hours are billable hours. Lawyers spend time running their offices, paying their bills, attending legal seminars and bar meetings, and doing other nonprofitable work. Unlike a medical doctor, an attorney spends very little time with the client, compared to the number of hours that he must spend in legal research, on the telephone, consulting with others, and going to court.

If you do not agree with the attorney's final bill, do not be afraid to ask for an itemized accounting of the services for which you were charged. If the bill seems high, ask yourself whether you phoned your attorney unnecessarily, or if you demanded that an agreement be reworded, even though you were advised that it was an inconsequential matter. Any changes made to documents require retyping by the secretary and reviewing by your attorney, by the opposing counsel, and by the opposing party. Ideally, you should make sure that your attorney has all the facts required at the very beginning.

Remember the following pointers whenever you believe that a legal situation might arise:

1. Keep good and accurate records for future use.
2. Take photographs of any pertinent location or automobile, of any injuries, and even of any witnesses. Take a picture of the crowd.
3. Try to get the names of witnesses and their addresses, places of employment, and telephone numbers.

There are times when, in an effort to keep legal costs down, you can utilize other available agencies. This can usually be accomplished by telephone, thus limiting delays before consulting an attorney and avoiding any waiving of your rights. For example, if you have an income tax matter, feel free to call the Internal Revenue Service for free advice. If you have a problem with your work, such as nonpayment of wages, call the state unemployment office or the local Federal Wage and Hour Division of the Department of Labor.

INITIATING A LAWSUIT

A suit is instituted by the filing of a complaint, which is a statement of the alleged wrongdoing of the defendants and a short statement of the injuries to the plaintiff. (It should be noted that, in states requiring a notice of claim, the fact of filing such notice, or any fact alleging legal excuse for not filing it on time, must be stated in the complaint.) In most jurisdictions, a legal notice stating your claim must be filed within 30, 60, 90, or 180 days after injury when suing a governmental entity. If this is not filed on time, you lose your right to bring the claim. It is well to check local laws to determine whether it must be filed with the county commissioners, with the county clerk, with the city clerk, with the secretary of state, etc. Again, this *must* be filed on time or you lose your right to make your claim.

When the defendant receives a complaint, which is served by the sheriff together with a summons, is sent through the mail, or is tacked on his door, he should immediately turn it over to an attorney or insurance agent, who will in turn deliver it to his attorney. The defense attorney will then probably interview the defendants and prepare and file an answer to the complaint. If an injury has occurred, do not hesitate to bring your complaint to an attorney.

Most plaintiffs' attorneys work on a contingent fee basis (a percentage of the award). The attorney gets nothing if you get nothing. This percentage varies, depending upon the point in the proceedings at which the award comes (before trial, after a jury verdict, or after the verdict is appealed to a higher court). In any case, the person who brings the action will be responsible for out-of-pocket expenses for filing fees, medical reports, accident reports, etc. The contingent fee has been aptly called the "poor man's key to the courthouse door."

As soon as the plaintiff's attorney gets the initial phone call from the injured party or, for the purposes of this book, from the parents of the injured party, he should immediately check local statutes to determine what, if any, notice is required, as well as the statute of limitations (the time limit beyond which no suit can be brought). If timely notice is required and the due date passes, the plaintiff's attorney should check for statutory excuses for failure to file.

At the first meeting with the plaintiff, the attorney will begin by taking a complete statement of the facts as related by the injured party, by members of his family, or by immediate friends who accompany the party to the office. If necessary, the attorney will go to the hospital, or wherever the victim is, to personally take the statement. Next, the attorney obtains copies of any accident reports arising out of the accident. The attorney will immediately contact any witnesses and take their statements, just as your insurance adjuster would do if you were named as a defendant.

Before the attorney sends out any notice letters, he will attempt to secure medical reports and hospital records, which normally offer more detailed and accurate information about the injury. Notifications are sent out to any prospective defendant, informing him of the attorney's representation of the injured plaintiff and his parents.

Investigative work consists of going to the scene of the accident, taking photographs, interviewing witnesses who have not already been questioned, obtaining any physical objects that contributed to the accident, obtaining medical reports, and checking school records.

Upon completion of this preliminary investigation, the adjuster representing the insurance company and the attorney for the plaintiff will attempt to negotiate a fair settlement. (A law professor once stated that a good settlement is one which satisfies neither party.) If the case is not settled after a period of time (usually months of negotiation and further investigation), the plaintiff's attorney will file suit and the defense attorney will file an answer. An answer is a brief statement of general denial, together with any affirmative defenses such as contributory negligence, assumption of risk, or other affirmative allegations. When the answer is filed containing the affirmative defenses, the plaintiff must then file a reply, admitting or denying those affirmative allegations. The answer and the reply are served only on the attorneys and not on the parties.

After suit has been filed, the process of *discovery* commences. Discovery consists of taking depositions from the other party and from witnesses. A deposition is sworn testimony of a party or witness taken before a court reporter, who is also a notary public, while the attorney for each side is present. Each attorney questions the witness as though they were in a courthouse. The depositions are typed and may be read to the jury during the trial.

Further, a set of typed questions may be submitted to either party to be answered under oath. These are called *sets of interrogatories.* A *motion for production of documents* may be filed to produce such things as the personnel file of the coach or student, or for any other documents desired by either party. A physical examination of the injured party may be obtained upon the defendant's motion, conducted by a physician of the defendant's choice.

While discovery continues, both attorneys will check the law and prepare *briefs* in support of their respective positions. A brief is a summary of the law from the governing state as it applies to the particular facts of the case. The attorneys check both the statutes (laws passed by the legislature) and case decisions from the particular state. If either side wishes a trial by jury, it will usually file a *motion for trial by jury* when it files the first pleading in court, be it a complaint or the answer thereto. If no jury is requested by either side, the witnesses are heard by the judge only, who makes the decision in the case.

It is usually at this stage, after the first pleading is filed, that depositions and other discovery processes commence. Again at this point, some serious negotiating occurs between the attorneys, in an effort to reach a fair and equitable settlement.

If the negotiations are unsuccessful, the court will issue a *pretrial notice.* This is an order by the court that the attorneys meet and write down both the points on which they agree and disagree. Then, at the pretrial conference, the court will make a decision for them on the points on which they cannot agree, thus determining both the issues that will be tried and the evidence to be allowed. At the pretrial conference, the court will usually set a trial date. (The terms "court" and "judge" are synonymous.)

In anticipation of trial, each attorney will prepare recommended instructions for the judge to read to the jury on the laws applicable to the case. These contain statements of law for the jury to apply to the facts of the case in reaching their determination. The judge decides which instructions will be given to the jury.

The attorneys will again interview the witnesses and arrange the most convenient time for them to appear and will then issue *subpoenas* for them to appear in court. A subpoena is an order of the court for a person to appear and testify as a witness.

THE TRIAL

On the day set for trial, the attorneys and their clients appear in the courtroom. The judge is on the bench, and the court reporter sits in front of the judge, taking down every word said with a stenotype machine, by recording, or in shorthand. If a jury trial has been requested, the prospective jurors are brought in and sworn to answer truthfully any questions asked of them.

The *voir dire examination* is then conducted. This consists of questioning by the judge and/or the attorneys as to the jurors' competence to sit. They are asked such questions as the following: whether or not they have any prejudices; whether they have any financial interest, including employment, in any insurance company insuring against liability; whether they or any members of their family have a disability or have ever had any claims for injuries to themselves or their family; whether they have had claims filed against them; and, in cases such as those discussed in this book, whether they have any close friends or relatives involved in education. Normally, some personal information is also sought regarding their own and their spouse's employment background.

Either side may "challenge" any person sitting on the jury, asking that they be removed. The judge decides each of these issues and decides who shall be excused from jury duty and who shall sit. The judge then swears the jury again. This time the jury is sworn to fairly try the case. After the jury is sworn, the plaintiff, or injured party, goes first. This is the rule because the plaintiff has the burden of proving, by a preponderance of the evidence, the injury and the negligence that he has alleged. The one who alleges must prove.

The plaintiff's attorney then calls his witnesses in any order he determines. Usually the liability witnesses who can testify as to how the accident occurred are called first, followed by the medical witnesses, who testify as to the extent of the injuries. The plaintiff is also put on the stand to testify, telling his story on his own behalf. All witnesses are sworn under oath to tell the truth before they testify.

When the plaintiff completes the presentation of his evidence, he "rests his case." At this point, the defense usually files a motion for the court to grant a judgment in behalf of the defendant for the reason that the plaintiff has failed to prove all of the necessary allegations in the complaint and has therefore failed to prove the case. If this is denied, the defense then proceeds with the presentation of its witnesses.

Each witness is examined by the attorney presenting him as a witness. This is called *direct examination* of the witness. This is immediately followed by *cross-examination* by the opposing attorney, in turn followed by *redirect examination* by the attorney presenting the witness.

When the defense has presented all its witnesses, including the defendants, the defense rests its case. The jury is then excused, with the admonition that they not discuss the case between themselves until they receive the law from the court.

The attorneys and the judge then *argue instructions.* This means that each attorney requests the judge to give the instructions on the law as outlined by that attorney. The judge hears arguments and determines which instructions on the law are to be given, usually including some additional instructions that the court will give *on its own motion,* meaning that the judge adds instructions on the law that he feels appropriate.

After the instructions have been approved, the attorneys present their *final arguments* to the jury. The final arguments are the attorneys' respective positions on how the jury should find in their verdict and why, applying the law to the facts in reaching their respective conclusions. After the final arguments, the judge reads the instructions on the law to the jury. The jury then retires to the jury room to deliberate or discuss the case until they arrive at a verdict. (In most states, the issue of whether or not there is insurance carried by the defendants is not admissible in evidence. Thus the jury is never told whether there is insurance to cover any judgment they might render.)

After the jury reaches its verdict, they notify the *bailiff,* who in turn tells the judge. The bailiff is the court attaché who assists the judge in keeping order in the court, and who tends to the jury, keeping anyone from talking to or disturbing the jurors. The judge returns to the courtroom, the jury returns, and the verdict is announced.

The trial is now over, although either side has the right to appeal to the court of appeals and, if still unsatisfied, to the state supreme court.

THE APPEAL

On appeal, the appellate judges review the records of the proceedings (as typed up by the court reporter) and *appellate briefs* of the law, which are filed by the respective parties. An appellate brief is a statement of alleged errors of law that occurred at the trial, together with citations of previously decided cases supporting the position. No witnesses appear, nor is any new testimony permitted in the appellate court.

Usually neither party is anxious to incur the expense of, or invest the time required in, the preparation, trial, and appeal of a lawsuit if it can be avoided by a reasonable settlement. Settlement negotiations begin at the time the first notice goes to the insurance carrier and continue until a final settlement is reached, even during or after the appeal.

TYPICAL PLAINTIFF'S ARGUMENT

Let us assume a hypothetical case in which Mary Ann Washington, age thirteen, slightly on the chubby side and with limited athletic ability, reluctantly attends her physical education class. Today they are to play field hockey. As Mary Ann moves toward the goal, another girl twice her size comes rushing at her and knocks her down, landing on top of her. Mary Ann lies motionless on the ground. An ambulance is called, and she is removed to the hospital with a broken neck, permanently paralyzed.

In arguing damages to the jury, her attorney states: "Ladies and gentlemen of the jury, Mary Ann Washington was age thirteen at the time of this injury. At age thirteen, she had a life expectancy of sixty years. Mary Ann was in the eighth grade, was receiving good grades, and was headed for high school and then college. You heard her parents testify as to their plans for her future. Those are no more.

"Consider that Mary Ann, as a college graduate, would earn an average of $20,000 per year over her lifetime (which we all know would increase with inflation and with promotions during those years). Assume she would be twenty-two years old at the time of college graduation and would retire at age sixty-five.

"We then, here on the blackboard, multiply that $20,000 per year times her forty-three-year work life expectancy, giving us $860,000. That is for her eight working hours only. Mary Ann, like you and I, could work another job for another eight hours a day and sleep eight hours. She wouldn't do that, as you wouldn't do that, because she would value those other eight hours more highly when used for leisure activities, just as we do.

"Each accident case or injury is unique and different, just as each piece of real estate is unique and different. Those of us who are called upon to evaluate accident claims have certain formulas to guide us, just as real estate appraisers have formulas to follow in measuring the square footage of the house, the size of the lot, and so on.

"The court will instruct you that, if you find for Mary Ann, you should consider the nature and extent of her injury and whether her injuries are temporary or permanent. We ask you to consider the physical pain and mental suffering experienced, and reasonably certain to be experienced in the future by Mary Ann as a result of these injuries. We ask you to consider the value of her lost time, earnings or salaries, and the loss or impairment of her earning capacity. Consider the reasonable expense of necessary medical care, treatment, and services that she has received, together with the reasonable expense of future medical care, treatment, and services. And consider also any disfigurement or deformity resulting from the injuries.

"In this case, we first consider the lost wages of $860,000. To that we add an equal amount for the eight waking hours of her disability or incapacity, or another $860,000. All of her past medical bills and all of the medical bills that her doctors have indicated would probably be incurred in the future should also be added.

"You are then ordered by the court to add a sum for physical and mental pain and suffering. To assist you in this, let me give you a common formula. We take one dollar per hour for her physical pain and suffering, plus one dollar per hour for her mental worry and concern over herself, called mental pain and suffering.

"Let us assume, for the sake of fairness, that she will have eight good, uninterrupted sleeping hours every night, during which she will not suffer. We then multiply the other sixteen hours per day times the two dollars per hour for physical and mental pain and suffering, for a total of thirty-two dollars per day, times 365 days per year, which gives us $11,680 per year, times the sixty years of her life expectancy to age seventy-three, which totals $700,800. To this the court has instructed you that you should add a figure for disfigurement or deformity, so we add another two dollars per hour for those, for a lifetime sum of $700,800 for disfigurement and deformity. These figures on the blackboard total $3,121,600, plus medical bills. This does not make any allowance for inflation over the next sixty years which, when compounded at eight or nine percent per year, accumulates to a rather large figure.

"Ladies and gentlemen of the jury, the testimony is complete. The doctors have done all they can for Mary Ann; I have done all I can for her. The only one who can do anything for Mary Ann now is you by your decision."

* * * * *

That is the way Mary Ann's lawyer would talk to the jury.

There would also be a separate claim on behalf of Mary Ann's parents for their losses, consisting of medical bills paid, nursing and other services contracted, for loss of Mary Ann's services, and loss of her love and affection.

Liability could be based on negligent or inadequate supervision, or for negligently permitting little Mary Ann to play opposite a girl twice her size and weight, in a contact sport where the physical education instructor reasonably should have foreseen that injury might occur to the smaller child.

Aside from arguing that the injury was the result of the negligence of the school, plaintiff's counsel should strive to eliminate a defense based on assumption of risk, by contending that the injury was intentional. He should argue that the risk was not of a nature ordinarily inherent in the sport.

It should be argued that the risk was not one naturally occurring in the game (which would have been assumed by the player), but rather was an extraordinary risk of which the player had no knowledge and, therefore, did not and could not have voluntarily assented. A contestant does not assume the risk of another's negligent act. Plaintiff's counsel should contend that the risk was unusual and not reasonably foreseeable, and that the injured player had no knowledge of such risk. The plaintiff should allege that she did not know, or have reason to know, of any such danger in advance. The plaintiff should charge that required protective measures for the particular sport (as outlined in Chapters 4, 5, and 6 of this book) were not followed. The precautions taken, if any, were insufficient to guard against a danger that the coach should reasonably have foreseen. Plaintiff also should allege that she was a *business invitee* and therefore was owed the duty of reasonable precautions for her safety while on the premises.

In the law of most states, persons who enter or use a premises are divided into three legal categories: trespasser, licensee, and invitee.

A *trespasser* is one who goes on another's premises without permission. This includes retrieving a ball from another's land. A possessor of land owes the duty to a trespasser to refrain from willfully or intentionally injuring him once his presence is known; otherwise, there is no duty owed to a trespasser. When a trespasser is discovered, there is a duty to warn him or her of any concealed dangers.

A *licensee* is anyone who enters another's premises for curiosity, convenience, or entertainment, with the occupier's permission. A social guest falls into this category. The duty owed to such a person is to refrain from gross negligence and willful or wanton misconduct. Willful or wanton misconduct is gross negligence, that is, almost an intentional act with total disregard of consequences. The legal duty is to refrain from intentionally injuring the person. A licensee accepts the premises as they are found.

An *invitee*, or a *business invitee*, is one who comes upon another's property to bestow an economic benefit to the possessor. This includes anyone who enters another's premises at the occupier's invitation to transact business, to perform some act to the advantage of the occupier, or to perform an act to the mutual advantage of both the invitee and the occupant (such as a customer in a store). In return for this "service," the possessor of the property must refrain not only from gross negligence, but also from ordinary negligence. This duty includes using ordinary care to maintain the property in a reasonably safe condition for the use of business invitees, as well as the duty of inspection to make certain it is reasonably safe.

To determine if a duty exists, the courts have been known to look to the following three elements: (1) the likelihood of injury; (2) the magnitude of the burden of guarding against injury; and (3) the consequences of placing that burden on the chosen defendants. Following these lines, the court will determine if the defendant had notice of a dangerous condition that could give rise to foreseeability of injury, such that a reasonable person would have taken precautions (such as something spilled on the floor). To this is added the requirement of using greater care when dealing with children of tender years.

Every plaintiff's attorney should establish fully that the defendant had a duty to the injured person.

TYPICAL DEFENDANT'S ARGUMENT

Two of the most generally relied upon defenses in sports injury cases are (1) incurring or assumption of risk on the part of the player, and (2) contributory negligence of the player. Any defense attorney will immediately look for evidence to support these arguments. A key element in argument for assumption of the risk is that a participant in a contest assumes all risks inherent in the sport. This includes any extraordinary risks of which the person is aware, that is, any foreseeable risks of injury.

Defense counsel frequently stresses that the injured plaintiff wanted to play the game, knew the game, and understood the possibility of being injured. While there is a general rule that a participant in a contest assumes the risks inherent in the game, there are many exceptions. This does not mean that the player assumes the risk of injury resulting from someone else's negligence; nor does he assume any extraordinary risks unless he is fully aware of them ahead of time. Defense counsel will argue that the plaintiff knew of the dangers of the sport, knew of previous injuries, and proceeded to play the sport anyway.

Defense counsel should be ready to combat the plaintiff's allegations (that the injury was intentionally inflicted and that the plaintiff did not voluntarily assent to such a risk). Showing either *contributory negligence* on behalf of the injured player, or assumption of the risks inherent in the athletic activity, serves to establish that the injury was not the fault of the defendant, coach, or school. Contributory negligence is negligence on the part of the injured plaintiff that contributed to causing the injury.

It is a fact of life that the defense will have a harder time establishing assumption of risk or contributory negligence when the plaintiff's injury is serious. The defense should, however, attempt to minimize the damages by establishing, through the defense's doctor, that the injuries are not as serious or as permanently disabling as the plaintiff alleges.

In the hypothetical case of Mary Ann's injury, incurred while playing on the hockey field, the defense attorney would probably argue along the following lines: first, that there was proper supervision. In a class of forty children, there were twenty on the field. There is no way that a teacher, even in close proximity to the colliding students, could have prevented the injury. The law requires physical education classes for everyone, and there was a reasonable breakdown or separation by size of players, in that only one class or grade was on the field at the time. The school could not afford more than one teacher per class.

Second, defense counsel would argue that when Mary Ann decided to play in the game, she thereby voluntarily incurred the risk of such injury and therefore cannot recover for same. Third, counsel would contend that Mary Ann, in abruptly stopping on the playing field or in failing to watch who was running where she planned to run, was contributorily negligent and should, therefore, be barred from recovering. Fourth, counsel would argue that such injuries are just normal incidents of such a contact sport. If anyone was in a position to prevent the collision, it was clearly Mary Ann, who had the last opportunity to do so.

A good defense attorney, representing a teacher or a school district charged with negligent supervision, will always try to establish that the teacher's presence or the taking of precautions could not have prevented the injury.

Counsel for the defense should seek a jury determination of no negligence on behalf of the person in charge at the time of the injury. Evidence should be introduced to show that such person was qualified to perform the functions involved, and that there were sufficient supervisory personnel present (who did everything required, as outlined in Chapter 4 of this book).

Following the general principle that the mere happening of an accident is not negligence, the only way that a school entity could be found liable for an injury would be to show that some duty owed to the injured party was breached. Where the supervisory personnel are found not to have been negligent, the school entity cannot be held liable on the theory of *respondeat superior*, that is, that an employer is responsible for his agent's acts done within the course of his employment. A school entity can only be found liable for a child's injury when the injury results from a breach of some duty it owed to the child.

When a suit is brought for an injury caused by a dangerous condition, the attorney for the defendant should establish that the defendant had no knowledge of such a dangerous condition. This can be accomplished by introducing evidence that no similar accident had previously occurred over an extended period of years. Defense counsel would be sure to mention that certain protective measures were in fact taken to guard against such an injury as did occur. An allegation that any danger was open and obvious to all present, and therefore assumed, would also be of some assistance to the defense's argument.

As another means of defense, the attorney should determine whether or not notice of claim was filed in a timely fashion.

Where a party appears to have been injured while being removed from the location of the injury, defense counsel should be sure to specify that the persons moving the victim were only acting as ordinarily prudent persons would have acted under the same circumstances.

In the case of injury to a spectator, a good defense attorney will always check state laws to determine whether spectators are considered invitees or licensees. This legal distinction determines the degree of cautionary procedures that must be taken to protect those spectators. When a fee is charged or tickets are sold, spectators are usually classed as business invitees.

In a suit brought by a spectator injured while watching a game from the sidelines, the defense attorney should be sure to specify that the precautions taken by the authorities were adequate. This may be done by establishing that the injured party had previously watched, or had some experience with, such a game, including events that had occurred earlier in the ongoing contest.

JUDGE'S INSTRUCTIONS

Attorneys should be aware of any rules violated at the time of injury. The defense attorney should seek an instruction similar to the following: "A knowing violation of a safety rule by a student or spectator constitutes negligence on the part of said person."

The judge's instructions to the jury should represent a neutral statement of the law as it applies to the facts. A typical sampling would be as follows: "While the general rule is that participants in an athletic event assume the risks normally associated with the sport, it is necessary to determine whether the magnitude of the risk assumed outweighs the value that the law attaches to the activity itself. It is not necessary to prove that the very injury that occurred was foreseeable by the school authorities (that is, the party in a position to do something) in order to establish that the defendant's conduct constituted negligence. Negligence is established if a reasonably prudent person would have foreseen that an injury of the same general type would be likely to occur under such circumstances."

In cases of personal injury, the term *proximate cause* means that cause which, in natural and continuous sequence, unbroken by any efficient intervening cause, produces injury or damage complained of, and without which the result would not have occurred. (Proximate cause is usually a question for the jury to determine.)

There is a doctrine in the law called *res ipsa loquitur*, which means "the thing speaks for itself." This doctrine may come into effect under certain conditions in a negligence case. In order for the doctrine to apply, the following conditions must have existed at the time of the occurrence in question: First, the plaintiff was injured or damaged as a proximate result of the occurrence. Second, the instrumentality causing the injury or damage was under the exclusive control of the defendant. Third, the occurrence was of a sort that usually does not occur in the absence of negligence on the part of the person in control.

As an example, an airplane of which the defendant airline company has exclusive control could crash, leaving no survivors. In such a situation, "the thing speaks for itself." Since the occurrence of the crash itself is probative of negligence, it is said to infer negligence, thereby satisfying the burden of proving negligence. The defendant would then have to show, by a preponderance of the evidence, that no negligence was present.

In such a case, the judge's instructions might be something like this: "Since such an accident would not usually occur in the absence of negligence, you may infer that the defendant airline, which was in control of the airplane at the time of the accident, was negligent. You may consider this inference, together with all the other evidence in the case, in arriving at your verdict."

As a pertinent example, consider the case of Ramona Blackburn and two of her friends, who were riding in the rear of a school bus. As the bus passed over a newly constructed roadway and bridge, the rear wheels encountered a severe bump. The three students in the last seat were thrown upward, hit the ceiling, and, on the way down, Ramona hit her mouth on the metal railing in front of her.

The court recognized that when any ordinary bump is encountered, children frequently bounce off their seats. Insufficient evidence was presented to show that the driver had negligently operated the bus, or to show that a separate, unknown third party caused the road's defect. But the court found the owner and driver of the school bus to be responsible on the grounds of *res ipsa loquitor*. In this contest, "the thing speaks for itself" means: (1) that the instrumentality (the bus, not the bumpy road) that caused the injury was under the exclusive control of the defendant; (2) that the circumstances were such that common knowledge would justify the inference that the injury would not have occurred in the absence of negligence.

When *res ipsa loquitor* applies, the injured party will have established a *prima facie* presumptive case of negligence against the defendant. The court ruled that whenever there is a severe jolt, such as a bump of sufficient force to knock one against the ceiling, which is not incident to the normal operation of the conveyance, the doctrine of *res ipsa loquitor* properly applies. (*Blackburn* v. *Boise School Bus Company,* 508 P. 2d 553 [Idaho, 1973].)

The reader will find additional examples illustrating the common, everyday language describing the law, such as the judge uses in his instructions to the jury, throughout this book.

DEFENSE'S ARGUMENT TO THE JURY

The following represents a summation of the evidence, an application of the law to the facts of the case, and the conclusion that the defense attorney wishes the jury to adopt.

The previous discussion outlined an argument for the injured plaintiff. What follows here is an outline of some of the points that defense counsel would make in behalf of the coach, teacher, trainer, or official, as the defendant. For purposes of illustration, it has been assumed that the defendant is a coach.

First, defense counsel would attempt to overcome the natural sympathy for the injured party, which is a factor in all injury cases. Defense counsel will ordinarily express his deep and heartfelt sympathy for the plaintiff, while at the same time reminding the jury of their oath to determine the case based only upon the facts and the law and independent of feelings of sympathy or anger. Defense counsel will sympathetically express his concern for the injured party, but also his concern for the innocent defendant who did not cause the injury.

Counsel would then point out the absence of any preponderance of the evidence, that is, the absence of any proof that anything the coach or school did or did not do was the cause of the injury. He would stress that no witness testified to alleged negligent wrongdoing on the part of the school board, the coach, or anyone connected with the school as a cause of the injury.

Counsel would stress the coach's background and his knowledge in the field of endeavor, such as high school, college, or professional training, as well as his years of experience and efforts to keep up with new developments through postgraduate study, journals, or attendance at institutes. Further note would be taken of the coach's competence to supervise a number of students in a class or on a team, and the presence of any assistant coaches, trainers, student coaches, student trainers, etc. The coach's position as a teacher in the school would also be discussed.

The many hours the coach donated in training and exercising the team should be brought to the jury's attention. The use of protective measures and instruction on the safe way to play a game would also bear mention.

Defense counsel would stress a coach's policy of enforcing rules and seeing to the safety of school facilities and would cite the coach's long career free of any serious injuries to his players. Further mention would be made of the individual attention the coach had given to all participants, as he taught and trained them to develop good safety habits, as well as the coach's custom of educating students in the risks involved and in avoiding these risks. The jury would also be reminded that the opponents were evenly matched, and that it was a hard-fought but fair game.

Counsel would note that, in any contact sport, there is a normal injury rate inherent to that particular sport. It should be stressed that the coach had no prior knowledge of the particular incident or dangerous condition that precipitated or might have contributed to the injury, and that the coach did not have, and could not have had, an opportunity to avoid this particular injury under any circumstances.

It should be established that students are participating in more dangerous, more complex feats of athletics today than they did in former years. It should be emphasized that, if the coach saw a student doing something improper, he was quick to correct and discipline the offending student, and that the coach always required that activities be conducted in the safest way.

Due to television and formal athletic programs, students are more experienced and advanced in their own knowledge of athletics, as well as of the dangers connected thereto. Counsel would stress the great number of elementary, high school, and college programs available in athletics that were not available twenty, thirty, or forty years ago.

It should be noted that the subject type of accident can occur no matter what safety precautions were taken, and that the accident was not caused by any negligence of the coach. The coach did not *cause* the injury to the player.

The jury should also be told that the participant knew of the limitations of the safety mats, shoulder pads, or other safety device involved, and that the participant understood why students are required to use the devices. Participants generally know of other injuries that have occurred to students while using the same equipment and playing the same game, and they thus fully appreciate the risks of engaging in the particular sport and assume such risk voluntarily when they decide to participate.

Defense counsel would note the benefits of participating in sports, such as character building, outlet for competitive spirit, the ability to work with others as a team, outlet for the desire to excel, etc. After making these points, the attorney would point out the detrimental effect of personal injury suits on athletics.

If applicable to the sex of the plaintiff, it should be stressed that boys are inclined to assume risks even greater than those involved in the subject sport when they get into fights or participate in unsupervised sandlot athletics. The comparative safety of organized sports should be contrasted to the dangers of a pickup game on a sandlot. It should be stressed that there are certain risks inherent in any of these activities that cannot be entirely eliminated, even with excellent coaching, equipment, and facilities. Good supervision cannot guarantee that the player will not be injured. Neither the school nor the coach is an insurer or guarantor of player safety.

Jurors are acquainted with the dangers in sports when they see, on television, players lying on the field like wounded gladiators, and they will duly accept the concept of assumption of risk, which is probably the strongest defense in an athletic injury case. *Consent* is another excellent defense in such cases. By participating in the game, each player consents to the brutality and risks naturally inherent in the game.

It should be made obvious to the jury that, like themselves, the participant fully appreciated the hazards and dangers in the venture he undertook and that by playing the game, the participant voluntarily assumed all risks and hazards normal to the game. Then it should be strongly reiterated that, when the injured plaintiff assumed the risk, he lost all ability to recover, even if the defendant school or coach had been negligent. This is the key in a defense based on assumption of risk.

It should also be argued that, even if the injured plaintiff did not have actual knowledge of the particular danger or instrumentality that allegedly caused his injury, he is still barred from recovery if, in his ordinary use of due care for his own protection, he reasonably should have known of such danger (the principle of "constructive knowledge").

It is not sufficient to establish so-called negligence on the part of the coach. It must also be established that the negligence, if any, was the proximate cause (as defined earlier) of the injury. For example, the coach may have been temporarily out of the area at the time of the injury. However, it must be established, by a preponderance of the evidence, that his presence would have prevented the injury and that his absence was the cause of the injury, rather than some other cause such as participation in the game.

To effectively explain this principle to the jury, the defense counsel would draw an analogy to an everyday experience in life. For example, two cars hit in a head-on collision and one of the cars has no taillights. It is obvious that failure to have taillights is negligence, but that negligence had nothing to do with the head-on collision, since the front of each car was involved in the accident. Failure to have taillights was certainly not the proximate cause of the collision, and so it is that mere negligence alone is not sufficient to establish liability.

It must be established by the injured plaintiff, by a preponderance of the evidence, that the negligence, if any, was in fact the proximate cause of the injury.

Another available defense is that of *last clear chance.* This means that even though the coach may have been negligent, if the injured party had the last clear chance to avoid the injury and failed to do so, then the injured party cannot recover from a negligent coach for the injury. The jury should be told that the burden of proving negligence, proximate cause, etc., rests with the injured plaintiff, and that if there is failure of proof on any one of these elements, the jury's verdict must be for the defendant.

In some areas, the so-called *locality rule* applies. This means that the coach is held only to the reasonable standard of care exercised by other coaches in the same or similar localities. For example, a coach in a little country school is not held to the same high standards as a complete coaching staff in a large metropolitan school. (In this regard, defense counsel and all others involved should be aware of the trend toward applying the same national standards in every locality. This trend has arisen due to increased efficiency in communications via television, sports journals, and other means of education.)

The second best defense, after assumed or incurred risk, is *contributory negligence.* As stated previously, contributory negligence is the failure of the injured plaintiff to use reasonable care to avoid injury. Defense counsel should point out that, in this case, without the action of the injured plaintiff in failing to properly look out for and guard himself, or in performing some other act or failing to perform some other act, the plaintiff proximately contributed to the injury. Contributory negligence is an absolute defense.

In some states there is a trend toward *comparative negligence,* whereby the jury compares the negligence of the defendant to the negligence of the plaintiff in arriving at a verdict. In some states, the amount of the verdict is reduced by the percentage of negligence chargeable to the injured plaintiff.

Where comparative negligence exists, it completely replaces contributory negligence. When a jury brings in a verdict, they also bring in a statement as to the percentage of negligence allotted to the plaintiff and the percentage allotted to the defendant. The injured party collects a dollar amount in proportion to the defendant's proportion of negligence. For example, if the defendant is found sixty percent negligent and the plaintiff forty percent contributorily negligent, the injured party will be allowed to collect sixty percent of the award.

The second and third forms of comparative negligence differ only in situations where the plaintiff is found to be fifty percent contributorily negligent. This means that, in some jurisdictions, when the plaintiff is fifty percent negligent, he is completely barred from any recovery at all; in other jurisdictions, he will be allowed to collect the entire amount of the verdict.

The defense should restate to the jury every bit of evidence that tends to show that the injured plaintiff was aware of the danger of the particular sport he was playing, that is, that the plaintiff fully appreciated the risk, that he knew serious injury could result, that he had seen or heard of others seriousiy injured while engaging in such activity, and that such injuries are inseparable from the game being played.

In conclusion, it should be reemphasized that the coach was a good disciplinarian, exercised good standards of supervision and instruction, and was not required to prevent every injury that might arise in the arena.

Limitations on Liability Immunity

CHARITABLE IMMUNITY

The law dealing with *charitable immunity* has been developed primarily by the courts and has been, at best, in a state of flux, if not confusion. Charitable immunity means that a charitable organization cannot be held liable for its negligence or the negligent acts of its agents or personnel.

Some courts have completely abolished charitable immunity; other courts favor it; still other courts limit immunity to the trust assets of the charitable organization, in order to protect trust property, which is held in trust for the charitable purpose only and not for the payment of judgments. The law varies a great deal from state to state. The modern trend is to abolish all immunity, whether charitable, governmental, or other, and to hold everyone equally responsible for their acts.

Some courts have refused to allow insurance companies that charge premiums to charities to insure against liability to hide behind the defense of charitable immunity, thereby holding such organizations liable to the extent of their insurance.

In some cases, courts have distinguished *corporate negligence*, meaning the wrongdoing of the organization itself, as opposed to negligence of one of its employees. Courts have held that the charitable organization is not responsible for the negligent acts of its agents but have held the agent responsible for his own negligence. Some courts have held that the beneficiaries of charitable activities, the recipients of the charity, cannot enforce tort or negligence claims against the charity. They have held that, in consideration of receipt of the charitable help, there is a waiver of liability against the charity, or they indicate an assumption of risk on the part of the party receiving the benefits of the charity.

Employees of charitable institutions are generally covered by Workmen's Compensation statutes in the various states, which limit their ability to recover but make it easier to recover without proof of negligence. This issue has arisen mostly with regard to parochial schools and hospitals operated by religious groups.

GOVERNMENT IMMUNITY

Governmental immunity is based upon a theory that "the king can do no wrong." Government immunity means, generally speaking, that school districts, school boards, or authorities in charge of public schools are immune from tort liability in the absence of legislative enactment or judicial abrogation of the doctrine of governmental immunity. This means that, according to the common law, nobody can sue the government or any of its agents. In most states, however, this law is being changed, either by the legislature or the courts, to allow an injured party to sue the government and its agents. Public elementary schools, high schools, and colleges fall within this category.

Nonliability, or immunity, has been applied to injuries to pupils alleged to have resulted from dangerous conditions at buildings or school grounds, dangerous or defective appliances, unsafe transportation, negligent acts, or failure to act on the part of officers or agents, as well as from lack of, or inadequate, supervision on the part of teachers or others in charge of pupils.

TORTS CLAIMS ACTS

As a general principle, resting upon public policy, the sovereign state, its subdivisions, or agents cannot be sued without the consent of the state. However, most states have given their consent in what are commonly termed *torts claims acts*.

Most state torts claims acts are patterned after the federal Torts Claims Act (28 United States Code, Section 1346 [b]), which permits suits against the United States for "negligence or wrongful act or omission of any employee of the government while acting within the scope of his office or employment, under circumstances where the United States, if a private citizen, would be liable to the claimant. . . ." The United States is not liable for claims based on the exercise of a "discretionary function or duty" by a government agency or employee (such as a decision to build a dam or a road).

When we speak of governmental immunity, we recognize it as being applicable to subdivisions of the state, such as counties, cities, public school corporations, or any other public agency of the state.

School corporations or other agencies in charge of public schools have, by particular laws passed by the legislatures or by court decisions, been held liable for personal injuries due to negligence or failing to adequately supervise pupils while under their control. Statutes (laws passed by the legislature), as well as regulations by boards of education (both state and local) regarding supervision of pupils have been the basis of liability for injuries resulting to pupils when such laws or rules were violated by the person in charge.

GOVERNMENTAL VERSUS PROPRIETARY ACTIVITIES

Some courts have distinguished between proprietary and governmental activities in determining immunity from suit. Some courts hold that governmental immunity applies to governmental acts, such as exercising governmental powers in making and enforcing police regulations for the prevention of crime, the protection of property, public health, and education of the young. Proprietary functions, such as the operation of a public utility or a public golf course, have been held to make the municipality liable. Courts have attempted to distinguish between governmental acts that only a government can perform (such as police protection) and proprietary functions (such as operating a water or light company for money).

One test applied is whether the tort was committed when action was being taken for the common good, such as caring for the poor, as opposed to operating a gas company for a profit. Courts have held that there is no liability for governmental action taken for the common good, but that there can be liability for actions performed for money.

There is no known legal theory that shields a public official, e.g., a teacher or police officer, from liability for his own negligence — for example, a police officer beating a person. Teachers have not been held liable for the good-faith exercise of discretionary powers but have been held liable for their ministerial acts. Where the act requires judgment or discretion, such as the establishing of certain rules and regulations, the courts have found no liability for errors of judgment. These usually pertain to prospective matters, such as things to be done in the future.

Judicial or judgment matters usually require discretion, and sometimes even a hearing, before a determination is made. Courts usually grant immunity for these judgments. Ministerial duties are generally those requiring absolute obedience to the rules, and courts will generally find liability for breach of these. School officials may be held personally liable for failure to perform ministerial duties that are required of them, such as the purchase of insurance when required by law.

Courts have held schools liable for their breach of ministerial duties, such as injury caused when acting in pursuance of a plan that is faulty, or caused by a state of disrepair at a building, or caused by a nuisance existing on the property or in the school building.

SUITS BROUGHT BY CHILDREN AGAINST THEIR PARENTS

Generally speaking, parents have immunity from suits by their own children. Recently, however, courts have even been allowing children to sue their parents for negligence when the child is injured during the course of the parent's business activity. The basis of family immunity is found in the preservation of family harmony. When a member of the family dies, some states have allowed suits against a negligent family member under the rationale that the family unity or harmony will not be disrupted. The courts are beginning to recognize that which we all know, to wit, most of these injury accidents are covered by insurance and family harmony will not be disrupted. In fact, family harmony might be improved with compensation for the lost member of the family.

Only a half-dozen states retain complete charitable immunity. And almost all states have abolished governmental immunity to varying degrees. Naturally, all of the cases and law in this book apply to cases where governmental immunity does not apply.

LIMITATIONS ON LIABILITY AND DEFENSES

Indemnity is a right that inures to a person who has discharged a duty owed by him but which, as between himself and another, should have been discharged by the other. For example, I am an assistant manager of a racketball club. I am sued after someone slips on a puddle negligently left by an employee. After paying the judgment, I can turn around and sue the employee who left the puddle for the damages I have suffered or paid out. Likewise, the owner of the club could join with me or the employee as a codefendant if my negligence also contributed to the accident.

Indemnity also comes into play if a child is injured by a school bus due to faulty maintenance by a garage. The school would then pursue the garage for indemnity, or repayment of the damages paid to the injured student.

Academic freedom, like all other freedoms, is limited. For example: I have the freedom to use my property as I please. However, I may not use my property in such a way as to damage my neighbor by burning tires or keeping wild animals on the premises. Likewise, the limits of academic freedom are exceeded when statements or behaviors impinge upon the rights of others.

For every freedom or right there is a corresponding duty. Freedom of education is no exception to this rule. With greater freedom of education goes greater responsibility and the duty of providing a good education, which includes a safe education. Complete elimination of all high-risk activities is not the solution. Awareness of which actions involve greater risks, however, is a beginning to solving the problem.

As Mr. Justice DeBruler of the Court of Appeals of Indiana stated:

> It should be emphasized here, however, that schools are not intended to be insurers of the safety of their pupils, nor are they strictly liable for any injuries that may occur to them. The duty imposed by this legal relationship is a practical recognition by the law that school officials are required to exercise due care in the supervision of their pupils. . . .
> . . . that while they are neither an insurer of safety nor are they immune from liability. It is not a harsh burden to require school authorities in some instances to anticipate and guard against conduct of children by which they may harm themselves or others. (*Miller* v. *Griesel,* 308 N.E. 2d 701.)

This generally states the law in all of the states throughout the country, to the effect that school authorities may be required, in some instances, to anticipate and guard against conduct that they, as professionals, can reasonably foresee, based upon the teacher's superior knowledge gained from prior classes and the actions of students therein. So if a teacher sees a student doing harm to himself or other persons, there is a duty, as the reasonable teacher in charge, to take some reasonable actions to prevent the child from harming himself or others.

Contributory negligence is the term given to the negligence of the injured party (as defined in Chapter 2). In states with contributory negligence laws, it usually bars the injured party from any recovery in a lawsuit, that is, a defendant will not be held liable for injuries if contributory negligence is successfully proven. About thirty-eight of the fifty states have tempered this rule by applying the principle of *comparative negligence* in the place of contributory negligence. Comparative negligence allows the judge or jury to apportion the damage award among all parties whose negligence contributed to the injury (see Chapter 2).

Assumption of risk (also discussed previously) is the most common defense and is the basis for most verdicts for the defendant.

Further, there can be either joint or individual liability for injuries. If two persons each contribute, by their acts, to a plaintiff's injury, each is liable for the entire injury, even though his act alone might not have caused it. If a school bus stops and does not put out the "Stop" arm or sign, and another car is speeding and strikes a child who has just alighted from the bus, both drivers would be concurrently negligent.

JOINT TORT-FEASORS

Joint tort-feasors are each liable to the injured party for all damages. A person is a joint tort-feasor if he assists and/or contributes to the commission of a tort by another. For example, a teacher negligently allows water to escape onto the gym floor, and the teacher in charge of the succeeding class negligently fails to remove it. Each would be held liable for the entire damage stemming from a resulting injury.

In common law, the release of one joint tort-feasor relieves all. But some courts now hold that it depends upon the intent of the parties and wording of the release as to whether or not the injured party has released one and can then sue the other. *Contribution* is sometimes allowed between joint tort-feasors. This means that a judgment may be rendered against one wrongdoer, who may legally obtain contribution from another who is not sued in the original action. Such an event is based upon the theory that it would be unfair for one person to pay all the damages and the other wrongdoer to pay none. One joint tort-feasor cannot recover from another joint tort-feasor if the second tort-feasor has immunity of some type, such as charitable immunity or governmental immunity.

The current trend is toward contribution among joint tort-feasors. *Several liability* means that the damages are apportioned between two persons whose independent acts cause different injuries to the injured party, assuming that the jury or judge is able to determine which person's negligence caused which injury. If the jury or judge cannot reasonably make such a distinction, each is liable to the injured plaintiff for the whole injury or all the damages. They would then have recourse against each other for contribution.

Occasionally there is a shifting of responsibility, say, when a person's negligent act is superseded by another person's intervening negligence, thereby relieving the first negligent party of liability. As an example, a contractor negligently installs wiring in a health spa, resulting in a short in the whirlpool. The electrical contractor finishes the job and no longer has any control over it or right to inspect it. Over a period of time, the insulation wears off and the whirlpool becomes charged with electricity, resulting in injury to a user. The negligence of the owner of the health spa, in failing to inspect or failing to make certain that the premises are reasonably safe for its paying customers, will result in liability of the owner, which will relieve the contractor of his original liability.

SOURCES OF LEGISLATION

As mentioned previously, there are two sources of laws that govern us. One source is the legislatures in the various states and the Congress of the United States. Laws passed by legislatures are called statutes. The other source of law is prior case decisions by judges and juries in similar cases.

One of the purposes of legislation is to establish a standard of conduct. A violation of these laws or standards usually results in liability for negligence. A good example of this is to be found in our traffic laws. The federal Department of Health and Welfare is now establishing a rather complete set of standards and enforcement procedures, similar to OSHA (Occupational Safety Health Act) guidelines and safety standards for industry.

EMPLOYER LIABILITY AND WORKMEN'S COMPENSATION

Employer liability acts and Workmen's Compensation acts in the various states modify and restrict the use of the common law defenses of assumption of risk, negligence, and contributory negligence.

Most employees in most states are covered by Workmen's Compensation. This means that if a person is injured within the scope of his employment (not off on a lark of his own), he will be compensated by his employer's Workmen's Compensation insurance. The theory behind Workmen's Compensation is that every employee shall be covered regardless of his or her fault. It is true "no fault" insurance. The employees give up receiving an adequate award for their injuries in exchange for receiving compensation for all their injuries. The injured employee need not prove negligence, and defenses such as contributory negligence, assumption of risk, and others are abolished by most Workmen's Compensation Acts in exchange for the limitations on recovery.

Most teachers and coaches, as employees, are covered by Workmen's Compensation insurance. Often, in addition to Workmen's Compensation, the coach, teacher, referee, or other injured person has an additional cause of action against another party other than his employer — which the injured party frequently fails to pursue with his attorney.

INJURED COACHES AND TEACHERS MAY SUE

When a coach is injured in a school bus accident, he can collect his Workmen's Compensation. He can also collect for his medical bills from automobile insurance on his own car, which was parked at home at the time. This personal insurance covers him or any member of his family when involved in any automobile accident, including the school bus accident. He also can collect from the third party who crashed into the school bus. Further, he may be able to collect from the bus manufacturer, who previously may have been held liable for negligently failing to install seat belts in school buses, or from some other defendant who is required by law to respond in damages to such an injured teacher.

Many states have state torts claims acts, similar to the federal government's Torts Claims Act, which allow suits against state employees such as teachers. Some of the laws limit the amount of money that can be recovered under the torts claims laws. Other laws allow suits only for the amount of the insurance carried by the school district. Liability may also be predicated upon the violation of any rules or regulations prescribed by the school board, the state superintendent of public instruction, or other administrative officials.

STATUTES OF LIMITATIONS

Most state torts claims acts, under which most of these actions are brought, have a very short *statute of limitations* for the filing of notice of claim. This means that when someone is injured on the school premises or public property, or through the negligence of a governmental agent such as a teacher or coach, they must, usually within 180 days, file a notice of claim with that governmental agency and serve a copy on the attorney general of the state, the county attorney, or whoever else is involved. It is well to check local statutes in this regard, for such actions are governed by extremely short statutes of limitations. Statutes of limitations state that, unless a notice of claim is filed with all the proper authorities required by the statute, within the time specified by statute, the action can never be brought.

CHILDREN AND CONTRIBUTORY NEGLIGENCE

The majority of states have laws stating that a minor under the age of seven years is incapable of contributory negligence. Further, most states have laws stating that a minor between the ages of seven and eighteen is to be held to a different standard of conduct than an adult, namely, they are usually held only to that degree of care ordinarily exercised by a child of similar age under the same or similar circumstances. It is often well to check not only the state statutes and case decisions, in order to determine what law is applicable to the case, but also to check the local municipal, city, or county ordinances that apply.

BUILDINGS AND GROUNDS LIABILITY

In the law, liability for the negligent maintenance of buildings and grounds is termed *premises liability*. When a person is injured on any premises, what is the liability? The answer in most jurisdictions depends upon the status of the person injured — was the person a trespasser, a social guest, or a business invitee? (These terms were discussed in Chapter 2 but are redefined here for the reader's convenience.)

A *trespasser* is a person who enters the premises of another without permission. Every unauthorized entry to land or a building of another constitutes a trespass. Such entry need not be in person but may be performed by casting something onto the land involved. An owner or occupier of property is under no duty to a trespasser until his presence is known or should reasonably be known. Then the owner or occupant has only the duty of not willfully or intentionally causing injury to the trespasser. However, when the owner or occupant has actual or constructive notice that a trespasser is in a helpless situation or in a position of danger, he is under a duty to use ordinary care to avoid injuring such trespasser. (The above represents the broad, general concepts of law but will vary from state to state.)

A *social guest* or *licensee* is one who, for his own convenience, curiosity, or entertainment, enters the premises of another with the owner's or occupant's permission. A person invited by an employee without authority becomes, at most, a mere licensee when he acts on the invitation. An owner or occupant of property is under no duty to a licensee until his presence is known or should reasonably be known. Such a social guest (or licensee) accepts the premises as he finds them. The owner or occupant has only the duty of not willfully or intentionally causing him injury.

An *invitee,* sometimes called a *licensee by invitation,* is a person who enters the property of another, with the expressed or implied invitation of the owner or occupant, either to transact business with such owner or occupant, to perform some act that is to the advantage of such owner or occupant, or to perform some act to the mutual advantage of the two parties. The terms *invitee, business invitee,* and *licensee by invitation* generally have the same legal connotation. An owner or occupant owes the duty to use ordinary care to maintain his property in a reasonably safe condition suitable for the use of those who come upon it as invitees. The owner or occupant is not an insurer of the safety of persons coming on the premises.

STUDENTS AS BUSINESS INVITEES

A student is generally considered to be a business invitee on the school premises and therefore is owed the duty of reasonable care and of reasonably safe premises. A person's status may change when he goes into an area of the premises that he is not authorized to enter. Thus an invitee, such as a student, may become a mere licensee when he goes into the boiler room. Some courts might even hold him to be a trespasser.

Sometimes it is necessary, in order to show liability on the part of the school, to establish that a negligent condition existed long enough for the school to have remedied it, or to reasonably have discovered it and remedied it. The mere fact that injury occurs on school premises does not, in itself, establish negligence on the part of the school. It is necessary that the injured party present evidence of negligence on the part of the school authorities before liability is established.

Schools have been held legally responsible when they violated a building code, resulting in a dangerous condition and an injury. In one case, a school was held liable when injury resulted from a defective elevator. On the other hand, another school was held not liable when injuries were suffered due to defects in electrical wiring, despite an alleged failure to provide proper fire escapes.

Pupils have sucessfully sued a school for injuries occurring in school shops where proper safety devices or machine guards were not provided, as well as for injuries resulting from machinery disrepair and defective or inadequate equipment furnished by the school.

Many suits have been brought for playground injuries. Courts have generally held that there is no liability for injuries occurring during the use of standard playground equipment that was properly maintained. Liability has been recognized when injury has resulted from poor lighting or an icy sidewalk.

ATTRACTIVE NUISANCE

Courts frequently find liability based upon an *attractive nuisance*, even in the case of trespassing children, if the school had knowledge that children frequently played there and that the children would probably not discover or realize the risk involved in such play. The great majority of American jurisdictions have adopted the so-called attractive nuisance doctrine. This doctrine has sometimes been called the *playground rule* or *dangerous instrumentality rule*.

The *Restatement of Torts* discusses these points as follows:

> . . . a possessor of land is subject to liability for physical harm to children trespassing thereon caused by an artificial condition upon the land if:
> 1. The place where the condition exists is one upon which the possessor knows or has reason to know that children are likely to trespass; and
> 2. The condition is one which the possessor knows or has reason to know, and which he realizes or should realize, will involve an unreasonable risk of death or serious body harm to such children; and
> 3. The children, because of their youth, did not discover the condition or realize the risk involved in intermeddling with it or in coming within the area made dangerous by it; and
> 4. The utility to the possessor of maintaining the condition and the burden of eliminating the danger are slight as compared with the risk of children involved; and
> 5. The possessor fails to exercise reasonable care to eliminate danger or otherwise to protect the children.

This is the type of law that would be applied in a case where a school maintained a swimming pool but left it unlocked and unguarded. The courts would be prone to recognize the swimming pool as an attractive nuisance and would recognize the propensity of children to use it.

In Montana, an eleven-year-old boy brought an action against the board of trustees of the school district to recover for injuries sustained in a fall. The boy was riding his bicycle beneath a monkey bar on school property, and he fell to an asphalt surface when his hands slipped as he grabbed for a horizontal bar. The court held that a case of legal liability might be made under these facts. It was for the jury to decide, since there were a number of issues in question as to whether the monkey bars involved an unreasonable risk of death or serious bodily injury to the boy; whether a boy of plaintiff's age and intelligence should have perceived the danger; whether the school custodian's observation of children's activities on the monkey bars put the school on notice of the risks; and whether the burden of eliminating the danger by procuring a protective ground covering was slight as compared to the risks involved.

From this we learn that teachers, coaches, proprietors, or others involved with children in their recreation, should be ever vigilant for dangerous conditions and should correct them immediately.

PUBLIC AND PRIVATE NUISANCES

Separate and apart from the principle of an attractive nuisance are public nuisances and private nuisances. A *public nuisance* is an unreasonable interference with the land, in such a way as to affect the general public's interest in the areas of health, safety, comfort, peace, convenience, or morals. A *private nuisance* is an unreasonable interference with the enjoyment of land.

When a public nuisance exists, a private individual is not allowed to recover for an injury received unless his injury is different in kind from the injury received by the public at large. If a person operates a hot rod track that causes noise, odor of burning rubber or exhaust fumes, heavy traffic coming and going, and bright lights at night, he could be held guilty of creating a nuisance.

Special relations give rise to duties to aid or protect other persons. One who is required by law to take, or who voluntarily takes, custody of another person, under circumstances such as to deprive the other person of his normal opportunity for protection, is under a duty to take reasonable action to protect that person against unreasonable risk of physical harm, to give him first aid after he knows, or has reason to know, that he is injured, and to care for him until he can be cared for by others.

For example, A is a small child sent by his parents to B's kindergarten. In the course of the day, A becomes ill with scarlet fever. Although recognizing that the child is seriously ill, B does nothing to obtain medical assistance, does not take the child home, and does not remove A to a place where help can be obtained. As a result, A's illness is aggravated in a manner which proper medical attention would have avoided. B is subject to liability to A for aggravation of his condition.

By the same token, if an athlete is injured and the coach recognizes, or reasonably should recognize, that there is a serious injury, he has a duty to immediately render first aid or obtain medical assistance. If he fails to do so and, as a result, the patient's condition is aggravated or worsened, or the healing process is hampered, the coach can be held liable.

This rule of law also has application to teachers in special education or in charge of mentally retarded or physically disabled children.

/ 4 /

Legal Duties and Responsibilities

Generally speaking, liability exists for any and all injuries resulting from negligence. The practice of safety is the best way to prevent liability. It is the duty of a teacher or proprietor not only to practice safety in order to avoid liability and for the protection of students or customers, but also to go one step further by teaching safety practices.

NEGLIGENCE

Negligence on the part of either party to a lawsuit is the failure to do what a reasonably careful and prudent person would have done under the same or like circumstances, or the doing of something that a reasonably careful and prudent person would not have done under the same or like circumstances. In other words, negligence is failure to exercise reasonable or ordinary care.

Reasonable or ordinary care, on the part of both the plaintiff and the defendant, is such care as a reasonably careful and ordinarily prudent person would exercise under the same or similar circumstances.

As defined in Chapter 2, contributory negligence is the failure of a plaintiff (injured party) to use reasonable care to avoid injury to himself, which failure is the proximate cause of the injury for which he seeks recovery. Contributory negligence has also been defined as a plaintiff's conduct that is a legally contributing cause, cooperating with the negligence of the defendant, in bringing about the plaintiff's injury. Under the laws of some states, a child under seven years of age cannot be guilty of contributory negligence.

As we have seen, in most states a child under the age of majority is bound to exercise such care for his own safety as would ordinarily be exercised by a child of like age, knowledge, judgment, and experience under the facts, circumstances, and conditions disclosed by the evidence. It therefore becomes incumbent upon the coach, teacher, or person in charge to give explicit instructions. To ensure that these instructions are actually communicated to the children or persons involved, they should be posted on signs or handed out in printed or mimeographed form.

Remember also that crippled children, mentally retarded children, and other handicapped persons are only required to exercise ordinary care commensurate with their mental, physical, and emotional competence. The law states that while due care or ordinary care is measured by the care that a person of reasonable prudence would ordinarily exercise under like circumstances and conditions, this is not true where the actor is disabled in some way. The care that must be exercised by such a person is measured by the care that a person with such disability, of like age, knowledge, judgment, and experience would ordinarily exercise under similar conditions and circumstances.

In general, when a child is old enough or mature enough to know the difference between danger and safety, and when he is of sufficient age and intelligence to realize and appreciate that a certain course of conduct is attended by great danger, it may be safely said that he can be chargeable with contributory negligence. Knowledge and appreciation of the danger or risk of injury are essential in order for a child to be guilty of contributory negligence.

PARENTS' DERIVATIVE CLAIMS

When a child is injured, a parent has what is called a *derivative claim* for the child's injuries. This means that the claim of the parent derives from the child. Therefore, if the child is contributorily negligent, his negligence not only bars his own recovery, but also the parents' ability to recover.

INCURRED RISK

When a person knows of a danger, understands the risk involved, and voluntarily exposes himself to such danger, that person is said to have incurred the risk of injury. Many courts use the terms *assumption of risk* and *incurred risk* interchangeably. Usually, however, the doctrine of assumption of risk applies where contractual relations exist. The doctrine of incurred risk would apply where the relationship is noncontractual, tortuous, or negligent.

In determining whether a plaintiff incurred the risk, the court would consider the experience and understanding of the plaintiff — whether the plaintiff had reasonable opportunity to abandon or leave the situation or to take an alternative course available to him, and whether a person of ordinary prudence, under the circumstances, would have refused to continue and would have abandoned that course of conduct or that activity.

In the district court of Colorado, a football player brought an action against a player from an opposing team for negligence and reckless misconduct. During the course of a professional game, the defendant struck the plaintiff in the back of the head out of frustration and anger over the interception of a pass intended for the defendant. The court held that the level of violence and the frequency of emotional outbursts in professional football games were such that plaintiff must have recognized and accepted the risk that he would be injured by such an act as that committed by the defendant, and that even if defendant breached a duty that he owed the plaintiff, the plaintiff could not recover because he must be held to have assumed the risk of such an occurrence. (*Hackbart* v. *Cincinnati Bengals, Inc.*, 435 F. Supp. 352.)

Consider that this case arose in 1977. It is doubtful, if this case were tried again today, that the outcome would be the same. It should be remembered that no two cases need come out the same, since no two alleged negligent acts, injuries, or juries are exactly alike.

Where one voluntarily and knowingly places himself in a certain environment or undertakes to use a certain instrumentality and, as a consequence, receives an injury, his right to recover therefrom may be defeated by the doctrine of incurred risk, even though he may have exercised due care. This means that when one decides to play football and is injured, even though he is very careful himself, his right to recover may well be defeated by that doctrine.

It is important to thoroughly understand the defense of incurred or assumed risk, since these are the defenses most commonly used in athletic injury cases.

The doctrine under discussion may be restated as follows: One who knows of a danger arising from the act or omission of another and understands the risk therefrom, and who nevertheless voluntarily exposes himself to it, is precluded from recovering for an injury that results from the exposure.

The incurring of risk must be truly voluntarily. If continued exposure to a known risk of injury is due to a lack of reasonable opportunity to escape after the danger is appreciated, or if continuance of exposure to the danger is the result of influence, circumstances, or surroundings that are a real inducement to continue, the doctrine does not apply, since the exposure is not in a true sense voluntary. The burden of establishing incurred risk is upon the defendant.

For example, various court decisions have ruled for incurred risk in cases where a person continued to ride in a car in thick and dangerous fog, the danger of which must be anticipated, or continued to ride in a defective car, such as one without lights or with an obviously drunken driver, given a reasonable opportunity to abandon the journey. Under such circumstances, it can be reasonably assumed that the risks will continue unabated.

If there is an opportunity to abandon the pursuit of an athletic activity at some point that would provide shelter and an opportunity to do something else, or do it in another way, the jury might conclude that the athlete who continues to play incurred the risk by continuing. One must voluntarily and willingly take a risk by refusal to take advantage of a reasonable and safe opportunity to abandon the pursuit of the game. The doctrine of incurred risk involves a voluntary choice of the individual between a course of action known to be dangerous and one that is not dangerous.

Where one voluntarily and knowingly *places* oneself in a certain position and undertakes to use a certain instrumentality and is thereby injured, his right to recover may be defeated under the doctrine of incurred risk. For example, if a pole vaulter uses a pole designed for a lighter person because it bends more easily and offers more whip, and if it breaks and he falls and injures himself, he may then be said to have knowingly used a dangerous instrumentality. In such a case, the athlete's right to recover may be defeated under the doctrine of incurred risk.

When a coach or teacher is injured, the defense used against him would more properly be termed *assumption of risk* because of the employer/employee contractual relationship between the coach and the school board. An employee assumes all the ordinary risks incident to the work for which he is employed, including those risks that are open and obvious to observation and that can be seen and appreciated by an ordinarily careful and prudent person. However, an employee does not assume extraordinary risks of which he is ignorant, which are not obvious, and which cannot be readily seen and appreciated by an ordinarily careful and prudent person.

As discussed in other chapters, in a Workmen's Compensation insurance claim by an employee against his employer, the defenses of contributory negligence and incurred risk are not available to the defendant employer or his insurance carrier.

RESPONDEAT SUPERIOR

When a teacher is negligent, the school administration, such as the principal, vice-principal, school board, and the like may also be held liable under the theory of *respondeat superior*. This is sometimes referred to as the *principal and agent theory* of liability, which means that the principal is liable for the acts of his agent. Translated, this means that the school board or school administration will be liable for the acts of teachers.

A general *agent* is a person who, by agreement with another called the *principal*, acts for the latter and is subject to the control of the latter. By this we do not mean only the principal of a school. Principal, as used here, includes a school principal, the head of a department, the school board, the school corporation, the municipality that runs the school, or the proprietor of a business. It is anyone who is a supervisor or employer of a teacher/agent or employee/agent.

In contrast, an *independent contractor* is a person or corporation who or which renders service in the course of an independent occupation, representing the will of the employer only as to the result of the work, and not as to the means by which it is accomplished. An independent contractor is one who makes an agreement with another to perform a task, retaining to himself control of the means, method, and manner of producing the result to be accomplished, neither party having the right to terminate the contract at will.

An agent exists when a principal has control of the manner in which the job is done, that is, the details of how it is done. In an independent contract situation, the independent contractor has control of the manner of doing the job and the details of how it is to be done.

Principals, meaning employers, may be held responsible, independent of any acts of any agent, if they have been negligent in the selection of an agent (for example, if they select a person as a coach who has a known propensity for child abuse). They may also be held responsible if they select a teacher, coach, or other agent who is not adequately trained in safety or in the subject to be taught.

For example, if a health spa employs someone to operate a reducing machine and that person does not know how to safely operate it, and if a person is injured using the machine, the employer may be held liable. By the same token, if a school employs someone to teach gymnastics who is not qualified and, as a result, a student is injured, the school may be held liable, independent of the principal/agent relationship.

The jury is usually provided with a definition such as the following: "A general agent is a person who, by agreement with another called the principal, acts for the principal and is subject to control by the principal." The jury would be further instructed that "a corporation can act only through its officers, employees, or agents. Any act or omission of an officer, an employee, or an agent, acting within the scope of his authority, is the act or omission of the corporation." Further, "an agent is acting within the scope of his authority if he is engaged in the transaction of business that has been assigned to him by his principal."

When a janitor or coach negligently leaves a trampoline in the gymnasium and a child is injured playing thereon, the agent (the janitor or coach) is usually sued along with the principals. The principals may include the school principal, superintendent, school board (as a group or individually), a dean, or college president. Anyone who is in charge, has supervision over, or has control over the agent might be held liable.

Often the agent is not even sued, or the case against the agent is dismissed during the trial. The injured party has the option of suing any or all of the possible principals.

In 1939 a New York court ruled (in *Thompson* v. *Board of Education,* 280 N.Y. 92, 19 N.E. 2d 796) that a school principal was not liable in a case where a fourteen-year-old girl sued the teacher and principal for injuries incurred while descending a stairway with twenty-four other children. In this case, a boy was running down the stairs and collided with the plaintiff, causing her to fall. The teacher in charge of the children had taken the girls out of class and started them down the stairs. When the head of the line reached the bottom of the stairs, the teacher went back to the classroom, such that the accident happened while the teacher was absent.

The court held that there was no proof of negligence on the part of the teacher, but that the principal was liable. Plaintiff's complaint alleged negligence in allowing overcrowding and unsupervised roughhousing by the boys. The appellate court reversed the decision, stating that the principal was not liable because he had exercised such general supervision as was reasonable. The court said supervision by the principal consisted of the following:

1. He held regular conferences with his thirty-four teachers; ingress and egress of the pupils, dismissal of classes, and safety procedures were discussed, and rules were laid down at these one-hour conferences.
2. He established a rule that teachers were to see to the entire dismissal of a class.
3. He told the teachers to place themselves in a strategic position during dismissals.
4. He instructed teachers to use their discretion as to whether to lead, be in the middle, or be at the rear of the class, according to where they would exercise greatest control of the class.
5. He instructed the teachers to admonish pupils against jostling and any other behavior detrimental to their safety. In supervising the overall school, the principal personally observed dismissals, regularly inspected the stairways and corridors, shut down stairways he found unsafe until repaired, directed children to go down the stairway that gave the fastest and safest egress, and forbade the use of outside stairways in bad weather.
6. He followed the general course of practice in well-regulated schools.

In supervising the plaintiff's class, the principal put a mature teacher with twenty-nine years experience in charge, limited the class to twenty-five pupils, modified the program of this class to avoid loss of time because these pupils were behind in their studies, and provided this class with almost the private use of the stairway, avoiding the heavy traffic on the other stairway.

In supervising the pupils, the principal personally admonished children whenever he witnessed unruliness on exiting, talked to them in his office, spoke to the teacher when he was not satisfied with a dismissal, and sent for the parents to come to his office when appropriate.

Principals (in the legal sense) are responsible only for acts of an agent that are performed within the scope of the agent's authority, that is, within the scope of his employment. For example, a coach may drive students to a game as a part of his job or a normal incident of it, which would place liability on his principals. If he invites the team to his house on Saturday to go swimming, he is clearly acting outside the scope of his authority or duties. He may still be a teacher, agent, or employee of the school, but he is clearly acting on his own.

Principals (including school principals, superintendents, school boards, deans, college presidents, or others) have rarely been held responsible for acts of an independent contractor, and then only if they were negligent in the selection of the independent contractor, if they were negligent in giving directions to the contractor, or if they were negligent by providing him with defective equipment. As a general rule, there is no liability on the part of principals, once they have selected an independent contractor, for any acts of the contractor. By definition, an independent contractor is not his employer's agent. The independent contractor is in control of his own work, usually having independent financial responsibility and insurance.

On March 13, 1965, Cumberland High School won the right to participate in the Wisconsin state basketball tournament, which was to be held March 18–20 in Madison. The principal arranged for three buses to carry the students, faculty, and chaperones. On an interstate highway en route to Madison, one of the buses struck a car from the rear. The car belonged to a Cumberland High School faculty member, Matthew G. Lofy. Mr. Lofy was killed, and his wife and children were injured as a result of the accident. Suit was filed against the school district, the municipality, the transportation company, the bus driver, and their insurance companies. Wisconsin had a law that the school district "may provide transportation" for extracurricular activities. The school principal signed a "commercial charter coach order" to rent the buses with drivers.

The bus driver and his principal, the bus company, were held liable, but the school district, municipality, and their insurance carriers were held not liable, since the bus driver and the bus company were said to be independent contractors and not agents of the school or municipality.

The test to determine responsibility for an injury is: who should have anticipated the harm, and could he have acted, before the harm occurred, to prevent it?

There has been a recent trend to hold board members personally liable. Thus it would be wise for school districts to make sure that the corporation carries insurance to protect individual members of the board, as well as the corporation itself. This is best accomplished by asking the attorney or insurance agent for the school board to make certain that adequate and proper insurance is carried in a sufficient amount.

SUPERVISION: ADEQUATE OR NEGLIGENT?

Many judgments have been based on negligent supervision in lawsuits brought against teachers, coaches, and officials. Even when negligent supervision is not the major charge in such suits, however, it is almost certainly a subordinate issue.

The law reads that a coach or teacher of a physical education class or, for that matter, any other class, has a duty to *adequately* supervise the students under his charge. Trying to specifically define that duty is like trying to define the duties of a parent, since teachers have been said to stand *in loco parentis* (to be substitute parents) to their pupils.

To explain this, we will describe in specifics the duty owed, a breach of which constitutes negligence. Then we shall examine some cases and try to define that legal duty further and more specifically. It will not help to address this in broad generalities or broad legal concepts. Therefore we will apply it to fact situations within physical education, recreation, and coaching.

A duty to supervise includes, but is not limited to, the duty to properly instruct. This means that before one permits a student to go out for recess or to participate in a gymnastics event, one must make certain the he has been properly instructed, not only in the manner of doing the activity but in how *not* to do it. In other words, a coach has a duty to see to it that a participant does not do something wrong in ignorance because the coach has negligently failed to instruct him.

The concept also includes the duty to protect students from unsafe activities. This means that if a student is seen doing something that the older, more learned coach recognizes, or reasonably should recognize, as being beyond the scope of the participant's ability, or as being done in a dangerous way, the coach has the duty to stop that student immediately, so as to prevent him from harming himself.

As an example, take the case of a student who did not know what he was doing and was attempting to pole-vault without sufficient mats. A court ruled that it was the duty of the coach to stop him, even to the point of tackling him as he ran to execute the vault.

A coach has the duty to determine whether an activity is too risky and, if in his judgment it is, to ensure that the student avoids the activity.

With regard to equipment, it is not sufficient for a coach or trainer to say, "There is the equipment room. Select a uniform that fits you and report to the field." Courts have held coaches responsible when players wore improperly fitting helmets that resulted in severe neck injuries and for similar equipment injuries. The coach must fit the gear properly to the participant.

While the coach is not a medical examiner, he does have the duty to observe, to read medical reports submitted by participants, and to be aware of any disabilities of participants. A teacher was held responsible by a court for permitting a student in a physical education class to somersault over a horse when she had a physical limitation resulting from childhood polio.

(This case was tried by one of the authors and will be discussed in greater detail later.)

The coach also has a duty to make certain that the players are properly matched. Liability has been found where a much larger girl participating in a sport severely injured a much smaller girl. This concept includes the duty to ensure that participants are positioned far enough apart to avoid colliding with one another.

The coach has a duty to be aware of the background and experience of participants, and to be personally familiar with the ability of participants. And the courts have ruled that a coach or physical education instructor has the duty to bring a student along slowly, starting with the very simple skills and working up gradually. Liability has been found where a student was permitted to do a forward somersault off equipment at tryouts for a gymnastics team without first demonstrating ability to execute skills leading to this move.

It is the duty of the coach to have experience and knowledge in the activities he teaches. It is the duty of the school board, as legal principals in the principal-agent sense, to ensure that the coach is adequately trained and has the background and experience to coach the specific activity for which he is responsible. The coach has a duty to know what is needed in the form of skills before permitting an athlete to progress to more difficult feats. And the coach is responsible for knowing the norms or standards required in a certain sport.

In *Gardner* v. *State* (22 N.E. 2d 344), a New York court ruled that failure to adequately instruct in the proper method of performing a headstand resulted in injuries to an eleven-year-old girl, due to negligent supervision. A California court held a physical education instructor liable for negligent supervision when a seventeen-year-old girl, doing a dive-roll over two persons kneeling on the floor, suffered injury while the instructor was watching. The court said the jury could find negligence if the teacher failed to adequately test the participants before letting them try this stunt. (*Bellman* v. *San Francisco High School District*, 81 Pac. 2d 894.)

In *Ceda* v. *Board of Education* (152 N.Y. St. 2d 356), a pupil in a gymnastics class was swinging on the horizontal bars, fell, and was hurt. The court found no liability, stating that general supervision would not have avoided the accident. The court said the requirement of supervision of the specific apparatus would be unreasonable and that risk of falling was assumed by the participant.

In another case, an eleven-year-old child was injured playing on the rings during a gymnastics class. The child stood up on the rings, fell backwards, and injured her back. The court said the instructor was guilty of negligent supervision in failing to adequately demonstrate the stunt, failing to adequately instruct the spotters, and failing to keep the apparatus in full view during the class (in violation of a school policy).

We have attempted to be as clear and specific as possible in this discussion. But above all, it should be remembered that a coach or teacher in charge has a duty to know all the things that a reasonably prudent coach or teacher, under the same or similar circumstances, would have known.

It is the duty of the person in control to maintain control. This includes the duty to discipline. It is not enough to tell the class or team members the rules. Rules are worthless unless they are enforced, and the coach or teacher is the enforcer. If there is a lawsuit and all the students testify that the coach permitted horseplay in the shower room, the coach may be held liable if he failed to see that the students were protected from themselves.

There is a duty on the part of the coach to warn students of any hazards on or about the premises or playing field. This requires the coach to make a reasonable inspection of the premises, so that he will be aware of any hazards, to correct them if possible, or to *adequately* warn all students and any spectators of the existence of such hazards. It may even be advisable to call off a game.

Whose duty is it to clear the swimming pool in the park when there is lighting? Obviously it is the duty of the one in charge. This same basic principle applies when any other known or observable hazards are present.

The duty to inspect means to make an "adequate" inspection. Adequate is defined as "what a reasonably prudent person, under the same or similar circumstances, would have done."

There is a duty to protect the players from unsafe activity, whether it be horseplay in the locker room or overly aggressive, rough, unsafe play on the field.

The courts have ruled that there is even a duty on the part of a teacher or coach to anticipate acts of children and adolescents and to understand and know in advance how they will act. This does not imply reading minds. It simply means that when you deal with children every day, the coach (like the parents on a jury) knows that children do foolish and irrational things. As a substitute parent, the coach has a duty to anticipate these acts and prevent them from happening if "a reasonably prudent person, under the same or similar circumstances, would have so done." (This phrase is intentionally repeated throughout this discussion because it is the broad, general, basic standard for judging a person's duty, and because it is always part of the instructions on the law that the judge reads to the jury in explaining a person's duty at the time of an accident.)

Courts have said that peer pressure and pressure from the coach should be weighed when considering the ability of students. It should be recognized that, when trying out for a team, young persons are under significant pressure to go beyond what they reasonably should do. This is not to say, however, that a jury would not realize that a good coach has a duty to push athletes to their limit and to make winners out of them.

The physical or recreation educator or coach should have sufficient first aid training and knowledge of medicine to know not to move an athlete with a neck injury. He also needs to know what to do in case of other emergencies.

THE CASE OF BRUCE DIKER

In a suit brought by Bruce Diker (a minor) and Louis Diker (his father and natural guardian) against the city of St. Louis Park, Minnesota, the supreme court of Minnesota ruled that there was no duty to provide supervision. The facts of the case were as follows:

On February 6, 1959, Bruce Diker, then ten years of age, sustained serious injury when struck near the eye by a puck while playing hockey at a public skating rink maintained by the defendant. The Minnesota supreme court (*Diker* v. *City of St. Louis Park,* 130 N.W. 2d 113) stated:

> The evidence offered at trial does not sustain the finding of negligence. . . . The rule is well established in Minnesota that a private person operating a place of public amusement is under an affirmative duty to make it reasonably safe for his patrons, and that the obligation of due care includes supervision and control of others on the premises whose actions may cause injury, at least where the defendant has actual or constructive knowledge of the activities involved.
>
> There is a difference between that relationship which exists between a municipal corporation and a person making use of a park or playground provided without charge, on the one hand, and that which exists between the owner of a private enterprise conducted for profit and its patrons, on the other. A person who pays for admission has more reason to expect that supervision will be maintained and adequate equipment provided as partial consideration for the admission charge. Proprietors can adjust such charges to spread their cost of protection among those benefitted by it. A municipality, in contrast, provides recreational facilities to people generally, and if no admission charge is made, the cost of measures to prevent possible injury must be carried by the public in the form of taxes.
>
> If the identical precautions are required in this situation, as are to be expected from a private owner, operating for a profit, the result may be that public funds will be spent for protection from a remote hazard, easily avoided by the users, which could be spent with greater overall benefit to make healthful recreation more widely available. The general requirement is the same in the one case as in the other; that is, "due care under the circumstances." But the facts are that the responsible authorities in allocating available public funds must balance the need for extending and maintaining recreational facilities against the need of guarding against foreseeable dangers to those using certain of them . . . a circumstance which must be considered in determining the acts or omissions which do or do not meet the precise standards. Therefore, a precedent which controls in testing facts by the standard of care owed to a business invitee, while helpful, is not necessarily controlling.

The court then went on to rule: "It is our opinion that a municipality making a skating rink available for the general public without charge has no duty to provide supervision of those participating in the games being played on the ice and no duty to provide equipment for such games."

However, the court also stated: "If it assumes such a duty [supervision or equipment], it must apply reasonable care to perform it adequately." The ruling continued:

There is no evidence that defendant assumed supervision over persons skating and playing on the ice at the time and place in question. The supervision which had been afforded was limited to that provided by referees and voluntary coaches while games were in actual progress; a "warming house attendant" was stationed at the rink, but his responsibility was the supervision of activities occurring in the warming house. The city had not assumed the responsibility of supervision of "practice sessions" such as the one in which Bruce Diker was participating when hurt, and in our judgment, a finding of negligence cannot be based on its failure to do so.

However, the court went on to say: "But the city did assume the duty of furnishing equipment to the boys who played hockey at the rink. Face masks were not provided. If, at the time of the accident, masks were available, which could have prevented the occurrence of this injury, the jury could have found that the failure on the part of the city to *include* [emphasis added] a face mask in the equipment provided by it constituted negligence proximately causing the injury sustained by Bruce Diker."

Mr. Leroy Theis, employed by the defendant, was on duty the evening of the accident. He had some acquaintance with Bruce Diker, having observed him at the community center on a number of occasions. He was charged with possessing knowledge that Bruce was immature and probably not skilled as a hockey player. Mr. Theis knew that Bruce intended to play goalie in a game with boys ranging in age from ten to eighteen.

Mr. Theis also knew of the hazards involved. He testified: "I told him that I wouldn't advise him to go out into the goal to act as a goaltender, because he was not a regular goaltender, and he told me . . . Well, I can't repeat the words, but he just told me to give it [the goaltender's equipment] to him, so I gave it to him. . . . I advise all boys that are not regular goalies not to go in the goal. They have no business there."

He gave such advice, he said, because he knew "that it is a dangerous thing to do."

Nevertheless, Mr. Theis gave Bruce the equipment then on hand, including a chest protector, shin guards, and gloves. Following this occurrence, a face mask was added to the equipment and made available by the city, but we cannot tell from the record whether a protective mask adequate to prevent injury of the type involved in this case was obtainable by the city at the time of the injury. The court ruling continued:

The burden of presenting this evidence was on the plaintiff. The record indicates the possibility that facts relevant to this question could be produced in the event of a new trial. It is our conclusion, therefore, that the matter should be retried and permitted to show, if they can, that the defendant city was negligent in the performance of its *assumed* [emphasis added] duty of providing the equipment to those using its skating rink for the purpose of playing hockey and that this failure, if there was one, was the proximate cause of the harm.

Generally speaking, one who participates in a game assumes the inherent risks in the contest. If plaintiff is to be held to the same standard of care or risk comprehension as an adult, it is clear that a verdict should have been directed for the defendant. In Minnesota, the hazard of being struck by a flying puck is held to be of the same nature as the danger of being hit by a baseball insofar as spectators at games are concerned. . . .

Since the puck is round with a flat bottom and top, it is not always possible for a particular player to determine the direction the puck will take when in flight, nor how high it will rise. Any person or ordinary intelligence cannot watch a game of hockey for any length of time without realizing the risks involved to the players and spectators alike.

Hockey is played to such an extent in this region and its risks are so well known to the general public, that as to the question before us, there is no difference in fact between the two games as far as liability for flying baseballs and pucks is concerned.

We are dealing here, however, with a boy only ten years of age.

. . . children, through childish inattention, may fail to observe conditions which an adult might reasonably be expected to discover. Even if they know of the condition, there may be risks which it may not be reasonable to assume that children will appreciate.

The close line of demarcation which separates contributory negligence or assumption of risk *as a matter of law* [emphasis added] from an evidentiary situation which is for determination by the jury, is illustrated by two recent cases from the state of Massachusetts.

Before discussing the two Massachusetts cases cited by the Minnesota court, a word is in order regarding the phrase *as a matter of law*. This is a key phrase found in many such cases. When a court rules contributory negligence as a matter of law, or assumption of risk as a matter of law, it means that there is no fact question involved. Thus the court rules, as a matter of law, that the facts indicate absolutely one way or the other. The judge is saying that this is not an evidentiary or fact question to be submitted to the jury for a decision, but rather the judge rules as a matter of law that the plaintiff was in fact contributorily negligent.

In so doing, the judge takes the fact question away from the jury and rules that in no way could reasonable minds differ from the ruling, since it is such an obvious ruling to make. In the reverse situation, the judge would feel that there is evidence on both sides and would allow the jury to decide the question as an evidentiary matter.

To state the principle in another way, it means that the facts are so overwhelming that, even if the jury were to decide the other way, the judge would overrule the jury and make his original ruling. For example, there might be overwhelming evidence of assumption of risk of possible head injury in a case involving a boxing match. In that event, the judge would probably rule, as a matter of law, that there was an assumption of risk, thereby removing the assumption of risk question from consideration by the jury.

In general, the jury (if one has been requested by either side) is the finder, determiner, or "judge" of the facts, and the trial judge determines the law. Rulings made as a matter of law are the exception to the general rule.

To return to the case of Bruce Diker, the court cited the following cases:

> In *Pouliot* v. *Black* (170 N.E. 2d 709), it was held as a matter of law that a ten-year-old plaintiff hit by a golf ball while "shagging" on a driving range was contributorily negligent in light of his testimony indicating that he knew the danger of being hit. On the other hand, in *Farinelli* v. *Laventure* (172 N.E. 2d 825), a ten-year-old plaintiff at a roller-skating rink was held not to be contributorily negligent as a matter of law when knocked down by other skaters whom she had previously observed "doing the whip." A court there said under the circumstances of that case, the plaintiff's conduct must be judged in the light of her immaturity and the lack of the caution and judgment natural to her youth.

The Minnesota court continued with citation of another case:

> In *Aldes* v. *St. Paul Ball Club, Inc.* (88 N.W. 2d 94), the plaintiff, a twelve-year-old, was struck by a flying baseball at St. Paul Baseball Park. The minor had been induced to leave the seat assigned to him and sit in a box seat by an employee of the defendant. The court, after noting that plaintiff was well acquainted with the dangers inherent in open seats and aware that misdirected balls generally land in the box seats, said ". . . while it is evident from his own testimony that plaintiff could have appreciated the greater dangers involved in occupying a box seat if he had paused to consider them at the time . . . it is not clear that he did so, and we see no reason for holding him to the same standard of sober reflection which we would require of an adult. The workings of the mind of a boy of his age are not susceptible to ironclad rules. For this reason, the law imposes upon him the duty to act only with the degree of care commensurate with his age, experience, and judgment."

In *Roy C. Pasentino* v. *Board of Education of the City of New York*, the court issued the following explanation:

> From the testimony of the injured plaintiff, it appears that the reason he was hit by the flying puck was that he "froze" and was unable to duck to evade it. The shot traveled the distance of forty feet. If he had not "frozen," it is probable that he would have been able to avoid being hit. There is nothing in the testimony to indicate that he had experienced such difficulty before and nothing to indicate that he had been hit in the face or head on any prior occasion. To a person of mature judgment, the possibility or even the probability that an unskilled goalie with limited skating ability would freeze in the path of a flying puck would seem to be readily anticipated. However, with respect to a plaintiff not yet eleven, we feel that the jury could find as it did, apparently, that because of his youth, he should not be precluded from the recovery as a matter of law.
> Finally, the defendant assigned as error refusal of the trial court to let the jury consider the defense of contributory negligence on the part of the father of the injured boy. Such a defense, if established, could bar recovery of medical expenses caused by the accident. The evidence in the record indicates that the father permitted the boy to play hockey at the community rink and provided him with some hockey playing equipment. There is no evidence that he knew he was playing in a particularly dangerous position as goalie. There is no evidence to indicate that he knew that the equipment

provided was inadequate to protect the boy against being hit in the face by the flying puck when stationed in the nets for the purpose of obstructing the flight of these missiles. In the absence of such knowledge, there was a failure on the part of the defendant to maintain his burden of proving contributory negligence on the part of the father as a matter of law.

Here we see the concept of *guilty knowledge* being stressed by the court, when it states that the absence of such guilty knowledge relieves the father of any contributory negligence.

The case was reversed and a new trial granted. Ultimately, the New York supreme court, appellate division, reduced the $1.8 million verdict to $1 million and affirmed the judgment.

* * * * *

In summary, when considering the issue of adequate supervision, the courts will consider whether or not the student or player was acting on directions of the teacher or coach, the foreseeability of injury, any intervening causes (such as acts of fellow players), the possibility of prevention, and the contributory negligence or assumption of risk by the injured party.

MALPRACTICE

Negligence on the part of a teacher or coach may be called *malpractice*. This means failure of a teacher or coach to exercise that degree of reasonable or ordinary care and skill in the performance of his profession that is normally possessed and exercised by a teacher or coach engaged in the same line of work. Negligence may consist of performing some act that a teacher or coach should not have performed under the circumstances, or the failure to do something that should have been done under the circumstances.

LOCALITY RULE

Some states still apply the *locality rule*, which means that a teacher would be held only to the reasonable or ordinary care and skill exercised by other teachers in the same locality, such as in the same state or within the same school corporation.

A coach or teacher may also incur liability as a principal (in the legal sense of the term) when he delegates a task to an assistant coach or to a student helper. When a coach or teacher appoints a subagent, he may be held responsible as a principal for the negligent acts of his agent or subagent. The teacher's employer may also be held responsible for the negligence of the teacher's agent or subagent.

A teacher and his school may be held liable for failure to *adequately* inform the students of safety rules, for example by posting signs or supplying the information at the point of use. Safety rules are fine in themselves; however, there is a duty to communicate them to the consumer, ultimate user, or participant in an athletic event, in order to avoid liability. It is not sufficient to establish such rules; it must also be shown that they were communicated to participants.

IN LOCO PARENTIS

It is common to say that a teacher stands *in loco parentis*. As defined previously, this principle means that the teacher or coach who is present is given, by law, the status of a parent, with some of the parent's privileges. These privileges, given to aid in the education and training of a child, do not extend beyond matters of ordinary conduct and discipline. Among the duties owed to an athlete by a school entity are the following:

1. Providing proper instruction for the activity.
2. Providing proper equipment for the activity.
3. Making reasonable selection of participants.
4. Providing proper supervision of the game.
5. Taking proper precautions to guard against postinjury aggravation.

A school entity's duty to use care relative to spectators would not be as great for an intramural activity as it would be for a formal scholastic contest with another school in which admission is charged and a larger crowd attends. If a grade school conducts an activity on its playground, it is not necessary that the school erect physical barriers to hold back spectators, since to do so could have prevented the athletic event from being staged.

Prudent teachers will find that courts will protect them. Only negligent teachers need fear the courts.

PRODUCT LIABILITY

Product liability refers to the liability of a manufacturer, processor, seller, lessor, or anyone furnishing a product that causes injury to another. Liability is predicated on negligence, breach of warranty or, most recently, strict liability.

When one manufactures or sells an article, by operation of law the product carries certain guarantees called *implied warranties*. In addition, there may be some written guarantees called *express warranties*. Implied warranty means that the law requires that a product sold must be reasonably fit for the purpose for which it is sold. Negligence means that there is some hidden danger or defect in the product.

One of the necessary elements of a product liability case is to properly and adequately identify the defendant manufacturer or seller as the one who truly manufactured or sold the product, and to show that there was a sale. Sale here simply means to place the product in the ordinary channels of commerce, as for example by retail sale, lease, or other commercial transaction. This would include furnishing a football helmet to a player at a school or furnishing a treadmill to a jogger at a health spa.

Courts have held that one who puts out a product bearing a trade name, for example Sears, Roebuck & Co., is liable as a manufacturer, even though that person or company had somebody else manufacture it. The actual manufacturer can also be brought in as a party-defendant. Usually, in a product liability case, courts will only hold liable one who is in the business of furnishing such products. If a private person is simply selling a used car, he is not held to the same standard as one who is in the business of selling used cars. That a product is defective or ultrahazardous must always be proved in a product liability case.

Defective simply means that something is wrong, does not work, or is faulty about the product involved. *Ultrahazardous* means more than dangerous. For example, a butcher knife may be dangerous, but hook that knife onto a rotating motor and leave it exposed without a guard, and it then becomes *ultrahazardous*. In such a case, liability would be recognized if someone were injured by such an ultrahazardous product.

In order to prove a product liability case, it is necessary to prove that the product, at the time of injury, was in substantially the same condition as it was when it left the manufacturer's or seller's hands. That is to say that it had not undergone any major change that contributed to the injury. The manufacturer is not responsible for any injury caused by modification of the product. If the modification is minor and did not contribute to the injury, then the product is considered to be in substantially the same condition as when it left the hands of the seller.

Frequently it is possible to sue a manufacturer of a component part that causes injury, say, the manufacturer of electrical controls on a baseball pitching machine. One would then bring an action against both the manufacturer of the controls and the manufacturer and/or seller of the pitching machine.

For purposes of discussion, take a case of food served in a school cafeteria to a varsity team. There is one broad, general rule (with numerous exceptions) that might help in recognizing liability. Very generally speaking, it is easier to establish liability if one finds a foreign substance in the food. For example, if one finds a fish bone in a slice of bread and it causes injury, that is a foreign body and liability is much easier to establish. If one finds a fish bone in a fish meal that leads to injury, it is extremely difficult to prove liability. The same principle applies if a foreign body is found in a piece of machinery, such as metal shavings in a brake shoe.

The mere occurrence of an injury does not prove a defective product case. But when there have been a number of injuries arising from the use of a product, these may be taken to show evidence in a defective product case. Evidence of malfunction of a product before an accident may also be evidence of some defective or dangerous condition.

By the same token, the continued use of the same type of product by many other persons without any untoward results may be shown as evidence that the product was in fact not defective. Further, prolonged use of the same product without injury may be shown as evidence by the defense. Proof of care in the manufacture of a product, in the handling of it by the seller, or the testing and inspecting of it prior to sale, may be shown as evidence in behalf of the defense in a product liability case.

Expert testimony and scientific analyses are frequently used in product liability cases. Sometimes experiments are conducted with a product or similar products to establish the presence of a defect or ultrahazardous condition.

Product defectiveness may not be shown by evidence of postinjury change in the product. This is because public policy encourages change to make a product safer, and such change cannot be used as evidence against the one making such change.

PROXIMATE CAUSE OF INJURY

Whatever the grounds for liability, whether negligence, warranty, or strict liability, it is always necessary to prove what is termed *proximate cause*. Proximate cause means that the defect in the product must have been the cause, or a contributing cause, of the injury.

Expert evidence is usually required to establish a defect and proximate cause. By expert evidence we mean the statements of an engineer or someone acquainted with the product who can give his expert opinion as evidence. (Ordinarily, witnesses are not allowed to give opinions when testifying. They can only testify as to facts perceived with the senses. However, expert witnesses, who are qualified by virtue of training and experience in the particular field, are allowed to give opinions as evidence.)

A product liability case can also be based on the negligent wrongdoing of a manufacturer, seller, or person placing the product in the channels of commerce. Negligence is the failure to use due care, as in the manufacture, handling, shipping, or delivery of the product that results in damage to it or a defect in it. For example, if a pole to be used in pole vaulting has a crack or other defect that results in injury, the manufacturer may be held responsible for negligence in the manufacturing process or the inspection process.

Sellers generally have the same duties as manufacturers, that is, the duty of reasonable care in handling the product. This has been held to apply to used as well as new products. An injury caused solely by ordinary wear cannot be a basis for liability.

LIABILITY DISCLAIMERS

Disclaimers of liability and contracts, intended to exempt persons from liability for their own negligent acts that might occur in the future, are usually void as violative of public policy. The courts will not uphold such releases of liability in advance of negligence for two reasons: First, it would create carelessness if someone knew that he could not be held responsible for his negligence; it could even encourage him to act in a negligent manner. Second, it would be unjust to require the consuming public to agree in advance to release someone from their liability for their negligence. For example, it would be unjust for an airline to require a coach and players to sign a release of liability for possible airline negligence before they would be allowed to board a plane.

Disclaimers of liability in connection with a sale have been held effective, for example where a used car is sold "as is." Such disclaimers usually disclaim implied warranties rather than act as a release from future negligence.

In product liability cases involving the sale of ultrahazardous items, such as weed killer, butane gas, and drugs, the courts have stated that "reasonable care" is care proportionate to the danger involved.

A manufacturer is generally not held liable when a product is not used in a normal manner, is misused, or is used for a purpose other than that for which it was made. However, some courts have gone so far as to hold a manufacturer liable if a misuse was reasonably foreseeable.

CONTRIBUTORY NEGLIGENCE IN PRODUCT LIABILITY CASES

Contributory negligence is a defense to a negligence action arising out of product liability, since the same laws of negligence apply in product liability cases as in other negligence cases. An exception would be in a jurisdiction where comparative negligence is the law. If a person uses a product that he knows to be defective or dangerous, he may be held contributorily negligent and be barred from recovery, or he may be held to have incurred the risk.

Contributory negligence is not a defense to breach of warranty or strict liability. However, misuse of a product is a defense.

While the manufacturer or seller has the duty of testing and inspecting an article for defects, the consuming public does not have such duty. The consumer, however, will be barred from recovery if he knows of the defect. One who voluntarily assumes a known risk of injury from a known danger is barred from recovery. As previously defined, this is called assumption of risk or incurred risk. The doctrine of assumption of risk has no application where the product was used by one who had no knowledge of the risk involved in using it. The duty of inspecting and testing extends to component parts, including containers.

A manufacturer has a duty to test and inspect his products for defects. He also has the duty to test any component parts and packing. If a dangerous product is manufactured or sold and the danger is not obvious, the manufacturer or seller has a duty to warn of the danger. However, the fact that a product might cause injury does not raise a duty to warn of something that is obvious. In most jurisdictions, the warning extends beyond the purchaser and must go to the ultimate user.

The Texas civil appellate court ruled that a cause of action was stated by a lady who, after using a vibrating reducing machine, learned that she had kidney stones and that the machine aggravated her condition. The court stated that this was enough to bring action against the defendant for failure to warn of the extent of danger in using their machine. (*Shugar* v. *Pat Walker Figure Perfection Salons International*, 541 S.W. 2d 511.)

Courts usually find that the seller has a superior knowledge of the dangerous characteristics of a product, and this is the basis for the duty to warn the buyer or ultimate user. Giving an adequate warning can be a good defense.

It is important to remember, in product liability cases, that the liability of the manufacturer or seller runs not only to the purchaser, but also to other users. This means that if a school is the purchaser of equipment and furnishes it to a team for use, the team members become the users, to whom the liability of the manufacturer extends.

It should be noted that liability in this field may also extend to nonusers who are injured by virtue of a defective product, for example someone standing near a pitching machine who is hit by the machine arm. These are sometimes referred to as persons being in the "zone of danger."

Obvious Dangers

A manufacturer is not obliged to warn against every hazard or every conceivable possibility of use. A manufacturer or seller has no duty to warn of a danger that is open or obvious, or that is either known or that should have been known by a person who regularly uses the product. A hammer, with no defect, may hurt someone. Any knife can cut someone. A stove can burn a hand. If a user mistakenly hits the gas pedal rather than the brake pedal, a car accident can occur. You can stab someone with a lead pencil, or someone can slip and fall on the pencil. However, there is no duty to warn of such possibilities.

As an example, in the case of *Jamieson* v. *Woodward and Lothrop* (355 U.S. 855), the federal court in Washington, D.C. denied the claim of a purchaser/user against the manufacturer/seller of an elastic exerciser that slipped off the user's foot and injured his eye.

The purpose of a warning is to protect from danger; therefore, the warning must be adequate under the circumstances. An inadequate warning is no warning at all. The warning must be in proportion to the potential danger or seriousness of potential injury. The warning must be accurate, readily noticeable, strong enough, and clear enough. This means that the warning should be of a degree of intensity that will cause caution. In giving a warning, one should consider the seriousness of the consequences and the likelihood of an accident occurring.

In one relevant case, a seller of an incinerator furnished the buyer, a school district, with operating instructions. The seller also instructed a school custodian as to its operation, warned the plaintiff against the danger of overloading the incinerator, and warned the plaintiff not to look into the door to see if refuse was burning. The warning was deemed sufficient. (*Parker* v. *Heasler Plumbing and Heating Company*, Wyo. 388 Pacific 2d 516.)

By itself, failure to warn is not sufficient to create liability. In addition, it must be proven that the failure to warn was the proximate cause of the injury. The defense may contend that the failure to warn was not the cause of the injury; in other words, that the failure to warn did not result in the accident. The defense would also contend that a particular danger, of which there was no adequate warning given, was not the cause of the injury but, rather, that there was another cause.

If a product bears a warning and is safe if the warning is followed, the product is not defective and there is no liability for failure to give adequate warning.

Courts have consistently ruled that the manufacturer is not an insurer with regard to his product and injuries arising from it. Courts have found that there is no duty on the part of the manufacturer to design an absolutely safe product that is accident-proof. Conversely, some courts have found liability for negligent design, such as with the Pinto gasoline tank cases.

Res ipsa loquitur, as we have pointed out earlier, means that "the thing speaks for itself." The circumstances of an accident may be such that they raise a presumption or permit an inference of negligence on the part of the defendant. If the accident was one that, in the ordinary course of events, would not have happened in the absence of negligence, then that is evidence of negligence. The application of this doctrine requires three things: First, the accident was of a kind that does not ordinarily occur unless someone was negligent. Second, the instrumentality causing the injury was in the exclusive *control* of the defendant. Third, the plaintiff was free of contributory negligence.

"Control" is the key word here. In these cases, control simply means that when the container or product was negligently made and sealed, it was in the hands of the manufacturer.

As an example, take the case of a hand grenade fuse manufactured in Iowa. The grenade was assembled in Texas, and an injury occurred in Georgia, where it exploded in the hand of the plaintiff. The court held that *res ipsa loquitur* applied in this case.

In a Louisiana action against a manufacturer and wholesaler of a saddle girth buckle that allegedly broke, causing plaintiff to fall from the horse, there was evidence that, sometime after the accident, one-half of the crossbar was broken. An expert testified that, in his opinion, a sharp impact load broke it. The court ruled that this presented no more than the possibility of defect and was insufficient. The court further stated that, because of lack of control by the defendants, *res ipsa loquitur* could not apply. (*Lewellyn* v. *Lookout Saddle Company*, 315 Southern 2d 69.)

BREACH OF WARRANTY

Product manufacturers and suppliers may be held liable for *breach of warranty*. In a breach of warranty case, it is not necessary to prove negligence, and contributory negligence is usually no defense in such cases. Some jurisdictions do allow contributory negligence as a defense; other jurisdictions allow the same evidence (as would prove contributory negligence) to show that the plaintiff's action, rather than the defendant's breach of warranty, was a proximate cause of the injury.

"Puffing," or "dealer talk," is usually not considered a warranty, but rather mere seller's talk. It is not considered a basis for liability. However, in a sale, there is generally an implied warranty of merchantability and an implied warranty of fitness for the particular purpose for which a product is sold.

A manufacturer can be held *strictly liable* (that is, liable without negligence) when an article he places in the channels of commerce proves to be defective or unreasonably dangerous. This usually has application only to a party who is in the business of manufacturing or selling, and then only when the product is used without substantial change to same.

The Rawlings Manufacturing Company of California manufactured a baseball catcher's face mask. A professional player wore it and alleged that he suffered injuries when a ball went through the mask. The evidence showed that it was worn about eighty times prior to the injury, and that the plaintiff kept it in an equipment bag with other equipment. Thus it was shipped from city to city when the team traveled. Further, it was often struck by foul balls. The player checked the mask frequently before, during, and after games for defects and found none, but did find some dents. When he caught foul-tipped balls, he frequently dropped the mask to the ground.

On the day of the injury, the pitcher threw the ball, the batter swung and fouled it back, and the ball hit the mask of the plaintiff. The injured plaintiff testified that he didn't see the ball after the batter fouled it, and that he fell to the ground, his eye bleeding. The injured plaintiff testified that a weld at the top of the mask was broken when it was struck by the ball, and a bar at the top of the mask was pushed back such that the ball could pass through and hit him.

A defense witness testified that he inspected the mask and found that it was bent out of shape, some welds were broken, and the mask appeared to have been struck several times. It was pointed out that the defendants had no control over the mask after they manufactured it and it was delivered to the player. The witness further testified that the mask appeared to have taken a beating and was in a different and much less safe condition than when it left the manufacturer's control. Another defense witness said the mask appeared to have been well used and to have been hit hard.

The injured plaintiff got a verdict, but it was reversed by the court because the evidence was not sufficient to prove that the mask was in a defective state when it was delivered. The court ruled that no inference could be drawn, under the strict liability law, that the defendant manufacturer placed a defective product in plaintiff's hands under this set of facts. (*Roseboro* v. *Rawlings Manufacturing Co.*, 275 Cal. App. 2d 43 [1969].)

IMPLIED WARRANTY

Implied warranties, or warranties that are required by law of a manufacturer or seller, cannot be disclaimed or limited by the manufacturer or seller.

The tendency of the law is toward allowing recovery by bystanders. In one case, strict liability was available as a remedy to a boy injured in a school yard when a 1968 Thunderbird accelerated out of control. The alleged defect was that the motor mounts broke, allowing the engine to shift and bind the accelerator linkage. The boy recovered a judgment in Iowa in 1977. (*Haymersen* v. *Ford Motor Co.*, 257 N.W. 2d 7.)

The *Restatement of Torts* is a general codification of the law of negligence. In section 402B, it states:

> When engaged in the business of selling chattels, one who by advertising, labels, or otherwise, makes to the public a misrepresentation of a material fact concerning the character or quality of a chattel sold by him is subject to liability for physical harm to a consumer of the chattel caused by justifiable reliance upon the misrepresentation, even though (a) it is not made fraudulently or negligently, and (b) the consumer has not bought the chattel from or entered into any contractual relation with the seller.

/ 5 /

Administrative Procedures for Avoiding Lawsuits

Administrative procedures are the first line of defense against initiation of lawsuits against physical education and athletic departments, as well as their personnel. Employment of appropriately prepared personnel, with experiences matched to their responsibilities and with attitudes, values, and temperaments appropriate to their teaching or coaching assignments, will decrease the number of situations that may lead to lawsuits.

It is the responsibility of the physical education chairperson and of the athletic director to periodically conduct clinics, to distribute memoranda, and to establish procedures that will inform teachers and coaches of safety procedures, and that will enhance and sustain their awareness of unsafe conditions. Administrators should establish and distribute, in printed or mimeographed form, agreed-upon procedures to be followed when injuries or sudden illness occurs, for the transportation of students, for medical examinations, for research and physical fitness testing, for selection and maintenance of equipment, and for use of school facilities by outside groups.

Administrators of recreation, physical education, and athletic programs will aid themselves in avoiding legal problems by becoming familiar with the local statutes that affect their programs. Many state coaches' associations and state professional associations of physical educators have established committees to abstract and report on the implications of state laws that bear upon these areas. Obviously, administrators must also understand the implications of certain federal statutes for the conduct of programs in their charge. These will be discussed in detail in Chapter 6.

77

Finally, the administrator must be able to secure the cooperation of teachers, coaches, students, parents, the principal, the superintendent, the dean, the school board, spectators, and the community. The degree of success experienced by the athletic administrator in this process will be determined in part by his personality and popularity. However, certain techniques and procedures have proven helpful. Some of these will be presented later in this chapter.

SELECTION OF PERSONNEL

The first step in the selection of personnel is preparation of a job description. The job description should include a listing of safety procedures to be followed in the specific activities to be taught or coached. Further, it should specify the knowledge, skills, and understandings required of the job-holder for safe and liability-free teaching and/or coaching.

Teachers or coaches of swimming should hold valid, up-to-date certification by the Red Cross, Y.M.C.A., or Y.W.C.A. in senior life saving or water safety instruction. Teachers of scuba courses should be appropriately certified. Football coaches should understand the physiology of heat-stroke and the procedures for the prevention of this major killer of athletes. They should also understand the potential consequences of spearing for the vertebral column and the spinal cord. Further, they need to understand the dangers of using players with a history of concussions.

Teachers and coaches of men's and women's gymnastics must know progressions and spotting procedures if they are to minimize injuries. They need to know the physical and skill prerequisites for the execution of the skills taught. They should be certified by the U.S. Gymnastic Safety Association. Further, experience as a member of an intercollegiate gymnastics team is highly desirable and, perhaps, should be mandatory.

The teaching/coaching technique of a person instructing students in gymnastics is a most important consideration. Gymnasts, like athletes in other sports, generally perform best and progress most rapidly when they are highly motivated. Thus the ability to motivate students is a most important quality in the teacher or coach of gymnastics. However, a driving, pushing gymnastics coach might lead gymnasts into attempting skills for which they are not ready. In executing a block or tackle in football, the greater the force the player utilizes, the more effective the block or tackle. In gymnastics, excessive force may produce an overspin leading to disastrous consequences. Consequently, there are times when the gymnastics coach must restrain gymnasts from attempting certain skills.

The point being made here is that the administrator, in selecting personnel to serve as teachers or coaches of gymnastics, must look for different personal qualities and approaches to coaching than when looking for coaches of football, lacrosse, or ice hockey. A "Bear" Bryant personality and approach to the coaching of gymnastics might produce a few champions, but it would also likely produce a greater number of concussions and fractures. The sports program administrator must be familiar with differences in the demands of coaching various sports.

The authors feel that written and oral examinations on relevant subject matter would objectify the selection process. Prospective lawyers are required to pass the bar examination; why shouldn't prospective physical educators and coaches be required to demonstrate knowledge of their job responsibilities? This procedure would decrease the number of young people who suffer serious and debilitating injuries. Further, it would improve the stature and respectability of the professions involved in teaching and coaching human movement. As a further advantage to such examinations, institutions preparing teachers of physical education and coaching would be greatly motivated to improve the quality of their programs, since graduates who did a poor job on the exams would not be placed.

Until such written examinations are prepared, administrators should hire only graduates of schools turning out well-qualified personnel. At this writing and, by all indications, for a number of years to come, it is a buyer's market. The best-qualified people are most deserving of employment. The administrator who truly wishes to serve the students and the community will extend himself to find the best-qualified person possible for any position. This mandates that the search be wide and vigorous, and it eliminates the hiring of friends out of loyalty or the selection of inbred graduates or personnel already "on board" (unless they are better qualified than the other candidates).

Members of departmental committees established to select candidates should endeavor to purge themselves of any bias. Some committee members may fear that selection of a person more highly qualified than themselves may result in a delay in their own promotion. Others may fear an upgrading of the quality of departmental personnel, since then they may not look as good. For these reasons, administrators should review all the work of departmental selection committees.

SCHOOL SAFETY PROGRAMS

The school administrator, usually a superintendent, has ultimate responsibility for the safety of all students, faculty, and staff in all school programs. The "buck" stops at the desk of the superintendent.

The school superintendent is responsible for implementing the policies set by the school board. In smaller communities, he may assume direct responsibility for the school safety program; in medium and larger school districts, he usually will appoint a safety supervisor to act as his representative in the area of safety. Principals in individual schools will coordinate their safety efforts with those of the superintendent and/or his representative. Likewise, the school district supervisor of athletics and physical education must coordinate his efforts to reduce injuries in athletics, physical education, and recreation with those of the safety supervisor for the school district.

The School District Safety Supervisor

Yost lists the following specific activities of a safety supervisor:[1]

1. Help the entire school staff see safety education as an integral part of the curriculum.
2. Develop instructional guides for use by all teachers.
3. Identify the safety needs of pupils and plan cooperatively.
4. Appraise existing curricular content for safety education adequacy.
5. Know the sources of current safety materials for both student and teacher use.
6. Work with teacher-sponsors of school safety organizations (safety councils, safety patrols, safety committees, and safety clubs).
7. Use accident reports as a preventive, defensive, protective, and/or constructive device.
8. Inform the school staff of legal aspects involved in safety.
9. Secure the cooperation of out-of-school agencies for service and assistance.
10. Guide teachers in selecting safety education materials.
11. Publicize and interpret the school safety program to the public.
12. Exert leadership in organizing and conducting emergency drills.
13. Cooperate with the school administrator and regulatory agencies in removing building and general safety hazards and in planning for future activities.
14. Appraise the suggestions and criticisms of community groups regarding the school safety program.
15. Cooperate with community agencies in serving as a speaker, in supplying the names of speakers, and in securing instructional aids.
16. Keep informed on the latest developments in the safety field.
17. Cooperate with the school administrator in conducting in-service educational programs for all staff members, including custodians, bus drivers, and luncheon personnel.
18. Assist and encourage teachers to undertake safety research projects.
19. Take an active part in community safety activities, for they have an influence on the total school safety program.
20. Evaluate the school safety program.
21. Enforce safety rules and regulations and administer consequential disciplinary action.
22. Present personnel progress reports relevant to safety program goals.
23. Develop criteria for use in personnel selection.
24. Supervise or assist in the selection, training, and education of qualified staff members.
25. Evaluate and rate safety staff and instructional personnel.
26. Inspect environment and evaluate safety services to assure adherence to legal regulations.

---

[1]Charles Peter Yost, "An Introduction to Administration and Supervision," in *Administration and Supervision for Safety in Sports, Monograph #1, Sports Safety Series,* American School and Community Safety Association of the American Alliance for Health, Physical Education, Recreation, and Dance (1977), pp. 22–23.

The school principal can help reduce the number of accidents in physical education, recreation, and athletics by avoiding large classes and avoiding the expeditious, but dangerous, practice of placing students of different grades and ages in the same physical education class. He should also expedite repairs to equipment, supplies, and facilities and approve structural changes in facilities to promote safety.

The Director of Physical Education and Athletics

The chairperson or director of physical education and athletics, working in close cooperation with the school district safety supervisor and the individual school safety officers, is responsible for safety in his program. Pechar points out that his responsibilities include:[2]

1. Adoption of a uniform procedure for the reporting, recording, and investigation of all accidents within the program.
2. Provision for inspection and maintenance of safe equipment and facilities, including safe storage.
3. Provision of first-aid and emergency care for all injuries, as well as any indicated follow-up medical treatment.
4. Securing of certified and qualified teachers, coaches, trainers, and officials.
5. Formation of an accident prevention and injury control committee.
6. Provisions for safe transportation of athletic teams and other sports participants.
7. Formulation of special emergency procedures for fire and other disaster emergencies.
8. Approval of the course of study in physical education, as well as the contests scheduled for the athletic teams and other sports participants.
9. Adoption of recommended procedures for crowd control at athletic contests.

Pechar goes on to point out that physical education teachers, coaches, and trainers are in a position to instill in their students desirable attitudes, knowledge, and skills concerning safety. Activity leaders, teachers, and coaches are aware of the importance of classification and grouping of students with regard to skill level, size, weight, and physical condition, since these factors influence the probability of injury. Grouping by age, weight, skill level, and physical fitness is especially important in combative and body-contact sports such as wrestling, boxing, and football.

Participants must be made aware of the hazards of an activity, the consequences of unsafe actions or conditions, the importance of observing the rules of the game, the importance of mastering skills in their progressive order of difficulty, and the need to develop a high level of physical fitness. With the legally required integration of the sexes and the physically and

---

[2]Stanley F. Pechar, "Administration and Supervision of Institutional Contests," in *Administration and Supervision for Safety in Sports, Monograph #1, Sports Safety Series,* American School and Community Safety Association of the AAHPERD (1977), p. 28.

mentally handicapped, including mainstreaming, this procedure assumes great importance. ("Mainstreaming" is the legal requirement to integrate physically disabled or mentally retarded children, to the fullest extent of their abilities, into the ordinary, normal course of life.) The instructor should work these items into his course outline, syllabus, and lesson plans.

The physical education and athletic department should develop a system for inspecting and testing equipment and facilities, and for taking corrective action where deficiencies are found. In physical education, this process should be completed before the beginning of the school year; in athletics, it should be completed before the first practice session for the particular sport. The results of such inspection and testing should be reported to all participants, that is, assistants, players, etc.

In-Service Preparation of Faculty

Regular departmental meetings seem to occur all too frequently and are often tedious. The agenda is often long and safety and avoidance of liability are usually regarded as of peripheral interest. However, a lawsuit alleging negligent action usually receives considerable school and public attention, which can be harmful to the department and the school. Furthermore, lawsuits can be expensive; awards have ranged as high as $2.5 million.

The authors strongly recommend that physical education and athletic departments establish safety committees to study and report on safety, liability, state and federal statutes, and accident prevention and reporting. This committee should be chaired by a departmental safety coordinator.

The Athletic Safety Coordinator

The safety coordinator and his committee should assume responsibility for the following:

1. Establishment of a philosophy, objectives, and policies of the school sports safety program and interpretation of this program to faculty, administrators, service personnel, students, and parents.
2. Interpretation of relevant state and federal statutes, building codes, and executive orders.
3. Establishment of an accident reporting system, review and interpretation of accident data, and recommendations for measures to decrease the incidence of accidents.
4. Preparation and selection of teaching aids for children and faculty designed to decrease the incidence of accidents.
5. Periodic inspection of sports facilities and equipment, leading to recommendations for increased safety.
6. Establishment of procedures to be followed in the event of injury.
7. Investigation and recommendations for selection of athletic accident insurance.

8. Study, selection, and recommendations for purchase of appropriate safety education materials, such as posters, motion pictures, filmstrips, and charts.
9. Presentation of clinics on injury prevention in the various athletic and recreational activities.
10. Establishment of criteria for selection of safe equipment and facilities.
11. Establishment of regulations for the use of school facilities by outside groups (with regard to safety and accident prevention).
12. Arrangements for advisory services from physicians, attorneys, health educators, and insurance specialists.
13. Arrangements for the inventory and inspection of all sports equipment at the conclusion of athletic seasons, and replacement of defective equipment to ensure that no player is issued defective equipment at the start of the following season.
14. Inspection of bleachers and grandstands by manufacturers' engineers.
15. Recommendations concerning safe storage of equipment.
16. Recommendations regarding both indoor and outdoor playing surfaces.
17. Recommendations for maintenance of hygienic and safe conditions in the swimming pool and shower rooms. (These should include proceduresto control fungal infections, rules of behavior for students and athletes, cleaning procedures, control of temperature of shower water, recommended construction modifications relative to safety, and considerations in the event of fire.)
18. Recommendations from a safety standpoint regarding size of classes for various activities.
19. Recommendations regarding program planning to ensure the selection of activities that are safe for students of each sex, age, and level of ability.
20. Provision for the implementation and enforcement of all the above recommendations, since the school can be found liable for failure to do so.

FACILITIES AND EQUIPMENT SAFETY

Many athletic and physical education facilities now in use were constructed at a time when programs were less diversified and enrollments were much smaller. Many facilities have insufficient outdoor play space, and many are located along major roads, with heavy traffic and the consequent hazards to students.

The changes in standards and levels of expectation relative to facilities are illustrated by one of the authors' experiences at Ohio Wesleyan University in the early 1950s. One of J.A. Baley's duties was to serve as swimming coach. The swimming pool had been constructed according to the standards of days gone by; it was slightly over sixteen yards long, was located under the men's shower room, and was reached by way of a trap-door and a steep ladder. Ceiling height was approximately eight feet. But as times progressed, the need for a more diversified program was strongly felt, and during the next year, a much safer, twenty-five-yard pool was constructed, with six lanes and three diving boards.

Unsafe features of older buildings can sometimes be remedied. In other cases, these features can be compensated for through education of the users or by installing protective equipment such as padding and safety glass. Unfortunately, these measures cannot be taken in all cases.

When new facilities are constructed, there should be no unnecessary hazards. When an injury occurs due to a hazard in the design or construction of the facility, a lawsuit could follow, alleging negligence in the planning or construction. Hazards can be avoided through careful planning and supervision during construction, involving the architect, landscape architect, planning committee and its coordinator, community governmental offices, school board, the park commission, and the community planner. The plans for the athletic facilities must fit into master plans for the community.

Facility Design

The first step in the design of a facility is site selection. Safety of the participants and spectators should be a major consideration in site selection. Traffic, terrain, and access must also be considered. To aid in site selection, a building or facility committee should be formed. This committee should include representatives from *all* groups that will use the facility.

One person should serve as coordinator of the proposed facility. This coordinator would act as a liaison between the administration, architect, contractors, and building committee, on the one hand, and the teachers, parents, and student groups that will use the facility, on the other. It is unlikely that the architect will be highly familiar with the hazards involved in the various activities conducted in the facility. Thus it would be the responsibility of the coordinator to point out to the architect or builder any construction or design features that might present hazards.

All members of the planning committee should carefully review the architect's plans at each step from the standpoints of function and safety. After a general contractor has been selected and as work progresses, monthly inspections of the site and meetings of the planning committee should be conducted. An insurance agent should either sit on the committee or be called in to inspect the plans and construction for safety recommendations and suggestions that might reduce insurance premiums.

Traffic circulation and control must be planned in such a way as to: (1) reduce congestion in corridors, stairwells, locker rooms, and spectator areas; (2) minimize noise in certain areas of the building; (3) facilitate building supervision; (4) provide for safe and efficient movement of individuals; and (5) allow future building expansion. The plans for traffic flow within the building must consider the movement of participants from lockers to shower rooms, from shower rooms to swimming pools, from locker rooms to athletic training rooms, and to the various spectator areas.

Corridors should be a minimum of five feet wide to accommodate peak traffic loads and wheelchairs. They must be free of all obstructions and be well lighted. Fire extinguishers, water fountains, telephones, and other equipment should be recessed into walls. Corridors should terminate at an exit or a stairwell in a case of fire. Where it is necessary to install gates or doors for security purposes, these should be equipped with panic or signal releases.

Nonslip-surface ramps are preferable to steps for small variations in floor level. The rise in any ramp should not exceed one foot for every twelve feet of length.

Stairways must have a minimum width of four feet. Two-lane main stairways with a central handrail are recommended. A stair landing should be provided for at least each sixteen steps. Further, there should be a change of color to indicate changes in floor level.

Shower and locker rooms can be located to serve as buffers between offices and participant areas. State and local building codes should be consulted to ensure that heating, cooling, ventilation, lighting, and electrical systems meet local standards; electrical service must also meet the national electric code of the National Board of Fire Underwriters.

The power entrance should be located in a specially designed room that is accessible only to authorized maintenance personnel. All main service panels, switches, light and power panels, and meters should be located in this room. Secondary control panels should, of course, be located where they are convenient to personnel opening and closing the building. Independent circuits must be provided for distinct areas in the building, such as the swimming pool, wrestling room, and handball courts. Three-way switches should be provided at each end of each corridor, at the foot and head of all stairs, and at the entrance to classroom areas and the various activity areas.

Night-lights should be provided for areas requiring security, such as the swimming pool, gymnasium, and locker rooms. Night-lights are also recommended for corridors, stairwells, classrooms that contain expensive equipment or hazardous materials, and parking areas. Since it is more important to protect people than equipment, all lights should have a protective shield. Vapor-proof lights must be used in shower rooms, locker rooms, swimming pools, and other areas of high humidity. Sun-glare must be eliminated in activity areas.

A telephone must be provided to facilitate calling off-property emergency services.

Locker room floors should be of a nonslip, impervious material and should slope toward the drain. A textured floor finish will help prevent falls.

Facilities should be so designed that they are easily maintained. There should be no exposed belt-ends, electrical wires, moving parts, small holes, sharp edges, or other dangerous conditions.

The gymnasium should be so planned that during multiple use one activity does not interfere with another. A minimum ceiling height of twenty-four feet is recommended. Windows in the gymnasium must be shatterproof and translucent. There must be no protrusions from the walls. Structural facing tile to a height of seven feet is suggested for ease in cleaning, and padding should be provided where necessary.

A storage room large enough to accommodate all equipment should be planned. Gymnastic and certain other equipment such as pitching machines, trampolines, and hanging rings should not be left in an unsupervised gymnasium. Adequate ventilation is obviously essential.

For recommendations regarding the construction of swimming pools from an injury prevention point of view, the reader is referred to Chapter 7.

The collapse of bleachers has led to many deaths and injuries. Thus administrators must give serious consideration to the erection and maintenance of bleachers. Demountable bleachers should be erected only by reliable workmen who carefully follow the directions of the manufacturer. They should not be placed on soft or wet ground. Seat stringers and A-frames should be wired in place. Permanent bleachers should be inspected prior to their season of use by a competent engineer. Both types of bleachers should be inspected regularly for protruding nails, splinters, and broken boards.

Doors that swing into play areas should be reversed, or doorstops should be installed to prevent their opening fully into these areas. Signs should also be painted on the doors, cautioning persons to open the doors slowly. Showers should be equipped with mixing valves, and the water temperature should never exceed 100° F.

Sports equipment should be inspected and inventoried at the end of each particular season. Defective equipment must be repaired or replaced. A form requesting repair of equipment or a facility should be available. This form should be completed in duplicate by the instructor, with one copy sent to the administrator and the other filed by the teacher. This procedure will be helpful to the teacher in the event of an injury and lawsuit.

When the gymnasium is used for a school dance, powdered wax should not be put on the floor, since this makes the floor dangerously slippery for classes or games. Boric acid powder is better for dances, because it is easily dissolved in water.

Unslaked lime should never be used to line fields, due to the danger of skin burns. Lines of white tape, securely attached to the ground, provide safer markings.

The following list consists of policies regarding the safety of facilities, equipment, and supplies. These policies were recommended by the American Alliance for Health, Physical Education, Recreation, and Dance.[3]

---

[3]Charles Peter Yost, *School Safety Policies* (Washington, D.C.: American Alliance for Health, Physical Education, Recreation, and Dance, 1968), pp. 18–21.

1. Facilities, equipment, and supplies should be designed for hard use, thus reducing their accident potential.
2. In the design, layout, and selection of facilities, equipment, and supplies, the age level, sex, maturity, and skill level of participants should be considered.
3. The surfacing of various areas of playgrounds — blacktop, turf (natural or synthetic), tanbark, loose dirt, or other material — should be appropriate for the activities.
4. Schools should require protective equipment and should insist on its use in appropriate activities in the program.
5. Personal and protective equipment must be carefully fitted to ensure maximum safety for each participant. This is especially true in vigorous body-contact activities and applies to all levels of activity.
6. Sufficient equipment should be purchased to ensure immediate replacement in case of damage or wear in activities presenting hazards to the participants.

The authors would add the following three items to the list:

1. In the design, layout, and selection of facilities, equipment and supplies, consideration must be given to participants with various handicaps.
2. Playgrounds should not be paved.
3. Adequate supervision is mandatory. (This point is discussed at length in Chapter 7 and 8.)

Playgrounds

Playground safety is principally a matter of providing well-planned facilities and adequate supervision. The U.S. Consumer Product Safety Commission estimates that over 167,000 children receive emergency-room treatment annually as a result of injuries associated with playground equipment.[4] Most such injuries are lacerations and fractures from falls from slides and climbing apparatus onto a hard surface.

The most important factors that determine the safety of playground apparatus are selection, anchoring of the equipment, maintenance, and children's understanding and practice of the safe use of the equipment. The children's size, age, and level of motor development should be major determinants in selection of equipment.

When planning for location of the equipment within the playground, it is important to maintain space between units sufficient to permit control of traffic and to make the equipment accessible. This implies either significant playground size or limitation of the amount of equipment. Ideally, the area used by younger children should be fenced off from the sections used by older children. It should be unnecessary for either age group to cross the

---

[4]U.S. Consumer Product Safety Commission, *Hazard Analysis: Playground Equipment* (Washington, D.C.: The Commission, April 1975).

other group's areas, or to cross game courts or free play-areas, in order to reach the apparatus area. To facilitate safe movement of children to and from various pieces of equipment, lines should be painted on the surface to indicate "danger zones" around the pieces of equipment.

Both the equipment and the general area should be inspected daily for missing bolts, sharp edges, glass, holes in the surface, and other potential causes of injury. Children should be taught to participate in this process by reporting broken or malfunctioning equipment and by placing debris in garbage cans. Student patrols may be organized for this purpose.

Repairs to equipment should be made promptly. Broken or hazardous equipment should not be used until necessary repairs have been made. Daily inspections should look for loose fastenings, worn and broken parts, the need to lubricate moving parts or ball bearings, any need for refilling of landing pits, signs of wear in supporting parts, and the covering of concrete foundations with several inches of sand or soil.

Many accidents are due to improper use of equipment. To discourage children from performing unsuitable stunts and games, or from general roughhousing, adequate supervision is necessary at all times. Student patrols under the guidance of the playground director can be of great help in this regard.

The National Safety Council recommends that the following general practices be followed throughout the apparatus area:[5]

1. No roughhousing.
2. No games such as tag, king-of-the-mountain, etc., to be played on or around apparatus.
3. No throwing of debris on the playground or on the apparatus.
4. No pupil removal of sand, tanbark, or other material that has been placed as a landing surface under apparatus.
5. No apparatus should be used when wet or ice-coated.
6. No apparatus should be used unless a supervisor is present.
7. Children should use only the apparatus designed for their age group.
8. Youngsters must learn to take turns in using the various units of apparatus.
9. Children should not enter the danger zones of apparatus when others are using it.
10. Only those using or waiting to use apparatus should be within the apparatus area.

Parents of children using the playground should receive copies of the rules.

Swings

Swings should be set in concrete to avoid tipping over. The top pipe must be perfectly horizontal so that the swing swings straight and does not twist. If the area under the swings is earth, it must be raked smooth daily; if the

---

[5]National Safety Council, "Playground Apparatus," Safety Education Data Sheet No. 69. Reprinted with permission of the National Safety Council.

surface is tanbark or similar material, it must be filled and leveled as necessary. The saddle, or canvas, seat has been found safer than wood or metal seats, because it discourages standing on the seat while swinging, and because, if it hits a child, generally there is no injury. Chair-swings should be provided for children of nursery-school age. Swings set at different heights should be provided for primary-, intermediate-, and upper-grade children.

The following rules regarding swings are recommended by the National Safety Council:[6]

1. Sit, do not stand or kneel.
2. Hold on with both hands.
3. Do not push anyone else in a swing, and do not allow anyone to push you.
4. Only one person in a swing at a time.
5. All those using swings in a given unit should face the same way.
6. Come to a stop before leaving the swing.
7. Don't climb or play on the frames.

Additional rules include refraining from twisting swing-chains and refraining from walking too closely to the front or back of a moving swing. Swings should be no closer than six feet to fences, walks, and sandboxes.

Slides

Playgrounds should have a six-foot slide for children of primary-school age and an eight-foot slide for older children. Slides should be set in concrete and should be inspected daily to ensure that braces are firm, that steps are in good condition, that the bed and sides have no projecting nails or screws, and that there are no rough spots. Wooden slides must be oiled frequently. The pit containing sand or tanbark at the foot of the slide must be kept level and free of debris, and the sand or tanbark must be kept loose and resilient.

The following rules should be posted and promulgated:[7]

1. Climb the steps to the slide one at a time, and keep a safe distance behind the person ahead of you.
2. Be sure, before starting down, that the slide is clear.
3. Slide one person at a time, sitting up, feet first, and do not hold onto the sides as you go down.
4. Get away from the foot of the slide as quickly as possible.
5. Do not climb up the sliding surface or the frame of the slide.

Seesaws

Although seesaws, or teeters, are popular with primary-grade children, they are not recommended for intermediate-grade students, who often attempt

[6]Ibid.
[7]Ibid.

unsafe stunts on this piece of equipment. To protect the fingers and hands of children, it is recommended that the fulcrum of the seesaw be enclosed. Attachments at the fulcrum should be secure and protruding nails or screws should be removed. Boards should be replaced if they splinter or crack.

Children should be taught the following rules:[8]

1. To sit facing each other.
2. Not to stand or run on the board.
3. To keep feet from under the board.
4. To avoid bumping.
5. To warn partners before dismounting.
6. To get off the board when it is in a horizontal position.

Giant Stride

Many recreational specialists believe that the hazards of the giant stride outweigh its advantages. Those who endorse its use recommend that it be used only by children in the elementary grades and above. The giant stride should not be used without supervision. The ladders should be removed after play hours. The pole must be firmly anchored, and the ground around the pole must be kept level. The pole, attachments, and splices should be inspected daily.

The following rules should be observed:[9]

1. Everyone should start at the same time.
2. Each person should hold firmly to one rope or chain, and to one only.
3. No two youngsters should attempt to hold onto the same rope or chain.
4. Children should not try to cross the chains.
5. There must be no overtaking of the person ahead.
6. Youngsters should not put their feet through the rungs of the apparatus.
7. On letting go of the chain, send it easily to the center pole; be careful not to hit the people ahead of or behind you.

Climbing Structures

The area under climbing structures should be surfaced with a soft, resilient material, which should be kept level and at least six inches deep. Daily inspection should assure that the bars will not turn. Children should not be permitted to use this equipment when the bars are moist or wet. They should always grasp the equipment with the thumb opposite the fingers, rather than alongside them, and should hold on with both hands except when moving to a new position. Overcrowding should not be permitted. No child should use a horizontal ladder or bar that he is unable to reach by himself without standing on an object or being lifted.

---

[8]Ibid.

[9]Ibid.

The National Safety Council offers the following rules for safe use:[10]

1. Know how to grip the bar.
2. Start at the same end of the apparatus and move in the same direction.
3. Keep a safe distance behind the person ahead and watch for swinging feet.
4. Refrain from any kind of speed contests on the apparatus or from trying to cover large distances in a single move.
5. Know how to drop, landing on the feet with knees slightly bent.

* * * * *

Certain playground equipment should be avoided, for example, equipment with open-ended hooks (especially S-hooks), with moving parts that could crush fingers, and with rings with a diameter of more than five inches or less than ten inches, which can entrap a child's head. Children should not be allowed to run or play with sharp, dangerous objects in the mouth or hand. Knives, sling-shots, BB guns, and other dangerous items should not be permitted on the playground. Craft tools must be left in the craft area or shed.

Children should receive instruction in playground safety during the primary grades, that is, before they reach the sixth or seventh grade when the incidence of playground injuries is highest. Including children in an "opening clean-up" helps to develop safety consciousness and a feeling of pride in their playground.

COPYRIGHT LAW

As a result of improvements to, and reduction in the price of, copy machines, as well as the increased cost of textbooks and a decline in the lecture method of teaching, it became obvious that changes in the copyright laws were necessary. The Copyright Act of 1909 simply was not providing adequate protection for holders of copyrights, because copying of their material became so widespread that sales of their writings were substantially affected.

Consequently, since January 1, 1978, a completely new copyright law has been in effect in the United States. The requirements and restrictions of the new law, as presented in *Circular R21, Reproduction of Copyright Works by Educators and Librarians,* are abstracted in the following. (A copy of this circular may be obtained from the U.S. Copyright Office of the Library of Congress.)

Teachers may make a single copy (after requesting permission) of a chapter from a book, an article from a periodical or newspaper, a short story, short essay, or short poem (whether or not from a collective work), and of a

---

[10]Ibid.

chart, graph, diagram, drawing, cartoon, or picture from a book, periodical, or newspaper, if the copy is for scholarly research, use in teaching, or preparation to teach.

Teachers may also make one copy for each student in a class, provided that the copying meets the tests of brevity and spontaneity and the cumulative effect test, and provided each copy includes a notice of copyright.

The test of *brevity for prose* is a complete article, story, or essay of less than 2,500 words, or an excerpt from any prose work of not more than 1,000 words or ten percent of the work, whichever is less, but in any event a minimum of 500 words. The test of *brevity for poetry* is a complete poem, if less than 250 words and if printed on not more than two pages or, from a larger poem, an excerpt of not more than 250 words. The number of words permitted may be exceeded to finish a line of poetry or of any unfinished prose paragraph. One chart, graph, diagram, drawing, cartoon, or picture per book or periodical issue is permitted.

According to the cited circular, the test for *spontaneity* is met if the "copying is at the instance and inspiration of the individual teacher, and the inspiration and decision to use the work and the moment of its use for maximum teaching effectiveness are so close in time that it would be unreasonable to expect a timely reply to a request for permission."

The test for *cumulative effect* limits copying to one course in the school. Not more than one short poem, article, story, essay, or two excerpts may be copied from the same collective work or periodical volume during one class-term. Multiple copying is limited to nine times for one course during one class-term. These limitations do not apply to current news periodicals and newspapers, or to current news sections of other periodicals.

The following are prohibited:

1. Copying to create, to replace, or to substitute for anthologies, compilations, or collective works. A charge of replacement or substitution may be lodged if excerpts are reproduced and used separately but their cumulative effect is replacement or substitution.
2. Copying of "consumable" works such as exercises, tests, test booklets, answer sheets, and workbooks.
3. Substitution of copying to avoid purchase of books, publisher's reprints, or periodicals.
4. Repeated use of the same item by the same instructor over several semesters.
5. Charging students for copies beyond the total cost of photocopying.

CROWD CONTROL

One of the many responsibilities of athletic directors and directors of recreation programs is planning and preparing for athletic contests or entertainments that will draw a large number of spectators. A most important facet of this responsibility is crowd control. It is the responsibility of the athletic or recreation director to minimize possible spectator injuries. The probability that one or more spectators will be injured is great simply because of numbers. There is also the possibility that many people may be hurt as a result of unforeseen occurrences, such as riots or collapse of bleachers. While the probability of a lawsuit is not as great as it is in some other areas of responsibility, no director wants to see someone injured if it could have been avoided.

Crowd control has become increasingly difficult because special interest groups frequently use public gatherings as a highly visible podium for publicizing their point of view, and because spectators today often want to become participants in the spectacle. Some schools in large cities have found it advisable to discontinue night games. Greater numbers of police are being used at athletic contests. If disruptive elements are permitted to interfere with the tranquility of athletic contests, the situation will worsen until it becomes necessary to prohibit spectators or to discontinue the contests.

The first step in preparing for crowd control is the planning and provision of adequate facilities. The facilities should be so planned as to allow ready flow of traffic for pedestrians in the stands and the walkways surrounding the facility, and for vehicular traffic on approach roads and in the parking lot. Lighting should be adequate, with no unlighted areas. Landscaping should not provide hiding places for muggers, thieves, or rapists. Signs indicating the desired flow of traffic should be short, easily understood, and clearly visible.

Ticket windows should not be so near the admission gate that lines at the ticket office become ensnarled with lines going through the admission gate or elsewhere.

Players, officials, and coaches should be separated from the spectators by appropriate fencing. Rest room facilities should be adequate to accommodate the largest probable attendance. In the case of indoor facilities, smoking areas should be indicated. Run-down, unclean, graffiti-covered facilities invite vandalism; thus rest rooms, hallways, and all other parts of the facility should be kept clean and painted. Preparation of the facilities should be completed at least two hours prior to game time.

The person in charge should develop policy statements, guidelines, and regulations for crowd control in cooperation with all others who will be involved. This would include, in a school situation, school administrators, coaches, faculty members involved in the sports program, directors of youth athletic programs that use the facilities, the director of campus security, the local police, and local emergency services (fire and ambulance). When changes or modifications are made in these policies, all the above groups should be informed. The policies should be kept effectively up-to-date by yearly evaluation and should be adequately published or posted.

Sportsmanship as a Means of Crowd Control

People are educable. Social behavior, ethical behavior, and sportsmanship are learned and, as such, can be taught. The teaching of sportsmanship can proceed through many avenues. Avenues other than the classroom include, but are not limited to, the example of the coach and players, comments made in the event program and in news releases, announcer's comments, slogans, mottoes, sportsmanship awards, lectures, and distribution of a sportsmanship code. A flag-raising ceremony and singing of the national anthem prior to contests will help to develop positive attitudes.

To enlarge the educational arena, coaches and athletic directors should seize opportunities to talk to civic groups such as the Kiwanis, Junior Chamber of Commerce, Civitans, and others. In such talks, they should comment on the importance of player and spectator performance. There are colleges at which the spectators applaud skillful play by the opponents, and this practice has not been found detrimental to the performance of the home team. The sportsmanship code mentioned above should receive wide circulation — in newspapers, in event programs, and on bulletin boards in the school and in public places.

* * * * *

Those responsible for crowd control — security officers, local police, ushers, and assigned faculty — should all be at their posts before the gates are opened. Ushers should be identified by armbands or caps and should confiscate confetti, horns, bottled drinks, fruit, or other objects that can be thrown. Concession stands should sell drinks in paper cups. An experience at a professional baseball game in Cleveland at which beer was sold, and which was postponed because marauding fans overran the field and destroyed property, should convince anyone that beer should never be sold at athletic contests.

Troublemakers should be removed only by uniformed police. The person in charge should never engage in a shouting match with disorderly people in the stands. The police should bring these people to a quiet room where the director or others in charge can talk to them. The uniformed police and others involved in security should have a walkie-talkie system.

The athletic director should insist that coaches refrain from arguing with officials or in any way demonstrating disagreement or displeasure with decisions. There is probably nothing that influences a crowd toward disruptive behavior more than the behavior of a coach. Good officials will not change their calls due to such antics anyway. The athletic director should only employ capable officials, since the quality of officiating substantially influences the behavior of spectators.

Advance sales of tickets will help avoid congestion at the gate. Concession stands may be open before and after the game and at half time, but they should be closed during play. Traffic to and from concession stands can be controlled by means of roped-off routes.

A doctor or emergency medical technician should be present at all games, and an ambulance should be in or near the arena, but out of sight of the spectators (if feasible). The athletic trainer for each team should have a stretcher, and oxygen tanks should be on hand. A first aid station, manned and fully supplied, should be located inside the arena or near the rest rooms.

Crowd control problems are more likely to occur at doubleheaders, which should therefore be avoided. The seating capacity of stadiums or gymnasiums should not be exceeded. Well-known faculty members should sit behind the visiting fans in order to reduce harassment by the home fans. There should be an ample number of well-marked exits to clear the area quickly. Uniformed police can expedite traffic movement both in the stadium and in the parking lot.

SPECTATOR INJURIES

The liability of a stadium owner or other sports establishment for injury to a patron is called *premises liability.* An owner or promoter who sells tickets to a business invitee, who pays admission to get in, owes the ticketholder a duty to exercise reasonable care to ensure that the premises are reasonably safe.

If there is a dangerous hidden condition existing on the premises, there is a duty to give adequate warning to patrons. There is also a duty to provide sufficient supervision of the crowd. The owner of a stadium has a duty to keep the aisles free of persons and hazards.

Liability usually turns on the issue of foreseeability. If a landowner, promoter, or person in charge could reasonably have foreseen that there might be pushing by the crowd or overcrowding that might result in injury, then he had a duty to eliminate that danger or to protect the patrons from it. If, for example, there had been drinking and rowdiness at prior games, at which persons had been pushed or injured, the test of foreseeability would be met.

It is difficult to set down hard and fast rules establishing the duty of a proprietor. A Missouri appellate court ruled: "Ordinary care is always a relative term, and in every case must be determined by what the conduct of an ordinarily prudent person would have been under the same or similar circumstances." (*Murphy* v. *Wintergarden and Ice Company,* 280 S.W. 444 [1926].)

The duty of the proprietor is to ensure that patrons are safe from slippery ramps, assaults in rest rooms, falls due to poorly lighted stairways, etc. Again, the proprietor must be aware of, or reasonably should have been aware of, the dangerous condition.

Courts sometimes rule that the proprietor must have had notice that was actual or constructive. *Actual notice* means that he admits that he knew.

Constructive notice means that he reasonably should have known (for example, where there has been a similar problem in the past, such as falls or drunken, rowdy, or disorderly crowds). This duty extends to safe ingress and egress, for example, in the parking lot.

The duty of a proprietor in the exercise of reasonable care also includes the duty to warn of any hidden dangers, such as electric lines or holes in the ground or flooring. The proprietor also has the duty to make a reasonable inspection of the premises to discover any unsafe conditions.

In short, the proprietor must be certain that he is not inviting people to enter his premises and to pay him for the privilege, when he might be inviting them into a dangerous situation. This is one reason why all doors in public buildings must open outward. Thus, if the crowd is pushing the door, it will open and people can exit safely, whereas if the door opened inward and the crowd was pushing from behind, it would be impossible to open the door.

It is especially important to note that the duty of a proprietor charging money for use of his premises includes protection of customers from the acts of other customers. This includes a duty to anticipate and to reasonably foresee acts that might cause injury.

There is an affirmative duty to protect a patron against dangers caused by the negligence of the proprietor's employees or of his customers where, as a reasonably prudent man, he should have foreseen the possible occurrence and probable result of such negligent acts. Courts have gone on to say that the care required is commensurate with the risk involved. The owner has a duty to exercise precaution, care, and skill commensurate with the circumstances for the use intended.

In *Quinn* v. *Smith Company* (57 Fed. 2d 784), a California court ruled: "It goes without saying, in fact is not disputed, that proprietors of bathing pools owe to their patrons a duty to exercise due care, not only in providing a safe and proper place as such, but in policing and supervising the place to protect those coming there from wanton and unprovoked assault and injuries at the hands of other persons there."

But the courts also rule that the proprietor is not an insurer. This means that he is not absolutely liable in all cases, but rather only when it can be established that the proprietor failed to use due care under the circumstances.

Courts have said that where there is an increased likelihood of injury to persons of certain classes, such as children and elderly persons, then the precautions required must be commensurate with such increased likelihood of injury.

For liability to attach, the proprietor's superior knowledge of the danger must be established. For example, the proprietor would be guilty of negligence if he knew of a defect (such as a weak or cracked wooden bleacher) by virtue of its having been there for a long time, given that he had had an opportunity, upon reasonable inspection, to discover it and remedy it but had failed to do so.

The courts have said that the mere occurrence of an accident does not establish liability, because the owner of the premises is not an insurer against all accidental injuries. Accidents are compensable only when negligence can be established, and negligence is based upon foreseeability or notice (guilty knowledge). As previously mentioned, this notice can be actual or constructive. If there is a danger that might have been found by the exercise of reasonable care, such as a thorough inspection, guilty knowledge can be established or imputed to the proprietor.

In the case of *Hawkins* v. *Maine and New Hampshire Theater Company* (132 Maine One), the Maine court stated that:

> . . . the obligation, which the proprietor of a theater or amusement enterprise owes to his guests, has been thoroughly set forth. He must guard them not only against dangers of which he has actual knowledge, but also against those which he should reasonably anticipate. The failure to carry out such duty is negligence. A recovery may be had, even though the willful or negligent act of a third person intervenes and contributes to the injury, provided such act should have been foreseen.

Some courts have established liability based upon the *res ipsa loquitur* rule, as previously discussed.

The reader will recall that the defendant property owner must have had exclusive control over the injury-causing element. For this reason, the courts have been reluctant to apply the *res ipsa loquitur* rule where customers have been injured due to crowding or pushing by other customers.

A Maryland court, in the case of *Eryerly* v. *Baker* (168 Maryland 599), held the defendant property owner liable for a defect in the construction or maintenance of the premises. A customer was injured when he was struck by a revolving door pushed by another customer. The court said that the proprietor invites the public to come on his premises to do business with him, and that he is held to a positive, affirmative duty to protect the customer against dangers arising from any defect or unsafe condition of the property. This is pretty generally the law throughout the country.

In Texas, a court held that the jury should decide whether the proprietor was negligent in the case where a customer, entering the establishment through a reversible turnstile marked "Entrance," was struck by the turnstile hard enough to throw the plaintiff down and injure him when someone on the other side of the turnstile reversed it with speed and force. In *Latson* v. *Winegarten, Inc.* (83 S.W. 2d 734), the court ruled that by posting the signs "Entrance" and "Exit," the proprietor assumed a duty to prevent any reverse use of the turnstiles.

Many claims have arisen in which one patron assaults another. In general, there is no liability on the part of the property owner, promoter, school, or other person or agency in those situations. Going back to the foreseeability test again, the courts have said that there is no lack of supervision in failure to protect the patron unless prior incidents would have made it appear likely that a patron might experience injury through the repetition of such incidents. Such a case has been held to have put the proprietor on notice that he had better do something and afforded him the opportunity to do so.

The Hotel Astor, in New York City, did not have a doorman to control entrance through the revolving door. At the time of a national football game, the lobby was full; everyone was in a gay, carousing, hilarious mood. An elderly lady was injured severely when a couple of young men rushed through the revolving door playing "football." The lady recovered a judgment against the Astor. (*Chubart* v. *Hotel Astor Inc.*, 5 N.Y. State 2d 203.)

In Savannah, Georgia, some boys were roughhousing on the stairway of a theater. The proprietor had knowledge of this because the boys had caused a disturbance during the performance. In *Brown* v. *Savannah Theater Company* (36 Georgia App. 352), the court said that the liability of the proprietor was a question for the jury to determine.

At a Florida swimming pool (a profit-making venture), a patron was knocked into the pool as a result of a pushing and shoving match between several other patrons. In *Quinn* v. *Smith Co.* (57 Fed. 2d 784), the federal court ruled that the proprietor owed not only the duty to use due care and the duty to provide a safe place, but a duty to police and supervise the place to protect patrons from injury caused by other persons.

A New York court went even further in *Esposito* v. *St. George Swimming Club* (255 N.Y. State 794), stating that a proprietor is obligated to take precautions to prevent injury when one patron dives before another emerges from the water. The court based this on the fact that the proprietor solicited large numbers of people for profit, and that he therefore must be vigilant to protect them.

Generally speaking, there is no liability on the part of the proprietor for the *natural* jostling and pushing of crowds seeking entrance to a ballgame. The exception is where the defendant proprietor had reason to be aware of, or should have been aware of, uncontrolled or violent conduct on the part of customers. The proprietor must have a reasonable opportunity to anticipate violence and an opportunity to protect the patrons from it.

A Massachusetts court, in *Lord* v. *Sharer Dry Goods Company* (204 Mass. 1), stated that:

> . . . it cannot be said that a merchant is negligent simply because he has his store crowded with customers, because, while the store is crowded, he directs their attention to some part where they can get good bargains. That is what the store is for and while it is not difficult to conceive a case where the path to which the customers are called may be so dangerous, and the place itself may be so dangerous as to make it the duty of the merchant to warn the customers, we do not think that under the circumstances of this case there was any such duty resting on the defendant.

This case involved a boy who was pushed down a stairway by a crowd rushing toward a bargain counter.

The court further stated that "the stairs were of ordinary construction, and the merchant had the right to assume that, under the circumstances, there was no reason to anticipate any danger to those upon them."

A Kansas court, in dismissing a petition for damages due to the over-crowding of the defendant's "Ice Palace," said that "crowds are common in theaters and other places of amusement. That there may be some jostling in such crowds is inevitable. That someone may fall and sustain injury or cause injury to others, always is a possibility." (*Shayne* v. *Colosseum Building Corporation,* 270 Ill. App. 547.)

The Kansas court ruled that the evidence was insufficient to establish any negligence on the part of the defendant's servants, agents, or ushers. The court said that "the jostling, laughter, moving about, yelling, conversation, shouting, verbal tilts, or even betting on a boxing exhibition were the ordinary incidents of such a performance" and were not sufficient to put the defendant on notice that an altercation would arise and put the crowd in a panic.

A verdict for the president and fellows of Harvard College was upheld against an injured plaintiff named Waterman (290 Mass. 535) for injuries sustained during a football game at the college stadium. Waterman, seated on the rear, or topmost, bench, rose with the crowd during an exciting moment and stood on top of the bench he had been occupying. The people in front of him pushed backward, and he stepped back onto a ledge board, which gave way. He fell, straddled a supporting beam, and was injured.

The court ruled that the injured plaintiff had not been invited to use the open space behind his bench, and that the defendant, Harvard College, was not required to anticipate that he would do so or that he would stand on the bench, making it possible for him to be forced backward. The court thus ruled that the accident was not foreseeable. The court said Harvard College had no reason to anticipate that the crowd would become disorderly and surge against the plaintiff.

At the Saratoga Racetrack in New York, some bettors rushed to place a bet, resulting in jostling and pushing in the grandstand and a patron injury. Liability was denied in *Futerer* v. *Saratoga Association* (31 N.Y. State 2d 108). The court said that the ardor of patrons desiring to place bets somewhere below the grandstand would naturally incline them at times to be impatient and hasty in their movements. To prevent them from hurrying along an aisle would be impossible without a guard for every patron. The defendant could hardly anticipate and could not prevent, by any ordinary means, a large group rushing along an aisle in a compact body.

In *Ramsey* v. *Fontaine Ferry Enterprises, Inc.* (234 S.W. 2d 738), a Kentucky court held the operator of an amusement device not liable for injuries to a female patron in a collision of scooters. There was no foreseeability, no evidence that the rink had notice that the patron was encountering any unusual hazards, and no reason to avoid the accident by turning off the current. The court ruled that:

> . . . the injured person consented to the dangerous undertaking; the device is arranged to provide thrills for its users by bumping into or dodging each other. There is no other lure. The game has its hazards, but one cannot be ignorant of them. Plaintiff entered the scooter for the purpose of engaging in the frolic. She deliberately exposed herself to the contingency which occurred. If, by the conduct of another patron, she was exposed to an unusual hazard, no one could have been better acquainted with the fact than she. While the management had control of the electric current used by all of the scooters to propel their vehicles, she had independent control of the motion of the scooter she was using. She could have stopped it and alighted from it, and by so doing, could have eliminated herself as a target in the prankish game the youth persisted in playing. . . .
>
> Under the circumstances, we are of the opinion that the plaintiff assented to the engagement which brought about her injury and in such circumstances the law will enforce the maxim *volenti non-fit injuria* [no legal wrong is done to him who assents].

The court thus ruled contributory negligence was a bar to the plaintiff's recovery.

Assumption of risk also has been held to bar recovery, that is, one who plays a game is presumed to assume the risk of the game. This is limited to the ordinary risks inherent in the game and not to unusual hazards.

A California court, in more than one case, said that a patron of a roller-skating rink did not assume the risk created by the reckless action of other skaters, which action was capable of being prevented by guards stationed on the rink for the protection of patrons. (*Thomas* v. *Studio Amusements, Inc.*, 58 Calif. App. 2d 538.) In *Hairston* v. *Studio Amusements, Inc.* (86 Calif. App. 2d 735), the skating rink owner was held liable for injuries for negligent failure of the guards to take any action after the patron fell and was injured.

A New York court held an ice-skating rink liable when an injured patron testified that he had been thrown to the ice by another skater who had, for a time prior to the accident, been cutting in and out while having a race with some friends. In *Bloom* v. *Dalu Corporation* (54 N.Y. State 831), the court said: "While there is a certain amount of danger in a sport, it may not be said, as a matter of law, that in a skating enclosure, plaintiff must assume the risk of being struck by a reckless skater where defendant in the exercise of due care, might have protected plaintiff from the injury."

Here we see a general rule emerging, namely, that to hold the owner liable, you must show that he or his agents had the opportunity to have notice of a dangerous condition (foreseeability), had the opportunity to correct it, and failed to do so.

Such dangerous conditions are so common that those who patronize such places are presumed to know of them. To permit crowding in a place of amusement is in itself not negligence. Merely permitting a crowd in a place is never, by itself, sufficient to create liability. There are crowds at every athletic function, and if there aren't, there are supposed to be.

In *Thurber* v. *Skouras Theaters Corp.* (112 N.J. 385), the court held the proprietor of a motion picture theater not liable to a seventy-three-year-old woman who was injured when she was pushed down in an aisle by some other patrons in the crowd. The court said that there is no duty to prevent overcrowding of amusement places. The New Jersey court ruled:

> . . . we cannot close our eyes to the fact of common knowledge that motion picture theaters repeat the same picture at intervals during the day and evening and that each exhibition is concluded by many persons leaving the building and many others who have been held back taking their places. Incident thereto is the hurry to obtain seats and of this all patrons are well aware. From all that appears, we have just such a situation here presented. There was, however, nothing in the proofs to suggest that the crowd was other than usual when a popular picture is being shown, or that its conduct was out of the ordinary, or of a character calculated to endanger the plaintiff who with others was seeking to procure seats.
>
> It is not the crowding, which of itself imposes no duty, but danger that is likely to arise therefrom which poses liability. What was the danger to be apprehended here? There was nothing unusual about the crowd or its actions. When the ropes were withdrawn, those waiting to enter passed through. It is said that they hurried, but hurry consisted of walking fast, certainly nothing to suggest to the ushers that danger threatened.

An Indiana court, in *Cory* v. *Ray* (115 Ind. App. 50), said that overcrowding does not of itself constitute negligence, since crowds are a part of our everyday life in populous centers, and patrons of places of amusement must be held to assume the risk of the dangers normally attendant thereto.

But liability can arise where the proprietor could have foreseen that a customer might suffer injury from the pressure of a crowd. In the law, one can usually find a case with very similar facts that resulted in the opposite verdict, unless it is very clearly distinguished.

There have been a number of cases where it was held that failure to prevent crowding constituted negligence. This is true where the crowd was attracted by advertisements, where the crowd could reasonably have been anticipated to be rowdy, and where the proprietor failed to provide for proper crowd control.

An Ohio court ruled that a defendant theater owner failed to properly handle a crowd that knocked down an injured plaintiff waiting in the lobby for admittance to an auditorium. (*Mears* v. *Kelley*, 59 Ohio App. 159.) The court said:

> We believe the law to be that those who operate amusement places must exercise reasonable care to meet hazards and dangers which may reasonably be anticipated. One who invites persons upon his premises must properly protect those accepting the invitation. In this day and age when managers and proprietors of places of amusement and other places invite the public, and thereby cause great crowds of people to be amassed to-

gether, it would be violative of the common rules of humanity to say that
no duty is imposed upon those proprietors and managers. For their own
profit, they bring crowds together and must exercise ordinary care to protect and guard these people from the "crowd spirit" which always prevails.
Since they owe such duty, it clearly becomes a jury question, under a
proper "charge" of the court [instructions on the law] as to whether the
proximate cause of an injury to a person did or did not arise through a
breach of duty.

A New Jersey court, in *Williams* v. *Essex Amusement Corp.* (133 N.J. 218),
said that while overcrowding alone does not constitute negligence, it may
become negligence when the actions of the crowd are out of the ordinary or
such as to endanger the safety of other patrons.

In general, the proprietor is not liable for negligence or intentional injury by another person. However, liability can attach where the existence of
the dangerous condition is known or foreseeable, or where it reasonably
should have been known or foreseen, and where the proprietor failed to
take necessary or reasonable precautions.

A Missouri court told the St. Louis National League Baseball Club that
they could not, without liability, allow activities of third persons (that were
dangerous to patrons) to continue after they knew of their existence or,
where in the exercise of reasonable care, they could have known of them
and could have protected patrons by controlling or preventing the activities.
(*Hughes* v. *St. Louis National League Baseball Club*, 359 Missouri 993.)

At a roller-skating rink in Georgia, a skater was run down by another
skater who, disregarding two warning signs at the entrance, brushed close to
the plaintiff in an attempt to frighten him. The Georgia Appellate Court, in
the case of *Swope* v. *Farrar* (66 Ga. App. 52), said that the proprietor was not
entitled to assume that the warnings would be sufficient under all circumstances, and that the proprietor had to provide or use such additional means
of protection as an ordinarily prudent man would have provided. The *adequacy* of the warning was at issue.

LEAGUES AND CONFERENCES

In the United States, institutional athletics began on an informal basis in
colleges and universities. Interested students gathered on grassy areas of the
campus to relieve the tedium of classrooms and study and to satisfy the need
for vigorous physical activity and competition. College faculty and administrators felt that control or supervision of these activities was not their responsibility.

The popularity of such contests and the number of spectators increased,
and teams representing one institution began to challenge teams from other
institutions. Players of outstanding skill who were not students were recruited to play on teams. Some players enrolled at universities in order to
participate in athletics but seldom attended classes. Others played on college

teams for six to nine years. Some athletes changed colleges every year because the alumni or fraternities of other universities made better offers.

University administrators then realized that they had better assume control of this rapidly growing phenomenon. At first they employed former athletes as coaches, most of whom had not earned a degree. These coaches did not hold faculty rank or tenure. Few of them understood the ethical, educational, or health aspects of athletics. Gradually, the educational qualifications of college coaches improved, primarily as a result of the writings and speeches of leaders in physical education who had been coaches. The necessity for the formation of leagues and conferences to control problems that could not be controlled by the individual institutions became more obvious.

During the 1920s, athletics experienced a tremendous growth, both in the number of participants and the number of spectators. However, this growth magnified the problems that aroused concern among educators. In 1905, President Theodore Roosevelt had been asked by a group of private school headmasters to call for a meeting of the coaches at Yale, Harvard, and Princeton to "persuade them to undertake to teach men to play football honestly."

During that same year, the death of a player prompted the chancellor of New York University, Henry McCracken, to call a meeting of the leaders of the nation's colleges. At a follow-up meeting, the Intercollegiate Athletic Association of the United States was formed, which today is famous as the National Collegiate Athletic Association (NCAA). Many conferences at the high school and college levels were organized to establish rules and regulations to ensure equity in competition, to promote the best possible educational experience for the athletes, and to protect athletes from injury. These conferences performed commendably but, understandably, were greatly interested in promoting their sports.

The general public and, consequently, the courts have felt that the rulings of these leagues and conferences were inviolate. In fact, it has been felt that the behavior of participants in sports was immune to laws that provide limits to the behavior of people in all other areas of life. As Huizinka has pointed out, play is conducted in an area and in an aura that are outside the mundane world.[11] Until recent years, very little litigation was instituted against athletic associations and, when it was, the plaintiff seldom won the suit.

Athletic associations today are increasingly named as defendants in lawsuits. However, the plaintiffs are still not winning their suits very often. The courts have ruled that interscholastic athletic competition is outside the protection of due process. Further, the courts have stated that a student does not have a federally "constituted right" to participate in interscholastic or

---

[11]Johan Huizinka, *Homo Ludens: A Study of the Play Element in Culture* (Boston: Beacon Press, 1950).

intercollegiate sports. The only exception to this is when the student's rights under the equal protection laws (Title IX) are violated.

Almost all association rules prohibit a transfer student from competing for one year. Courts have ruled that associations have passed this rule because of past problems, that the association rules apply to students, that the association was voluntary, and that members agree to abide by the rules of the association when they join.[12]

In general, the courts have felt constrained to support regulations adopted by school authorities responsible for the administration of school programs. The courts have felt that they do not have the authority to interfere in the conduct of athletic association business, unless conditions of fraud, collusion, arbitrariness, or invasion of personal or property rights exist. This has characterized the opinions of courts in cases of residency requirements, cases of attendance at summer sports camps, and cases where students were caught with intoxicating beverages or otherwise in violation of rules of good conduct. In general, the courts support the authority and right of athletic associations to make rules that are *reasonable.*

When state athletic associations assign unto themselves the formulation of rules in areas that have been delegated to local school boards by a state legislature, the courts will not support the athletic association. Rules that require judgment or discretion, which are the domain of the school board, cannot be delegated to athletic association. If state athletic associations want to avoid litigation, they must review their rules and regulations and make changes necessary to bring them up-to-date.

LAWS AFFECTING RECREATION AND PARK AGENCIES

Almost all the laws discussed in this text are of import to managers, directors, and leaders of recreation programs, both public and commercial. The same is true of almost all safety procedures suggested to avoid liability. The broad scope of the responsibilities, activities, and services of public recreation agencies makes it important that recreation leaders possess an understanding of relevant laws.

This section will discuss those laws that have a special bearing upon the conduct and administration of recreation programs. This includes laws as they relate to personnel administration, public relations, and contracts.

Civil Rights

Title VII of the Civil Rights Act prohibits discrimination on the basis of race, color, religion, sex, or national origin in areas of employment, including

---

[12]*Bruce v. South Carolina High School Athletic Association,* Opinion No. 19441, June 1972.

hiring, firing, promotion, transfer, compensation, and admission to training programs. The Act affects employers, employment agencies, unions, and labor/management committees.

The Equal Employment Opportunity Act of 1972 expanded coverage of Title VII to include employees of state and local governments, of educational institutions, and of private firms that employ more than fifteen people. The Equal Employment Opportunity Commission (E.E.O.C.) was established to enforce the requirements of Title VII.

President Lyndon B. Johnson's Executive Order 11,246 added the requirement that contractors must develop a written affirmative-action plan and must establish integration goals in terms of employment of females, blacks, Spanish-Americans, and American Indians in proportion to their percentage of the population. The executive order also required contractors to establish timetables to achieve equal opportunities for those selected groups.

In this regard, state and local governments are required to file a detailed annual report. A sample of the appropriate reporting form is presented as Figure 5-1.

PERIOD FROM ____ 19 ___ TO ____ 19 ___ .						MALE					FEMALE				
NAME	POSITION TITLE	SALARY OR GRADE	JOB CATEGORY	TYPE OF APPOINTMENT	DATE OF APPOINTMENT	WHITE	BLACK	SPANISH AMERICAN	AMERICAN INDIAN	OTHER	WHITE	BLACK	SPANISH AMERICAN	AMERICAN INDIAN	OTHER

JOB CATEGORY
1 - Officials/Administrators
2 - Professionals
3 - Technicians
4 - Protective Service Workers
5 - Paraprofessionals
6 - Office and Clerical
7 - Skilled Craft Workers
8 - Service/Maintenance

TYPE OF APPOINTMENT
OP - Original Probationary   P - Provisional   E - Emergency   EX - Exempt or Unclassified
T - Temporary

Agencies employing workers must also develop an affirmative action plan, which must include a policy statement regarding discrimination. The policy statement must list specific objectives regarding employment of women and minority groups and designate a person or department responsible for administering the affirmative action program.

Agencies can use a number of procedures to facilitate the implementation of affirmative action, including the following:

1. Request employees to refer qualified persons for openings.
2. Advertise openings in newspapers and other media, particularly those oriented to minority groups.
3. Use private employment agencies.
4. Recruit at colleges and universities.
5. Inform civic and social organizations serving minority groups of any vacancies.

Administrators of recreation programs should be aware that, during interviews of female candidates for positions as well as on application forms, it is illegal to ask:

1. If the applicant is married.
2. Her maiden name.
3. The age of her children.
4. Where her husband works.
5. Age of the applicant.
6. Date of birth.
7. Prior diseases.
8. If ever arrested.
9. Membership in clubs, societies, and lodges.
10. Where applicant was born.
11. If candidate has a disability.
12. Military experience.

When establishing employment policies, recreation directors, like other employers, must ensure that interview boards include females, blacks, and Hispanics, as well as white males. Stated educational and experience requirements for the positon may not exceed those required to perform the job satisfactorily. Written, oral, and practical examinations must be related to the assigned tasks.

Discrimination Against the Handicapped

It is also a violation of the law to discriminate against the handicapped. A 1948 amendment to the Civil Service Act prohibits discrimination against the handicapped in federal employment. Sections 501 and 503 of the Rehabilitation Act, passed in 1973, require recipients of federal funds to take affirmative action in hiring and promoting the handicapped. In 1977, Section 504 of this act was implemented (the Vietnam Era Veterans' Readjustment Act), making it mandatory that affirmative action be taken in the employment of disabled veterans.

In recognition of increased longevity, as well as vigor and productivity extending into the sixth decade of life, the Federal Age Discrimination Act was passed in 1967. This act prohibits discrimination against those in the forty to sixty-five age bracket; in 1978, amendments extended protection from mandatory retirement to age seventy.

Fair Labor Standards Act

Howard and Crompton point out the many ways in which the Fair Labor Standards Act (F.L.S.A.) of 1938 influences policies of recreation departments.[13] They list the following questions as examples of the influence of this act:

> Must I pay the minimum wage to all my seasonal staff?
>
> Do our camp counselors qualify for the minimum wage?
>
> What are the allowable deductions against the counselor's hourly wage for room and board?
>
> I've asked my lifeguards to be "on call." Must I pay them?
>
> If I ask the lifeguards to report fifteen minutes early to change into swim wear, must I pay them?
>
> How do I know if my recreation supervisor qualifies for overtime pay?
>
> Am I required to pay employees during their fifteen-minute coffee breaks? How about lunch periods?
>
> If an employee works seven consecutive days at ten hours per day, must I pay him overtime if the seven days fall into two separate weeks, e.g., Thursday through Wednesday?
>
> Does an employee have the right to examine his personal file?
>
> Can I require an employee to go home if she is ill?
>
> Can I require my playground leaders to be well groomed, including removal of mustaches, beards, long sideburns, etc.?
>
> Our aquatics director was injured at our employees' annual softball game. Must I pay her Workmen's Compensation?
>
> Can I require my park crews to buy needed safety equipment, such as hard hats, safety shoes, glasses, etc.?
>
> Can I require a physical examination, loyalty oath, and fingerprints at time of employment?

Increasingly, effective administration of recreation programs, as well as educational programs, becomes a matter of knowing the laws because legislation and the courts encroach more and more upon the decision-making process. Where there is even the slightest suspicion of liability, the person

[13]From Howard, Dennis R., and John L. Crompton, *Financing, Managing and Marketing Recreation and Park Resources* © 1980 Wm. C. Brown Company Publishers, Dubuque, Iowa, p. 170. Reprinted by permission.

who believes he has been harmed will experience no difficulty in initiating a lawsuit.

And because of the large number of attorneys and the increasing number graduating each year, more attorneys are willing to take cases on a contingency basis, that is, their fee will be based on a percentage of the final settlement (approximately thirty to forty percent). The plaintiff has nothing to lose except his time, and the attorney is rewarded financially according to the size of the settlement. Howard and Crompton state that insurance companies apparently prefer to raise their rates rather than fight the system, since they can justify increases in rates to boards by showing the amounts of their payments.

Bills are now being introduced in legislatures to limit awards for injuries, to require that litigation be initiated within a specified time, to establish maximum fee schedules for attorneys, and to deny claims in product-related injuries if the product was of a certain age at the time of injury or if it had been significantly modified.

Torts and Negligence

This section will review some aspects of tort law especially relevant to the conduct of recreation programs.

A *tort* is a wrong, that is, a wrong done to the plaintiff, or injured party. The act of the defendant (the *tortfeasant* or wrongdoer) may not have been intentional, but could have been the result of negligence. In order to establish negligence and consequent liability, the plaintiff must prove to the judge and jury that: (1) there was a duty owed to the plaintiff; (2) there was a breach in the standard of care by the defendant; (3) there was a causal relationship between the breach in the standard of care and the injury; and (4) some injury occurred.

The court decides whether the defendant owed a legal duty to the plaintiff while the jury decides the remaining three elements. Legal duty is not to be confused with moral duty. The standard of care is sometimes measured against the local standards extant in the line of work or profession of the defendant. However, there seems to be a trend toward measuring the care provided against national standards. The standard of care would not be the same for a recreation volunteer or aide as it would be for a paid professional. The standard of care owed by the allegedly negligent defendant to the plaintiff is also determined by their relationship. The three basic relationships — trespasser, licensee, and invitee — have been defined previously. Two are redefined here for the reader's convenience.

An adult *trespasser* is one who enters the property or land of another without permission. The owner of the property, in this instance, has no obligation to assure a reasonably safe environment. The owner, however, may not create hazardous conditions, especially if the property has a history of trespassers. The owner may be declared liable for harm to children if there is a condition that is attractive to them. These cases of *attractive nuisance* usually involve children younger than twelve years of age. The determining factor is whether a child of the relevant age could be expected to appreciate the risk.

Social guests, salespersons, and canvassers are examples of *licensees.* The owner must inform licensees of any dangerous conditions that are not obvious. Generally, a recreation director can be held liable in all the ways we have discussed for teachers, coaches, and business proprietors. These laws and legal duties apply to the "person in charge."

People working in recreation are vulnerable to negligence claims in a number of areas. These include buildings and grounds, equipment, program, qualifications of personnel, methods of instruction, and auxiliary services such as first aid.

The recreation director who approves blueprints may be a defendant, along with the architect, engineer, and contractor, since attorneys invariably name as many defendants as possible to enhance the probability of winning the suit, as well as to be able to collect a large amount for damages. The same applies when the recreation department signs purchase orders for equipment that may become an issue in a product liability suit.

The recreation director may also become a defendant if a hazardous activity, beyond the level of the given age group, is included in a program, thus causing injury to a child. Such situations might occur in rock climbing or mountain climbing, spelunking, or scuba diving. And the director may be involved in a suit if he employs unqualified people, for example, if he hires someone to serve as a lifeguard who is not certified, or if he employs an uncertified person to teach scuba.

Finally, the director must have someone on his staff who is certified in first aid. All staff and volunteers should be provided with mimeographed or printed instructions on emergency care procedures.

Following are a number of random suggestions for recreation workers that will be helpful in avoiding charges of negligence. The list is merely suggestive and is by no means complete.

1. The level of instruction and progressions used by directors and assistants should be appropriate to the age of the children involved.
2. Contestants must be matched against competitors of similar age, size, and skill.
3. Used or inferior protective equipment must not be used.
4. It is better to err on the side of excessive supervision than to have inadequate supervision.
5. In many states, those involved in dispensing alcoholic beverages become liable for the actions of intoxicated patrons. If alcoholic beverages are served at a banquet sponsored by the recreation department, and if an

inebriated participant kills someone with his car on his way home, recreation department personnel may be named in a suit by the injured parties.

6. When the recreation department provides transportation to one of its affairs, it must exercise care. Use of volunteers and parents to transport the participants does not absolve the department of liability if the drivers are negligent.

7. Before leasing land and/or facilities to a vendor, inspect the facilities to ensure that there are no unseen hazards.

8. When permitting school districts to use recreation and park facilities, a written agreement should be drawn up that indicates who is responsible for maintenance and repairs of equipment, facilities, and grounds and that indemnifies for injuries. An indemnifying agreement or indemnifying clause in a contract or lease states who shall be liable and agrees to hold the other party free from liability for injuries occurring on the premises.

    For example, a school owns the premises and leases them to a promoter for a concert. As part of the lease, the promoter agrees to carry insurance, agrees to hold the school harmless for any injuries occurring on the premises, and agrees to reimburse the school (indemnify) for any financial loss by, or judgment against, the school. This is to say, the promoter agrees to insure the school against any loss arising out of personal injury during the term of the lease. A similar agreement should be prepared and signed by both parties when buildings, athletic fields, or picnic facilities are rented to social or civic groups.

9. Insurance coverage should be reviewed to make certain that the recreation agency is covered for liability claims (especially when the premises are leased out), that the amount of coverage is adequate, that all job classifications are covered, and that part-time employees, volunteers, and interns are covered.

10. Copyright laws should not be violated when preparing brochures, bulletin board displays, and materials for programs, or in the use of poetry, music, or photographs.

11. An attorney should be consulted whenever there is uncertainty regarding the legality of planned actions. Caution is called for when contracts over $500 are drawn up, when planning contests and lotteries, and when using copyrighted material.

PLAYER AND SPECTATOR VIOLENCE

In recent years, violence increasingly has become a part of contact sports. While particularly evident in ice hockey and football, violent incidents have occurred in soccer, baseball, basketball, horse racing, and other sports.

At a Florida high school football game, an argument between an assistant principal and the rival school's business manager ended when the business manager shot and killed the assistant principal. At a baseball game at the Cleveland, Ohio, Municipal Stadium, hundreds of drunken, marauding fans went on a rampage, attacking players, umpires, and one another.

At Churchill Downs, during the Kentucky Derby, hundreds of drunken youths broke through a fence and threw paper cups and beer cans at the horses as they raced down the backstretch. And four members of the Philadelphia Flyers hockey team were brought up on assault charges as a result of a brawl during the Stanley Cup playoffs in 1975.

Also in 1975, David Forbes, of the Boston Bruins hockey team, was indicted for aggravated assault by a Hennepin County (Minnesota) grand jury. The offense carries a potential penalty of imprisonment for from zero to five years and/or a $5,000 fine. During a game in Bloomington, Minnesota, between two National League teams, a fight broke out between David Forbes and Henry Boucha of the North Stars. Both men were assessed penalties and sent to their penalty boxes, where Forbes made numerous threats against Boucha.

At the expiration of their penalty time, when the game was no longer in progress, both men were returning to their respective team benches when Forbes, skating from the right rear of Boucha and carrying his hockey stick in his hand, punched Boucha on the right side of the head, the butt-end of the stick striking Boucha just above the right eye. Boucha dropped to the ice, stunned and bleeding profusely. Forbes then pounced upon Boucha, punching him in the back of the head, and then grabbed the back of Boucha's head by the hair and pounded his head upon the ice until he was restrained by another player. Thousands of spectators and even the announcers and players were shocked by Forbes's brutality.

Although the court declared a mistrial because the jury was unable to reach a unanimous verdict, the case is significant because it may portend an increase in the number of court cases dealing with violence in sports. The greatly increased concern over violence in sports in recent years is manifested by the large number of articles on the topic appearing in professional journals. Is this increased concern due to an increase in sensitivity to violence, an increase in violence, a decrease in public acceptance of violence, or to a greater effort on the part of attorneys to bring cases of aggravated assault into the courtroom? In former years, the courts tended to avoid involvement in such cases.

Should the courts become involved in judgment of player behavior during athletic contests? What are the pros and cons of such involvement from the sociological, philosophical, pragmatic, and legal points of view? The physical educator and coach must concern himself with these questions, since it is highly probable that inter-collegiate athletes may also be indicted on charges of aggravated assault.

Articles by attorneys representing the two sides of the Forbes case appeared in the January 1977 issue of *Trial* magazine. In these articles, both attorneys discussed many facets and ramifications of the case that should be enlightening to coaches and physical educators.

Among the points made by Ronald L. Meshbesher, chief defense counsel for David Forbes, were:[14]

> The crucial difference making sports unique is that violence is intrinsic to sports activity in a way that makes legal intervention difficult.
>   Among the important features of current sports that must be acknowledged are:
> a. Their organization as a business enterprise.
> b. Their increased importance as a feature of leisure society.
> c. Their increased visibility through electronic media.
> d. Their recognized influence on the behavior and values of youth.

The author cited the results of a statewide survey in Minnesota that included an inquiry on fighting in professional sports. Respondents preferred league discipline over court punishment by 61 percent to 26 percent, while 5 percent believed both forms of control should be utilized. Meshbesher continued to say:

> Although several cases of assault in hockey remain to be tried, and although there is some indication that criminal law intervention has influenced rule changes in the sport, we argue that sporadic criminal prosecutions are not an effective long-term solution and that the peculiar characteristics of criminal law and procedure reduce its effectiveness as an initial response to sports violence problems.
>   Sports violence trials have raised the question of whether the sport or the individual is on trial. Thus, the individual can be seen as the "scapegoat" for the level of violence in the sport and, by some standards, unjustly punished.

The defense counsel pointed out that there is no public or legal agreement over who should be held responsible and punished in cases of occupational and corporate conduct when the individual acts within a legitimate organization and in accordance with the requirements of his role. Advocates of defendants in such cases feel that, whether following unwritten rules of the job or direct orders, the individual is not solely responsible for his conduct. They illustrate their point by citing a study conducted several months after the Lt. Calley trial, which showed that fifty-eight percent of the people surveyed disapproved of criminal sanctions for an individual acting in a legitimate role and following what he believed to be *at least implicit orders*. They indicated that contemporary sports involve the *explicit* expectation that violent conduct is part of the game.

---

[14]Lyle Hollowell and Ronald L. Meshbesher, "Sports Violence and Criminal Law," *Trial*, January 1977, pp. 27– 32.

During the Forbes trial, the defense attorneys attempted, unsuccessfully, to have an expert witness testify concerning the effect of the intense emotional processes on a player in a competitive contact sport. An important consideration, as far as the jurors' decision was concerned, was whether the assault occurred in play or out of play. Those voting for conviction stated that, had the incident occurred in play, they would not have voted as they did.

The defense lawyers lamented the judge's decision to deny their request that the jury be instructed to consider the context of the incident in determining criminal intent. That is, the defense wanted to show in evidence and have the jury consider as extenuating circumstances the aggressive nature of ice hockey, the supercharged emotional atmosphere of the game, and the lifelong learnings of ice hockey players regarding physical contact and fighting.

The defense allowed that, although there is some evidence that criminal prosecutions have been a force in decisions by the National Hockey League Players' Association to urge League leadership in establishing new rules and penalties aimed at reducing violence and fighting in hockey, it is unfortunate that this worthy goal may be achieved at the expense of individual justice.

The defense went on to propose a solution to the problem of excessive violence in sports. They proposed a "cooperative effort among the federal and state governments to establish either a federal sports commission, state sports commission, or both." This approach, they believed, would provide primary *review* of sports-related matters by a regulatory board and provide for criminal sanction through referral of extreme cases only as a *last resort*.

Gary W. Flakne, County Attorney for Hennepin County, who prosecuted David Forbes, also wrote an article for *Trial* magazine on the Forbes case.[15] Flakne and his coauthor, Allen H. Caplan, disagreed with Meshbesher regarding the advisability of establishing sports commissions or councils for the control of violence. These authors pointed out that token fines or penalties would have little impact. They wrote: "Furthermore, to suggest that the governing body of a particular sport determine adequate sanctions for a quasi-criminal or criminal act would be tantamount to granting the board of directors of General Motors jurisdiction over the determination of guilt or innocence and the appropriate punishment for one of the employees who, while on the job, killed his foreman."

It was pointed out that "the rationale in support of the encroachment of the criminal justice system into the world of sports is derived from the proposition that no particular segment of society can be licensed to commit crime with impunity." They cited Lord Justice Bramwell's instructions to the jury in *Regina* v. *Bradshaw* (Cox C.C. 83 [1878]), a criminal prosecution

---

[15]Gary W. Flakne and Allan H. Caplan, "Sports Violence and the Prosecution," *Trial,* January 1977, pp. 33–35.

resulting from a death during the course of a soccer game. In this case the court ruled:

> No rules of practice of any game whatever can make that unlawful which is unlawful by the law of the land . . . no persons can by agreement go out to fight with deadly weapons, doing by agreement what the law says shall not be done, and thus shelter themselves from the consequences of their acts.

In their article, the prosecutor and his assistant wrote: "Obviously, the same act, had it occurred outside the arena, would yield certain criminal prosecution. Since it receives only a token penalty inside the arena, there is no real compelling force to curtail that type of conduct. So the psychological conditioning drilled into the body-contact athlete flourishes."

The authors then went on to deny that the entry of the criminal justice system into the sporting arena would bring about the demise of sporting events, contending that execution of a bone-crushing block or tackle in football or a punch in boxing, executed within the rules of the game, could not be successfully prosecuted in criminal court, because participants in body-contact sports consent to the possibility of injury (assumption of risk) as a result of acts committed by opponents, which acts are in accordance with the rules of the game. Further, where assault resulted in serious injury, the courts have held that the public has a stronger interest than does the injured person who "requested" injury.

In sports, the rules, regulations, and equipment are designed to avoid serious danger of life or limb; nevertheless, serious injuries do occur. Consequently, as stated by the abovementioned court, "the presence or absence of serious bodily injury as the standard for determining whether a defendant will be able to invoke the defense of consent becomes wholly unrealistic." Instead the question is whether the defendant was guilty of criminal intent (whether he intended to injure), and whether or not he was in compliance with the rules of the game.

* * * * *

We have reported the Forbes case and the rationale of the attorneys on both sides in rather lengthy detail. Since this was the first time a professional athlete had been tried in the United States on a game-based criminal charge, it would serve as a precedent. That the case *was* brought to court is an indication of the extent of concern over violence among people outside of sports.

If the people involved in sports do not take steps to remedy the situation, people in the federal or state governments or the law *will* take steps to do so. Through a review of this material, the authors hope that the reader will gain a better understanding of how attorneys view the problem of violence in sports from their perspective.

Readers interested in gaining additional insight and information regarding violence in sports are urged to read Appendices VII, VIII, IX, and X to H.R. 79035, Congressman Ronald R. Mottl's 1980 proposal for a sports violence act, as well as testimony presented to the Subcommittee on Crime.

Longtime physical educators and coaches are surprised and discouraged by recent levels of sports violence and brutality, by disdain for athletics as a means for development of ethical character and sportmanship, and by the admiration received by players and coaches who are cunning in circumventing rules and regulations. One of the major points of physical educators and coaches as proponents of sports programs has been that the programs contribute not only to physical fitness and improvement of health, but that they develop socially worthwhile qualities (such as a sense of fair play, obedience to rules and regulations, cooperation, civic responsibility, and ethical and moral behavior).

Evidence of the importance earlier attributed to development of the above qualities is provided by statements of pioneers and leaders in the development of school physical education and athletic programs, as well as by position statements of professional associations in physical education and sports. J.B. Nash defined physical education as an aspect of the total educational process that utilizes inherent activity drives to develop organic fitness, neuromuscular control, intellectual powers, and *emotional control.* Delbert Oberteuffer's fifth principle of physical education states: "The teaching of values on the ethical-moral plane must assuredly be as definite and planned for as those of skill."[16]

David K. Brace listed fifteen values that can accrue to participants in a well-conducted physical education program.[17] He advocated teaching of "concepts of fair play and respect and consideration for the shortcomings or achievements of opponents through sports."

One portion of the *Platform for Physical Education* of the AAHPERD (American Alliance for Health, Physical Education, Recreation, and Dance) reads: "So that all the educational values of interscholastic athletics may be secured for youth, athletics should be administered and conducted by school officials and teachers who are primarily concerned about the welfare of participants."[18]

There is a chasm between the ideals and standards expressed above and those expressed in the following quotations:

> Players die like flies in football; why is everybody up in arms over violence in hockey? (Fred Shero, Head Coach of the Philadelphia Flyers)

---

[16]Delbert Oberteuffer, "A Decalogue of Principles," *Journal of the American Alliance for Health, Physical Education, Recreation, and Dance,* January 1947, p. 37.

[17]David K. Brace, "Physical Education Experience in Relation to Cultural and Educational Values in a Dynamic Society," *Professional Contributions No. 6,* American Academy of Physical Education, November 1958, p. 30.

[18]W.K. Street and Simon McNeely, "A Platform for Physical Education," *Journal of the American Alliance for Health, Physical Education, Recreation, and Dance,* March 1950, p. 21.

>   If you can't beat them in the alley, you can't beat them on the ice.
> (Conn Smythe, President, Toronto Maple Leafs)
>   I only wish I had one man I could have sent after Mikita to send him
> back to Czechoslovakia in a coffin. (Don Cherry, Head Coach of the Boston
> Bruins)

With coaches and team presidents offering such points of view, it is not surprising that players feel encouraged to give physical expression to their feelings of frustration and anger. Some coaches and owners of football and ice hockey teams, like the promoters of roller derbies and professional wrestling matches, may believe that violence increases gate receipts — and it may. However, people involved in professional sports have a responsibility to refrain from contaminating the moral environment of their society, just as chemical and other industries have a responsibility to refrain from contaminating the physical environment.

Professional athletes serve as role models for athletes in college, high school, and youth leagues, not only in the manner in which they execute the skills of their game, but in all areas of behavior. Children will mimic not only the batting style of Reggie Jackson, but also the football style, or even the way of drinking cola, exhibited by "Mean" Joe Green. If an athletic hero uses a certain brand of after-shave lotion, many of his fans will buy the same brand. This is why successful professional athletes are paid large sums to endorse products.

Generally speaking, the more vivid an experience, the greater the learning. Sports have great potential as a modality in teaching social behaviors because they are visual and often emotionally charged. Whether they want to or not, and whether they are aware of it or not, participants in professional sports are powerful teachers. Will these athletes elect to teach socially desirable and ethical behavior, or will they elect to carry us back to the decadent Roman gladiatorial contests that contributed to the fall of the great empire?

Sports began as one form of play. In the life of every professional sportsman, his participation in the sport began as play. The most recent, inclusive, and comprehensive analysis of the phenomenon of human play was made by John Huizinka in the previously cited book *Homo Ludens* [Man the Player]. This work is highly respected and often quoted by writers on physical education, athletics, and recreation. Perhaps Huizinka can provide some guidelines in helping to determine the appropriateness of judicial intervention into sports.

Huizinka sees play as pervading most of man's activities, as predating recorded history, and as being an attitude, or way of perceiving, an activity. Play is a manipulation or conversion of reality into images. It is an effort to bring order and beauty to man's activities. The play mood is one of rapture and enthusiasm. It elicits feelings of exultation or tension, with mirth and relaxation following the action. Huizinka writes: "As civilization becomes more complex, more variegated, and more overridden, and as the techniques of production and social life itself become more finely organized, the old cultural soil is gradually smothered under a rank layer of ideas, systems of thought, and knowledge, doctrines, rules and regulations, moralities and conventions which have lost all touch with play."[19]

Play demands absolute order. It endeavors to bring into life a temporary perfection and beauty. The important element in most play is to prove oneself superior. Superiority tends to confer on the winner superiority in general. The winner and his supporters gain honor and esteem. Victory represents triumph of good over evil and salvation for the winning group or individual.

When an act of violence is performed outside the rules of the game, the spirit of play is violated because the order and beauty of play are violated, because there can be no mirth and relaxation following play, and because reality impinges upon images. Forbes's angry and vicious attack upon Boucha violated the spirit of play.

But the intrusion of courts of law into the area of play also violates the spirit of play. Those involved in sports cannot have it both ways: they cannot have the social protection that play provides while violating the spirit of play. Perhaps sports, at least on the professional level and in large universities, can no longer be classified as play. Perhaps, at these levels, sports are being taken too seriously. Perhaps there is too much regimentation and systemization, too little spontaneity and carelessness, and too much emphasis on profit. If this is true, the courts have no less duty to become involved in sports than they do in other forms of commerce and industry.

If those involved in sports, and particularly those in professional sports, wish to stem the movement of the courts and the law into the sports arena, they must exercise greater control through their leagues, commissions, presidents, and coaches. This control must be directed toward maintenance of the "ludic spirit," which includes education for ethical and sportsmanlike behavior. This educational process will take place through rules, the enforcement of the rules, publicity releases, and exemplary behavior on the part of those involved in professional and other upper-level sports.

Coaches and athletic directors, particularly those at large universities, must give the above points serious consideration if the further intrusion of the courts into interscholastic and intercollegiate athletics is to be checked.

Law enforcement does not stop at the gate of any sporting arena. There are no special pockets of immunity where the law of the land does not apply. When we speak of violence in sports, we are not speaking of the injuries that normally occur in the course of a rough-and-tumble body-contact sport played according to the rules of the game; we are speaking of conduct that society does not tolerate in any other setting.

If a player is injured in regular play in a body-contact sport such as hockey, football, basketball, or wrestling, there is no, and should be no,

---

[19]Huizinka, *Homo Ludens*, p. 75.

responsibility, either criminal or civil. It is only when a player seriously violates the rules of the game, when he commits an assault and battery upon another player, that the law should intervene. Players, both professional and amateur, are also citizens and as such are subject to the laws of the land. A citizen-player has as much right to the protection of the law and of the police during play as does the citizen-player when he is walking through the parking lot to his car.

The law should not, and does not, hold its citizen-players responsible in tort or criminal law for the rough-tough, violent conduct that is normal for a sporting event. So-called sports violence is that which occurs when one citizen-player violently attacks another, with or without a weapon, and seriously injures or kills him. The law of the land holds him accountable to his fellow citizen.

If a citizen in the stands, watching the game, takes a hockey stick and beats his fellow citizen in the stands into unconsciousness, he is legally responsible. There is no reason why a citizen-player should not be entitled to the same protection of the law: the citizen-player and his family suffer the same loss. If a fight erupts in the street outside the stadium between rival players, there is no question that civil law would apply to the conduct of those citizen-players. If a fight between players breaks out during a game, the players are still under the protection and requirements of the law.

A case in point comes to mind. The New York Rangers and the Boston Bruins were playing hockey when a fight broke out. One of the Ranger fans reached over the protective glass and punched a Bruins player. A group of Bruins players then went into the stands with their fists and sticks waving and got into a fifteen-minute melee with a group of spectators. This is the type of sports violence that demeans the game.

In the previously discussed case of Rudy Tomjanovich and the Houston Rockets versus California Sports, Inc. (owner of the Los Angeles Lakers), the National Basketball Association fined Laker Kermit Washington $10,000 and suspended him for sixty days. As the reader will recall, this case arose when Tomjanovich went to help break up a fight between one of his teammates and Washington. Washington turned and hit Tomjanovich in the face, breaking his jaw and fracturing his skull.

Tomjanovich sued and his wife, Sophie, sued for damages and loss of consortium of her husband. The jury rendered a verdict of $1.8 million in general damages and $1.5 million in punitive damages. The defense claimed that Washington was acting in self-defense and that Tomjanovich had assumed the risk. The jury ruled that the blow struck by Washington was far beyond any type of conduct permitted by the rules and customs of the game, and that Tomjanovich did not consent to this type of conduct.

In prosecution of this type, the defendant commonly pleads self-defense. This means that the law allows anyone to meet force with equal force in defending himself. Another defense often employed is implied consent to violence when one voluntarily engages in a contact sport, knowing that serious injury, though not likely, is certainly a real possibility. Still another defense is that the injury was accidental and "part of the game." Another is that the defendant was acting with an involuntary reflex and was not really responsible. Still another is that there was provocation that brought about the assault or battery.

* * * * *

From the above cases we can see a trend for courts to hold the defendant responsible if his acts go beyond the rules of the game in purposely injuring or attempting to injure an opponent.

Violence is not limited to hockey, however. In one football contest, Terry Bradshaw, of the Pittsburgh Steelers, passed to teammate Franco Harris. The Oakland Raiders' George Atkinson came up behind another Steeler receiver, Lynn Swann, and hit him with his forearm at the bottom of the helmet. Swann suffered a brain concussion and was unable to play for the next two games.

In the case of *Hackbart* v. *Cincinnati Bengals,* also discussed previously, a lower court ruled that Hackbart had no claim. The facts were that Charles "Booby" Clark, angered because his Bengals were losing, hit Denver's Hackbart on the back of the head when Hackbart was down on one knee after play had ceased. (The officials didn't see it happen.) Hackbart suffered three broken vertebrae, some muscular atrophy, and a loss of reflexes and strength in his arm. In ruling against Hackbart, the lower court said that participants in this type of violent activity assume the risks, even if another player's conduct violates the rules of the game.

The Tenth Circuit Court of Appeals overruled that decision, stating that the general customs of football do not allow that kind of violence outside the rules. They also ruled that the defendant's team could be held accountable. When an agent (a football player), acting within the scope of his employment (playing football), performs a negligent or wrongful act, his principal or employer (a football team and its corporate owner) may be held responsible for the damages incurred by the injured plaintiff-player.

This is the same basic law that applies to every other corporation. The law of the land is the same whether applied to the playing field, the streets, or the corporate boardroom. This is only fair and reasonable when one considers whether it is fair for Hackbart to pay for all damages caused by Clark, or whether Clark and the Bengals team should pay.

But again, sports violence is not limited to professional contests. For example, a goaltender on an amateur soccer team and his father brought a court action for injury sustained at the hands of an opposing player during a match at Duke Child's Field in Winnetka, Illinois. The plaintiff, Julian Nabozny, was the goaltender for the Hansa team. The defendant, David Barnhill, was playing forward for the Winnetka team. Both teams were composed of high-school-age players.

During the course of the game, a Winnetka player kicked the ball over the midfield line. Two players, Jim Gallos of Hansa and the defendant of Winnetka, chased the free ball. Gallos reached the ball first. Since he was closely pursued by the defendant, Gallos passed the ball to the plaintiff in the Hansa goal. Gallos then turned away and prepared to receive a pass from the plaintiff.

Nabozny, in the meantime, went down on his left knee, received Gallos's pass, and pulled the ball to his chest. The defendant, Barnhill, did not turn away when Gallos did, but rather continued to run in the direction of Nabozny and kicked the left side of the plaintiff Nabozny's head, causing severe injuries.

All witnesses agreed that the defendant had time to avoid contact with Nabozny, and that the plaintiff observed the rules of the game by remaining at all times within the penalty area (a rectangular area between the eighteen-yard-line and the goal). Four witnesses testified that they saw Nabozny in a crouched position on his left knee inside the penalty area. Nabozny testified that he actually had possession of the ball when he was struck by Barnhill. One witness stated that the plaintiff had the ball when he was kicked. All other witnesses stated that they thought Nabozny had possession of the ball at the time.

Nabozny called three expert witnesses. Julius Roth, coach of the Hansa team, testified that the rules under which the game was being played prohibited all players from making contact with the goalkeeper when the goalkeeper has possession of the ball in the penalty area. Possession is defined in the Chicago area as the goalkeeper having his hands on the ball. Under the applicable rules, any contact with the goalkeeper in possession in the penalty area is an infraction of the rules, even if such contact is unintentional. The goalkeeper is the only member of the team allowed to handle the ball in play so long as he remains in the penalty area. The three experts agreed that the contact in question in this case should not have occurred.

As a further point in the case, it was indicated that head injuries to goalkeepers are rare in soccer. But as a result of being struck, plaintiff Nabozny suffered permanent damage to his skull and brain.

In *Nabozny* v. *Barnhill* (334 N.E. 2d 258), the court said the initial question was whether or not a legal duty existed between the defendant and the plaintiff. The court ruled as follows:

> This court believes that the law should not place unreasonable burden on the free and vigorous participation in sports by our youth. However, we also believe that organized athletic competition does not exist in a vacuum. Rather, some of the restraints of civilization must accompany every athlete onto the playing field. One of the educational benefits of organized athletic competition to our youth is to develop . . . discipline and self-control.
>
> Individual sports are advanced and competition enhanced by a comprehensive set of rules. Some rules secure the better playing of the game as a test of skill. Other rules are primarily designed to protect the participants from serious injury.

For these reasons, this court believes that when athletes are engaged in athletic competition, all teams involved are trained and coached by knowledgeable personnel; a recognized set of rules governs the conduct of the competition; and a safety rule is contained therein which is primarily designed to protect players against serious injuries. A player is then charged with a legal duty to every other player on the field to refrain from conduct proscribed by such safety rule. A reckless disregard of the safety of others cannot be excused. To engage in such conduct is to create an intolerable and unreasonable risk of serious injury to other participants. We have carefully drawn the rule announced herein in order to control a new field of personal injury litigation. Under the facts presented in the case at bar, we find such a duty clearly arose. Plaintiff was entitled to a legal protection at the hands of the defendant. The defendant contends he is immune from tort action for any injury to another player that happens during the course of a game, to which theory we do not subscribe.

It is our opinion that a player is liable for injury in a tort action if his conduct is such that it is either deliberate, willful or with a reckless disregard for the safety of the other player so as to cause injury to that player, the same being a question of fact to be decided by a jury.

Defendant also asserts that plaintiff was contributorily negligent as a matter of law, and therefore, the trial court's direction of a verdict in the defendant's favor was correct. We do not agree. Evidence was presented to show that plaintiff was in the exercise of ordinary care for his own safety. While playing his position, he remained in the penalty area and took possession of the ball in a proper manner. Plaintiff had no reason to know of the danger created by the defendant. Without this knowledge, it cannot be said that plaintiff unreasonably exposed himself to such danger or failed to discover or appreciate the risk. The facts and evidence reveal that the play in question was of a kind commonly executed in that sport. Frank Longo, one of plaintiff's expert witnesses, testified that once the goalkeeper gets possession of the ball in the penalty area, "the instinct should be there" [in an opposing player pursuing the ball] through training and knowledge of the rules to avoid contact with the goalkeeper. All of plaintiff's expert witnesses agreed that a player charging an opposition goaltender under circumstances similar to those which existed during the play in question, should be able to avoid all contact. Furthermore, it is a violation for a player to simply kick at the ball when a goalkeeper has possession in the penalty area even if no contact is made with the goalkeeper.

. . . We conclude that the trial court erred in directing a verdict in favor of the defendant. It is a fact question for the jury. This case, therefore, is reversed and remended to the Circuit Court of Cook County for a new trial consistent with the views expressed in this opinion.

(This opinion was written by Justice Adesko of the First District Division Appellate Court of Illinois.)

In most of these cases, we see a trend for courts to find liability not when there is simply a violation of the rules of the game, but more specifically when there is a violation of the safety rule, that is, a rule of the game meant to protect the participants.

Another case in point relates to America's all-time leading sport, baseball. The prominent baseball case is *Bourque* v. *Duplechin* (331 South 2d 40). This case occurred in Louisiana where some adults were playing in an amateur softball league. The plaintiff sued for negligence when a runner left the baseline to hit the plaintiff, a second baseman, "intentionally bringing his arm up under the plaintiff's chin." Had the plaintiff been standing on the baseline, he might have been held to be contributorily negligent or to have assumed the risk. But he was four or five feet off the baseline. The court found the defendant baserunner, Duplechin, liable for substandard and negligent conduct.

The court ruled that the defendant, Duplechin, had a duty to play softball in the ordinary fashion, without unsportsmanlike conduct or wanton injury to other players. The court said Bourque, the second baseman, did not assume the risk of contact since "he was so far away from the base as to be a violation of a duty to play the game in the ordinary manner." In other words, the court ruled that Bourque did not assume the risk (of Duplechin running out of his way in order to run into him at full speed) when he was four or five feet from the baseline.

This is not a case of the ordinary type of violence that some sportscasters dramatize when they announce a professional game. Such sportscasters tell us, for example, that the injury rate for football players is one hundred percent. They justify rough play with clichés such as, "men are men," "boys will be boys," "outlet for aggression," and "sports are excellent training and good, clean fun." Sports provides many benefits, but when it goes beyond the bounds of good, clean fun and takes the form of a malicious attack, the action must be penalized.

Policing of sports is required. There is policing of the bar association, by the courts and by the bar association itself, with possible disbarment of lawyers who violate the rules. In the medical profession, policing is accomplished through the medical society and individual hospital staffs by removing hospital privileges from a negligent doctor.

If those in sports do not take affirmative steps to police their own organizations from within, they will find themselves in court more frequently. Positive steps must be taken. If this is not done, state and even federal laws will be passed to dictate what is right and wrong and how the game is to be played. There are already moves in the Congress, as well as in various state legislatures, for such laws. Senator Mottl's sports violence bill has already been mentioned.

The authors agree with Joe Brown, Director of Information for the National Football League, when he said: "We feel it is better to police the sport ourselves than to have it policed by outside courts." We also agree with baseball commissioner Bowie Kuhn, who said: "Baseball does a good job of controlling violence."

But such statements are not sufficient. Positive steps must be taken to establish rules to govern and police sports or it will be done by the courts, legislatures, and others. It is incumbent upon those involved to draw a line delineating where legitimate aggressive play ends and illegal conduct or true violence begins. Those in sports must speak out. There are already ruling bodies that have established rules for fairly playing the games and for the protection and safety of participants. What is required now is one more small step for man and a giant step for sports, namely, stating in a legislative, positive, and affirmative way what violence will not be tolerated by sports professionals. (Rules established for professionals will trickle down and become the accepted rules for colleges and schools and will ultimately be accepted in the courts as a basis for measuring liability — if the legislative task is performed fairly.)

The law has already accepted the Uniform Commercial Code, Uniform Accounting Practices, the electrical code, the rules of the National Football League, and similar standards or quasi-laws to govern the conduct of professionals. Steps have already been taken in a positive direction by the American Law Institute in its research of the law. In this regard, the reader is referred to Section 50, Comment B, which states in part:

> Taking part in a game manifests a willingness to submit to such bodily contacts or restrictions of liberty as are permitted by its rules or usages. Participating in such a game does not manifest consent to contacts which are prohibited by rules or usages of the game if such rules or usages are designed to protect the participants and not merely to secure the better playing of the game as a test of skill. This is true although the player knows that those with or against whom he is playing are habitual violators of such rules.

The following illustrations are offered:

> A, a member of a football team, tackles B, a player on the opposing side. A's conduct is within the rules of the game. A is not liable to B.
>
> A, a member of a football team, ttackles B, an opposing player, while he, A, is "offsides." The tackle is made with no greater violence than, or different from, that permitted by the rules, although he is guilty of a breach of a rule. A is not liable to B.
>
> A, while tackling B, deliberately drives his knee into B's abdomen, rupturing his spleen. A is subject to liability to B, whether the tackle was or was not otherwise within the rules and usages of football.

Spectator Violence

In a paper presented at the 1981 national convention of the American Association for Health, Physical Education, Recreation, and Dance in Boston, Cheffers, Wood, and Meehan reported the results of their comprehensive study of sports spectator violence.[20] They concluded that the violence demonstrated by spectators at sports events is of a different nature than violence of the players. They said: "The context within which violent behav-

---

[20]Don Cheffers, David Wood, and Al Meehan, "Sports Spectator Violence: Origins, Recogniton, and Control." Unpublished report presented at the National Convention of American Alliance for Health, Physical Education, Recreation, and Dance, Boston, 1981.

ior occurs among spectators is governed by the normative order [rules] of every life [society], not by the rules of the game. Thus behavior such as wrestling someone to the ground is 'assault' within the former order and a 'fine tackle' in the latter."

The authors cited the recommendations of Glenn C. Leach, presented in his text *Spectator Control at Interscholastic Basketball Games*:[21]

1. The schedule of games should take place during the afternoons.
2. The number of tickets sold should be slightly under the capacity of the gymnasium.
3. Strong supervision at games from athletic directors and teachers is much more important than the use of special police.
4. Long-term and short-term recommendations for avoiding disturbances that get out of control are equally important.
   a. To educate the student body on the rules and ethics.
   b. To explain controversial decisions quickly and quietly when they occur.
   c. Interpretations of officials' calls, etc., can be displayed on the score-boards.
   d. Reports should be submitted to the conference or league after each game. Hostile or unnecessary poor acts of behavior should be reported to the conference, discussed at the conference level, and appropriate action taken.
   e. Coaches and athletic directors should hire competent officials in the first place.
   f. The schools should educate the press on not only the results aspect of their interscholastic games, but more vital forms of information such as total numbers participating, ethics of the local competition, support services, parental backing, and any other detail designed to promote balanced reporting at the local level.
   g. The general public and parents, in addition to officials, coaches, and players, should be included in invitations to rule-interpretation sessions and to clinics.
5. Strong actions, required in emergency situations, should not be avoided:
   a. Troublesome players should immediately be withdrawn from the game.
   b. Troublemakers in the stands should be barred from any future games and should be removed immediately from the games in which they are being troublesome.
   c. Troublesome teams should be eliminated from future schedules.
   d. It appears that each new generation, and indeed each new team, needs to be reminded that the game is the most important thing, and other considerations (winning, monetary rewards, scholarship atten-

---

[21]Glenn C. Leach, "Spectator Control at Interscholastic Basketball Games," cited in Cheffers, Wood, and Meehan, "Sports Spectator Violence," op. cit. pp. 8–10.

dance, etc.) are secondary. Although this point appears, unfortunately, moralistic, it still needs to be made.

e. Immediate stoppage of games should take place if disturbances get out of hand. Games should not be allowed to proceed if they are out of control.

Cheffers et al. add one further recommendation to those made by Leach:

f. Troublemakers arrested for acts of vandalism within the stadium should be made to work on whatever reconstructive activities are needed to restore the facility.

The same authors add that among professional sports teams, the question of crowd control is not as simple. They suggest the following to help professional organizers:

1. Local, national, and international press and television networks should be requested to reward alternative behaviors, and not to dwell unnecessarily on acts of violence. Related to this point is the inordinate preoccupation the press has for rankings. There appears to be little doubt that the indulgence of the press in describing first placings, over and above the means by which that victory was achieved, has educated crowds to really believe that victory is the essence of a game. Victory is only the essence of the game if both teams strive towards it within the spirit of the game. A team that wins a game in points, having violated the spirit and rules of the game, is not a winner, and that should be emphasized by the press, continuously.

2. Games should not be permitted to take place in areas which have become degenerate, or at times which are considered dangerous. The nationally televised Monday night NFL "Game of the Week," presided over in circus fashion, is believed to be held at a dangerous time from a spectator control viewpoint, and has to be considered highly suspect.

3. Stoppages during a game have an important effect upon the crowd. Natural stoppages occur where injury to a player takes place. This was illustrated when Fred Lynn, the Boston center fielder in 1975, while chasing a ball hit the wall with such solid contact that he fell to the ground. The crowd stopped dead, acting as one concerned person, until they were sure that Lynn was unhurt. A second point, of course, is that contrived stoppages, like an injury to a player, can, at the discretion of a referee, still the crowd.

4. A return of respect to players as human beings needs to occur. One wonders how much longer the intervention of lawyers, contractors, major business concerns, and economic interests can continue to predominate. Perhaps it is expecting too much to have such intervention from outside interest groups, and to have spectator control at the same time.

5. When winning becomes primary, and what is achieved predominates over how it is achieved, then a disrespect for the whole game ensues. Inversely, when two teams go at it in close, hard-fought activity, usually both teams are respected for the excellence of the game. What happens on the field will always affect what happens in the crowd, sometimes critically.

LEGAL RESPONSIBILITIES OF TOP EDUCATIONAL ADMINISTRATORS

Superintendents and principals are not named as defendants as frequently as are other school personnel, primarily because they have few direct contacts with students. However, administrators are liable under the general principles of tort law for their own acts of negligence. Most legal actions against administrators have involved rules and regulations, equipment and facilities, supervision, due process, and operation of the school. These areas are discussed throughout this text.

In other words, if rules or regulations promulgated by the administrator are cited as a cause of a student injury, the administrator may find himself a defendant in a lawsuit. For example, if exceptions are allowed to the rule that teachers may never leave a class unsupervised, and if a student is injured while the class is unsupervised, the administrator could be declared liable.

In some states, school administrators may be charged with negligence under the doctrine of *respondeat superior* (master and servant, or master and agent). This doctrine imposes liability on an employer or boss when an employee fails to use ordinary care, when the administrator has been negligent in supervising subordinates, or when he has directed the subordinates to perform an act that results in a tort.

In the past, school districts have been immune from liability under the principle of governmental, or sovereign, immunity. This principle, along with charitable immunity, comes from English law. It arose in England out of the belief that the king, or sovereign, was an emissary of God, and since God could do no wrong, the king could do no wrong. The doctrine was extended such that those representing the king in governmental duties also could do no wrong.

Common law doctrine has forced those wronged to press their suits against teachers individually, since they could not sue the immune school district. However, some states have passed save-harmless, or hold-harmless, statutes, by which a teacher on trial for negligence is furnished an attorney and, if found guilty, the school district pays the cost of the award for the teacher.

The end result is that school boards should carry liability insurance to provide protection for members of the school boards, as well as for teachers.

One argument for retention of the common law doctrine in tort cases is that governments do not have adequate funds to pay for the tort claims that could be brought against a school district. Another argument is that once a principle has been accepted by the courts, it must stand (*stare decisis*).

On the other hand, arguments are increasingly made for abandonment of this common law doctrine. Some argue that medical and other costs arising out of injuries to students are as much operating costs for a school as are costs for electricity, heat, buildings, and books. Opponents of the common law doctrine ask why the student or teacher should pay the costs of injuries when other costs are paid out of the school budget. They argue that if a school is liable for breaking a contract, it should be liable for breaking a student's leg.

/ 6 /

Student and Faculty Rights

Several decisions by the Supreme Court between 1969 and 1975 have forced administrators and teachers, including physical education teachers and coaches, to consider student rights. In *Tinker* v. *Des Moines Community School District* (1969), the Supreme Court stated that students do not "shed their constitutional rights at the schoolhouse gate." In this case, the wearing of black armbands to protest the war in Vietnam was found to be a protected mode of free expression. This decision came at the height of the civil rights movement in the high schools.

In *Goss* v. *Lopez* (1975), the Supreme Court ruled that education is a property right of students that cannot be denied without due process of law, as guaranteed under the Fourteenth Amendment. This ruling requires schools to establish hearing procedures that students can utilize *before* being suspended. The procedures must include a statement of the charges, provision to the student of the supporting evidence (if the student requests to see the evidence), and the opportunity for the student to present his defense against the charges.

The ruling extends the rights of due process into the schools. The majority of the Court felt their decision would not impose an unfair burden upon school administrators, as indicated by their opinion: "In holding as we do, we do not believe that we have imposed procedures on school disciplinarians which are inappropriate in a classroom setting. Instead, we have imposed requirements which are, if anything, less than a fair-minded school

129

principal would impose upon himself in order to avoid unfair suspensions." Realizing that suspension from school is "not only a necessary tool to maintain order but a valuable educational device," the Court required only "an informal give-and-take between student and disciplinarian."

Shortly after its decision in *Goss* v. *Lopez*, the Court handed down its opinion in *Wood* v. *Strickland*. This ruling adds teeth to the prior ruling, since it creates the possibility of money damages being levied against a school board and school administrators for violating the civil rights of students in suspension cases. The language of this Supreme Court decision requires that the educator act in "good faith" and defines this term as knowing, within the bounds of reasonableness, what a student's constitutional rights are.

The Court ruled as follows: "In the specific context of school discipline, we hold that a school board member is not immune from liability for damages under the civil rights statute known as 42 USCA 1983 [United States Code Annotated], if he knew, or reasonably should have known, that the action he took within his sphere of official responsibility would violate the constitutional rights of the student affected. . . ."

The Tinker, Goss, and Wood decisions require that educators regard students in a new, nontraditional light. This acquisition by students of certain constitutional rights has produced a different relationship between school authorities and students. Educators who have used discipline as an authoritarian tool to secure absolute obedience must now employ a higher order of professional judgment and imagination. The disciplinarian will have to communicate with the student.

Corporal Punishment

In *Baker* v. *Owen* (1975), the Supreme Court supported a lower court ruling permitting school officials to employ corporal punishment, in spite of parental objections, to restrain or correct pupils and to maintain order. The Court's opinion stated: "So long as the force used is reasonable — and that is all that the statute here allows — school officials are free to employ corporal punishment for disciplinary purposes until, in the exercise of their own professional judgment or in response to concerted pressure from opposing parents, they decide that its harm outweighs utility." The Court did not attempt to define the term "reasonable force."

To protect the student, the Court ruled that the following procedures must be followed:

> First, the use of corporal punishment must be approved, not in each individual instance but in principle, by the principal before it may be used in a particular school. Second, except for those acts of misconduct which are so antisocial or disruptive in nature as to shock the conscience, corporal punishment may never be used unless the student was informed beforehand that specific misbehavior could occasion its use, and, subject to this exception, it should never be employed as a first line of punishment for

misbehavior. The requirements of an announced possibility of corporal punishment and an attempt to modify behavior by some other means — keeping after school, assigning extra work, or some other punishment — will insure that the child has clear notice that certain behavior subjects him to physical punishment. Third, a teacher or principal must punish corporally in the presence of a second school official [teacher or principal], who must be informed, and in the student's presence, of the reason for the punishment. The student need not be afforded a formal opportunity to present his side to the second official; the requirement is intended only to allow a student to protest, spontaneously, an egregiously arbitrary or contrived application of punishment. And finally, an official who has administered such punishment must provide the child's parent, upon request, a written explanation of his reasons and the name of the second official who was present.

Participation in Intercollegiate Athletics

In *Regents of University of Minnesota* v. *National Collegiate Athletic Association* (1976), an appeals court reversed a lower court decision that the opportunity to participate in intercollegiate basketball was a property right and consequently entitled to due process guarantees. The lower court had stated that participation on an intercollegiate basketball team could lead to a highly remunerative professional career and, further, that intercollegiate competition is an important part of a student athlete's educational experience.

In this case, three basketball players had been accused of infractions of NCAA rules but were cleared of charges after the University of Minnesota held due process hearings. When the university refused to suspend the players, the NCAA imposed a prohibition on all the university's athletic teams. It appears the courts are reluctant to impose their judgment on athletic associations and refused to do so in this case.

In *Colorado Seminary* (University of Denver) v. *National Collegiate Athletic Association* (1976), the Court concluded that student participation on intercollegiate athletic teams was not at the level of constitutionally protected property rights or liberty sufficient to invoke the process guarantees. However, the Court stated that a hearing by the NCAA was required before it sanctioned the university.

Search and Seizure

Physical education and athletic personnel are advised to establish a policy with regard to inspection of lockers and rooms. In establishing a policy, they should secure legal counsel to ensure that the policy conforms to state and federal law. As an example, one relevant law requires that students be informed, at the beginning of each school year, of the reasons for search and seizure.

The Fourth Amendment of the U.S. Constitution provides students with protection against unlawful search and seizure of themselves and their property. The amendment states: "The right of people to be secure in their persons, houses, papers, and effects, against unreasonable searches and seizures, shall not be violated, and no warrants shall issue, but upon probable cause. . . ."

The courts attempt to strike a balance between a student's right to be free from unreasonable searches and seizures, on the one hand, and the institution's responsibility to maintain order and discipline through reasonable rules and regulations, on the other. In recent years, there has been a trend to place greater weight on students' rights.

The Fourth Amendment protects individuals from the police by requiring that law enforcement officers secure permission of a judge or magistrate prior to a search. The judge then decides, on the basis of reasonableness, probable cause, and necessity, whether the request should be granted. However, law enforcement officers do not require a judge's approval for a search if consent is secured, if an emergency exists, or if the search relates to a lawful arrest.

School officials may conduct inspections for purposes of health and safety. However, it is illegal to conduct searches and seizures for drugs, for stolen articles, or for other purposes without the student's consent (except in emergencies such as bomb threats). Although the institution may or may not utilize the evidence secured in an illegal search in its own disciplinary proceedings, such evidence is not usually admissible in court.

A statement in a dormitory contract, permitting college officials to search rooms without search warrants, even though signed by the student, may not excuse college authorities from securing a search warrant. In *Smyth v. Lubbers* (398 F. Supp. 777 [D.C. Mich. 1975]), the judge stated that a search warrant should have been secured by the college if they had "reasonable cause to believe" that students were violating college regulations or general laws. In this case, the college officials found a substance alleged to be marijuana in the rooms of five students. To prevent a college disciplinary hearing, the students filed a civil rights suit in federal court, contending that their Fourth Amendment rights had been violated.

The court held that for Fourth Amendment purposes adult college students have the same privacy rights in their dormitory rooms as any adult in his own home; a student's Fourth Amendment rights cannot be waived by a statement in a rental contract; a college may not search dormitory rooms without probable cause and, unless there is an emergency, without a warrant; and, further, evidence secured during an illegal search may not be used in college disciplinary proceedings.

Somewhat different conclusions were reached by the court in *Morale* v. *Grigel* (45 L.W. 2287 [D.N.H. Nov. 9, 1976]). In this case, university employees searched all dormitory rooms for stolen goods. The room of one suspected student was searched, and although the stolen property was not found, marijuana and a pipe were found and confiscated. A disciplinary hearing was held, and the student was suspended. The student filed suit, maintaining that the marijuana seized resulted from an illegal search and that, consequently, his admission of marijuana possession should not have been permitted in the college disciplinary hearing.

While the court did hold that the search was illegal by virtue of the student's Fourth Amendment rights, it also held that, although the evidence found as a result of an illegal search would be inadmissible in criminal proceedings, it was admissible in college disciplinary hearings.

The case of *State* v. *Kappes* (550 P. 2d 121 [1976]) further confuses the issue of search and seizure. In this case, the court ruled that no unlawful search had taken place when a student was convicted of possession of marijuana on the basis of its discovery and seizure by student advisors, who had been making a routine room investigation. The court stated that the student advisors were not "tainted with the degree of governmental authority which will invoke the Fourth Amendment." The student advisors had provided entry to the room to university and law enforcement officials who, upon entry, found the pipe and marijuana in plain sight.

Dress Codes

Some coaches believe that esprit de corps is of great importance to the success of their teams. Some further believe that uniform dress requirements for away games and even on campus will help to develop esprit de corps. The authors concede that this practice can develop team pride and unity, as well as serve for good public relations. However, coaches are advised, on the basis of court decisions, to observe the following cautions when intiating dress codes.

First, the dress code should be arrived at through democratic processes that involve students, parents, administrators, and faculty. And second, enforcement procedures should include some form of due process. That is, the student should be given oral or written notice of the charges; the school authorities should give the student an explanation of the evidence in their possession; and the student should be given an opportunity to present his side at a hearing.

Private schools have greater freedom from constitutional restrictions than do public schools. Students who take their objections to dress codes to court usually invoke the Fourteenth Amendment. One court has expressed the opinion that on entry into college the student's level of maturity is sufficient to tip the scale in favor of the individual, as opposed to the institution's responsibility for his education. The decision was reached in the case of *Lansdale* v. *Tyler Junior College* (470 F. 2d 659 [5th Cir. 1972], certiorari denied, 411 U.S. 986 [1973]).

Academic Policies and Decisions

The courts have been reluctant to impose their judgment over that of educators in academic matters. This has not been true of disciplinary dismissal proceedings, which they have reviewed and continue to review. It is unlikely that an educational institution would be successfully prosecuted in the areas of awarding grades or requirements for a degree, if the institution follows a reasonable set of regulations and procedures for these functions, and if it provides a review process for students to contest academic decisions.

Judicial reviews of academic decisions have addressed charges of arbitrary and capricious action. But most of these cases have been won by the educational institution, since almost all schools have some form of appeals process available to students dismissed for academic reasons. Furthermore, the student must prove that the school acted arbitrarily or capriciously in order to win the case.

Lawsuits brought against educational institutions demanding damages for poor teaching or inadequate course content have been largely unsuccessful. In one case, a court ruled: "The achievement of literacy in the schools, or its failure, are influenced by a host of factors which affect the student subjectively, from outside the formal teaching process, and beyond the control of its ministers. (*Peter Doe* v. *San Francisco Unified School District*, 60 Col. App. 3d 814 [1976].)

Grades are a sensitive issue to students. Faculty and school administrators have certain responsibilities in this area, including the following:

1. The institution should have written policies concerning grading procedures, cheating on examinations, and plagiarism on term papers.
2. The faculty should inform students of attendance requirements, grading procedures, standards of performance, and penalties for turning in assignments late.
3. Grades must be posted with care and within a reasonable time after the conclusion of the term.
4. Student records should be accurate and confidential. The criteria set forth in the Family Educational Rights and Privacy Act of 1974, as well as in the Privacy Act of 1974, must be followed. The first of these acts provides that federal funds be denied to any school that denies parents the right to inspect any and all official records, files, and data directly related to their child.

   A student over eighteen years of age, unless his parents claim him as a dependent for income tax purposes, is the only one to whom files may be released. Information in the files may not be released to others without written permission from the parents or the student. If the parents or student believe the files contain inaccurate material, a hearing must be held within a reasonable time and before an impartial hearing officer, at which the student may present his side of the story. An explanation may be inserted into the file by the student or parents.

   The Privacy Act of 1974 prohibits new uses of the social security number by all governmental agencies — federal, state, and local. Private agencies are exempt. The purpose of the laws is to eliminate tracing a person's identity through his social security number. Students cannot be denied admission to a public institution, nor can they be denied any other legal right, due to refusal to disclose their social security number. As an example of the provisions of the cited act, it would be a violation to use social security numbers when posting grades on bulletin boards or office doors.

When dismissing a student for academic reasons, faculty and school officials are advised to exercise caution to avoid placing a stigma on the student that can be detrimental to future opportunities. A court could hold that the student was deprived of a significant constitutional liberty interest and that due process is required. Condemnation of the student through wording in letters or forms, such as "lacks intellectual ability," "lazy," "poor personal hygiene," "indolent," or "poorly motivated," which may deny the student other opportunities, can result in a charge of deprivation of one's interest in liberty. Reasons for academic dismissal should refer to inadequate performance.

In *Horowitz* v. *Board of Curators of University of Missouri* (538 F. 2d 1317 [8th Cir. 1976]), the court found that the dismissal (without a hearing) of Horowitz, a medical student, for poor personal hygiene, erratic attendance at clinics, and lack of rapport with patients, "imposed a stigma or other disability that foreclosed freedom to take advantage of other employment opportunities." The court declared that the student had been stigmatized in such a way that she would be unable to continue her medical education, and that her ability to find employment in any field related to medicine was impaired. The court ordered the university to hold a hearing at which she could utilize her due process rights by rebutting the arguments used in her dismissal.

FACULTY RIGHTS

Throughout this text, we have discussed the responsibilities of physical education faculty, coaches, and athletic program directors. In view of all the mentioned legal responsibilities, it would not be too surprising if some of these professionals opted for other, less demanding fields of endeavor. However, teachers, coaches, and officials are also protected by the law. This section presents a discussion of the rights of these professionals.

Free Speech

As long as it is not harmful to the educational process, faculty and administrators at public institutions may exercise their right of free speech and other first amendment rights. However, when speaking or writing publicly, they should identify their statements as personal opinion or expressions of official position.

Dress Codes

The courts have usually ruled against dress and grooming codes at public institutions. In a case involving a faculty member of a public junior college who was fired for violation of a regulation banning beards, both the trial court and the appellate court held in favor of the faculty member. However, in another case of a dress code requiring teachers to wear a shirt, tie, and jacket, a teacher claimed a constitutional right (of free expression) to wear a turtleneck sweater. The appellate court at first supported the faculty member, on the basis that his Fourteenth Amendment liberty interest and his First Amendment interest had been violated. However, the court then decided to rehear the entire case and vacated the decision, holding that a public school board may impose reasonable regulations governing the appearance of its teachers. (*East Hartford Educational Association* v. *Board of Education*, 4.05 F. Supp. 94 [D. Conn. 1975]; 97 S. Ct. Judicial Highlights, p. 2 [2nd Cir. Feb. 22, 1977], no. 76-7005 [2nd Cir. August 19, 1977].

If school officials desire a dress code for faculty, they should involve those who will be affected in formulating such a code. And the code should include a statement of the need for the code and its purpose. The code will have less chance of being successfully challenged in the courts if it sets standards relating to health or educational order.

Employment Issues

Contrary to public opinion, an untenured position carries few legal rights. The employee cannot expect further employment, a notice of nonreappointment, or a hearing. The employer is not required to give reasons for nonreappointment. An untenured position is generally viewed as a probationary period of employment. The legal relationship between the employer and the untenured employee is limited to whatever was agreed to between the two parties. Administrative officials usually serve at the pleasure of the employer and may be released at any time. Term contracts are generally prepared and signed by both parties for nontenured faculty employees. While the untenured may not be fired for expression of free speech, an untenured person must prove that such a termination resulted from exercising this right.

If it is proven that the two parties shared an expectancy of future employment, due process is required. Due process is also required when evidence shows that a charge was made that might place a stigma on the person's good name and reputation, such that it foreclosed future employment opportunities or seriously damaged the person's standing in the community.

Courts rarely order an educational institution to grant tenure. Nevertheless, colleges and universities should understand the procedure for grant of tenure and should be aware of the positions courts have held in tenure-related cases.

The most common form of tenure is called contractual tenure, which is the result of a series of formal review procedures. The first step is a review of the candidate's academic and scholarly competence, conducted by members of the candidate's department through a departmental tenure and promotion committee. Most often, several selected areas (such as teaching effectiveness, contributions to the department, college, and community, and professional leadership) are evaluated, sometimes on a point basis. The departmental chairman generally can participate on this committee only on an ex-officio basis. The recommendation of this committee may then be forwarded to a college or university tenure and promotion committee, or it may be forwarded directly to the academic dean of the school or college of which the department is a part. The dean then forwards his recommendation to the college or university president, who adds his recommendation and passes the case on to the highest governing body, usually a board of trustees.

Only the person or body having specific power to grant tenure may do so. This is customarily the board of trustees. The department and college tenure and promotion committees generally focus their evaluation on the performance and qualifications of the faculty member. The dean, president, and board of trustees must evaluate the need of the institution for the faculty member's services. The higher-level officers must consider faculty-student ratios, funding, anticipated future objectives and trends, and percentage of tenured faculty. (If all members of a department are tenured, little flexibility to move in new directions is permitted.) These officials would also consider the candidate's length of service. (Almost all institutions of higher education require three to seven years of satisfactory probationary service prior to granting of tenure.)

The granting of tenure is not official until the highest governing body has made its decision. In one relevant case, an outgoing university president informed a faculty member in writing that he had in effect been granted tenure by being continued "without term." However, the new president informed the faculty member he would not be rehired, and the professor demanded a hearing. The court in this case dismissed the professor's suit on the basis that "only the board may elect an individual to the faculty and only the board may confer the equivalent of tenure by electing a faculty member 'without term.' "

Trustees may delegate authority to the president to deny tenure, but they cannot delegate power to grant tenure. Tenure may not be conferred upon a faculty member as a result of the failure of administrative officers to notify the individual that tenure was not granted. However, the courts may require some form of redress, such as additional period of employment or the payment of some money damages, as did occur in the case of *Gorman* v. *University of Miami* (Case No. 75-3697, 11th Cir., Dade Cy., Fla., 1975).

The courts have also ruled that a faculty member has no right to be included in faculty committee meetings during which his tenure is discussed. (*Stebbins* v. *Weaver*, 396 F. Supp. 104 [W.D. Wis. 1975].)

If a faculty member is properly notified of denial of tenure but then, at his own request or for the convenience of the institution, is awarded another term appointment, he may not contend that he has been granted tenure. (*Kilcoyne* v. *Morgan,* 405 F. Supp. 828 [E.D.N.C. 1975].)

Some states and colleges provide de facto tenure when they state in the faculty handbook or a similar source that teachers are awarded tenure after a stipulated number of years of satisfactory service. Tenure is not granted on a system-wide basis unless policy statements, faculty handbooks, contracts, or other official sources specifically so state.

Termination of Tenure

Tenure can be terminated only for adequate cause. "Adequate" or "just" cause may be determined by reference to professional documents, such as the *Statement of Academic Freedom and Tenure* of the American Association of University Professors (AAUP) and the Association of American Colleges, or by reference to collective bargaining agreements.

Adequate cause includes professional incompetence, moral turpitude, bona fide financial exigency, and discontinuance of a program or course of study. The AAUP statement cited above defines moral turpitude as "behavior that would evoke condemnation by the academic community generally," and not behavior that would be condemned by the people in the particular community.

The institutions must provide reasons why tenure is terminated, and the person terminated must be permitted to attend the hearing and to rebut the evidence presented against him. An institution may terminate tenured faculty on the basis of financial exigence; however, the institution must show that the financial exigency is real and that it is the reason for termination of tenure.

When a number of faculty are to be released, the school administration has the right to determine which teachers to release and which to retain. (*Levitt* v. *Board of Trustees of Nebraska State Colleges,* 376 F. Supp. 945 [1974], p. 170.) However, a hearing must be provided for tenured faculty to be terminated at which they can present arguments for their own retention and for that of other faculty. (*Brady* v. *Board of Trustees of Nebraska State Colleges,* 376 F. Supp. 945 [1974], p. 171.)

Seniority rights during such periods of retrenchment become especially important. Some systems permit the employer to retain persons with special skills while releasing others with more seniority. (*Smith* v. *Regents of University of California,* 130 Cal. Rgstr. 118 [1976], p. 172.)

Promotions

Courts have avoided interceding in decisions involving promotions, believing that these judgmental decisions are best left to college administrators.

However, the institution must follow its own rules and avoid arbitrary or malicious actions.

Resignations

Letters of resignation should be sent to the authorized person. In general, this is the person or body who has the authority to hire, fire, and promote personnel. This is usually the school board in public schools, and the board of trustees in colleges and universities.

Retirement

An individual may not be discharged because of age; however, he may be required to retire if he will have a pension. An appellate court, in reversing a decision of a lower court, pointed out that the primary purpose of the Age Discrimination in Employment Act (ADEA) of 1967 is to prevent age discrimination in hiring and discharging workers, but that retirement with an adequate pension is generally regarded with favor. This court found that a bona fide employee benefit plan gave an employer the option of retiring employees before age sixty-five against their wishes and that this was not in violation of the ADEA.

Faculty Evaluation and Promotion

A large number of lawsuits and complaints filed with federal agencies concern allegations of discriminatory practices in recruiting, hiring, and treatment of faculty, administrators, and other educational officials. A number of laws, acts, and statutes, in addition to the Fourteenth Amendment of the Constitution, are cited as a basis for the suits and complaints. Suits may arise out of job descriptions, advertising of job openings, interviewing procedures, selection of candidates, terms of employment, or collective bargaining procedures.

Discrimination in Hiring

To avoid accusations of discrimination in hiring, a description of the job should be written, along with the minimal qualifications required. The qualifications should be closely related to the responsibilities of the position. (The requirement of a doctoral degree when not really necessary for a position may lead to allegations that this requirement is aimed at preventing minorities or women from applying for the position.) Job announcements should state the salary or salary range and should indicate whether the appointment will be for a limited time or whether it involves a possibility of tenure.

The equal opportunity laws require that educational institutions receiving federal funds seek qualified minorities and women if such groups are underrepresented in the work force. For this reason, job openings should be advertised in newspapers and journals that will reach qualified minorities and women. For jobs in the physical education and recreation fields, announcements should also be sent to placement offices and to chairpersons of physical education departments that prepare physical education teachers, coaches, and recreation leaders. Affirmative action laws require that job openings be advertised to increase the number of people who learn about them.

The statutes require that the job interview be conducted in a nondiscriminatory manner. Questions should be centered strictly on qualifications for a position, as manifested by educational preparation, references, and employment experience, as these factors relate to the responsibilities of the position. Questions regarding marital status, children, birth control practices, spouse's attitude toward the job, etc., are likely to be judged as other than job-related.

A Wyoming court reasoned that a school board does not give up its freedom to choose the teacher it wants just because it advertises for a teacher. (*Sheffield* v. *Sheridan County School District No. 1*, 544 P. 2d 870, [Wyo. 1976].) The Supreme Court of Wyoming overturned the decision of the Wyoming Fair Employment Commission when it stated: "If it turns out that for reasons of economy, one applicant can fulfill the needs of the district at a cost substantially less than another applicant, even though the rejected applicant may on paper possess the greater qualifications, a selection of the less expensive teacher cannot be said by any board or court to have been the result of discrimination based on sex."

This court concluded that a school board may select a teacher who has the ability to perform additional duties, such as coaching, and may select a teacher who is personally more attractive to it without being charged with discrimination.

Title IX of the Federal Elementary and Secondary Act prohibits recipients of federal aid from classifying a job as being for males or females, or from maintaining separate lines of progression, seniority lines, career ladders, or tenure systems based on sex. Teaching certificates are not issued based on sex, and physical education is no exception to this rule. For this reason, a person cannot be denied a position teaching physical education to the opposite sex by reason of locker room duties or having to touch students (as in spotting in gymnastics and tumbling).

Collective Bargaining

Chairpersons of physical education departments and athletic directors are not usually directly involved in collective bargaining unless they are elected to a union office. However, an understanding of the collective bargaining process, as well as of the laws and statutes affecting it, can be helpful to such professionals. Community recreation directors, on the other hand, are very likely to become involved in collective bargaining at some point in their professional careers.

The National Labor Relations Act, administered by the National Labor Relations Board (NLRB), provides the legal guidelines for collective bargaining at private educational institutions, which are included in the NLRB's jurisdiction because they have a substantial impact on interstate commerce. Included in this jurisdiction are all private institutions with a gross annual revenue (from all sources except contributions not available for operating expenses) of not less than $1 million.

Due to the First Amendment principle of separation of church and state, the courts have held that the NLRB does not hold jurisdiction over secondary Catholic schools. Additionally, the courts have ruled that if secondary church-related schools are too sectarian to receive government aid, they are too sectarian to be regulated by governmental agencies. Further, the NLRB has no jurisdiction over public institutions that receive financial assistance from the state but not from the federal government and/or are regulated by the state.

Public Employee Labor Relations Acts have been passed in many states. Public institutions in those states are covered by these acts rather than by the National Labor Relations Act.

An *agency shop* is one in which the employer and the union have negotiated a clause in their agreement whereby an employee in the certified bargaining unit who does not wish to join the union, need not do so. However, such an employee must pay the regular union dues, and the union will represent the nonunion employee in grievances. A *union shop*, on the other hand, requires all employees in the unit to become union members after a specified date.

With few exceptions, students are not eligible to be members of a bargaining unit, the reason being that the "stipends" students receive constitute a living allowance rather than compensation for services and, further, that the work of the students is part of their instructional program.

Good-faith bargaining requires that the employer and the bargaining agent meet and confer but does not require either party to make concessions. Parties must bargain with an open mind and a sincere intention to reach an agreement. Bargaining in good faith is required in most bargaining statutes.

A refusal to discuss mandatory subjects of bargaining can be evidence of bad-faith bargaining. *Mandatory* bargaining subjects include: wages, hours of work, and conditions of employment that are not accepted as management prerogatives (such as pay for summer teaching, insurance benefits, effects of eliminating a department, selection of employees for layoff, retirement, and employee injuries). *Permissive* subjects are those that the parties may negotiate if they choose to do so.

After a bargaining agreement is reached, copies should be given to all employees and managers. Most state and all federal laws require that members of the union receive copies. It is good practice to meet with all management personnel to explain the provisions of the agreement and to answer questions. Similar meetings for employees should be conducted by the bargaining agents. Particular attention should be given to the grievance procedure, since it is often as important to employees as are wage issues.

When the employer and the bargaining agents are unable to reach agreement, unsolved grievances may be submitted to an impartial arbitrator. While some collective bargaining agreements accept an arbitrator's finding merely as recommendations, most such findings are final and binding and may be enforced through the judicial process.

Although statutes and most collective bargaining agreements prohibit strikes, strikes do occur in the public sector (police, firemen, and workers in public schools and institutions of higher education). Many states have passed legislation that makes strikes by public employees illegal. Striking employees may be dismissed and, unless the employer agrees to rehire fired strikers, they have no legal right to their former jobs. Penalties may also include loss of tenure, fines, or incarceration for failure to return to work following court injunctions to do so. Rehiring of fired strikers is sometimes arranged as part of an overall strike settlement.

Contractual Protection for School Administrators

Athletic directors and chairpersons or deans of departments, schools, or colleges of physical education, health, and recreation are classified as administrators. As such, they serve at the pleasure of the employing body, but some have sued successfully after being fired. Tenure for these administrators is based on the 1940 *Statement of Principles On Academic Freedom and Tenure* of the American Association of University Professors. This document emphasizes that the purpose of tenure is to protect faculty members in the classroom and in scholarly research. Courts have held that these purposes are not served by awarding tenure to administrators. As a result, administrators are subject to arbitrary dismissal, transfer, or pay cuts.

Over the years, administrators began to see the advantage of contractual protection, and school and college boards came to realize that a waste of human resources resulted from unnecessary turnover in administrators. New administrators must be recruited, trained, supervised, evaluated, and allowed to gain experience, all of which require time and money. Thus boards began to see the advantages of three- to five-year contracts for administrators. They also began to assess job descriptions, to evaluate job candidates more carefully, and to use probationary periods of employment before making a more permanent commitment.

Contractual protection for administrators is provided at the elementary and high school levels to a greater extent than at higher levels. However, the trend is toward providing educational administrators at all levels a more protected employment relationship. In higher education, chief executive officers are usually given contracts for three to five years.

The American Association of University Administrators (AAUA) was founded in 1970. In 1975, it adopted a statement of professional standards for administrators in higher education. These standards pointed out both the responsibilities and rights of administrators. Under the rights of administrators, the AAUA statement listed several conditions of employment, such as a written statement of the conditions of employment that would cover salary, fringe benefits, term of office, process of review, notice of renewal or continuation, and responsibilities of the position. There will likely be increasing reliance upon the AAUA's professional standards as protection for administrators' rights at institutions of higher education.

Athletic directors and deans of schools or colleges of physical education, health, and recreation are administrators and, consequently, are subject to the same laws and rulings as are other administrators. They should know that in the absence of a contract they may be required to accept a cut in salary, to accept a reduction in their contract from twelve to ten months, or to accept a transfer to another post at the end of a term contract. When an administrator does not have a contract, he may be terminated without due process or reasons given.

Due process is required if the administrator is terminated during the term of the contract. However, when dismissal procedures at public institutions are conducted in a manner that might damage the reputation or career of the individual, due process is required. When educational institutions give financial exigency as a reason for termination, they usually must prove that they were suffering economic distress of sufficient magnitude to require cuts in their budget.

/ 7 /

Procedures for Reducing the Incidence of Injuries

When policies and procedures concerned with safety are written and distributed to students and faculty, the incidence of accidents and injuries is almost certain to decrease. And the fewer injuries, the fewer tort actions taken. Further, in the event of a lawsuit against a coach, physical educator, or recreation director, printed policies and procedures placed into evidence will reinforce the case of these professionals.

Obviously, it is not sufficient to merely draw up such policies and file them in a folder. They must be distributed to all faculty and students and should be prominently posted near the site of relevant activities. The policies and procedures must be followed by all personnel, and the faculty must insist that they be followed by students.

This chapter presents sample policies and procedures for a number of sports and recreation areas. It is recommended that these be studied, adapted to the situation at the particular institution, and then printed, distributed, and posted. Coaches and physical educators who follow these policies and procedures are not likely to be sued successfully.

ARCHERY

Students should understand that while archery is an enjoyable recreational activity, a bow and arrow are not toys. They can be lethal weapons when carelessly used and are capable of causing serious injury and even death. Deer and other big game are brought down with a hunting arrow. A hunting arrow can penetrate three feet into a sandbox — twice the distance of a bullet from a Garand rifle. Even an arrow released by a child's bow can penetrate the eyeball, causing loss of sight.

Students must be informed of procedures they are required to follow whenever using the archery range, whether in class, during free play, or in intramural or team competition. Ignorance of the regulations cannot be used as an excuse in the event of injury to self or others.

An indoor archery range is preferable to an outdoor range, from the safety point of view, because it is easier to control entry to the range by nonparticipants, and because students are more easily supervised. Entry to the range should be limited to an area behind the shooting line; doors in front of the shooting line should be locked. Objects that might cause deflection of arrows should be removed from the range. Windows forward of the shooting line should be closed and covered with a material that will prevent arrow penetration. A nylon net, rug, or other material that will stop an arrow should be suspended behind the target line.

On the other hand, outdoor ranges provide the aesthetic advantages of open space and fresh air. They also make it possible to shoot at greater distances and to add clout shooting and archery golf to target shooting. When selecting the site for an outdoor range, look for a hill or embankment toward which arrows can be shot. The area should be clear of trees, wires, fences, and other obstructions. There should be an area behind the target bales that is twice the length of the longest shooting yardage. Nonparticipants should not be permitted access to the range. Barriers and signs around the range should warn people not to enter.

Guidelines for Students

1. Aim arrows downward while nocking (placing the arrow notch on the bowstring).
2. Wait for the signal "nock arrows" from the person in charge before doing so. Do not nock arrows until all persons are behind the firing line.
3. Wait for the signal before releasing arrows.
4. Remain behind the firing line until the signal "retrieve arrows" is given. If an arrow falls just beyond the firing line, do not retrieve it until the signal is given.
5. When two or more people are shooting at the same target, only one person at a time should draw arrows from the target, while others stand back at a safe distance. An arrow pulled out of the target quickly and forcefully may fly backward and strike persons standing too near.
6. To withdraw an arrow from the target, the left palm should be placed against the target with the index finger on one side and the second finger on the other side of the arrow. The arrow should be grasped near the target with the right hand and removed by exerting equal pressure with each hand.

7. Do not use split or defective bows or arrows. Your instructor will provide replacements. Bows should be checked periodically for cracks and stress marks. (Stress marks appear as frosted areas in fiberglass and laminated bows.) Discard any worn strings.
8. Always use an arm guard and a finger tab or gloves.
9. Your clothing should have no pockets, buttons, or ruffles, and you should not wear jewelry or pins — any of which might snag the bowstring.
10. Your bow and all arrows to be used should be matched. A heavy bow will cause a low-spined arrow to crack. If you are uncertain whether they match, ask your instructor for help.
11. Check the fistmele (distance between the bow and string). It should be six inches, or roughly the equivalent of the fist with the thumb extended upward from the fist. Insufficient fistmele will cause wrist slap; too much may cause the bow to break.
12. Use arrows and bows of a length appropriate to your size. To determine arrow and bow length, measure the distance between the fingertips of both hands by standing with your back against a wall with both arms raised sideward horizontally. Then refer to the chart below.

Spread Measurement	Arrow Length	Bow Length
57–59 in.	2–23 in.	Not under 4'6"
60–62 in.	23–24 in.	Not under 4'6"
63–65 in.	24–25 in.	Not under 5'0"
66–68 in.	25–26 in.	Not under 5'0"
69–71 in.	26–27 in.	Not under 5'6"
72–74 in.	27–28 in.	Not under 5'6"
75–77 in.	28–29 in.	Not under 5'9"
over 77 in.	30 in.	Not under 6'0"

13. To avoid muscular strain, use the large muscles of the back and shoulders when drawing, rather than the small muscles of the fingers and forearms.
14. Discard cracked or splintered arrows and those to which the feathers are not securely fastened. A loose feather can penetrate the bow hand of a shooter.

Guidelines for Instructors and Administrators

1. Examine equipment weekly for defects.
2. Ensure that bows and arrows are matched.
3. Make certain that the range of lengths of bows and arrows is adequate to meet the range of student sizes.
4. Inform all participants of all safety procedures. Distribute printed material.

5. Provide an adequate backstop (bales of straw, hill) behind the target area.
6. Rope off the shooting area.
7. Locate the archery range away from pedestrian and motor traffic.
8. Never leave bows and arrows where children or careless persons might handle them.
9. Keep bows and arrows locked up when not in use.
10. Assign only qualified people to teach archery.
11. Assign students to a specific target, with no more than four students to one target.
12. The space between shooters should be such that they do not interfere with one another.
13. Instruct students to step back one pace behind the shooting line after releasing an arrow. When the shooting line is clear, the instructor may give the signal to retrieve arrows. Obviously no student should be permitted to retrieve his arrows while others are shooting.
14. If students are shooting at different distances, the target bales should be moved while all shooters use the same starting line.
15. Arrows falling immediately in front of the shooting line should not be retrieved until the cease fire signal has been given.
16. The step-through method of stringing a bow is safer than the instep method. With the former, one leg is placed between the bow and the bowstring, and leverage is provided by the thigh at the center of the bow.
17. The instructor should stand behind, or at one end of, the shooting line. When giving individual instruction, he should stand behind the student.
18. In archery golf, everyone should stand behind the person taking a shot. (The targets in archery golf represent the holes in golf, and participants move in sequence through the eighteen "holes.")
19. For clout shooting, a space completely free of barriers and at least 150 yards by 100 yards is necessary. (In clout shooting, participants shoot arrows upward, attempting to have the arrow drop into the center of the target on the ground.)

BASEBALL AND SOFTBALL

Although few deaths can be attributed to baseball or softball, the incidence of injuries is quite high, especially to beginning players. In particular, directors and coaches of Little League teams must concern themselves with prevention of injuries.

Although there has been no discernible trend toward lawsuits directed at officials and coaches of Little League teams, the overall trend seems to indicate a great probability that more suits in this area will be initiated.

A survey of the frequency and causes of injuries among professional and college baseball players indicates that sprains accounted for 27.3 percent of the injuries, strains 18.7 percent, contusions 16.9 percent, pulled muscles 11.3 percent, and fractures 8.3 percent.[1] The incidence of these types of injuries can be reduced by:

1. Properly conditioning the players.
2. Proper execution of skills.
3. Provision of suitable equipment and facilities.
4. Adequate supervision.

The game of baseball is not physically strenuous enough to condition players to meet any emergencies that arise during a game. For this reason, baseball players need to participate in a conditioning program, including jogging, running, and stretching during the off-season. Athletic directors should make certain that baseball coaches establish such an off-season conditioning program.

Adequate warm-up will also decrease the incidence of strains and pulled muscles. To ensure warm-up during a game:

1. Players should jog to their positions and to the dugout.
2. Outfielders, as well as infielders, pitchers, and catchers, should take warm-up throws before the first batter of the inning is called up.
3. Batters should take a few practice swings before stepping into the batter's box and should run out every play.
4. Pitchers should be replaced at the first sign of fatigue.

Baseball coaches should know the mistakes in execution of skills that are most likely to lead to injury. Some of the more important of these are listed below:

1. Failure by the pitcher to finish the pitch in a position to catch a line drive.
2. Failure by the catcher to keep his body in front of the ball.
3. Catcher unnecessarily close to the batter.
4. Catcher slow in removing mask on a pop fly, or failing to throw the mask away from the area to which he must move to catch the fly.
5. First baseman with foot on a corner of the base other than the inside corner when receiving throws from infielders. Placing the foot on the inside corner of the base will decrease the probability of a collision and also of having the foot stepped on.
6. Failure by the first baseman to relax the tagging arm when he is off the base due to a poor throw.

---

[1]Joseph Borzzne, Chauncy A. Morehouse, and Stanley F. Pechar, eds., *Monograph #6;* Warren Huffman, ed., *Monograph #3, Administration and Supervision for Safety in Sports,* Sports Safety Series, American Alliance for Health, Physical Education, Recreation, and Dance (Washington, D.C.: The Alliance).

7. Failure by infielders to keep the body low and to keep their eyes on the ball while fielding ground balls.
8. Outfielder colliding with the fence. The outfielder should run toward the fence but should turn around before reaching it and then relocate the ball.
9. Failure by outfielders to inform one another of who will take a ball. Players should call for the ball or indicate that they will permit the other player to do so.
10. Outfielder blinded by the sun. All fielders should wear sunglasses (shatterproof) on sunny days.
11. During the hitting of fungo flies, the receiver should be designated in order to avoid collisions between two players trying to catch the same ball.
12. Failure to wear a helmet while batting, either during a game or at practice.
13. Failure to keep the eyes on the ball when batting.
14. Throwing the bat. Huffman recommends that "bat throwers" be called out.[2]
15. Incorrect sliding techniques. Correct sliding techniques should be taught early, and the slide into first should only be used when the first baseman has been pulled off the base by a wide throw.
16. Head-first slide.
17. Incomplete slide. When the decision to slide has been made, it should be followed through to completion.
18. Lead runner on double play being struck by the ball. The lead man can avoid this by sliding to get under the thrown ball.

Catchers

Catchers suffer the highest incidence of injury. Foul tips, collisions at home plate, and the pounding that results from catching pitched balls may result in smashed fingers, broken knuckles, and bruised arms, among other injuries. The newer catcher's mitts with single and double hinges, snap action, and lightweight padding, eliminate the necessity of placing the bare hand over the ball immediately after the catch.

Two-handed catching makes the throwing hand vulnerable to injury from foul tips or wild pitches. The newer gloves permit the catcher to place the throwing arm behind the back with the knuckles resting on the buttocks. This position protects both the hand and the throwing arm. Huffman recommends that young catchers be taught the two-handed method and then, after achieving proficiency in this method, the one-handed method.[3]

Elston Howard recommends the following safety practices for catchers:[4]

---

[2]Ibid.

[3]Ibid.

[4]Elston Howard, *Catching* (New York: The Viking Press, 1966), pp. 4–9.

1. Place the forefinger of the glove hand outside the mitt or use sponge rubber inside to ease the impact of the ball. (The use of a golf glove inside the catcher's mitt for protection from the constant pounding of the ball has also helped to decrease injuries to the bones of the hand.)
2. Hold the rim of the glove with the bare hand or keep the bare hand folded and unclenched until the ball is in the mitt.
3. Keep in front of the ball. Shift the body with a quick shuffle or hop rather than move the glove. Never use a crossover step.
4. Assume a position far enough from the batter to rule out glove interference with the bat and to avoid being hit in the back of the head.
5. Get the mask off in a hurry to spot the ball on pop flies. The catcher should not throw the mask until the ball is spotted; then he should throw it away from the ball.
6. Teammates should give instructions concerning the proximity of barriers, obstructions, dugouts, and other hazards while a player is chasing a fly ball.

Pitchers

Pitchers suffer primarily from injuries to the pitching arm and the shoulder of the pitching arm. These injuries result from pitching styles that strain the arm and shoulder, from inadequate conditioning, and from throwing too hard for too long a time. Dugan makes the following recommendations for beginners who are trying to develop the smooth delivery that minimizes stress on the arm and shoulder:[5]

1. Keep the arm as straight as possible, with the back of the hand pointed downward on the fully extended backswing.
2. Do not permit the wrist to rotate until the arm is fully extended and as far to the rear as possible.
3. Finish the throw with the back of the hand facing forward on the follow-through.

Young pitchers who have not achieved full growth should be prohibited from throwing curve balls and should concentrate instead on development of form and control. Longer bones, such as those in the arm, grow at their ends from the epiphyseal plates. At the juncture of the ossified bone and the as yet unossified bone, and at the epiphyseal line where ligaments are attached, the joint is prone to injury until growth is complete.

Because the ligaments are stronger than the area around the epiphyseal line, certain movements may cause the epiphyseal plate to be partially separated. This can cause temporary or permanent damage to the bone: growth

---

[5]Ken Dugan, *How to Organize and Coach Winning Baseball* (New York: Parker Publishing Co., 1971).

may be slowed or accelerated; the growth plate may be moved out of position; and the end of the bone may become deformed. After the epiphyseal line disappears and ossification and bone growth are completed, throwing the curve ball may result in damage to the ligaments instead of the bone. This is not as serious as damage to the bone.

Batters

Batters face the hazard of being struck by a pitched ball. The batter should keep his eye on the ball and be completely relaxed from head to toe prior to delivery. On pitches that would strike a batter above the waist, he should drop to the ground. On pitches that would strike below the waist, he should jump up and forward or backward depending upon the direction of the ball. If being struck is inevitable, the batter should turn his back toward the pitcher to minimize damage.

Over-striding while batting decreases the batter's maneuverability and, consequently, his ability to avoid a pitch. When bunting, batters should keep the head and body outside the strike zone, and only the outer half of the bat should be inside the strike zone.

Base Runners

Base runners should run the base lines rather than make rounded loops. Most injuries to base runners occur while executing the slide. Players should be taught proper sliding procedures at the beginning of their training. Head-first sliding is hazardous, and any slide once initiated should be completed. Beginners should remove their shoes and practice sliding on dry grass or in sand while wearing hip pads and practice pants.

Equipment and Facilities

When planning the layout of a baseball field, consideration must be given to the field's orientation to the sun. Rays of the late afternoon sun should intersect the flight of the ball at approximately 90 degrees. Since major consideration must be given to the pitcher, batter, and catcher, the line from home plate to second base serves as the best reference axis. This axis should be at a right angle to the rays of the late afternoon sun.

All light poles should be outside the fenced-in playing area. Lights should be positioned high enough and be of sufficient brilliance to provide adequate light to all portions of the field. Fences behind first and third base should be high enough to stop wild throws. During batting practice, a baseball cage or backstop should be utilized. Only one batter at a time should be permitted in the cage.

Field maintenance is an important aspect of any safety program. Holes should be filled, and grass should be mowed regularly, with infield grass cut lower than outfield grass. Before each game, the infield should be thoroughly watered, and the pitching mound and home plate areas should be raked smooth.

Female softball catchers and male baseball catchers should be provided with, and required to wear, chest protectors that fit tightly and securely. Baseball pitchers should be required to wear a protective cap, both during practices and games. Provision should be made for a net to protect the pitcher from line drives hit during practice.

Indoor Batting Cages

Baseball teams at northern colleges must use batting cages if they are to be ready for the beginning of the season. However, the large number of injuries in the batting cage have caused baseball coaches to realize the necessity of measures to decrease injuries. The following procedures were suggested by Dick Young:[6]

1. Require both the pitcher and the batter to wear protective headgear, such as a football helmet.
2. Maintain adequate lighting (not less than sixty foot-candle power), with no dark spots.
3. Use only bright orange balls.
4. Permit use of the batting cage only when a staff member is present.
5. Protect the pitcher with a screen of wire mesh, four feet high and five feet wide.
6. Post rules of use outside the batting cage.

BASKETBALL

Basketball is one of the most popular sports in the United States, both from the standpoint of number of spectators and (at least among high school and college males) from the standpoint of number of participants. Like baseball, basketball is relatively safe, most of the injuries being contusions and abrasions from falls, ankle and knee sprains, and foot injuries. The most important procedures for decreasing the incidence of basketball injuries are:

1. An appropriate conditioning program.
2. Use of proper gear.
3. Provision of a safe physical plant with no unnecessary hazards.
4. Administrative procedures that consider the safety of players.
5. Teaching and coaching practices.

---

[6]Dick Young, "Safety in Your Indoor Batting Cage," *Athletic Journal*, February 1964, p. 36.

Basketball is a strenuous game that makes great demands for agility, quickness, and coordination. When players become fatigued, their agility, quickness, and coordination decrease. When fatigue sets in, players are more likely to fall and to collide with other players or objects. For this reason, players should develop a minimum endurance level sufficient to play a full game at peak efficiency.

A basketball conditioning program should include jogging, running, sprinting, and rope skipping. It should also include isotonic, isometric, and isokinetic exercises to increase muscular strength, particularly of the legs, arms, back, and shoulders. As muscles increase in size and strength, they offer greater protection to ligaments and to joints, since they provide the first line of defense against sprains and dislocations of joints by increasing stability of the joint. Further, muscles provide a resilient cushion for bones, decreasing the probability of bone bruises and fractures.

Guidelines for the Administrator

1. A minimum of twelve to sixteen feet of unobstructed space is required beyond the end lines and six feet beyond the sidelines.
2. No permanent bleachers, stairwells, fixed apparatus, or wall attachments should protrude within the above areas. If it is not feasible to eliminate such hazards, they should be covered with mats or pads.
3. Wall attachments should be recessed or padded.
4. Timer's and scorer's tables should be placed as far as possible from the playing area.
5. Baskets suspended from the ceiling or attached to walls are preferable to those supported by posts. When posts are already in place, they should be well padded.
6. Rollaway bleachers are preferable to permanent bleachers at floor level.
7. Racks should be provided for balls when not in use.
8. Floors must have a resilient, nonslip surface.
9. Arrangements should be made to have the floor mopped before every practice and game.
10. Floors in shower and athletic training rooms should provide good traction, even when wet.
11. Shower heads should be adequate in number to serve the largest possible number of users.
12. Shower handles and soap dispensers should be recessed.
13. Precautions should be taken to prevent the spread of fungal infections, bacterial infections, and contagious diseases.
    a. Shower and dressing areas should be mopped daily with a fungicide.
    b. Players should be provided with individual towels or with clean towels daily.
    c. Players should be permitted to use as much shower water as they wish.

  d. Players should not use a common drinking cup or glass. If there is no portable fountain, paper cups should be provided.
14. All players on interscholastic and intercollegiate teams should be covered by an accident insurance policy.
15. Only registered officials should be employed for varsity competition. Officials for intramural and recreational play should be required to attend a training course.
16. A team physician should be on call during practices and should be present during games.
17. Members of interscholastic and intercollegiate teams should receive a complete physical and dental examination prior to the season, halfway through the season, and upon completion of the season.
18. Players should not be permitted to resume practice after an illness or accident without a physician's permission.
19. If an athletic training room and a qualified athletic trainer are not available, the coach should be certified in first aid by the American Red Cross, and a complete first aid kit should be immediately available.
20. Each player's weight should be recorded before and after each practice session.
21. *All* team members should travel to games together on the same bus, plane, or train. There should be no exceptions.
22. Only qualified bus drivers or bonded carriers should be used.

Guidelines for the Coach

1. Shoes should be specifically designed for basketball, with nonslip tread, shock-absorbing properties under the heel and transverse arch, and adequate ventilation. All shoes should fit well.
2. Players should be required to wear two pairs of socks (thin socks under sweat socks).
3. Players should paint their feet with tincture of benzoin and then powder the feet.
4. Players should be provided with light hip pads and padded knee guards.
5. Players should be instructed to remove all jewelry before practices and games.
6. Safety or contact lenses should be used by players requiring glasses. Safety lenses should be firmly in place.
7. A warm-up drill of twenty to thirty minutes should be conducted before each game and practice session.
8. Early season workouts should progressively increase in intensity to a point where players are able to play a full game without a decline in efficiency. However, frequent rest periods should be provided since fatigue increases the probability of accidents and injuries.
9. Players with a history of recurrent ankle or knee injuries should have these joints wrapped before each practice session and game.

10. A coach or a qualified substitute should be present at all times during all practice sessions.
11. Players should be permitted to consume all the water they wish. Salt tablets should be provided to maintain saline balance.

BOWLING

There would be no injuries in bowling if a few simple rules were observed: thus the following checklist for the instructor. (Since few public schools or colleges have their own alleys, most using local commercial alleys, we will not provide a checklist for administrators.)

Guidelines for the Instructor

1. Inform students of the importance of selecting shoes (a) of the right size and (b) with a left shoe that has a smooth leather bottom (if the bowler is right-handed) to facilitate the slide on the last step of the approach. (The right shoe of left-handed bowlers should have the smooth leather bottom.) The opposite shoe should have a rubber bottom.
2. Beginners should use relatively light balls until the basics are learned.
3. The ball must fit properly. The finger and thumb holes should not be so loose that the ball may be released too early, or so tight that it may be lofted. Too much inward pitch of the holes, or holes located too close together, will also increase the probability of lofting the ball.
4. Students should change from street to bowling shoes prior to placing the ball in the rack. This will prevent tracking of dirt or moisture onto the lanes.
5. Students should inspect the approach for wet spots and dirt, and to test the approach before throwing the first ball.
6. Students should receive instruction (and demonstration) in the correct method for removing the ball from the rack. The ball should be turned so that the holes are on top. Then the hands should be placed on the sides of the ball, such that the fingers cannot be crushed between balls. Finally, the ball should be lifted out of the rack.
7. The bowler should not insert his fingers into the holes until he reaches the starting position.
8. When two bowlers are about to deliver the ball at the same time, the bowler on the right takes precedence.
9. After releasing the ball, a bowler should remain in his own lane.

BOXING

Boxing is unique: it is the only sport whose primary objective is to injure the opponent. Even in football, the primary objective is to get the ball over the goal line or through the uprights. In basketball, the goal is to put the ball through the hoop; in soccer and lacrosse, it is to put the ball through the goalposts; in track, speed skating, and swimming, it is to reach the finish line before the competition; in diving and gymnastics, it is to execute the most difficult skills with the best form. Only in boxing is the primary objective to inflict punishment upon one's opponent. A knockout is regarded as a superlative win.

A knockout is a concussion of the brain. With any concussion, there is tearing of blood vessels in the brain and consequent brain damage. Brain cells are replaced by unelastic scar tissue, which does not perform the same function as the healthy tissue it replaces. The damage resulting from concussions is cumulative and irreversible. With each succeeding concussion, there is additional damage, even if it is only hemorrhage. This is the reason that many professional boxers have the syndrome of slurred and thick-lipped speech, shuffling and stumbling gait, the appearance of confusion, and slow reactions.

Many years ago the American Alliance for Health, Physical Education, Recreation, and Dance condemned boxing. It was principally through this association's educational efforts that boxing was discontinued in school and college physical education programs, and in intramural, interscholastic, and intercollegiate athletic programs. It should also be discontinued in physical education programs of the military services, community recreation programs, and police athletic leagues.

FENCING

Historically, fencing was designed as a means for inflicting injury or death on an opponent. Today, the rules, equipment, regulations, and teaching techniques have almost brought the incidence of injuries to the point of negligibility, and in the last forty years there have been no fencing fatalities reported in the United States.

Foil, epee, and saber blades must flex in order to absorb impact. Further, the points must be blunted to conform to requirements. Fencers should put a slight bend in the blade to prevent injury to opponents and shattering of the blade. Participants should also apply a thin strip of adhesive tape to the tip of the blade so that if the tip breaks off it will be immediately apparent. (A large amount of tape on the tip of the blade will only succeed in making the weapon unwieldy.) The purpose of this piece of tape is *not* to prevent the blade from penetrating the mask or uniform. The prescribed diameter of the end is adequate to prevent this.

The wire of the mask must be rigid enough that (a) it will not bend inward upon impact and (b) it will not allow the blade to penetrate. Damaged, rusty, or weakened masks should be discarded.

The uniform should be of such weight and weave that it prevents penetration by a blunted blade. The more vulnerable body areas must have reinforced protection. During fencing with the epee, additional protective clothing must be worn under the uniform. Women, who compete only with the foil, must wear breast protectors of metal or other rigid material. All fencers are required to wear padded gloves on the fencing hand.

Since the rules do not specify the weight and penetration-resistance of fencing uniforms, masks, and gloves, nor the breaking point of weapons or the quality of steel in the blades, only quality equipment should be purchased. It is highly recommended that manufacturers of fencing equipment, in cooperation with fencing participants and coaches, quickly establish specific standards in order to avoid lawsuits.

Fencers should be required to wear all protective equipment during practice sessions as well as during competition. Officials should be knowledgeable and conscientious. They should immediately disqualify fencers for unsafe or unsportsmanlike conduct or for wearing unsafe or improper equipment.

New foil blades must be shaped before use. A slight downward bend of the first third (from the tip) is achieved by drawing the blade between the floor and the shoe while lifting the opposite end. This bend helps to absorb the impact upon touch, since the blade will bend further rather than transmitting the impact forward to the point and backward to the handle.

Students should not be permitted to fence unless a qualified supervisor is present. Wearing of protective undergarments is mandatory. Students should be instructed to relax the extensors of the elbow as the touch is made, and broken blades should be discarded. Because of the heat-retaining qualities of the uniform, heat stroke is a danger on days of high temperature and humidity, thus calling for frequent rest periods, less intense practice, and provision of adequate drinking water.

FIELD HOCKEY

Because field hockey requires striking a moving ball with a stick, often in close proximity to other players, some physical educators feel it is too dangerous to be included in a school program. But while injuries will never be totally eliminated, the incidence and severity of injuries can be reduced by use of proper equipment, development of proficiency in the fundamental skills, strict enforcement of rules, and proper maintenance of facilities.

Goal cages should not be constructed of wire mesh, since hard-driven balls are more likely to rebound and strike players near the goal. Additionally, when a player's momentum carries him into the cage, he is more likely to be injured when running into wire mesh than into netting.

Sticks with splinters should be sanded smooth and taped. Sticks with sharp edges should not be used. Players should wear shin guards. Shin guard straps, which buckle around the legs, should not be left hanging, since they may cause the player to trip.

Players should wear hockey sneakers with cleats for improved traction, thereby decreasing the probability of falling. (The rules prohibit the use of metal spikes, metal sticks, or protruding nails in boots or shoes.) Eyeglasses should have shatterproof lenses or be worn under a guard. Mouth protectors are advisable to protect teeth in the event of a collision or being struck by a ball. Goalkeepers should wear goalie pads, goalie boots, a glove on the left hand (of right-handed players), and a full face mask.

The field should be smooth, level, and free of stones or loose dirt. Sprains are more likely during play or practice on uneven ground. Loose dirt or stones may also cause the ball to rebound unpredictably, precipitating an injury. Sprinkler heads must have safe covers. Falls and injuries are more likely on a wet slippery field, so it is best to discontinue practice or games when the field becomes slippery.

Spectators may be injured if they are seated too close to the sidelines or too near the goal cages. Wings need room outside the sidelines for effective play and may collide with spectators seated too near the sideline. Further, officials may be hampered by spectators sitting near the sidelines. Balls rebounding from the goalposts may strike spectators seated near the goal.

Coaches should utilize a warm-up period for practice of skills and plays. Players should be thoroughly grounded in the fundamentals and should be taught to be constantly aware of the position of other players.

Coaches should ensure that players possess a high level of physical fitness, particularly cardiovascular endurance, since the probability of injury increases when players become fatigued. As in any sport, conditioning and training are the most important aspects in prevention of field hockey injuries. The conditioning program should include interval training, aerobic activities, and stretching exercises, as well as strength-building exercises such as progressive weight training, isometric exercises, and isokinetic exercises.

Competent and conscientious officials serve as a final line of defense against injuries. Prior to the game, officials should inspect the field, particularly for slippery areas in alleys and for depressions in front of the goal cages. Officials must enforce the rules strictly, especially those having to do with high-sticking, dangerous hitting and picking, undercutting the ball, hitting the opponent's stick, and hitting the ball without regard to another player's position. Rules should prohibit the wearing of pins, brooches, and similar items.

Facilities and Equipment

When games are played on artificial turf on hot days, the surface should be wetted down, since its temperature may be twenty to forty degrees higher than the air temperature. This will help decrease the likelihood of heatstroke. The water used for this purpose must be clean and free of bacteria, due to the danger of infected abrasions.

Lighting must be adequate for night games. Field lines should be easily visible, and the ball should be new or freshly painted. The fronts of goal cages should be painted white to enhance visibility. It is preferable that cages be constructed of wood rather than pipe, since wood gives on impact. If pipes are used, they should be padded.

The buckle-type shin guard should be used. This type has flaps that cover the ankles to protect them against bruises.

As with interscholastic and intercollegiate teams in any sport, field hockey players should be required to undergo a medical examination. During all games, a physician or qualified athletic trainer should be present. A telephone and well-stocked first aid kit should be on hand. The coach or athletic trainer should also have a complete and up-to-date list of all players' names, addresses, and home telephone numbers.

GOLF

A number of high schools and colleges offer instruction in golf, and many field interscholastic or intercollegiate teams. Relatively few schools or colleges manage their own golf courses and, consequently, must utilize a facility owned by another organization. However, they might be sued if the instructor or coach is held liable in the event of an injury.

The instructor or coach could be held liable if safety instructions have been incomplete, or if the students have been asked to do something of a hazardous nature. Although there is a low incidence of injuries in golf, accidents can be serious or fatal due to the high velocity of the ball and clubhead.

Guidelines for Coaches and Instructors

1. Practice shots should be limited to the area designated.
2. Players awaiting their turn on the practice tee and all others must stand to the hitter's right side, behind the ball, and a minimum of fifteen feet away.
3. On the first tee, players may take no more than three practice swings, and these may be taken only immediately before teeing off.
4. The ball should not be struck until the group ahead is out of range.
5. When another group plays through, the group ahead should seek a protected spot off the fairway, preferably with a tree between them and the tee, before the group playing through may hit.
6. The group playing through should be out of range before play is resumed.
7. No more than one person at a time should hit the ball.
8. Caution should be exercised when there is a possibility that the ball might rebound from a tree or boulder and strike a player.

9. Because shots from a sand trap are unpredictable, players should stand behind and to the left of the hitter if he is right-handed (behind and to the right of a left-handed player).
10. Foursomes should leave the green immediately upon completion of the hole and record scores on the next tee.
11. Balls should not be hit to the green until preceding players are on their way to the next tee.
12. A loud call of "fore" should be issued when the ball is moving toward a player or group of players. Players hearing "fore" should turn *away* from the direction of the call and lower their heads. Players should not turn in the direction of the call in an effort to see the oncoming ball. If a player hearing the call is near a tree or other obstruction, he should move to place himself behind it.
13. On hot, sunny days, players should wear a hat for protection from the direct rays of the sun.
14. In the event a lightning storm arises during play, play should be immediately stopped and players should secure protection in the nearest shelter, depression, deep valley, or dense group of trees. (Isolated trees attract lighting, as do steel-shafted clubs and umbrellas.) Clubs should be kept in the bag.
15. When workers are on the course, they should be warned before a ball is hit in their direction. The golfer should wait for an acknowledgement before hitting.
16. Caddies should never stand in the fairway to mark the point of aim on dogleg or blind holes.
17. Caution should be exercised when operating golf carts. Rental agencies must post regulations regarding their safe operation.

GYMNASTICS

A majority of athletic directors and physical education chairpersons have moved into their present positions from coaching major sports (football or basketball). Consequently, few have a genuine appreciation or reasonably thorough understanding of gymnastics. This, combined with anxiety over injuries and possible lawsuits, has resulted in such inadequate sponsorship of gymnastic clubs and teams in public schools that there are currently 6,000 privately operated gymnastic clubs in the United States. Thus, the private gymnastic schools are filling the vacuum created by the schools, which are failing to satisfy the interests and desires of children in this regard. The private clubs continue to grow in membership as well as numbers. Though membership fees are reasonable, they are prohibitive for most families with incomes below the median.

The incidence of injury in gymnastics is not as high as it is in many other sports. However, parents of children injured in gymnastics are much more prone to initiate lawsuits. This is because in contact sports such as football, ice hockey, basketball, and lacrosse, personal injury is regarded as an inherent characteristic of the sport and is accepted. This is not true with gymnastics.

The incidence of injuries in gymnastics could be reduced to an insignificant level if coaches and instructors were thoroughly knowledgeable and conscientious. Adherence to the following guidelines will considerably lower the incidence of injury.

Guidelines for Administrators

1. Employ only well-qualified people to teach or coach gymnastics. Experience as a competitor should be mandatory. A written or oral examination on spotting techniques and safety procedures would be advisable prior to employment. (Questions for such an examination could be taken from the *Gymnastics Safety Manual.*[7]) It would be preferable, however, that potential employees be certified by the United States Gymnastic Safety Association, just as lifeguards must be certified by the American Red Cross.
2. Purchase only high-quality equipment from reputable manufacturers. A quantity of mats sufficient to serve the needs of the largest possible class, when all equipment is in use, should be on hand.
3. Equip the gymnastics instructional area with adequate safety equipment such as safety belts, overhead belts, landing mats, and crash pads. Basic mats used in competition are $1-1\frac{1}{2}$ inches thick, landing mats are $3\frac{1}{2}-4\frac{1}{2}$ inches thick, and crash pads are $6-12$ inches thick. Crash pads and safety belts considerably reduce hazards when new skills are being learned. Mats should provide good traction, should be water-resistant, and should provide color contrasts in order that gymnasts can orient themselves as they approach the mats in somersaults or twists.
4. The various pieces of gymnasium equipment should be positioned in a manner that will minimize collisions between gymnasts.
5. The trampoline, rings, and horizontal bar should be used only under the supervision of a qualified instructor or a qualified student designated by the instructor. While this regulation tends to discourage participation, it is necessary due to the increasing incidence of lawsuits, and because inexperienced students are more likely to try stunts beyond their level of ability. The three mentioned pieces of equipment should be locked when not in authorized use.
6. Safety regulations should be posted in the gymnasium.
7. Some equipment is attached to the floor via floor plates during use.

---

[7]U.S. Gymnastic Safety Association, *Gymnastics Safety Manual* (The Association: 424 C Street, N.E., Capitol Hill, Washington, D.C. 20002).

These plates should be flush with the floor. They should be embedded in the underlying cement via long bolts, or the stress should be distributed over a large area (eight inches square) to the underside of the floor via a steel plate.

8. Administrators should encourage gymnastics teachers and coaches to attend gymnastic clinics.

Guidelines for Teachers and Coaches

1. Become certified by the United States Gymnastic Safety Association through attendance at one of their clinics. Information regarding clinics can be secured by writing to:

   Executive Director
   U.S. Gymnastics Safety Association
   424 C Street, N.E., Capitol Hill
   Washington, D.C. 20002

2. Learn the progressive order of difficulty or sequence of skills for all gymnastic events and insist that students master skills at each level before attempting stunts at the next level.

3. When teaching students a new skill, teach them spotting procedures for that skill.

4. Teach all students the correct use of the safety belt.

5. Teach all students the general principles of breakfalling, absorption of impact, and spotting. The following are five of the more important principles:

   a. Injury can often be prevented by distributing an impact over a greater surface area. This will result in an impact of fewer pounds per square inch.

   b. If possible, land on well-padded parts of the body (buttocks or thighs).

   c. Distribution of impact over a greater period of time will often prevent injury. This can be accomplished by moving into a forward, backward, or sideward roll, or by flexing the elbows, hips, knees, or ankles upon impact with the floor.

   d. When catching your weight on the hands during a backward fall, point the fingers forward so that the elbows can bend on impact.

   e. Tuck the chin in or turn the face sideward just prior to impact in a forward fall.

6. Insist that students be spotted at all times other than when executing stunts that have been thoroughly mastered.

7. Post safety regulations in the gymnasium and distribute mimeographed copies of these regulations to all students in gymnastic classes. Include questions on these regulations in written final examinations.

8. In the grading plan, include an item such as "Sportsmanship and Healthmanship" or "Ethical Behavior" (comprising ten to twenty percent of

the total grade). Include such items as willingness to spot and coach others, demonstration of determination tempered by good judgment, concern for safety, and willingness to accept instruction and coaching.

9. Make a thorough monthly check of all equipment, particularly swivel joints at the ceiling, overhead and traveling belts, and floor plates. Develop in students the habit of checking the security of width- and height-adjustments after each change in width or height.

10. Students using the trampoline should at all times have a minimum of four spotters — one at each end and one at each side. Spotters should be instructed to push the performer onto the bed (much like pushing a large beach ball) if it appears he will strike the frame or springs.

11. Spotters must at all times keep their eyes on the performer.

12. Trampolinists should learn all stunts with a low bounce before progressively increasing height as skill and assurance are gained.

13. Few inexperienced students have sufficient kinesthetic sense or ability to know positions of body parts or to have the coordination and agility to progress to forward and backward somersaults on the trampoline in the course of one semester. However, those who do should not be denied the opportunity to achieve at their maximum potential. Before students attempt somersaults, they should master all of the following skills:

> controlled straight bouncing
> jump and tuck
> jump and jackknife
> seat drop
> hands and knee drop
> back drop
> knee drop with half and full twist
> back drop with full twist
> cat twist
> kill spring
> jump and straddle toe touch
> jump and full pirouette
> knee drop
> front drop
> swivel hips
> back drop with half twist
> turntable
> cradle

Young gymnasts should master all of the preceding in various sequences:

> front over from the knees to the seat
> front over from the feet to the seat
> front over from the knees to the feet
> front over from the feet to the feet
> front somersault in the safety belt

      back somersault in the safety belt

      front somersault assisted (hand spotter)

      back somersault assisted (hand spotter)

Procedures for the execution of all of the above skills may be found in the *Handbook of Gymnastics in the Schools* by James A. Baley (Boston: Allyn and Bacon, Inc., 1974).

14. Obese or frail students should be discouraged from participation in gymnastics until they bring their body weight and strength to levels that will permit them to participate with reasonable safety.

15. Fatigue increases the probability of an accident during execution of gymnastic skills or exercises due to decreased coordination. Students should discontinue practice when fatigue begins to influence performance.

16. Warm-up and stretching exercises should precede practice sessions. Strength and endurance exercises should be conducted after practicing skills.

17. Loose-fitting clothing may snag on the equipment or be caught between the hands and the equipment. Consequently, girls should wear leotards and boys should wear snug trunks or gymnastic trousers. Students should not be permitted to practice in sweat suits, street clothes, or other loose-fitting clothing.

18. Skills should be learned with the equipment at low settings, when possible. For example, the rings could be at chin height, while the horizontal bar, uneven parallel bars, and parallel bars could be set at chest height. The balance beam should be at its lowest height.

19. Carbonate of magnesium (chalk) should be available and used at all times to prevent slipping.

20. Chalk buildup on equipment can cause tears of the skin on the palms of the hand. For this reason, the areas of chalk buildup should be sanded frequently.

ICE HOCKEY

People involved in ice hockey have done little to maintain records of the incidence of various types of, and causes of, injuries. This should be one of the first steps taken to decrease the incidence of injuries.

Ice hockey has, unfortunately, developed a reputation in recent years for being a brutal sport in which players frequently lose emotional control. Fights between players are frequent. Some players regard injuries and scars as badges of honor. Many disdain wearing helmets, despite evidence that several deaths could have been avoided by their use. Players complain of impaired vision, discomfort, and profuse perspiration as reasons for not wearing helmets. Nevertheless, helmets should be made compulsory at all levels of play, in practice as well as during games.

Promoters, managers, coaches, and players in professional ice hockey must try to change the image of the game. Instead of appealing to the baser instincts of people in order to sell tickets, they should emphasize the skill, speed, stamina, and teamwork required. If they do not do this, the incidence of lawsuits for vicious play will increase.

The practices recommended above must begin at the professional level because younger players, including college players, imitate the pros. The protective equipment of younger players is almost always inferior to that used by professionals, making the younger players more prone to injury. Teachers and coaches of ice hockey should, of course, teach sportsmanlike play. It is easier to teach aggressiveness and violence than to teach skillful play.

Facial cuts and loss of teeth frequently result from being struck with a stick or puck. Cuts from skates, incurred when falling to the ice, and bone bruises around the ankle and shin, resulting from contact with a flying puck, are common. Goalies, who must have little regard for the integrity of their own anatomy, suffer hand and facial injuries from stopping the puck. They also suffer groin injuries while doing splits to cover the goal.

The emotional behavior exhibited at games by coaches and players is exciting drama, but it also can elicit participation by the spectators, as they throw objects such as eggs, beer bottles, wood shavings, and coins onto the ice. This can cause injury when a player's skates are suddenly stopped while he is skating rapidly. Spectators should be educated regarding the hazards of such behavior, and police should closely supervise the crowd.

The Ontario Medical Association's Section on Sports Medicine studied injuries for fifteen- to twenty-one-year-old hockey players in Ontario in 1972–74.[8] A total of 542 injuries were reported and analyzed. Lacerations about the head and neck were most frequently reported, in spite of the requirement that players wear helmets. High-sticking, or striking the opponent's stick near his hands, was the principal cause of these lacerations. A large number of bone fractures of the hand indicated the need for gloves that offer greater protection.

The study concluded with the following recommendations:

1. Pad the grip-end of the stick.
2. More strict enforcement of high-sticking rules.
3. Use of shock-absorbing material behind the boards.
4. Increase the distance from the goal line to the end boards.
5. Combine a face and eye protector in the design of helmets.

Increased violence in junior and minor league hockey in Ontario, during 1973–74, resulted in the call for the investigation reported by William

---

[8]D.E. Hastings et al., "A Study of Hockey Injuries in Ontario," *Ontario Medical Review*, November 1974, pp. 686–92.

McMurtry.[9] The following were listed as the basic causes of violence:

1. The influence of professional hockey, especially the NHL, with its emphasis on winning, the use of violence to achieve victory, intimidation outside the rules, and the promotion of the sport by "selling" brawling.
2. The structure of the rules, which allows blatant interference, holding, tripping, slashing, and the like, thus laying the groundwork for fighting.
3. The lack of definition of objectives and purposes for amateur hockey, resulting in a wide variety of philosophies by coaches and parents alike, in turn contributing to the "win at any cost" mentality.
4. Poor training of referees, who do not enforce the rules, are inconsistent, and generally receive little respect from players, coaches, organizations, and fans.
5. The volunteer status of most coaches, who need more guidance and help through clinics. They fail to support the officials and lack control over their players.
6. A lack of respect, by the majority of players, for the rules and officials.
7. Parents and coaches as poor models of control, placing undue pressure to win on the players.

Guidelines for Players

John A. Conley offers the following suggestions to players to decrease the likelihood of injury:[10]

1. Keep your head up at all times. Learn to stickhandle and pass the puck without watching it.
2. Practice improving your peripheral vision so that you are aware of the total picture and where each player is situated.
3. Develop instinctive maneuvers in the corners and along the boards to prevent serious board checks.
4. When falling or being hit into the boards, protect your face and head with your arms and gloves.
5. Try to absorb the impact when hit by an opponent, unless the combination of your size and speed is much superior to his.
6. Spread out on the rink; do not overcrowd.
7. Do not lean on your stick. If you depend on your stick for balance, it is too easy to be upset.
8. Keep your stick below your waist and your elbows in. This will prevent injury to others and, ultimately, to yourself.
9. Keep moving on the ice. A stationary target is the easiest to hit.
10. Wear properly fitting protective equipment at all times. The one time you forget may be the time you are injured.

---

[9]William R. McMurtry, "Investigation and Inquiry into Violence in Amateur Hockey," *A Report to the Ministry of Community Social Services* (Ottawa, Ontario, Canada, 1974). Permission to reprint is granted by the Queen's Printer for Ontario and by the Ontario Ministry of Tourism and Recreation.

[10]John A. Conley, "Ice Hockey," in *Safety in Team Sports, Monograph #3*, Sports Safety Series, Joseph Borzzne, Chauncy A. Morehouse, and Stanley Pechar, eds., American School and Community Safety Association, American Alliance for Health, Physical Education, Recreation, and Dance (Washington, D.C.: The Alliance, 1977), pp. 43–44.

Guidelines for Administrators

1. Goal cages should give when hit forcefully. This will increase the time of absorption of impact and thereby decrease the probability of injury. Goalposts should not project too far downward. For younger players, they should not be attached to the ground at all.
2. Purchase all advisable personal safety equipment, including stockings, shin pads, pants, elbow and shoulder pads, sweaters, gloves, helmets, mouth protectors, and athletic supporters with metal cups.
3. Establish a procedure to ensure that all players are equipped with properly fitting equipment.
4. Purchase high-quality equipment for the goalie, including arm, shoulder, and leg pads, a wire mask, chest protector, helmet, and extra padding for the thigh and hip areas.
5. Do not allow face-molded masks, which do not provide adequate protection against a sharp-edged, hard rubber puck that reaches speeds of up to 110 mph. Norman and his colleagues investigated the impact qualities of several commercially available masks.[11] Their study showed that more than seventy-five percent of the total load transmitted through a mask from a direct blow to a contact point arrives on the contact point: that is, the mask does not disperse the load very effectively. It was found that the wire mask achieved the objectives of both force dispersion and reduction, while at the same time prohibiting loads from reaching the vulnerable forehead and cheeks.
6. Employ two well-qualified officials for every game. Officials should be fast on the whistle, particularly on the boards and around the goal, and should strictly enforce all safety rules.

Guidelines for Coaches and Instructors

1. Insist that players maintain a high level of physical fitness. Weight training and isometric exercise programs are particularly recommended.
2. Precede all scrimmages and games with fifteen to twenty minutes of warm-up exercises. Exercises should be selected that strengthen the hip extensors, hip abductors, plantar flexors of the feet, elbow extensors, wrist flexors, and muscles of the shoulder girdle. Efforts should be made to increase the range of motion in the foot, ankle, hip, and shoulder. Cardiovascular/respiratory endurance should be increased.
3. Teach players to protect their faces and heads with arms and gloves when down on the ice or against the boards.
4. Discourage players from high-sticking, slashing, cross-checking, and carrying sticks above waist level.

---

[11]R.W. Norman, Y. Sze Thompson, and D. Hayes, "Relative Impact: Attenuating Properties of Masks of Ice Hockey Goaltenders," *Biomechanics IV* (Baltimore: University Park Press, 1974), pp. 264–69.

5. Remind players that the slap shot is illegal. (In the slap shot, the puck is struck with great force and travels exceedingly fast.)
6. Discourage players from leaning on sticks since, when they do, they are more easily knocked off balance.
7. Teach and encourage fair play, obedience to the rules, and good sportsmanship.

SOCCER

There is a saying that the sun never sets on soccer. This is probably true since soccer is the world's most popular game and is played in all parts of the world. It is a game that requires great stamina and in which no protective equipment is used, although there is considerable body contact. Consequently, numerous injuries occur.

Guidelines for Administrators

1. In order to decrease the probability of collisions between members of opposing teams, purchase two sets of uniforms to provide color contrast. It is especially important that the jersey and stockings of players on opposite teams be of contrasting colors.
2. Although many players dislike wearing shin guards due to a supposed decrease in maneuverability, players should be urged to wear them. Lightweight shin guards are available.
3. Protective equipment for goalkeepers should be purchased, including elbow pads, knee pads, hip pads, and shorts with built-in padding. Baseball sliding pads also provide protection for the upper legs and hips.
4. Make certain there are no hooks or protrusions on the front of the goalposts or the crossbar.
5. Check the playing field periodically for holes, rocks, glass, or other hazards.

Guidelines for Coaches and Instructors

1. During practice or play on muddy fields, some players prefer to wear football cleats. The rules forbid this. Referees should check players' shoes before each game.
2. Coaches should require taping of players with injured or weak ankles and knees. Knee braces with metal hinges are available, although these do not provide as much protection as tape. Elastic sleeves for the knees and ankles provide little or no protection.
3. Goalkeepers should wear sweat suits during practice to eliminate abrasions and cuts that may be suffered during dives to save the ball.

4. When teaching beginning goalkeepers to dive, jumping pits or mats should be utilized.
5. Check the playing field for holes, glass, depressions, or other hazards before every practice and game. Holes and gulleys should be filled and leveled before play.
6. If the crossbar is attached to the uprights by means of bolts, the bolts should be checked to ensure that they are tight.
7. Practice or play should be postponed when the field is icy.
8. Everything being equal, the higher the level of physical fitness, the lower the probability of injury. The incidence of sprains of the ankles and knees is great among soccer players. Increased strength in the muscles whose tendons pass over these joints (quadriceps femoris, hamstrings, sartorius, gastrocnemius, tibialis anterior, peroneus brevis and longus, extensor digitorum longus, soleus and peroneus tartius) will decrease the probability of such sprains. Increased range of motion or flexibility will also decrease the probability of sprains. Consequently, soccer players should do stretching exercises and progressive resistance exercises such as leg curls, half knee-bends, toe rises, and leg presses.
9. Injuries are more likely to occur when a player is fatigued. Soccer is strenuous; therefore, soccer players need to develop a high level of cardio-respiratory endurance through endurance-type activities.
10. All scrimmages and games should be preceded by a warm-up.

SKIING

Increasing numbers of high schools are sponsoring ski clubs. College and university physical education departments are increasingly offering courses in skiing, usually during Christmas or intersession vacations. Departments of physical education are to be complimented for this effort to add to the number of lifetime sports being taught, and for keeping up with changes in people's recreational interests. However, they are also increasing their liability risk for several reasons.

The incidence of lawsuits against operators of ski resorts has increased. It is probable that schools and colleges that sponsor ski classes and clubs will also experience an increase in the number of suits brought against them. But these suits will not be successful if negligence cannot be proven.

Many school and college skiers are beginners. A study by Haddon, Ellison, and Carrol showed that, although beginners constituted only 21 percent of the group studied, they accounted for 55 percent of the injuries.[12] Females also incurred a disproportionate share of the injuries: females made up 35 percent of the group and accounted for 57 percent of injuries.

----

[12]W. Haddon et al., *Skiing Injuries* (Washington, D.C.: U.S. Department of Health, Education, and Welfare, Public Health Service, Division of Accident Prevention, 1976).

The number of suits against operators of ski resorts has increased to such an extent that the cost of liability insurance has become prohibitive for some. Surprisingly, however, the sport of skiing has an admirable safety record. Although it is a vigorous athletic activity practiced principally by nonathletes, most reports place the rate of reported accidents at between three and six injuries per thousand skiing man-days. This yields an accident rate of .3–.6 percent, which compares very favorably with the 20–30 percent seasonal rate reported in some high school and college contact sports.[13]

Except in skiing school classes, the skier is subject to few restraints regarding reckless skiing, lack of courtesy, difficulty of slopes he attempts, or crossing in front of other skiers. The following rules of the road should be taught and posted.

Selection of a Skiing Site

When a class instructor or advisor to a ski club is selecting a ski resort, consideration should be given to the following:

1. Are beginners shown how to board, and helped to get aboard, the lifts, at least for the first few times?
2. Are instructions posted for getting on and off the lifts?
3. Does the ski area offer either full-time, paid patrolmen or a voluntary ski patrol affiliated with the National Ski Patrol System? Is the ski patrol of adequate size? Are the members adequately trained?
4. Are uniform trail markings utilized to indicate the difficulty of trails?
5. Are the hills properly groomed?
6. Are first aid facilities adequate?
7. Is an ambulance available?
8. Is there a resident physician or is one readily available?
9. Are maps or map signs available to inform skiers of the several slopes and their level of difficulty?
10. Are facilities provided for locking ski equipment when not in use?
11. Does the ski area have a ski school directed by a certified instructor?
12. Is the number of instructors at the ski school sufficient to accommodate the group?
13. Do ski school classes have exclusive use of a designated slope?
14. What is the distance of the ski area and the condition of area roads?

Answers to some of the above questions for various ski areas can be secured from the National Ski Safety Research Group (126 Cresta Road, Colorado Springs, Colorado 80906).

---

[13]James G. Garrick and William C. Sears, "Skiing," in *Sports Safety*, Charles P. Yost, ed. (Washington, D.C.: American Alliance for Health, Physical Education, Recreation, and Dance, 1977).

Topics for Discussion Prior to Ski Trips

At least one week prior to a skiing trip, the group should meet for instruction and preparation. Lead-time is necessary to give students time to purchase and repair equipment, to have bindings adjusted, and to commence learning and practicing warm-up exercises. The following represents topics to be discussed and information to be presented during these sessions.

1. Do not ski in areas marked "closed."
2. Never ski alone; use the buddy system.
3. In the event a buddy is injured, place the skis upright in the snow so that they form an X slightly uphill from the injured skier.
4. Notify the ski patrol in the event of injury.
5. Do not attempt to move the injured person and do not remove ski boots. Ski boots provide excellent splints for ankles and fixation points for application of leg splints. Boots will also restrict swelling. The low temperatures on ski slopes serve to limit the amount of swelling and decrease pain. But because of reduction of pain, skiers are prone to underestimate injuries and to increase the severity of traumas by continuing activity.
6. Be familiar with the uniform trail marking system, including the meaning of the various shapes and colors of markings.
7. Observe skiing etiquette:
   a. Stops should be made only on the side of trails or slopes, never in the center of a trail.
   b. Use some kind of tether to prevent runaway skis.
   c. Look uphill before skiing onto a trail.
   d. Leave ample room when passing other skiers.
   e. Call "on your left" or "on your right" before passing another skier.
   f. Fill in holes caused by falls.
   g. Do not litter.
   h. Wait your turn for lifts.
8. Do not attempt speeds, turns, jumps, or trails beyond your present level of ability.
9. Novice skiers should not use the straps on ski poles while skiing. If a pole attached to the wrist is caught in deep snow or on a tree limb, the shoulder may become dislocated or the wrist injured.
10. Have ski bindings checked at a reputable shop. The bindings must be both installed and adjusted properly. They must be adjusted such that they release with application of equal force from the medial or lateral side. If different forces are required to effect release, the binding is not functioning properly.
11. Bindings should be adjusted such that the force required for release is not excessive. (A standard test is to have the skier stand in his boots, which are attached to the skis. The skis are then immobilized, and the

skier attempts to twist the boots from the bindings in both directions. If the force required is so great that pain is felt in the ankle, leg, or knee, the bindings should be adjusted to release with less force.)

12. The heels should release when leaning forward in the bindings at a point before discomfort is felt in the Achilles tendon.
13. One ski should always serve as the right ski, the other as the left.
14. Purchase locks for skis and poles.
15. Beginning classes should receive a demonstration and brief explanation of the fundamental maneuvers that will be taught on the slopes. The discussion should also include an explanation of the progressive order of skills to be learned.
16. Students should be questioned about any medical problems or injuries. Permission to participate should be secured from parents and personal physicians for those with medical problems or injuries.
17. The class should receive instruction in the care of boots, skis, and bindings. Ski edges should be sharp, and bindings should be lubricated with silicone lubricant. Mounting screws should be tightened.

Travel to the Ski Resort

Accidents on the way to a ski slope are more likely than in the case of other travel, due to weather conditions and because many ski slopes are in remote areas with icy, narrow, hilly, or mountainous roads. For this reason, the following recommendations are made with regard to such transportation.

1. Only licensed drivers sufficiently competent to drive safely on ice and snow should be used.
2. Adequate travel time should be allotted to allow for hazardous conditions and heavy traffic.
3. Ski equipment should not be carried in the passenger section of the vehicle.
4. Drivers should have sunglasses in the event of glare.
5. The driver should not wear ski boots.
6. Blankets, chains, sand, flares, a window scraper, and a first aid kit should be taken along for possible emergencies.

Upon arrival at the ski area, the instructor, who should be a skier and who must have the authority to discipline students, should check to ensure that all skiers have sunglasses and are dressed appropriately for the temperature. He should also check binding installations and adjustments and should ensure that all students have equipment to prevent runaway skis.

The instructor should point out to the students the location of emergency telephones, first aid room, rest rooms, warming facilities, closed areas, and a meeting site at which to gather at the end of skiing. The instructor should assign buddies and indicate the time of meeting, where he can be reached, and how to notify the ski patrol if help is needed. He should explain the levels of skill required to ski the various slopes.

The Rocky Mountains are a popular area for school and college ski clubs and classes. When groups come from low-altitude areas, however, it is necessary that they become acclimatized to the oxygen-poor atmosphere common to the high altitudes. Mathews and Fox point out that there is a reduction in endurance capacity, as measured by maximum oxygen consumption, of 3–3½ percent for every 1,000 feet ascended above 5,000 feet.[14] Endurance will improve with each day's stay at altitude but will never quite reach the level of endurance at sea level. Acclimatization takes 7–10 days at 9,000 feet, 15–21 days at 12,000 feet, and 21–25 days at 15,000 feet. The person in charge of groups traveling from low altitudes must consider these decrements in endurance and inform the group of this phenomenon and its effects.

The "wet look" fabrics seen increasingly on the ski slopes have increased the risk of injury. Skiers wearing this type of clothing, when falling on hard-packed or icy slopes, will accelerate during their slide to speeds sufficient to cause serious injury. Skiers wearing such clothing should be prohibited from using the steeper slopes.

Sample Legal Cases

It is estimated that some ten million people participate in snow skiing. This sport, like all others, is growing, and there are ski areas from New England to California.

Skiing is known to be a dangerous activity, and the number of accidents is increasing annually. There are more accidents in skiing than in football due to the greater number of skiers. Skiers seem to delight in taking unnecessary chances, and they are frequently not properly trained to participate in the sport.

Ski area operators have knowledge of these facts and, therefore, have a duty to take safety measures to prevent accidents. Assumption of risk is a common defense in many ski accident cases. That is, skiers are held to accept the dangers that are inherent in the sport and that are obvious to any participant. No one but the skier himself determines his ability to participate.

Skiers are business invitees who, as previously pointed out, are owed the highest degree of care known to the law, since they pay a fee for use of the premises. Some states have passed specific statutes regarding the protection of persons using ski areas and lifts. (Statutes relevant to a particular locality may be checked with trade associations.)

When a fee is paid, there is an implied warranty that the premises are reasonably fit for the use for which they are rented. Downhill skiers have

---

[14]Donald K. Mathews and Edward L. Fox, *The Physiological Basis of Physical Education and Athletics,* 2nd ed. (Philadelphia: W.B. Saunders Company, 1976), p. 350.

won lawsuits based on defects in, or improper adjustment of, rented equipment. They have recovered for breach of contract due to a failure to provide a safe place, safe equipment, or safe premises.

In a Colorado case, Roser, a skier, signed a stipulation relieving LTV Recreational Department, Inc. of all liability as part of the season pass he purchased. (*Rosen* v. *LTV Recreational Department, Inc.*, 569 F.2d 1117 [10th Cir. 1978].) Rosen was catapulted into a steel post, set in concrete and located in an open area, after colliding with another skier who had made a sudden, unexpected turn on a relatively flat area.

The court found that the stipulation Rosen had signed was really one-sided, a contract of adhesion offered to him on a take-it-or-leave-it basis. The court strictly construed the language such that the ski area operator would be exempt from liability for the negligence of other skiers, but he would not be exonerated for his own negligence.

The court found Rosen's injuries to be the result of "an independent hazard capable of producing liability regardless of a collision between skiers."

Since Rosen was only thirty-five years old and the father of two children, his award ($200,000) was upheld. He was in a full leg cast for eleven months, and a permanent arthritic condition that developed would continue to restrict his employability.

Liability has also been found on the part of the defendant for breach of a duty to provide competent and timely medical care. Violation of the duty to warn of existing hazards, as well as failure to prevent collisions that were reasonably foreseeable, have also resulted in liability.

In a New York case (*Jung* v. *State*, 186 N.E. 2d 569), a non-skier was held to assume the risk when she entered the ski area. The plaintiff was in a state-owned ski area but was not skiing. She fell in the area between the bottom of the ski slopes and the ski lodge, where she was staying with her family. The court pointed out that the place where she fell could not reasonably be kept free from snow or ice because of the nature of the sport. The court said the injured plaintiff assumed the responsibility when she ventured into an area that was obviously slippery.

In a related case, a novice skier, Mrs. Bagnoli, decided to go skiing with her teenage daughter. As forty-nine-year-old Mrs. Bagnoli waited for her instructor to return to the bottom of the hill, she adjusted her own skis. When the instructor arrived, he said to her, "Take this one" (indicating a chair on the lift), while she was still adjusting her poles. They slid into place at the chair lift, but Mrs. Bagnoli was knocked down when the chair lift hit her in the back. She received a spinal fracture.

As plaintiff, Mrs. Bagnoli alleged that the ski school and the operators of the facility were negligent in carelessly instructing her in the safe mounting of the ski lift. The court found for Summit, the defendant operator of the ski lift, saying that it was not responsible for the same degree of care as a common carrier, but rather was responsible for exercising a degree of care commensurate with the circumstances in the practical operation of a ski lift. The court found that the contract between the ski school and the state (which contract Mrs. Bagnoli wanted to admit into evidence in an effort to show the degree of care necessary on the part of Summit) was not admissible. It was found to be too vague to have any application.

One of the leading cases in this area, decided in 1961, arose from an incident at Mount Mansfield, Vermont. The case was *Wright* v. *Mount Mansfield Lift Incorporated* (Fed. Supp. 786). In this case, a moderately experienced skier, while skiing down a slope, struck a stump that was covered with snow and broke a leg. Plaintiff sued the ski lift company and hotel.

The court held that the duty of the owners of the premises was to warn the injured plaintiff, as an invitee on their premises, of any danger that reasonable prudence would have foreseen and that should have been corrected. The court found that that duty was fulfilled and found for the defendant.

A New York court, in the case of *Merenoff* v. *State* (131 N.Y. St. 2nd 491), denied liability where the plaintiff was struck by a ski that came off the foot of a participant in a ski jumping contest. The court said that such an injury could not reasonably have been foreseen and, therefore, the state had no duty to spectators to erect a net or fence to protect them.

Some courts have held that a chair lift is a common carrier and that a person riding on same for a fee is owed the highest degree of care. This is not true of a rope tow, however, where the duty is only to use ordinary care to protect the user. In a California skiing accident, a skier skied into the plaintiff, who was using the rope tow, and injured the plaintiff severely. The court ruled that the rope tow was not a common carrier and that the duty to the plaintiff was no greater than the duty owed her when she was skiing down the hill. Judgment was for the defendant. (*McDaniel* v. *Dowell*, 210 Cal. App. 2d 26.)

Courts often hold that there is an assumption of known risk. But courts are reluctant to deny an injured plaintiff recovery on a theory of assumption of risk when the injury was due to a latent or hidden defect not known to the plaintiff. Such a case was *Araphoe Basin, Inc.* v. *Fisher* (28 Colo. App. 580). A skier received a broken arm when the sleeve of her jacket caught on a stump that was protruding from a hanger bar on a ski lift.

In *Sunday* v. *Stratton Corporation* (390 Atl. 2d 398), plaintiff recovered $1.5 million for a ski injury. The Vermont Supreme Court ruled that poor trail conditions are not an obvious and necessary incident of skiing. The Stratton Corporation was held negligent for failing to give notice of hidden dangers. This was a substantial modification of the old assumption-of-risk doctrine. The court recognized that modern ski trails should be cleared, almost like a fairway on a golf course.

In this particular case, plaintiff was totally paralyzed from the neck down. The court held that it was negligence to allow tree stumps on the trail that could become covered with snow and hidden from the downhill skier.

The trend of the courts is to recognize that today's skier pays a high price and can expect the premises to be reasonably safe for the purpose for which the fee was paid.

TACKLE FOOTBALL

Injuries in football have long been an accepted element of the game. Many boys and young men have been proud to wear the "badge" of a football injury. Parents and the general public have also accepted these injuries. Coaches and teammates, when they wish to compliment a player, may refer to him as an "animal." And some players feel they have to hurt the opposition before they are hurt by them. Psychologists and psychiatrists have stated that extremely high levels of hostility — in fact, the ability to perceive one's opponent as a deady enemy — are crucial for success in body contact sports.

With the growth of the concept of accountability of manufacturers, physicians, and teachers, the incidence of lawsuits against football coaches has increased. Courts recognize that football coaches have certain duties to players, both before and during a game. When these duties are breached, the coach may be held legally responsible. Peter L. Obremskey,[15] attorney with the firm of Parr, Rickey, Obremskey, and Morton in Lebanon, Indiana, cites the following two cases to illustrate this point. These cases illustrate that courts will readily recognize a breach of duty (to players) as the basis for liability.

In *Mogabgab* v. *Orleans Parish School Board* (329 S. 2d 456 [1970]), the coaches were found liable for $40,000 in damages in a wrongful death action. The facts show that the deceased, a sixteen-year-old high school player, became weak and fainted during football practice on a hot afternoon. When he was taken into the school building, he was obviously weak and ill by virtue of the fact that he vomited. He was showered and laid on a blanket on the floor. The coaches denied repeated requests by a teammate's parents to call a doctor. This denial of medical treatment for, ultimately, two hours was the critical factor on which the coaches' liability was predicated. The player was suffering from heatstroke or heat exhaustion, which condition requires prompt medical treatment. The court ruled as follows:

> The best synthesis of the medical evidence is that heat damage works its wreckage upon the body in a continuum, causing progressive internal changes in the human system much as it causes progressive organic changes in a boiling egg. At some indefinite point in this continuum, the process of heat damage becomes irreversible, and past that point little can be done. All of this means that if appropriate medical assistance is available early, the

[15]Peter L. Obremskey, "Instructor's Duty Includes Supervision of Athletes," *The First Aider* (Gardner, Kansas: Cramer Products, Inc.), vol. 46, no. 6 (February 1977).

chances of survival are good. If it is long delayed, there is little hope. Once symptoms appear, each minute that passes without medical attention measurably reduces chances of survival.

In the Mogabgab case, treatment was delayed only two hours. However, as the player died the following day, the coaches' negligent failure to provide timely medical treatment rendered them liable for the death.

In the case of *Welch* v. *Dunsmuir Joint Union High School District* (327 P. 2d [1958]), the plaintiff, a high school football quarterback, was awarded $200,000 in damages for a coach's negligent conduct, based upon a breach of the coach's duty to render proper medical aid. The quarterback ran a quarterback sneak and was tackled. After the play, he was unable to get to his feet. The coaches suspected a neck injury and asked the player to move his fingers, which he was able to do. He was then carried to the sideline by eight players. When he was asked again to move his fingers, he was unable to do so, and from that point on he has been a quadriplegic.

In finding the coach negligent for moving the player, the court relied on undisputed medical testimony, maintaining that the extent of the injury was aggravated by moving the player from the field.

An Associated Press article in the *Home News* (New Brunswick, N.J.), of November 28, 1976, entitled "NCAA Lawsuits Are a Social Trend," points out that the NCAA spends an average of one thousand dollars a day on litigation, and that many see this as a social trend. In 1972, the NCAA spent $129,000 in legal fees; in 1973, $191,000; in 1974, $418,000. Although these legal fees were paid to enforce NCAA rules and decisions rather than for injuries, the figures present evidence of a general trend toward legal resolution of differences of opinion in the athletics area. It is highly probable that this trend will extend to an increase in the number of suits brought by parents and players against coaches for injuries suffered in football.

There are over 15,000 public and private secondary schools that sponsor organized football teams in the United States, and 1,200,000 young men participate. At the college and university level, another 100,000 participate. It has been estimated that 200,000 boys play on teams sponsored by various community and social agencies. In addition, many thousands play on sandlot or semi-organized teams. The grand total is probably two million players.

Leonard Larson states:[16] "There is no team sport anywhere in the world in which injury occurs more frequently than in American football." Klafs and Arnheim state that a high school football player, participating in a full season of practice and games, has a twenty percent chance of being injured during the season and an eight percent chance of incurring a serious injury.[17] The American Football Association, in its annual report for 1971,

---

[16]Leonard Larson, ed., *Encyclopedia of Sports Medicine* (New York: The Macmillan Co., 1971), p. 53.

[17]Carl E. Klafs and Daniel D. Arnheim, *Modern Principles of Athletic Training* (St. Louis: The C.V. Mosby Co., 1973), p. 5.

states that in that year there were a total of thirty-two deaths in football. Twenty of these were classed as "direct," while twelve were associated with "indirect" causes such as heatstroke, heart failure, or other systemic or secondary complications.

Knee Injuries

Over seventy-five percent of all athletic knee injuries occur in football. Every year about 140,000 high school football players suffer a knee or ankle injury. Approximately 50,000 of these result in knee operations.

The knee is particularly vulnerable to injury in football, due to the construction of the knee joint and due to the conditions under which football is played. The knee joint is extremely unstable laterally and is almost totally dependent upon the ligaments and muscles for its stability and integrity.

Unlike the hip and shoulder joints, the knee joint is very shallow, with the condyles of the femur resting on a very shallow depression on the upper end of the tibia. The large and strong ligaments of the knee joint (including the medial and lateral collateral ligaments, the anterior and posterior cruciate ligaments, ligament of Weisburg, and the patellar ligament) hold the femur, tibia, and fibula together.

But a major portion of support is also provided by the muscles whose tendons pass over the knee joint. These are the muscles which flex and extend the knee joint, such as the quadriceps femoris, iliotibial band, gastrocnemius, sartorius, semimembranosos, adductor magnus, semitendinosus, biceps femoris, and gracilis. For this reason, progressive resistance exercises (such as leg curls, half knee-bends, toe rises, knee extensor against resistance while sitting on a table, and leg abducting and adducting exercises against resistance) are highly recommended for all football players. Streching exercises to increase the range of motion of the hip joint also decrease the probability of knee injuries.

There is no doubt that lateral stress upon the knee joint is the major factor in knee injuries. Lateral stress originates primarily from opposing players during blocks or tackles, most often in a direction opposite to the direction of momentum of the injured player. For example, a player may cut to the right and be hit from the same side. His body has momentum to the right, his ankle is stabilized in the ground via his cleats, and the opposing player imposes a tremendous force inward against the right knee. Something has to give, and it is usually the ligaments of the knee, since the foot cannot slide across the turf.

The use of tennis shoes, removal of cleats, or installation of a swiveling type shoe would decrease the incidence of knee sprains. However, such gear would decrease traction, and players would fall more frequently and be unable to accelerate as quickly. Nevertheless, this would be true for players on both teams, and neither team would have an advantage.

A shoe manufactured by Wolverine World Wide, Inc. enables players to turn their legs upon impact, such that the knee flexes to facilitate absorption of impact. This shoe is equipped with a four-cleat torsion joint in the sole that can revolve 360 degrees. This feature enables the player to turn his foot, such that his knee will point in the same direction as the impact. The knee can then bend to absorb some of the impact.

Head and Neck Injuries

Roger I. Robinson studied head and neck injuries among players in the Eastern Collegiate Athletic Conference in 1972 and again in 1974.[18] Of the 117 ECAC colleges polled in 1972, eighty responded with usable data. Sixty-one reported injuries, and nineteen reported no injuries. The sixty-one colleges reported a total of 175 head injuries and 146 neck injuries. (Nine players suffered both head and neck injuries.) This gives an average of five or six head or neck injuries per reporting college. Robinson believes that a more accurate average would be seven or eight per college, in view of the fact that thirty-three colleges did not respond.

In his 1974 study, Robinson sent questionnaires to 110 ECAC schools, of which seventy-two responded. Fifty-one colleges reported a total of 190 head and 188 neck injuries. Based on these studies, Robinson makes the following recommendations:

1. Although football helmets are not designed for use as weapons, they give players a false sense of security.
2. Even though players are taught to place the face mask into the opponent's number, this is often impossible because of body position and because the player often lowers his head just before impact.
3. Field practice equipment should not be used to encourage use of the head.
4. Removal of the face mask would limit the amount of hitting with the helmet.
5. Coaches should instruct their players to slide the head when speed is involved.
6. Players should not be permitted to play for at least two weeks after a concussion and for at least an additional week if the brachial plexus stretch syndrome is evident. This time is needed for healing to occur. In the case of a concussion, blood that has leaked from ruptured blood vessels into the cerebral cavity must be reabsorbed.
7. The four-point chin strap should be used because it distributes impact over a greater area.
8. The use of neck rolls is questionable due to the possible lever effect with the neck roll acting as a fulcrum.

---

[18]Roger I. Robinson, "NCAA Football Head and Neck Injuries in Eastern Colleges, 1972 and 1974 Seasons," *Journal of Physical Education, Recreation, and Dance* June 1974, pp. 45–46.

Injuries to the brain and the cervical vertebrae are the most serious injuries because of the high probability of permanent brain damage in the case of concussion and of paralysis in the case of fractures of the cervical vertebrae.

Synthetic Turf

Athletic program administrators find artificial turf attractive because of its low maintenance requirements, its ease on cleaning bills (no muddy uniforms), and its versatility. It can be used eighteen hours a day with no preparation time lost between events. It has enhanced the lives of grounds crews, since it eliminates the need for mowing, watering, weeding, and fertilizing. Spectators enjoy its beauty. But almost all players dislike synthetic turf because of the greater incidence of injuries such as abrasions, sprained ankles, contusions, and concussions.

A study by Bramwell and Garrick showed an injury rate one-third higher on synthetic turf under wet conditions, and a rate double that of natural turf under dry conditions.[19] Synthetic turf is usually laid on an asphalt base, which does not have the resiliency of earth. This increases the probability of concussions. Artificial turf must have a thick padding, which raises its cost considerably.

Abrasions are more frequent and more severe on synthetic turf, and they are more likely to become infected. Proponents of artificial turf contend that the solution to this problem is simply to sprinkle the field before play and to require players to wear long sleeves, stockings, and adequate knee and elbow pads.

Increased traction on artificial turf increases the incidence of injuries to the ankles and knees. Again, artificial turf manufacturers have a solution to this problem. They advise the use of soccer shoes, shoes with rippled soles, or shoes with very short and flexible cleats.

It would seem that the best advice to give athletic directors regarding installation of synthetic turf is to hold off on installation unless all of the adjustments can be made. These would include extra padding under the turf, the wearing of appropriate shoes, willingness of players to wear extra clothing to prevent abrasions, extra padding on helmets, and pregame sprinkling of the playing area.

Guidelines for Administrators

1. Every player should be examined by a physician at the beginning of each season. The results of these medical examinations should be kept on file at the school.

---

[19]S.T. Bramwell and J.G. Garrick, "High School Football Injuries: A Comparison of Playing Surfaces," *Medical Science in Sports*, 3:5 (1971).

2. A medical history of each player should be completed and kept on file.
3. A history of several concussions should prohibit participation in football.
4. Players who have incurred an injury should be required to secure written approval of a physician and of their parents before being permitted to return to practice.
5. A physician should be immediately available during games and practice sessions.
6. Every school should have a qualified athletic trainer on duty during all practice sessions and games.
7. All schools should purchase appropriate athletic insurance.
8. The practice field should be inspected daily for potential hazards such as stones, glass, and holes.
9. Only competent officials should be employed.
10. The coach should be highly competent and safety-conscious. This is the most important element in decreasing the incidence of football injuries.
11. Only the best and safest equipment should be purchased.
12. The coach and/or equipment manager should discard old, worn, or unsafe equipment.
13. The coach should conduct a preseason conditioning program and encourage players to improve their physical condition between seasons.
14. Equipment necessary to conduct a physical conditioning program should be acquired.

Guidelines for Coaches

1. Complete an accident report or instruct the athletic trainer to do so for all injuries other than minor ones.
2. Prescribe an individual physical conditioning program to be followed between seasons for each player.
3. During hot weather, schedule practice sessions for early morning or late afternoon, when temperatures are lower.
4. Permit athletes to drink all the water they wish. Two teaspoons of common table salt per gallon of water, a 0.1 percent saline solution, should replace salt lost through perspiration.
5. Gradually acclimatize players to activity during high temperatures.
6. During hot weather, call for hourly rest periods of fifteen to twenty-five minutes.
7. Bear in mind that the higher the humidity, the lower the temperature necessary to produce heat exhaustion for a given amount of physical activity. During humid conditions, watch players for signs of impending heat exhaustion (stupor, awkwardness, or lethargy).
8. Select competent assistant coaches.
9. Report, both verbally and in writing (retaining a copy), any unsafe facilities or equipment.
10. Ensure that every athlete's equipment fits properly.

11. Do not permit players to "spear" opponents when blocking or tackling.
12. Never move a player, regardless of the circumstances, if you have reason to suspect a vertebral fracture.

TOUCH AND FLAG FOOTBALL

Of the 350,000 male college students who participate each year in intramural touch football, approximately 5,000 are injured seriously enough to require medical attention.[20] It is estimated that there is one death each year as a direct result of participation in touch football.

Touch football is one of the most hazardous games because it is played without protective equipment, because there is a great variation in the physical condition, size, and skill of players, because players seldom warm up, and because players are usually unaware of their physical limitations. Some play the game in the manner of regular football, and many possess little skill.

Many of the conditions that predispose to injury can be circumvented, eliminated, or corrected. Since the game today is seldom taught in physical education classes, the following guidelines are limited to those for directors of intramural programs.

Guidelines for Intramural Directors

1. If the number of participants permits, organize by weight classes and/or skill levels.
2. Prior to the season, hold a clinic to clarify the rules and to explain the applicable kinesiologic principles for prevention of injuries. (Attendance at this clinic by the team captain should be a precondition for participation.) These principles include:
   a. A wider base of support increases stability and decreases the probability of being knocked down.
   b. Lowering the center of gravity increases stability.
   c. Probability of injury as a result of impact, either with the ground or with an opponent, can be decreased by spreading the impact over a greater surface area or over a greater period of time. The surface area contacting the ground during a fall can sometimes be increased by turning to fall on the outside of the thigh or some other well-padded surface. Time of absorption of impact can be increased through rolling or through eccentric contraction of muscles.
3. Rules should be strictly enforced, particularly those concerning blocking and safety.

---

[20]Joseph Dzenowogis, "Touch Football," in *Safety Education*, 1st ed., A.E. Florio and G.T. Stafford, eds. (New York: McGraw-Hill Book Co., 1962).

4. Finances permitting, head gear and mouth pieces should be used.
5. Spiked or cleated shoes should be prohibited.
6. Game officials should instruct players to remove pens, pencils, and other hard objects before play begins.
7. Players who wear glasses should use safety glasses, and the hinge and bridge areas of all glasses should be taped or padded.
8. A warm-up should precede play.
9. Game officials should inspect the field for holes, stones, glass, or other hazardous objects.
10. Game officials should fill out accident reports for all injuries, whether sustained during play or as a result of a fight at the game site.

VOLLEYBALL

Volleyball may well be one of the safest of team sports. However, with the growth of the international style of play and power volleyball, the game has become more hazardous than previously.

The incidence of ankle and knee injuries can be reduced, while at the same time increasing players' vertical jumping ability, by having them follow progressive weight training for the legs. Fewer concussions from colliding with other players or with equipment will result if players are instructed to play their own area and to call for the ball. Equipment such as pipes under nets, crank handles, cables, official's stands, and chairs are collision hazards and should be removed.

Fewer abrasions will result if players wear long-sleeved jerseys and pads over the hips, knees, and the tailbone. The number of shoulder, elbow, and lower back injuries can be decreased by insisting on a warm-up prior to play, by improving player physical fitness levels, and by developing a higher level of skill.

WEIGHT LIFTING AND WEIGHT TRAINING

Many more males and females are participating in weight training than in former years. A greater number of males are also participating in weight lifting, particularly power lifting.

In most cases, participants learn procedures from one another. It is surprising that the injury rate is low in this activity, since it usually is an unsupervised activity conducted in the weight training room. This probably places even more responsibility upon the administrator.

A weight training and weight lifting clinic could be held at the beginning of the school year, at which body builders and competitive lifters could demonstrate proper techniques, including safety procedures. Regulations regarding safety procedures should be posted in the weight training room. A sample of such regulations follows:

1. Lifters should have a physical examination prior to beginning the program to uncover any problems relative to the heart, abdominal muscles, knees, or other joints that might be affected.
2. Collars should be checked for tightness before barbells are lifted. If a collar is not tight, plates could slip off one end to crush toes. The barbell could also become unbalanced, which could cause muscle pulls or strains.
3. A spotter should be utilized at each end of the barbell during such lifts as the overhead press, bench press, snatch, clean and jerk, and half-squat.
4. Maximum lifts should be preceded by a warm-up. This will decrease the probability of muscle pulls and strains.
5. Adequate room must be provided so that barbells cannot be dropped on other participants. No one other than the spotters should be allowed within ten feet of the lifter.
6. All participants should study posted instructions and illustrations of proper technique for the various exercises and lifts.

WRESTLING

Wrestling is an extremely vigorous contact sport. Consequently, injuries occur. At the World Amateur Wrestling Championships, 22 percent of all injuries incurred were to the head, 15 percent to the neck, 12 percent to the arms, 11 percent to the shoulder girdle, and 10 percent to the knee.

Guidelines for Administrators

1. Employ only the most highly qualified coaches and officials.
2. Provide adequate facilities. Fifty square feet of mat area per participant is recommended. Walls, posts, and any projections should be padded to a height of at least five feet.
3. Foam plastic mats are preferred. However, if canvas mats must be used, they should be covered with a material that does not easily cause mat burns. Abrasions from mats can become infected if the mat covers are not kept sanitary by daily cleaning and disinfecting. There are mats available with a paint containing an antibacterial additive, which guards against infection and fungus.
4. Foam mats and a six-inch plywood-base floor under the mats help to absorb shock.
5. Temperature in the wrestling room should be seventy to eighty degrees to reduce fatigue, which increases the probability of injury.
6. The janitor should be instructed in the procedures for daily cleaning and disinfecting of mats.
7. Adequate protective equipment, including elbow and knee pads and ear protectors, should be provided.

8. Coaches and instructors should not be assigned groups of more than twenty students.
9. Only officials who have passed both written and practical examinations should be hired.

Guidelines for Coaches

1. Thoroughly instruct participants in techniques, rules, and safety procedures.
2. Bring team members to a high level of physical fitness.
3. Require wrestlers to wear clean uniforms. Headgear and protective padding should be worn. Rings, watches, and other jewelry should be banned. Hair and nails should be trimmed.
4. Check daily to ensure that wrestlers cannot trip on a torn or loose cover or a space between mats.
5. Require a physical examination of each team member before the season begins and at the end of the season, as well as after any injury or illness before permitting return to practice.
6. A physician should be immediately available during all matches and practice sessions. Athletes with colds or infections should be prohibited from wrestling and should be cleared by a physician before returning to practice.
7. With regard to weight reduction, require wrestlers to conform to the recommendations of the American Medical Association's Committee on Medical Aspects of Sport.[21]
8. Permit athletes to drink all the water they wish, particularly when temperature and humidity are high.
9. Chairs, tables, clocks, clipboards, etc., must not be permitted in or on the wrestling area.
10. Wrestlers should warm up thoroughly before practices and matches.

Sample Legal Cases

The Rehabilitation Act of 1973 (29 U.S.C. Section 504) prohibits discrimination against an otherwise qualified individual in federally funded programs solely because of a handicap. This law applies to interscholastic activities of any school system that receives federal funds, even if no federal money is spent specifically for the programs. The relief provided by this statute is monetary as well as injunctive and is available to private individuals who have been wronged.

Richard Pool is one individual who successfully took advantage of this relatively new law. He was born with only one kidney. Aside from that, he

---

[21]American Medical Association, "Interscholastic Wrestling and Weight Control," in *Proceedings of the Eighth National Conference on the Medical Aspects of Sports* (Chicago: The Association, 1967).

was a healthy individual who had participated in wrestling for three years before being denied this right upon the advice of the medical director of the South Plainfield Board of Education. The Board's legal counsel concurred in the doctor's advice.

The Board of Education knew that Richard's parents had discussed Richard's wrestling with their family physician and had consulted with the Temple University Center for Sports Medicine and Sciences, as well as with the wrestling coach from Lehigh University, as to the types of frequency of wrestling injuries. The Board insisted on asserting their rational decision over the family's rational decision.

The court admitted that the Board of Education stood *in loco parentis* but ruled that this doctrine traditionally means that a school system must act in place of the parent when the parent is absent. The court found the Board acted contrary to the express wishes of the parents. The Board's duty in such a situation is to alert the participant and his parents to the dangers involved and to require that they rationally deal with the matter. The court stated:

> It is undoubtedly true that injury to Richard's kidney would have grave consequences, but so might other injuries that might befall him or any other member of the wrestling team. Hardly a year goes by that there is not at least one instance of the tragic death of a healthy youngster as a result of a competitive sport activity. Life has risks. The purpose of Section 504, however, is to permit handicapped individuals to live life as fully as they are able, without paternalistic authorities deciding that certain activities are too risky for them. (*Pool* v. *South Plainfield Board of Education*, 490 F. Supp. 948 [N.J. 1980] at 953–54.)

An example of the seriousness of injuries that can result from wrestling accidents is found in *Carabba* v. *The Ana Cortes School District #103* (435 PcRep. 2d 936 [Washington 1968]). In this case, a wrestling meet was sponsored by two student organizations. The referee noticed a separation between the mats and went to close the gap in order to protect the wrestlers in case they moved in that direction. When his attention was thus diverted for a matter of seconds, one of the contestants applied a full nelson to his opponent. As the referee blew his whistle and the buzzer sounded to end the round, the hold was broken. But Stephen Carabba had already suffered a severed spinal cord. His voluntary functions were permanently paralyzed below the neck.

SWIMMING

More than 100 million people participate in some water-related activity in the United States each year, and there are a total of over one million in-ground pools. Activities include boating, canoeing, fishing, scuba diving, water skiing, water polo, surfboarding, and springboard diving, as well as recreational swimming.

These activities take place in lakes, rivers, the ocean, and pools. The settings include the organized swimming pool, public beaches, summer camps, backyard pools, and undeveloped swimming areas such as ponds, abandoned quarries, and unprotected beach fronts.

Public schools operate more than 25,000 swimming pools. Few of the total of 8,000 drownings each year occur in school pools, even though school aquatic activities are regarded as high-risk activities. To date, there have not been many successful lawsuits in the aquatic area. This is because courts have usually determined that the victim's own negligence was a contributing factor, and because the courts have recognized (a) the dangers inherent in swimming and (b) the difficulty in controlling swimmers. However, there can be no assurance that such a legal disposition will continue. The number of suits is increasing and, thus, those in charge of aquatic activities must continue to be vigilant.

Directors of school programs and other organized programs can make substantial contributions to aquatic safety by improving students' aquatic skills, by informing them about aquatic hazards and how to avoid them, and by setting an example for safe operation of aquatic programs and facilities. The significance of such contributions is apparent when one considers that water-related accidents rank second only to motor vehicle accidents in causing deaths in the 4–44 age group in the United States.

There are presently over one million permanent swimming pools in the United States, most of which are residential pools. One out of four Americans goes boating at least several times each year. Another five million children have acquired small craft boating experience at camp programs each summer.

Boating fatalities (by drowning) constitute approximately twenty percent of the total number of lives lost each year as a result of water accidents. However, organized school, camp, "Y," and Red Cross instructional programs in swimming have decreased the number of drownings in unsupervised aquatic activities, in boating, and in residential swimming pool accidents.

* * * * *

There are a number of hazards involved in all aquatic sports. Consequently, the total number of guidelines that should be presented is impressive. Thus the guidelines offered in this section are broken down according to the various types of activities and settings.

Swimming Pool Design

1. When planning a swimming pool, make certain that it will be well designed and constructed, since the cost of correcting an error after the

pool has been completed is usually prohibitive. Study the plans thoroughly to make certain there will be no built-in hazards.

2. Provide for adequate parking space and safe pedestrian access to the pool.
3. Emergency vehicles should have easy access to the pool and filter room, even at times of peak usage.
4. Outdoor pools should be surrounded by a wall or fence at least six feet high.
5. A room to serve exclusively as a first aid room should be included in the plans.
6. The pool deck and the locker room floor should be at the same elevation (no steps).
7. The pool deck should be between six and twenty feet wide.
8. There should be a drain for every 250 square feet of deck.
9. A minimum of sunlight should reach the deck, since sunlight promotes the growth of algae.
10. A nonskid, but relatively smooth, surface should cover the shower and locker room floors and pool deck.
11. Fifteen square feet per person (at anticipated peak usage) should be provided for dressing areas.
12. Dressing cubicles for females should be a minimum of three feet square.
13. Equipment rooms should not be located within the locker room space, since children may be tempted to play in this slippery area.
14. The pool deck and shower room floor should slope toward the nearest drain, such that water will not collect at low spots.
15. Water depth should be indicated both on the edge of the deck and on the vertical walls on all four sides of the pool. Every foot of depth change should be indicated.
16. Depth change in the shallow area should not be greater than one foot for twelve feet of horizontal distance.
17. The bottom of the shallow area should be of nonslip material.
18. In the deep area, the slope should not be greater than one foot drop for three feet of horizontal distance.
19. The shower and dressing rooms should be at the shallow end of the pool.
20. The water depth at the line where the grade changes should be five feet. About one foot from this line, toward the shallow end, eyelets should be installed in the side walls to support a safety line, which should be in place as needed. The eyelets should be securely anchored and should be flush with the pool walls.
21. The diving area should be a minimum of thirty-two feet in width for a one-meter board and thirty-five feet for a three-meter board. The forward edge of the diving area should be at least fifteen feet from the forward edge of the diving board.

22. A one-meter board requires a pool depth of ten to eleven feet, while a three-meter board requires twelve feet. Platform diving requires a depth of fifteen feet.
23. The slope of the bottom of the diving area, the distance of the deepest position from the end of the diving board and the base, should be such as to provide safety for both long and short dives. The wider the base and the more gradual the slope, the greater the margin for error by the diver. The deepest portion in the diving area should be five feet from the forward end of the board.
24. Glass should be used sparingly in pools, lockers, and dressing rooms. There are many choices of alternate materials that are attractive and almost graffiti-proof.
25. There should be a minimum of one shower head for every forty persons, at peak usage. Water temperature, preferably controlled from an office, should range between ninety and one hundred degrees.
26. There should be a minimum distance of sixteen feet between the diving board and any ceiling (or projection from the ceiling).
27. The platform to the three-meter board should include a double rail on either side and back of the board and should extend forward to the edge of the pool to protect divers against falls from the board.
28. One-meter boards should not be less than ten feet apart and should not be less than twelve feet from the side of the pool.
29. Three-meter boards should not be closer than fifteen feet apart.
30. Boards should be firmly anchored at the inside end with bolts passing through the deck.
31. The fulcrum should be centered, level, and at right angles to the board.
32. The pitch of the board should remain constant in spite of different settings of the fulcrum. The pitch should range from level to not more than a one-inch rise.
33. The surface of the board should be a nonslip material, such as a sandpaperlike material or nonslip paint. Cocoa matting is not recommended because it becomes slippery and because when it becomes worn holes appear that may cause a diver to trip.
34. Underwater lights should be individually grounded to the junction box. Underwater lights of more than twelve volts should be double-grounded or equipped with a device to cut off the circuit.
35. Underwater lights should be flush with the walls.
36. Electrical wiring should not pass over the pool area. Power lines should be underground.
37. Electrical outlets should not be located within ten feet of the pool's edge.
38. The amount of light on the pool deck and the deepest end of the pool should be 100 footcandles. Excessive light will produce glare, which is especially hazardous in the diving area.
39. Pool load limits should be based on one person per twenty-five square feet of water surface.

40. Buoy lines should be stretched across the width of the pool twelve inches before significant depth changes.
41. The wading pool should be near the shallow end of the pool, but separated from it by a fence of three or more feet in height.
42. In public pools, there should be one elevated lifeguard chair for every 2,000 square feet of pool area, located as to minimize pool glare.
43. The filtration system should be capable of recirculating the entire volume of water in six hours.
44. The filter rooms should have a minimum of seventy-five footcandles of light, and there should be a complete change of air every four hours.
45. The filter room should contain a drainage pit, and the floor should be waterproof. Hose nipples should be provided on each wall.
46. All electrical equipment — motors, light fixtures, and receptacles — should be grounded.
47. The filter room should be fire-retardant, and all dry chemicals should be stored on wooden platforms.
48. A chain link fence at least six feet high should completely surround the pool. Gates at the main entrance should be at least six feet wide, and all gates should be self-latching.
49. Goggles should be worn whenever working with pool chemicals.
50. Maximum capacity for a pool should be 2,500 people (on the deck and in the water). Larger pools present excessive management and supervision problems. Instead of exceeding this capacity, communities are advised to build an additional pool.
51. In large community pools, the elderly and handicapped should be accommodated with steps from the deck into the pool. Handrails should also be provided. Separate times should be provided for use of the pool by the elderly and handicapped, although they should not be banned or discriminated against at other times.
52. Plans for new pools should call for a separate deep water well for diving. This will not only minimize collisions between divers and swimmers, but will also save water, since the main pool need be only eighteen inches to five feet in depth. A movable bulkhead at the four-foot depth can serve as one end for twenty-five-yard or twenty-five-meter races. (That is, the distance from the end wall at the five-foot depth to the four-foot depth is twenty-five yards or meters; beyond the bulkhead, the pool should slope to an eighteen-inch depth, where children and waders can cavort.)
53. Every pool should have a well-equipped first aid room.
54. Slides should be located in deep water only, with at least sixteen feet of clearance to the front and eight feet to either side.
55. Slides should be supervised at all times, and only feet-first entries should be permitted.
56. The pool design should allow for a continuous flow of water down the slide to prevent skin burns.

57. Wading pools should be adjacent to the shallow end of the large pool. They should have a maximum depth of eighteen inches, have an apron six to ten feet wide surrounding them, and be enclosed by a chain link fence three feet high (or a wall designed so that parents can sit on it while watching their children).
58. A lifeguard chair should be provided for every 2,000 square feet of pool surface. The chairs should be four to six feet above the pool deck and should be stable enough to permit the guard to dive from the chair into the pool. If there are two chairs at a pool, they should be located on opposite sides. Chairs should be so positioned that the sun is behind the lifeguard during the time of peak loads.

Pool Sanitation

1. Be familiar with local and state laws governing pool sanitation.
2. The turbidity level of the water should never exceed the point at which a six-inch black disc on a white field is not clearly visible in the deepest part of the pool.
3. Free chlorine residual and PH of the pool water should be measured at least every two hours while the pool is in use. A free chlorine residual of 0.6–1.0 parts per million and a PH of 7.2–7.6 should be maintained.
4. When chlorine gas is used, there should be an airtight duct leading from the bottom of the enclosure to the outside, with an exhaust fan capable of effecting a complete air change in one minute. A gas mask should be stored just outside the enclosure.
5. All electric switches should be outside the enclosure for the gas chlorinating system.
6. Algae growth should be controlled by frequent brushing and vacuuming and by superchlorination.
7. Maintenance personnel and lifeguards should be warned about the danger of explosion if water is spilled into a container of granular chlorine.
8. The pool should be cleared of all swimmers while "hand-feeding" chlorine into the pool.
9. A daily log of chlorine and PH measurements, as well as of numbers of swimmers, should be kept.
10. The recirculation and filtration systems should be capable of a six-hour turnover rate; the wading pool water should be completely recirculated every two hours.
11. Pool water should be regularly tested by the local or state health department.
12. The water level in the pool must be maintained above the gutters, especially in outdoor pools subject to greater evaporation, so that scum, debris, and other floating matter is effectively removed and the maximum diving depth is maintained.

Sample Safety Rules

1. No running on the pool deck.
2. Food and drinks are not permitted in the pool area.
3. Persons under the influence of alcohol or drugs are not permitted in the pool area.
4. Diving from the side of the pool into the diving area is prohibited.
5. A soap shower is required before entering the pool area.
6. Conversation with the lifeguards is prohibited.
7. Guards will prohibit persons with open wounds, sores, or skin infections from entering the pool.
8. The use of snorkles, scuba equipment, inner tubes, and air mattresses is prohibited.
9. Children may use flotation devices only in water below their chest height and only when an adult accompanies the child.
10. Only one person at a time is allowed on the diving board and on the steps leading to the board.
11. Double bouncing on the board is prohibited.
12. Diving sidewards off the board is prohibited.
13. No diving until the previous diver has surfaced and cleared the diving area.
14. Divers should clear the diving area as quickly as possible after surfacing.
15. Wrestling, tussling, and horseplay on the pool deck or in the water is prohibited.
16. Swimming is not permitted during electrical storms.
17. Only standard bathing suits are permitted. Cut-off jeans or similar street clothing is prohibited.

Guidelines for Administrators

1. Limit the number of swimmers to one person per twenty square feet of combined pool and deck area.
2. Provide one lifeguard for each 125 swimmers, with a minimum of two lifeguards whenever the pool is in use.
3. Each lifeguard station should be equipped with a ring buoy, a sixteen-foot pole, and a shepherd's crook or throwing line.
4. When lighted pools are used at night, an emergency lighting system should be provided for use in the event of an outage. As a minimum measure, each lifeguard station should be equipped with an operative lantern.
5. The first aid room should be equipped with cot, stretcher, blankets, and all necessary first aid supplies. Supplies should be replenished as they are used.
6. Employ only well-qualified lifeguards and maintain morale and discipline at high levels. Make certain that all personnel fully understand and

accept their responsibilities by requiring that they sign a complete job description prior to beginning work.

7. A staff training program should be conducted prior to pool opening, covering life saving, CPR, first aid skills, and pool maintenance procedures.

8. A pool manual should explain policies, rules, job descriptions, procedures, pay scales, employee benefits, and schedules.

9. To avoid the possibility that fatigue or boredom might lower the efficiency of lifeguards, they should not work more than an eight-hour day or a forty-eight hour week, should be given a ten-minute break every hour, and should rotate positions after each break. A one-hour lunch period should be scheduled for the midpoint of an eight-hour working day.

Legal Aspects

With over a million swimming pools in this country and more being added every day, there is bound to be an increasing concern over safety and liability in swimming pool accidents.

Generally speaking, the usual duty exists to use care in the operation of a swimming pool, whether it be a backyard pool or the YMCA. Some states have established different rules of liability for backyard pools and public pools that charge an admission fee. When a fee is paid, as has been discussed previously, the user of the pool becomes a business invitee and, in some states, is owed a higher degree of care than a social visitor.

The following section will be directed to the legal practitioner. The principles discussed, however, can be readily applied to those who are in a position to assure the safety of the premises.

Swimming pools can be analyzed from several viewpoints. One viewpoint concerns design; another is that of the construction of the facility. Finally, swimming pools can be analyzed from the aspect of the owner's or operator's duty. (The aspect of duty also applies to the construction and maintenance of the facility.) In the following discussion, pools will also be analyzed from a legal aspect, namely, what specific theory may be used to gain recovery for an injured individual.

* * * * *

From the *architect's* point of view, a swimming pool is a man-made tank that can be used for swimming and/or diving. It is this dual use that creates one of the greatest problems in the design and construction of pools. To begin with, the architect who designs the pool must design a large basin into which a dive can safely be made. This task is compounded by the placement of the diving board, which usually extends several feet beyond the edge of the basin.

When a person six-feet tall takes a few running steps, dives off the end of the pool, and ends up banging his head on the break in the pool, thus breaking his neck and severing his spinal cord, a large lawsuit is almost certain to follow. (The "break in the pool" refers to the wall or incline between the diving basin and the immediate rise to the shallow end of the pool.) The diver usually strikes this slanted wall at about a ninety-degree angle, which is the worst possible angle at which to hit it. There is usually not enough space between the point where the diver hits the water and the break in the pool for the water to sufficiently decelerate the diver's speed.

Since the diving board usually extends several feet out above the deep end of the pool, we find sufficient diving depth immediately beneath the board; but it takes a very accomplished diver to dive in this deepest area. The amateur diver often ends up at the shallow end of the basin, where there is greater probability of striking the incline.

For safety purposes, the bottom of the pool should be painted a light color to help the diver see where he can safely dive. When the sun or electric lights are reflecting off the water, the natural magnification property of water makes it extremely difficult, if not impossible, to see the variations in depth of the pool bottom. Thus the architect must be truly qualified to design a pool, and it is important for the administrator to check on the architect's experience in pool design.

Previous sections have stressed the importance of establishing a defendant's guilty knowledge (or prior notice). This can be either actual or constructive knowledge. In court, the architect-defendant would be questioned regarding his knowledge of any prior accidents or injuries due to a type of negligent design with which he is being charged in a case.

The architect would also be interrogated with reference to his knowledge of, or use of, any available standards, such as those of the National Swimming Pool Institute, the Amateur Athletic Union, the YMCA, or the Consumer Products Safety Commission. Failure to comply with these standards may be taken as evidence of negligence. It should be remembered that these are only minimum standards established by the industry or other organizations, some of which are clearly self-protective standards for the industry. An expert called by the plaintiff may testify that higher standards should have been applied.

Finally, from the architect's standpoint, it is essential that he inspect the pool after it has been constructed and/or during the course of construction to ensure that actual construction conforms to his plans.

The *builder* is held to liability for constructing a pool in keeping with the plans. It is important that he put the skimmer (through which the water exits the pool on its way to the filter) at the center of the pool and at such a height as to maintain proper depth. When the water level is lowered, the diving board is effectively raised and, as a result, the deceleration distance to the pool bottom is decreased.

In this regard, mere inches are very important. With an outdoor pool, sunlight and normal evaporation can change the level of the water over a period of time. It is essential that owners maintain proper water levels.

A permit should be issued for the installation of the pool, so that the local sanitary department can check compliance with local building codes and can check the filtration system and condition of the water.

The pool *owner* is an obvious party defendant. In court, the owner would be questioned about any previous accidents or prior complaints by parties using the pool. He would also be questioned regarding any cancellation of insurance or increase in insurance premiums due to addition to the pool of a diving board, or of a slide.

In many states, the *attractive nuisance* doctrine applies to swimming pools. This means that when one has something on his premises that will attract children, such as a pool, this can be considered an attractive nuisance with the result that the owner has a duty to take special precautions (such as fencing).

Most communities have an ordinance requiring fencing around a pool. These ordinances usually specify the height of the fence as well as the type of gate required, usually one that is self-latching so that little children will not wander into the pool.

In Arizona, a court held the owner liable when a five-year-old child drowned after apparently crawling through an opening in a hedge surrounding the pool. The court said that it would have imposed only a slight burden upon the owner to properly fence the pool. (*Giacona* v. *Tapley*, 5 Ariz. App. 494.)

It is interesting to note that more adults than children are injured on water slides. These slides range from six to ten feet high. Both children and adults frequently slide down head-first.

Water slides are often negligently placed at the shallow end, where children can utilize them. Thus when adults and children slide down head-first, they often hit their heads on the bottom of the pool. A warning attached to the slide, that one should not slide head-first, is grossly inadequate for little children. It is essential that slides be placed over water deep enough to allow for their normal use by adults as well as children. A slide would certainly fall into the category of an attractive nuisance.

When one owns a pool, supervision is essential. Running on a wet surface is hazardous, yet children, in the excitement of play, often run on the wet pool deck. Horseplay, wrestling, and throwing others into the pool are well-known activities of children. With this kind of guilty knowledge on the part of pool owners, it is essential that adequate supervision be furnished.

A pool owner, in order to be a good neighbor, may permit neighborhood children to use the pool. But the owner should require that a parent accompany the children at all times. This is good common sense.

Proper *maintenance* includes inspecting the premises for worn mats and mats that have rolled up at the ends, which might cause a person to trip and fall. Broken tile, cracks in the concrete, or broken or cracked wooden flooring or platforms may also cause the unwary to trip and fall.

The owner has the further responsibility to maintain the water in a safe condition, that is, to keep the water infection-free through the use of chemicals (without using so much that the chemicals cause injury or allergic reactions). Further, the water must be maintained not only at proper depth, but must also be clear and properly filtered so that the bottom is visible. This permits the lifeguard or person in charge to see anyone in trouble at the bottom of the pool. It also will help a diver judge the depth and thus avoid hitting the pool bottom.

A safety rope should be floated between the shallow and deep ends as a warning to nonswimmers and poor swimmers so that they will not enter water over their heads.

There are published rules and standards for lifeguards that cover training, maintaining order, and even the height at which they should be seated to provide full view of the pool and the surrounding area. The YMCA provides an excellent set of standards for lifeguards.

The very presence of a lifeguard indicates that a defendant had prior guilty knowledge or notice that inherently dangerous activities were involved. And where there is an inherently dangerous activity, many courts will apply the previously discussed rule of strict liability, that is, liability without fault.

It is essential that the lifeguard have adequate equipment, such as a pole or a float to throw to someone, and that he be properly trained in resuscitation and other lifesaving and first aid measures. Slip-and-fall cases frequently arise around a swimming pool due to wet, slippery surfaces. This can be solved by the use of nonskid material or strips, such as are used in bathtubs and showers.

The usual laws of premises liability apply to slip-and-fall cases in swimming pool accidents. Warnings must be given, especially where an inherently dangerous activity is involved. To be effective, a warning must be adequate to reach those persons who should be anticipated to use the pool or the surrounding area. For example, if the owner knows that persons who speak only a foreign language frequently use the pool area, he can be found negligent for failing to adequately warn if he fails to have signs in the appropriate language, as well as in English.

As Mr. Justice Holmes said: "What is usually done may be evidence of what ought to be done, but what ought to be done is fixed by a standard of reasonable prudence, whether it usually is complied with or not."

Rules for the use of the pool should be posted in such a way that they are obvious to any user. They must adequately inform the user. Not only must they inform, but they must be of sufficiently startling effect to attract the attention of the potential user.

For example, it is not sufficient to put a small number on the side of a pool to indicate depth. A rope stretched across the pool to indicate the end of shallow water is a much more adequate warning. Furthermore, as we shift to the metric system, the owner must remember that a number on the side of a pool may mean feet to one person and meters to another.

It is not uncommon to find a liquor bar at the pool of a resort, hotel, or in someone's backyard. Under such circumstances, it is a weak defense to contend that a person drowned or was injured due to a state of intoxication. Also, the person maintaining the premises should be aware that broken glass around the pool can cause severe injuries. Even when serving nonalcoholic beverages, it is wise to use paper or plastic cups (and dishes).

Good housekeeping is essential when maintaining a pool. Toys, roller skates, or other unusual objects should not be present on the premises, since they might cause serious injury due to falls on a hard surface or striking the edge of the pool.

Lighting can sometimes be a major factor in establishing liability. It is essential that a pool be adequately lighted in order to see anyone in trouble in the water. Many pools come equipped with lights under the water for this very purpose. This is especially important in deep pools and diving pools.

* * * * *

The following section discusses the liability aspect from the plaintiff's point of view and from the defendant's point of view.

From the point of view of the *plaintiff*, it is well to approach pool injury cases from an alternative liability standpoint, that is, from the aspect of negligence, strict liability, and breach of warranty, as well as premises liability. (An earlier section of this book discussed and defined these various theories of liability and the elements required to establish each.) Some, though not all, jurisdictions recognize all of these theories as applicable to swimming pool accident cases.

Expert testimony is essential to establish one of these theories. It is necessary to call a lifeguard or a diving instructor or swimming coach from the local YMCA, high school, or college, who can testify as to reasonable and applicable standards, as well as to his opinion as to wherein this particular defendant failed to meet the standards.

Of all these theories, probably the most acceptable to a jury is the negligence theory because negligence implies wrongdoing on the part of the defendant. In general, when wrongdoing can be established, the jury is more willing to find against the defendant and will presumably be more generous in its verdict.

The expert witness should visit the scene (and go through a few dives himself, for example, if a diving accident is involved). He should take measurements and thoroughly inspect the scene, such that he will be able to testify to any deviations from standards.

If an architect or builder is the defendant, it is important to have an expert witness with similar qualifications, who is qualified to express an opinion as to failure to comply with the reasonable standards applicable to the particular profession.

Again, the old bromide that a picture is worth a thousand words applies when trying to establish liability in these cases. The plaintiff should take pictures of the scene, even motion pictures reenacting the event. While it may be difficult to introduce these into evidence, it may be possible if the defendant should "open the door" on cross-examination. This means that the defense attorney might, in the course of cross-examining a witness, go into matters that can possibly be rebutted by the use of the pictures.

In considering the *defenses* available in a swimming pool accident case, it is important to first establish to the jury that there are many risks and dangers inherent in the use of a pool. In a pool, a human being enters an unnatural habitat — the water. Defenses such as assumption of risk and contributory negligence have their applications in swimming pool accidents.

Again, expert testimony on behalf of the defense is essential in defending one of these cases.

TRACK AND FIELD

Track and field is one of the safest of sports. With the exception of the pole vault, dangers to spectators are greater than to participants. Spectators are endangered because they try to get too close to the field events, especially the discus, shot, hammer, and javelin. The pole-vaulter is endangered by improperly landing from great heights and by having the pole break.

Guidelines for Administrators

1. Employ only knowledgeable and well-qualified coaches and officials.
2. Purchase poles in a variety of weights to accommodate pole vaulters of different weights.
3. Protect the rear and sides of the discus and hammer circles by chain link fencing so that spectators cannot be struck by wild throws.
4. Do not purchase multi-spiked, or "brush," shoes, since they can cause serious injuries during collisions and undue strain during curve running.
5. Purchase hurdles with padded or hinged tops for team practice.
6. Purchase raised pits for high jumping and pole vaulting. These pits should be filled with foam rubber pieces.
7. Contract for a qualified physician to be present at all meets and employ a qualified athletic trainer.
8. Purchase insurance or make it available to all track athletes.

Guidelines for Coaches

1. When selecting a pole for a pole-vaulter, consider not only the vaulter's weight, but also his handhold height and takeoff speed. The higher the handhold on the pole and the greater the takeoff speed, the greater the

stress on the pole and, consequently, the greater must be the weight of the pole.
2. Teach vaulters to land properly on the back.
3. Rope off the runways for the jumping events to avoid collisions between jumpers and spectators.
4. Rope off the areas of the throwing events and permit no spectators in these areas.
5. Insist that the discus, hammer, shot, and javelin always be carried, not thrown, back to the throwing circle.
6. Permit only coaches and trained managers to fire the starting gun, and insist that the gun always be held above the head when fired to prevent ear injuries or powder burns to the face or eyes.
7. Require hurdlers to pad the medial malleolus (inside ankle bone).
8. Each athlete should have a complete physical examination prior to the season.
9. All athletes should warm up before workouts and cool down afterwards.
10. Proper clothing should be required of all athletes.
11. Only teach the "Fosbury Flop" style of high jumping, which involves landing on the back, if there is a safe landing area such as an inflatable air cushion or raised pit filled with foam rubber pieces.
12. Instruct finish line officials not to run onto the track to spot finishers. Instruct timers to remain in position immediately after the conclusion of the race.
13. Require jumpers to use molded heel cups.
14. Train hammer throwers to periodically check the handle, wire, and swivel.
15. Cancel pole vaulting events during cold, windy, or rainy weather.

Pole Vaulting

In May 1967, Jack Johnson represented Fort Haze College in the pole vault event at a conference track meet. The officials at the University of Omaha, where the meet was held, used two wooden boxes to support the uprights. Once placed beneath the pole vault standards, the boxes were partially covered with a burlap bag filled with foam rubber.

In attempting to pass over the crossbar, Jack made a good flexion off the fiberglass pole. However, the carry (which is generated by speed) was insufficient, and he fell back, hitting the crossbar. Jack was injured when he landed on one of the boxes, which were specially built for the purpose for which they were being used.

The boxes facilitated the officials' job of moving the uprights without dislodging the crossbar. (Each competitor had a preference regarding the horizontal distance from the slideway in which he would place his pole.) Also, without the boxes, the crossbar could only be placed at fifteen feet, no higher. The conference record at the time was just one-quarter inch under fourteen and a half feet.

The *Restatement of Torts* (2nd, Section 291, page 54) states: "Where an act is one which a reasonable man would recognize as involving a risk of harm to another, the risk is unreasonable and the act is negligent if the risk is of such magnitude as to outweigh what the law regards as the utility of the act or of the particular manner in which it was done." (187 N.W. 2d 102.)

In the pole vaulting case, the court found the risk of harm from using the partially covered boxes outweighed their utility. Thus the University of Omaha was found negligent.

JOGGING

There have been phenomenal increases in the number of people of all ages and both sexes who jog regularly. Joggers are seen everywhere — on school tracks, on country roads, in suburbs, in industrial areas, downtown, up-town, and on the top of buildings. They are seen at all hours of the day and night, at all times of the year. They are seen out in the rain, sun, snow, ice, heat, and cold. High schools and colleges offer jogging in the physical education curriculum and as an extracurricular club activity.

The principles of safety should be taught in every jogging course, since injuries and damage to health can and do occur in jogging. Sprains, strains, joint injuries, heat exhaustion, frostbite, and collisions with automobiles are some of the unpleasant aspects of jogging.

Joggers should be reminded that roads were constructed for vehicles, not for foot traffic. Therefore, the primary responsibility for prevention of accidents on the roads lies with the jogger. Those in charge of jogging groups should learn and pass on the state traffic regulations and local ordinances pertaining to pedestrians. They should learn whether their state recommends pedestrians move with the traffic or against it, as well as which roads in their area are closed to pedestrians.

In any dangerous situation, the runner should move to the shoulder of the road. The runner should keep alert by using both eyes and ears. Wind and environmental noises (cars, jack hammers, etc.) often make hearing undependable; therefore, the runner must turn to look. Fatigue tempts a runner to depend excessively upon his hearing, because of the extra energy required to turn to look. When jogging on the side of the road toward approaching traffic, the jogger is endangered by cars passing one another at the point where the jogger is running, especially if the driver is blinded by the sun or oncoming headlights. Another hazard arises when approaching the crest of a hill, since neither the driver nor the jogger can see the other until the crest is cleared.

Under most circumstances, however, it is safer to jog toward opposing traffic, since oncoming vehicles can be seen better than when they are approaching from the rear, and since both driver and jogger have a chance to see the other and take evasive action to avoid collision. At intersections, the jogger must stop if the traffic signal so indicates. But even if he has the right-of-way, the jogger is advised to make eye contact with the driver waiting to enter the intersection, in order to be positive that the driver is aware of him. Remember, right turns are not allowed on red lights in many jurisdictions.

When running at night, joggers should wear white, light-colored, or fluorescent clothing. They should also add some reflective material to their clothing. The runner should move from one side of the road to the other as seldom as possible, but when necessary he should cross only at a right angle to the road, since it will be difficult to see a car approaching from the rear when crossing at an acute angle.

Fishing poles, two-by-fours, and other objects protruding from car windows can inflict injuries to joggers, as can articles falling from open trucks and dirt or gravel thrown by spinning wheels. Identification, including medical insurance cards and the names of those to contact in case of accidents, should always be carried.

Dehydration is a hazard during hot weather. Consequently, joggers must ingest adequate amounts of water to prevent heat exhaustion, which can lead to death. Cold weather presents the problems of frostbite and sore throats. Procedures to minimize these problems include wearing several layers of clothing, covering the head and neck, eliminating heat loss at the cuffs, ankles, and waist, breathing through the nose to warm the air before it reaches the lungs, and wearing a scarf around the mouth.

Before beginning a running program, joggers should undergo a physical examination to uncover any limitations. It may be best to initiate a jogging program on a nearby track until one's limitations are ascertained. All joggers should warm up with calisthenic exercises before jogging to minimize muscle strains. Large-busted female joggers should avoid excessive bounce and potential damage to tissues by wearing a well-fitted brassiere. Shin splints can be minimized by wearing footgear with thick soles and arches, as well as several pairs of socks (white cotton inside and white wool outside). Joggers should walk a block or two to warm up before running.

RACKET GAMES

Badminton and tennis are not hazardous games. There have been few, if any, lawsuits resulting from these games. On the other hand, squash, paddle ball, and racket ball are quite hazardous, due to the danger of being hit in the face or head with a racket.

In these dangerous games, one player may strike another with his hand, arm, or racket; players may collide with a court wall or wall projection; they may pull or strain muscles; and they may suffer cardiac failure due to undetected malfunctions. Procedures to minimize these hazards include the development of skill, sportsmanlike play, conditioning, physical examinations, removal of projections from the playing area, good court lighting, and keeping the floor skidproof.

In squash rackets, a short, low backswing and a checked follow-through will decrease the probability of striking an opponent with the racket; hitting the ball low will decrease the probability of hitting him with the ball. Lawsuits in the area of racket games usually result from a player being struck by either the racket or ball. The smaller the playing area, the greater the probability of a player being struck. Thus cutthroat and doubles play should be prohibited on undersized courts.

Few games are officiated but where they are officials should be generous in allowing a "let" (no loss of point or other penalty) if there is a question of interference. Lighting systems should be adequate. Wrist thongs should be utilized.

The National Society to Prevent Blindness recently recommended that players in racket games wear protective eyewear, even if they do not require glasses.

LACROSSE

Lacrosse is a vigorous, fast-moving, and competitive team sport that appears very hazardous. However, available statistics on the incidence and types of injuries show that the game is no more hazardous than soccer, baseball, wrestling, or basketball. Some fractures of the hands and clavicles occur, as do concussions and injuries to the mouth and teeth, but most injuries are sprains and strains of muscles in the ankles, knees, and shoulders.

Substitution of soccer shoes, which have shorter cleats, for football shoes will decrease the incidence of sprains of the ankles and knees. Since lacrosse requires that players make quick turns and spins, the shorter cleats will permit the players to turn with greater safety. The use of shoulder pads and careful officiating with regard to use of the crosse and body checking, as well as proper instruction in legal body checking and stick use, will decrease the incidence of fractures in the hands and clavicle.

Mouth guards will reduce the probability of a player suffering damage to the mouth or teeth. The rules of lacrosse require that shoulder pads and mouth guards be worn during games. However, the coach should also require players to wear them at all practice sessions.

The use of tape and weight training exercises for the legs will help to decrease the number of knee and ankle sprains.

Coaches can reduce injuries and the likelihood of tort actions arising therefrom by:

1. Checking fields regularly for ruts, holes, broken glass, and other hazardous conditions.
2. Supervising all practice sessions.

3. Having a qualified athletic trainer present at all practice sessions and games.
4. Having a physician on-call for all practice sessions and having him present at all games.
5. Ensuring that all players are covered by either a personal or school accident insurance policy.
6. Requiring that all players receive a complete physical examination at the beginning of the season. When injuries are improperly treated or diagnosed (or when the player returns to competition before the injury has healed), the damage may become chronic.

RESEARCH AND EXERCISE TESTING

Physical educators occasionally conduct graded exercise tests on adults for determining cardiorespiratory endurance in order to prescribe training intensities, to motivate participants, to measure the results of training, or to evaluate the effects of various modalities. These tests are usually conducted by well-qualified physical educators who possess a Ph.D. and who have been specially trained to conduct the tests in well-equipped physical fitness laboratories. These laboratories are equipped with ECG machines, gas analyzers, treadmills, and equipment seldom seen in physicians' offices.

Physical educators should only administer tests for which they are well qualified and even then under at least indirect supervision of a qualified physician. Legal risks and responsibilities are inherent in graded testing programs, and physical educators and exercise technicians should be aware of these risks.

A physical educator who performs an exercise test in a negligent manner may be liable to the participant or family members in the event of injury or death. If the examiner does not perform his duties according to commonly accepted standards, or if he fails to exercise due care, and if such failure is the proximate cause of injury or death, he may be declared negligent.

The Technical Group on Exercise Electrocardiography surveyed the procedures, safety, and litigation involved in approximately 170,000 exercise tests conducted primarily by physicians.[22] Of this total of 170,000 tests, only one resulted in legal action. Nevertheless, those administering exercise tests should observe the precautions described in the following discussion, since the incidence of suits may increase as it has in other areas.

Because of their contribution to public health and contributions to the advancement of human knowledge, these tests *should* be conducted. But

---

[22]P. Rochmes and H. Blackburn, "Exercise Tests: A Survey of Procedures, Safety, and Litigation Experiences in Approximately 170,000 Tests," *Journal of the American Medical Association*, 217:8 (1971), pp. 1061–66.

physical educators must know and follow the procedures necessary to avoid or minimize liability.

As Herbert and Herbert point out, if an examinee suffers a cardiovascular accident during an exercise test, the physical educator has from a legal standpoint proximately caused the injury if he failed to screen the individual or to obtain a medical evaluation.[23] These authors go on to state: "Other procedural omissions which might hypothetically lead to a legal determination of negligence include failure to adequately monitor the ECG, blood pressure, feeling and symptoms of effort, fatigue or distress, and other parameters deemed necessary for a safe test."

Before administering a test, a medical history, a twelve-lead resting ECG, and a blood pressure reading should be secured. Contraindications for administration of a stress test for adults are:

1. Unstable S-T segments and serious arrhythmia in the resting ECG.
2. Blood pressure of 160/95 or 200/110.
3. Extreme obesity.
4. Age above 30−40 (unless a physician is present to give approval).
5. Lack of a signed consent form.

The participant should be fully informed of, and be capable of understanding, all risks and dangers inherent in the test before being asked to sign a consent form. It would also be highly desirable to secure written consent from the subject's spouse and the attending physician. The subject's written consent imtroduces the legal element of assumption of risk, although it does not relieve the examiner of liability if it can be shown that he was negligent. If contraindications become manifest during a test, the examiner must stop the proceeding.

Federal statute 45 C.F.R. 46 protects the rights of human subjects "at risk" in experiments, demonstration projects, teaching programs, and evaluations. This statute requires not only informed consent of participants, but also the approval of an authorized institutional review board. This statute is monitored by the Department of Education, which may impose heavy fines and deny or withdraw federal grants or contracts from institutions that do not comply.

A human subject is "at risk" when exposed to the possibility of injury, including physical, psychological, or social injury. It is the duty of the institutional review board to:

1. Determine whether the risks are greater than the benefits and significance of the research.
2. Ensure that the rights and welfare of the subjects are protected.

---

[23]W.G. Herbert and D.R. Herbert, "Exercise Testing in Adults," *Journal of Physical Education and Recreation*, June 1975, pp. 17−19.

3. Assure that legally effective informed consent is secured.
4. Continue review of the project.
5. Ensure that risks to pregnant women and fetuses are avoided.

Informed Consent

The American College of Sports Medicine (ACSM) is the foremost association in the United States involved in sports and physical education research. The association is composed of physicians involved in sports medicine, research scientists in physical education, physiologists, and athletic trainers. From time to time, as a need is indicated, the association disseminates policy statements on research and training procedures. In their policy statement on human subjects and informed consent, the ACSM recommended that the following items be included in an informed consent form, as appropriate to a particular project:

1. A general statement of the background of the project and the project objectives.
2. A fair explanation of the procedures to be followed and their purposes, identification of any procedures that are experimental, and description of any and all risks attendant to the procedures.
3. A description of any benefits reasonably to be expected and, in the case of treatment, disclosure of any appropriate alternative procedures that might be advantageous to the subject.
4. An offer to answer any queries of the subject concerning procedures or other aspects of the project.
5. An instruction that the subject is free to withdraw consent and to discontinue participation in the project or activity at any time without prejudice to the subject.
6. An instruction that in the case of questionnaires and interviews, the subject is free to deny answer to specific items or questions.
7. An instruction that if services or treatment are involved in the setting or context of the project, they will be neither enhanced nor diminished as a result of the subject's decision to volunteer participation in the project.
8. An explanation of the procedures to be taken to ensure the confidentiality of the data and information to be derived from the subject. If subjects are to be identified by name in written documentation, permission for this should be included in the informed consent form or obtained in writing at a later date.

Further, if the subject is to be videotaped or photographed in any manner, the ACSM states that not only must the subject be informed of this, but he must also be advised as to who will have custody of such videotapes or photographs, who will have access to them, and what will be done with them upon completion of the study. The association goes on to say that the document must not contain a waiver of legal rights that releases, or appears to release, the investigator, project director, or institution from liability.

The ACSM editorial board expects physicians to comply with the principles set forth in the Declaration of Helsinki of the World Medical Association and in the case of psychological research with the principles established by the American Psychological Association (as stated in the publication *Ethical Principles in the Conduct of Research with Human Subjects*).

Need for Graduate Education

Physical education research has become increasingly important in today's world. To be sure that people, including medical personnel, understand the importance of physical education research, an educational program is appropriate.

For example, consider the value of research on human stress. The involvement of medical personnel and others in publishing results of such testing can help to minimize the potential risk to those in stressful situations. Such collaboration of journalists, athletic researchers, and medical personnel can lead to a better understanding of the role of exercise in health.

Anabolic and Androgenic Steroids

The American College of Sports Medicine has also issued a position statement on the use and abuse of anabolic and androgenic steroids in sports, based on a comprehensive survey and analysis of studies made throughout the world in the fields of medicine, physiology, endocrinology, and physical education. The association found that although positive effects of the use of testosterone-like synthetic drugs may sometimes occur because persons are led to expect such changes (the "placebo effect"), repeated experiments fail to support any initial positive effects.

In a summary of their survey, the editors of the ACSM's *Journal of Medicine and Science in Sports and Exercise* report that: (1) alterations of normal liver function have been found in eighty percent of one series of sixty-nine patients treated with C17-alkylated testosterone derivatives (oral anabolic-androgenic steroids); (2) five reports document the occurrence of peliosis hepatitis in seventeen patients treated with C17-alkylated androgenic steroids, and that seven of these patients died of liver failure; (3) thirteen patients taking C17-alkylated androgenic steroids developed hepato-cellular carcinoma.[24]

Studies have shown that administration of anabolic (tissue building) and androgenic (development of male secondary sex characteristics) steroids often reduces the output of testosterone and gonadotropins while reducing

---

[24]*Journal of Medicine & Science in Sports and Exercise,* Spring 1978, pp. 50– 52.

spermatogenesis in males. Administered to females (particularly those who are prepubertal or still growing), these steroids cause masculinization such as hirsutism, voice changes, and enlargement of the clitoris, as well as other symptoms such as acne, disruption of the normal growth pattern, and interference with the menstrual cycle.

These findings led the ACSM to take the following position:

1. The administration of anabolic-androgenic steroids to healthy humans below age fifty in medically approved therapeutic doses often does not of itself bring about any significant improvements in strength, aerobic endurance, lean body mass, or body weight.
2. There is no conclusive scientific evidence that extremely large doses of anabolic-androgenic steroids either aid or hinder athletic performance.
3. The prolonged use of oral anabolic-androgenic steroids (C17-alkylated derivatives of testosterone) has resulted in liver disorders in some persons. Some of these disorders are apparently reversible with the cessation of drug usage, but others are not.
4. The administration of anabolic-androgenic steroids to male humans may result in a decrease in testicular size and function and a decrease in sperm production. Although these effects appear to be reversible when small doses of steroids are used for short periods of time, the reversibility of the effects of large doses over long periods of time by humans are unknown. Use of anabolic steroids by females, particularly those who are prepubertal, is dangerous. Side effects include masculinization, disruption of normal growth, voice change, acne, hirsutism, and enlargement of the clitoris. It is suspected that use of anabolic steroids by females will detrimentally influence the reproductive function. . . .
5. Serious and continuing efforts should be made to educate male and female athletes, coaches, physical educators, physicians, trainers, and the general public regarding the inconsistent effects of anabolic-androgenic steroids on improvement of human physical performance and the potential dangers of taking certain forms of these substances, especially in large doses, for prolonged periods.

Physical Education Classes

Numerous court cases have arisen from issues and incidents involving physical education classes. The following guidelines summarize some of the more significant court rulings in such cases.

1. For reasons of illness or injury, students may receive permission to substitute other courses for physical education requirements and may not be denied graduation as a result.
2. Grades should not be determined exclusively on such subjective criteria as effort, motivation, or clothing worn to class. There must be a real

relationship between the objectives of the course and the evaluation and testing measures used.

3. Efforts to employ a teacher to instruct students of the same sex will be ruled discriminatory in court. Seniority lists, career ladders, and tenure systems must be free of sex bias.

4. When student enrollment drops significantly, courts will uphold the school board when it releases unneeded teachers. However, the courts usually recommend that the school board endeavor to use current personnel if possible.

5. In the area of attire and appearance of teachers, the courts give greater weight to the interest of the public than to the desires of the teacher. Courts generally reason that the school board has the right to determine whether a teacher's style of dress or hair length is detrimental to the educational process.

6. School boards may assign teachers reasonable extracurricular duties as part of their regular duties. If teachers refuse to perform such extra duties (such as supervision), school boards may dismiss these teachers and the courts will support the school board.

7. Teachers who leave classes unattended place themselves in jeopardy. A claim of negligent supervision was made when a student was injured while the teacher attended a required meeting, leaving the class in the charge of another instructor who had a class at the same time. In another case, a teacher left the class for only a matter of minutes and was in an adjoining room when an injury occurred.

   In reaching a decision, the court will consider the age of the students left unsupervised, the reason for the teacher's absence, and the length of the teacher's absence. The younger the students, the higher the degree of supervision expected by the courts.

   When an injury occurs in a physical education class, teachers face a dilemma. Instinctively they want to take the injured student for medical help. But when they do so, they leave the class unsupervised, and another injury may occur during the teacher's absence. Such a case occurred when the teacher took an injured student to the school infirmary and another student in the class was injured while the teacher was away. The lawsuit culminated in an award of $335,140 to the plaintiff. (*Miller* v. *Cloidt and the Board of Education of Borough of Chatham*, Docket No. L7241 62 [N.J.Super. 1964].)

8. Claims have been made against school administrators for failure to arrange adequate supervision of school premises, for failing to formulate rules and regulations for the safety of students, and for failing to ensure that such rules are enforced. The most heavily litigated area regarding school premises is the playground. Such litigation is initiated whether the injury occurred during class, before class, after class dismissal, after school, or during vacation periods. For this reason, school administrators must meticulously promulgate rules and regulations for use of play-

ground equipment. (Rules for the use of most playground equipment can be found in Chapter 5.)

Almost invariably, courts have found schools liable when the playground equipment was shown to be defective. Thus all items of playground equipment must be regularly inspected and carefully maintained.

9. Teachers must provide instruction in safety procedures for the activities they teach, and the activities must be taught in a safe manner. In soccer, for example, students should be taught to play the ball and to avoid collisions with opponents. In gymnastics, tumbling, trampoline, diving, and similar activities, skills should be taught according to a progressive order of difficulty. Where it can be shown that instructors failed to follow these precepts, the courts are more likely to rule in favor of the plaintiff.

Intramural Programs

Intramural programs serve large numbers of students, but usually only one faculty member serves as intramural director (although he may have a few paid student assistants). At a large university, on any school day or evening, there may be any number of team games in progress on the various fields and in the gymnasium, field house, swimming pool, wrestling room, handball or squash courts, and weight training room.

It is obviously impossible for an intramural director to provide on-site supervision at all these locations at the same time. Adequate supervision would mean that the intramural program be limited to no more than one game or event at any one time. In most cases, this would mean cutting the program by some ninety percent, without a corresponding cut in expenses, and the students would be denied worthwhile and healthful activities.

To somewhat alleviate this supervision problem, the incidence of injuries in intramural programs can be reduced through effective administrative procedures.

The liability of program administrators falls into three general categories that pertain to the type of person injured. These legal categories have been discussed in other sections but are redefined here for the convenience of the reader.

The first category of liability concerns the *trespasser*. This person has no affiliation with the activity and, consequently, there is no administrative liability in the event of injury. An example would be a high school student using the college weight training facilities in violation of posted signs indicating that the facility is for the exclusive use of the college's students.

The next level of liability arises with the *licensee*. The licensee is one who participates on property made available and who has permission to use the property. A participant in a corecreational program is a licensee. In this case, there is limited administrative liability.

The highest level of administrative liability involves the *invitee*. This is a person who is on the property for business for which the property is established. Participants in intramural programs are invitees because they have paid a fee in the form of tuition, lodging, or athletic fees.

The following are examples of administrative negligence that can lead to declarations of liability in the event of injury.

1. The use of uncertified lifeguards.
2. Fencing programs conducted without adequate protective equipment.
3. Use of gymnastic equipment without adequate mats.
4. Overcrowding of racket sports facilities (or any other facilities).
5. Performance on the trampoline without a minimum of four spotters.
6. Javelin, discus, or shot putting without safeguards to prevent people from wandering into the path of the projectiles.

Guidelines for Intramural Directors

The following guidelines will help to decrease the incidence of injuries in intramural programs.

1. Offer only those sports or activities for which adequate protective equipment and safe facilities can be provided.
2. Encourage intramural participants to develop the level of physical fitness and skill, as well as the attitudes, necessary to avoid injury.
3. Check playing areas for slippery conditions, holes, stones, glass, and projections into the field of play.
4. Make certain that playing areas are clearly marked.
5. Provide adequate playing space or modify the rules so that the games will conform to the space available. (Basketball courts with inadequate space at the ends and sides are particular hazards for participants.)
6. Inspect facilities regularly and in a systematic fashion.
7. Immediately eliminate any hazards detected.
8. Lock up gymnastic equipment when supervised activities are not in progress. If there is a separate room for gymnastics, lock this room when unsupervised.
9. Do not leave idle equipment near the area of play.
10. Consistently enforce all safety rules and regulations.
11. Do not permit injured players to continue play.
12. Do not permit the use of cast-off varsity equipment.
13. Use the most competent and alert officials possible. Encourage officials to employ a "fast" whistle.
14. Establish definite procedures to be followed in the event of an injury. Mimeograph these procedures, distribute them to key people in the program, and post them in prominent places in the various intramural areas.

15. Have telephones installed near the various playing areas so that first aid squads and medical aid can be summoned quickly.
16. With the aid of the school physicians, make a list of all injuries that require transportation to a hospital. This list should include head, neck, and spinal injuries, suspected fractures, heat exhaustion, and any others the school physician believes should be included.
17. Keep a well-stocked first aid kit at the site of all intramural activities.
18. Conduct an ongoing program to educate intramural participants in the rules for personal safety and the development of safety habits. This can be accomplished through the use of posters, lectures, slogans, and instructions in an intramural handbook.
19. Create an intern program in which physical education students can acquire work-related experience. If finances preclude the use of teachers or coaches, use qualified physical education interns for supervision of intramural activities.

OFF-CAMPUS PROGRAMS

The number and variety of off-campus physical education courses have increased in recent years. Off-campus courses such as skiing, horseback riding, and bowling provide students with opportunities to use facilities and benefit from instruction often not available on-campus.

One reason for the growth of these courses is a movement away from a general studies requirement in physical education and toward elective courses. When physical education becomes elective, the department must compete more vigorously for students; one way of attracting students in greater numbers is to offer courses in more popular activities. Other reasons include the increased attention to lifetime sports, an insistence upon more flexible scheduling patterns, and a general upgrading of the quality of facilities and instruction offered by private businesses.

But even if an activity is conducted on privately owned facilities and taught by instructors in the employ of a private enterprise, this does not absolve the physical educator and the institution of legal liability in the event of student injury. In some respects, the legal hazards are greater than in courses conducted on-campus. Off-campus courses must be conducted by the institution in a responsible manner, such that the safety of the student is protected, even though the institution's sphere of control is obviously more restricted.

As with on-campus courses, the physical educator must be shown to have been negligent relative to an injury in an off-campus course. This means that the administrator failed to behave in a reasonably prudent manner, as judged by standards of professional conduct. An injury does not result in automatic declaration of liability. Colleges and schools are not insurers of student safety, and college students are expected to exercise the same judgment and discretion as adults in caring for their own safety.

There are a number of *types of off-campus programs.* In one type, the facilities of a private enterprise are used while the instruction is provided by the regular faculty. In this case, details of the arrangement between the school and the business should be in writing. If both have an insurance policy, the written agreement should indicate whose insurance will cover students taking the course, although this does not bind the insurance company (which is not a party to the agreement).

By contract, you may agree to be responsible, but that does not enlarge your insurance policy to cover the new, extended liability that you, alone, have agreed to assume. In such a case, it is better not to sign such a contract, whether it be a hold-harmless or an agreement.

Such agreements should also indicate: (1) dates, times, and location of classes; (2) protective equipment to be provided; (3) quality of the equipment; (4) fee for use of the facility and its manner of collection; and (5) general liability coverages, including the underwriter, agent, amount, dates of expiration, and procedures for filing claims.[25]

It is the responsibility of the physical education department to exercise reasonable prudence in the selection of the site. When selecting a site for off-campus programs, the physical education department should consider: (1) safety of the route to the site; (2) design and maintenance of the facility; (3) size of the area; (4) adequacy of supervision; (5) availability of protective devices; and (6) observance of safety procedures. If the physical education department provides transportation to the facility, the laws regarding transportation of students must be observed (see Chapter 11).

A second type of off-campus arrangement is one in which the private enterprise provides both the facility and the instruction, but the faculty member is present at the site of instruction. In this case, all the admonitions presented above apply. In addition, the quality of instruction and the qualifications of the instructor must be assessed. The instructor must qualify for the title of specialist, and he must be certified (if there is a certification program in the subject). The physical education department in cooperation with the specialist must develop a course outline, which should indicate prerequisites for the course (including requirements for physical examinations), fees to be charged, course objectives, course activities, grading procedures, and rules for student behavior.

A third type of arrangement is called *contracting,* in which there is no faculty member present at the facility on a regular basis. Contracting is a relatively new educational method in which the student signs a contract with the teacher and the school to carry on a program of physical activity on an independent basis. Academic credit is awarded upon completion of the contract. The program may be conducted either on- or off-campus. Together, the student and instructor determine reasonable goals, and the student progresses at his own pace.

---

[25]Don E. Arnold, "Legal Aspects of Off-Campus Physical Education Programs," *Journal of Health, Physical Education, and Recreation,* April 1979, pp. 21–23.

The physical education department prepares student contracts, which state the course title, outline the subject matter, list course objectives in terms of observable behavior, describe course activities, and list rules and regulations. The contract should also include the cost to students, monitoring procedures, dates, times, and locations for periodic assessments of pupil progress. They should also describe procedures and specific criteria to be used in determining a final grade and specify the duration of the contract and any mutually agreed-upon conditions under which the contract should be negotiated.[26]

Outside agencies such as scuba schools, ski slopes, riding academies, and golf courses often provide both the facilities and the instruction, particularly when the educational institution has neither a facility of its own nor skilled and knowledgeable instructors. Where private agencies are used, the school administration should investigate and approve the agency and require periodic inspection of both its personnel and its facilities. An attorney should be employed to prepare a contract with the agency, and responsibility for liability should be placed on the agency rather than the school. The agency is responsible for its conduct when it is remunerated for its services, since it then assumes a proprietary function. A check should also be made with the school's insurance agent regarding adequacy of coverage.

The following guidelines apply to physical education departments that engage in contracting.

1. Contracts should include:
   a. A statement of course objectives.
   b. The evaluative criteria to be utilized and the date and location of tests of student progress.
   c. A description of the activity.
   d. The address of the site where instruction is to take place.
   e. The facilities and equipment available and a list of the equipment needed by students.
   f. A list of the instructional personnel and their qualifications.
2. The contract should be developed, monitored, and verified by a certified physical education teacher.
3. The contract should be signed by the student, by his parent or guardian, and by the school district or college representative.
4. The contract should include an estimate of any charges to the student for insurance and liability coverage.
5. It is advisable to permit only students with demonstrated responsibility to participate in contracting programs.
6. The physical educator should where possible do an on-site inspection of the facility.
7. The agency should understand that it is responsible and liable for the safe operation of the program.

---

[26]Ibid., p. 23.

8. The teacher and the school must carry adequate liability insurance.

9. Students should not be permitted to earn more than twenty percent of their required credits through contracting.

10. Students and their parents should sign permission slips, waivers, or release forms, even though these provide little legal protection. (A contract signed by a minor is legally worthless, as is a permission slip or waiver signed by the student. A minor may still initiate a lawsuit for medical expenses, loss in earning capacity, and for pain and suffering. And the amount awarded can appear astronomical. The minor can sue even though the parent signed the waiver, since the parent cannot legally waive liability for negligence that results in injury to a minor child. In such a case, however, the parent would probably relinquish the right to recover damages.)

11. School authorities should check with their insurance company to determine whether off-campus activities are covered.

/ 8 /

Safety in Outdoor Activities

CAMPING

Approximately one out of every six school children attends a summer camp each year. Approximately 16,000 organized camps, as well as the National Park Service, serve a large share of the 5–6 million people who go camping each year. Many of these people live in cities and are ill-prepared to cope with outdoor life.

Certain trends in organized camping have added to safety problems. First, camps are accepting younger children (sometimes as young as six), who require closer supervision. Further, there is an increasing number of unqualified camp operators, which increases the probability of errors in safeguarding the campers. Also, camps have greatly increased the number of campers that they serve, and the greater the number of campers, the greater the hazards. Finally, an increasing number of camps serve the handicapped, who are more susceptible to injuries and thus require closer supervision.

In view of the large number of campers, the great potential for injury to young campers, the young age of many of the counselors, and the inexperience of some camp owners and directors, it is surprising that the incidence of lawsuits brought against camps is not greater. This situation is not likely to continue, however.

School camps are legally required to meet the same obligations as schools. In the case of *Incorporated Village of Brookville* v. *Paulgene Realty Corporation* (200 NYS 2d 126 [1960]), the court stated: "If a so-called camp gets to the point where it is engaged exclusively in education, it becomes a

217

school no matter what appellation you choose. . . ." The court established that this day camp constituted a school in the traditional sense because it met the three criteria generally associated with schools: there were a curriculum, a qualified staff, and physical facilities to meet educational objectives.

Camp activities invariably include instruction and participation in sports and aquatic activities. Thus camp counselors, directors, and owners must be knowledgeable regarding safety procedures. (Safety procedures in sports and aquatics have already been discussed in Chapters 5 and 7. Readers involved in camping are advised to study these sections well.)

Counselor Training

Before campers arrive, the director should call a meeting of all counselors to present plans for camp safety and sanitation. These should include:

1. Safety procedures and methods of instructing campers in safety in the arts and crafts shop, on the waterfront, during overnight hikes, in sports and athletics, at campfires, in the stables, on riding trails, and around the camp in general.
2. The adequate dissemination of safety information, that is, safety instruction by means of bulletin boards, letters to parents, and camp newsletters.
3. Regular and complete safety inspections of camp facilities and equipment, as well as procedures to be followed for correction of any hazards discovered.
4. Safety procedures to be followed on camp buses.
5. Procedures for storage and use of gasoline and other flammable materials. Campers should not be permitted to use these materials. Flammable materials should be stored in a fireproof, vented storage place, and the key should be kept in the possession of one person only, who should be held responsible.
6. For day camps that pick up campers in the morning and return them home at the end of the day, drivers should be given routes, safety regulations, procedures to be followed in the event of an emergency, and other relevant information. Only qualified adult drivers should be used. Adequate liability insurance should be in force.

Before taking campers on overnight hikes, the following should be checked: the availability of a telephone within a reasonable distance; adequacy of first aid equipment; quality and quantity of food and water; health status of the campers; equipment belonging to the campers; and provision of special instructions for campers.

Safe campgrounds have pathways free of exposed roots and rocks that are adequately illuminated and have fire extinguishers strategically placed and in operating condition. Poison ivy, poison oak, tin cans, glass, and other hazardous objects have been removed, and craft tools and flammable materials are safely stored. A safe camp also will develop and enforce a safety code, will have sufficient bulletin boards on which safety rules and regulations can be posted, will use only qualified adult drivers for camp buses, and will carry liability insurance. A safe camp will require a health examination and parent statements before admitting a child, in order to be informed of any handicaps such as cardiac conditions, diabetes, asthma, epilepsy, enuresis, sleepwalking, or emotional disorders.

In a safe camp, campers are educated in safety procedures. Campers should be instructed to drink and eat only water and food approved by the camp staff. They should be taught to identify and avoid poisonous plants, snakes, dangerous animals, and insects. They should receive instruction in first aid procedures for common emergencies. Instruction should be given in the safe use of knives, axes, hatchets, saws, rowboats, canoes, camp tools, craft tools, riding equipment, and any other equipment that they might use. Campers should be taught safe methods for building and controlling fires for both cooking and heat. When walking on a highway at night, they should be required to walk on the extreme left, to carry a flashlight, and to wear something white.

The possibility of a serious fire at camp requires consideration, and plans for such a possibility should be made. Everyone should know his job. Fire drills should be organized and practiced. Rules concerning smoking and the use of matches should be rigidly enforced.

Planning Hikes

Hikes should be well planned. Following are several considerations when planning a hike:

1. Make certain that the hiking trail is safe. If none of the counselors has been over the trail, it would be well to have one survey the trail before the hike to ensure that there are no poisonous plants or dangerous holes.
2. Permit only those who are in adequate physical condition to go on the hike.
3. The hike will be more enjoyable if the group is composed of campers who are of similar age, physical capacity, and interests.
4. Campers should be properly equipped for the hike. They should have comfortable, sturdy shoes, two pairs of woolen socks, a raincoat, poncho, flashlight, matches, axe, compass, first aid kit, snakebite kit, blanket, and canteen, and other clothing appropriate to the conditions.
5. First aid kits should include gauze, antiseptic, bandaids, adhesive tape, triangular bandages, tourniquet, aromatic spirits of ammonia, scissors, scalpel, safety pins, and an ointment for poison ivy and burns. Halazone

tablets to purify water should be included if the water supply is questionable.

6. Counselors should carry all necessary maps and watches.
7. A contingency plan in the event of a camper becoming lost should be explained to the hikers previous to the hike. Hikers should be instructed to remain in one place if they become lost, to conserve their food and energy, to seek or build a shelter, and to build two smoke signal fires (since two columns of smoke are universally recognized as a distress signal). An alternative plan is to have fast hikers endeavor to find the home camp or a predesignated point, such as a lake or mountain, until nightfall and then to "hole up" and wait.
8. Hikers who have not had an immunization dose of tetanus toxoid should receive one. If any hiker suffers a cut, it should be treated properly and the hiker should receive a booster shot.

During the hike, the following safety procedures should be observed:

1. Hikers should be discouraged from wandering away from the group.
2. One counselor should be in the lead, while another brings up the rear. There should be one counselor for every six to twelve campers, depending upon their age.
3. Roll calls should be taken periodically, and a buddy system should be used.
4. When ascending rocky hills, the zigzag method should be used, but in such a manner that rocks do not roll down on those below. The zig should not be made until all hikers have completed the zag.
5. When walking on the highway, hikers should walk on the left side of the road in order to face oncoming traffic.
6. Avoid walking on the highway after dark. If this is necessary, hikers should wear something white and should carry a flashlight.
7. If hikers will be in the hot sun for prolonged periods, they should wear a light-colored, brimmed hat.
8. Pure water should be carried.
9. Hikers should be able to identify poison ivy, poison oak, and poison sumac.

Fire Hazards

If a one-floor dwelling (bunk or cabin) is used, there should be two exits. In a multi-level unit, there should be fire escapes and fire alarms. Most fire deaths occur in buildings, and people die because they don't know how to get out of the building. Fire drills are a necessity. Planned fire drills should be carried out when campers are in their bunks, in dining halls, and at sports and craft activities.

Counselors engaged in woodworking should be made aware of the fire hazard created by wood and paint dust. The careful handling of varnishes, which are highly flammable, should be learned by campers. Whenever possible, the woodworking and finishing should be done out of doors. If it must be done indoors, the work area should be well ventilated and located away from open flames.

Campers are often careless with electrical appliances. Cautions to be observed in this regard are:

1. Never allow a camper to use an electrical appliance while wearing a wet bathing suit.
2. Appliances such as irons, hair dryers, radios, stereos, and electric shavers should always be disconnected when not in use.
3. Never overload an electrical circuit.

The campfire, one of the most enjoyable camp events, can become an unpleasant experience. Campfires should be supervised at all times. Campfires can be dangerous under certain circumstances, such as:

1. Smoldering, unattended campfires.
2. Careless use of matches.
3. Lack of fire extinguishers.

Finally, campers should be aware of the danger posed by smoldering cigarettes. Many camps only allow counselors to smoke off duty and out of doors.

Missing Persons

Whether it is a camper or staff member, a missing person presents an emergency situation that must be dealt with immediately and systematically. When an individual is missing, a search should be made of the missing person's living area and all special camp areas such as those for swimming, boating, arts and crafts, etc. If the individual was last seen at the waterfront, the fire department or a rescue squad should be called while the search continues. Parents or family of those missing should be notified by the camp director when appropriate. To minimize the possibility of missing persons:

1. Have a bed check each night.
2. Hold a roll call each morning.
3. Use the buddy system during swimming, hiking, and other group activities.

Health Facilities and Supervision

Another aspect of camp safety is adequate health facilities and supervision. The camp infirmary should be well equipped. A separate infirmary area should be provided for those who are ill or injured. Supplies and equipment recommended by a physician should be purchased, and the premises should include provisions for hot water. There should be at least one bed in the infirmary for every 10–15 campers. There should also be at least one isolation bed, preferably in a separate room.

Some lights should be kept on in the infirmary after dusk for those campers or staff needing emergency care during the night.

A permanent record of all treatment should be maintained by the health staff, which should include a licensed physician and/or a registered nurse. Infirmaries should be staffed twenty-four hours a day.

The infirmary should have the telephone number of the poison control center in the area. There are two hundred such centers in the country, which are open twenty-four hours a day and which have readily available information regarding the toxicity of many commercial products. If the nature of the poison is unknown, the center can provide expertise for identification. Emergency rooms of large hospitals also serve as poison control centers.

The medical staff, through health supervision, can help maintain camp safety and sanitary conditions through routine checks of bunks, the kitchen, eating areas, washrooms, etc.

Camp Transportation

Many camps own and operate their own buses. They may also rent vehicles from local bus companies. Transporting campers in trucks is dangerous and should be avoided. To minimize danger, all camp staff should be instructed in transportation safety as part of their orientation. The staff can then convey this vital information to the campers during the season. (See Chapter 11 for a full discussion of transportation.)

General Safety Rules

Injuries are possible in almost any camp activity, but the following rules may be applied to all camp activities:

1. *Proper instruction.* Basic skills involved in activities should be thoroughly understood by beginners before the activity is attempted. Safety should be taught, not as an adjunct to the activity, but as an integral part of it.
2. *Proper equipment.* Safe equipment, adapted to the activity, is essential. Makeshift equipment causes accidents.
3. *Awareness of limits.* Counselors should know their own physical limits in terms of strength, state of health, and skill. They should also know the limits of the campers under their supervision. Counselors should be aware of campers' emotional limits. For example, what are their attitudes toward the activity at hand: fear, doubt, or uncertainty? Physical and emotional limits cannot be exceeded without danger.

4. *Regulations*. Counselors should understand the need for strict enforcement of regulations. Campers should be guided toward the observance of regulations through an understanding that safety rules are for their own protection.
5. *Adequate facilities*. Facilities should be safety-approved for the intended activity. An unsafe backstop on a rifle range, or an improperly laid out archery range, pose hazards for individuals using the facilities and for bystanders.

On the subject of riflery, which is offered at many camps, a check of local ordinances should be made, and children should be taught the basic safety rules for carrying and using a gun. Even when unloaded, the rifle should be carried with the muzzle held upright and the bolt in the open position.

Many camps also offer bicycling, with campers riding with counselors on trips of various lengths. The bicyclist must behave as though he were driving a car. He must be expected to control the speed and direction of his bicycle at all times and must observe many of the precautions applicable to an automobile. Bicycles should be equipped with safety equipment such as a headlight, tail reflector, horn, and good brakes. In general, the bicycle should be in good working condition. The speed at which a camper may ride depends upon the conditions of the road and the weather.

Camp Safety Legislation

Senator Abraham Ribicoff (D. Connecticut) introduced a bill (S. 583) to ensure camper safety by establishing federal standards for safe camp operation. The bill also provided federal funds and technical assistance to help states implement safety standards. The bill required camp operators to provide safe and healthful conditions, facilities, and equipment, as well as adequate and qualified instruction and supervision of camp activities.

The bill provided for establishment of an Office of Youth Camp Safety within the Department of Education, and provided for grants and consultative services to be made available to the states to encourage them to develop and implement safety standards. Camp operators could be fined for failure to correct violations. Camps covered by the legislation included residential, day, primitive, short-term group, troop, travel, trip, and federal recreation youth camps on public or private land. (A copy of this bill is included in the Appendix.)

AUTO CAMPING

Private, state, and national parks have greatly increased in number and are attracting millions of auto campers each year. These parks have allowed many families to visit distant points of interest by virtue of the savings in motel, hotel, and restaurant bills. Stack and Elkow recommend the following procedures for auto camping:[1]

1. Carefully plan travel time between campsites to avoid fatigue and worry.
2. Carefully follow the rules and regulations of each camping area.
3. Camp only in designated areas.
4. Use fire with a purpose — to warm or to cook. To prevent forest fires, put out all fires when not needed.
5. Supervise young children within the camp area to prevent their becoming lost.
6. Adapt to animal and plant life: neither tease nor feed animals; observe posted regulations; be aware of hazards such as snakes, poison ivy, and the many other dangers of outdoor life.
7. Consume only approved drinking water.
8. Swim only in safe areas, observing rules and regulations for safe swimming.
9. Keep first aid equipment in top condition.
10. Secure needed immunizations in advance of camping (tetanus, typhoid, etc.).
11. Treat all injuries and illnesses promptly. (The threat of tetanus from soil-contaminated wounds is always present.)
12. Use axes and knives only for the purposes for which they are intended.
13. Secure advice from qualified persons in areas where you do not possess adequate skills or knowledge.

FISHING

Some 34 million fishermen spend $2.5 billion annually in the United States on fishing equipment. These data imply that there are a lot of fishing enthusiasts.

A few of these fishermen drown, and almost all suffer injuries such as falls; bites and stings of animals, fish, and insects; cuts and lacerations from gear; burns from the sun, fires, cooking stoves, or lanterns; and puncture wounds from hooks.

Many fishermen are hooked during casting. The probability of being hooked or hooking others can be decreased by looking to the rear before casting, keeping a safe distance from those about to cast, wearing a wide-brimmed hat, and learning the proper way to remove a hook from a fish (for example, immobilizing a large fish before attempting to remove the hook).

Fishermen should learn to swim before going out in a boat. The boat should not be taken out when the weather is inclement or if it is threatening. If the weather turns bad when the fisherman is already out, he should immediately seek the nearest safe harbor.

---

[1]Herbert J. Stack and J. Duke Elkow, *Education for Safe Living,* 4th ed. (Englewood Cliffs, N.J.: Prentice-Hall, Inc., 1966), pp. 94–95. Reprinted with permission of Prentice-Hall, Inc.

BOATING AND CANOEING

Boating and canoeing are ever gaining in popularity. Many fishermen use rowboats on small lakes, and more and more people are discovering the joys of canoeing. Thus younger students and campers should learn how to row or paddle a boat, since it is unlikely that they will be taught elsewhere.

With regard to safety, the boat and oars should be in good condition. Rowboats should be equipped with pin-type oarlocks. Boating and canoeing should be permitted at camps only during scheduled times when a lifeguard is on duty. Campers should not be permitted to go out alone in a rowboat or canoe until they have demonstrated the skills to handle an emergency. Only qualified swimmers should be permitted rowing and canoeing privileges when a lifeguard is not on duty. Both rowing and canoeing should be prohibited when a storm threatens.

Canoeists should be able to swim for at least ten minutes while fully clothed; all others should wear approved life jackets. All canoes should carry life preservers.

The lower the center of gravity in a canoe, the less likely it is to tip over. For this reason, canoes should be provided with thwarts, since the canoeist will then be required to sit or kneel on the bottom of the canoe. A low center of gravity is basic to all canoeing skills. Canoeists should master all of the following skills:

1. Exchanging paddling positions.
2. Reentering the canoe from deep water.
3. Reentering a swamped canoe.
4. Rescue of a swamped or capsized canoe.
5. Assisting a tired swimmer.
6. Assisting a tired swimmer into the canoe.

On canoe trips, someone qualified in senior life saving by the American Red Cross should be assigned for each ten canoeists. Only those who have demonstrated a satisfactory level of skill, knowledge, and endurance should be taken on the trip. Rubber boots or other heavy boots should not be worn in the canoe. A vessel for bailing should be placed in each canoe, and canoes should not be loaded beyond their capacities.

Canoeists should remain with capsized canoes and should know how to right them, how to remove the water, and how to reenter them. In the event of capsizing, weak swimmers can hold onto the canoe while the strong swimmers push it to shore. Canoes should never be towed behind a motorboat. Neither canoes nor boats should be allowed in a swimming area.

SKIN AND SCUBA DIVING

Skin and scuba diving have undergone dramatic growth in recent years. Some eight million people have experienced the fascination of skin diving.

Skin and scuba divers should complete a course of instruction before making their first dive. They should always dive with a partner with whom they have worked out a signal system. They should not dive when they are not feeling well or are fatigued and certainly not when they have a sore throat, cold, sinus infection, or ear infection. Divers should not eat or drink before diving and should particularly avoid gas-forming food and drink, since pressure at depth causes expansion of gases.

Anyone contemplating diving should first undergo a thorough physical examination. Divers should keep themselves in top physical condition. Moderation in speed of swimming, depth of dives, and time in the water should be exercised. Only approved and properly fitting equipment should be used.

Diving equipment should always be checked before diving. Divers should have a float on the surface and should take an inflatable float on the dive. Divers should avoid holding their breath during the last thirty feet of ascent, since this can rupture the air sacs and blood vessels of the lungs.

Gabrielson, an internationally recognized authority on aquatics, has presented the following safety rules and instructor guidelines:[2]

1. Know the movements of the water: tides, currents, and surf.
2. Know the type of bottom: mud, shell, rock, sand, or coral.
3. Know the depth of the water.
4. Know the storm characteristics of the area.
5. Always stay with a group, or at least one other person. Know where the others are at all times. Have a system of hand signals to be utilized if audibility is poor.
6. Before starting out, inspect all rubber fittings and safety equipment. A moment of time may well save a life.
7. Excessive shivering is a signal to stop diving. Cold water induces rapid fatigue, and the diver could become exhausted when he is far from the beach.
8. Be thoroughly familiar with the latest methods of artificial respiration.
9. Sound is magnified under water. A diver should always be aware of speeding power boats in a fishing area and should always look up before surfacing.

---

[2]M. Alexander Gabrielson, Betty Spears, and B.W. Gabrielson, *Aquatics Handbook*, 2nd ed. (Englewood Cliffs, N.J.: Prentice-Hall, Inc., 1968), p. 131. Reprinted by permission of Prentice-Hall, Inc.

Guidelines for Instructors

1. Be sure that facilities for the course are safe. Do not attempt to teach in open-water areas.
2. The first concern of the course should be safety.
3. Do not neglect theory in the course content. Design the course around the use of the equipment.

WATERFRONT CAMPS AND PUBLIC BEACHES

Many of the guidelines suggested for the design, operation, and regulation of swimming pools (Chapter 7) apply to waterfront camps and public beaches. Some additional considerations specific to these settings are offered in the following.

1. Consideration should be given to water quality when selecting a lake site for possible development of a waterfront camp or public beach. Water samples should be taken to the local health department for chemical and bacteriological analysis. If the body of water is not too large, chlorination may be possible.
2. The bottom of the swimming area and beach should be free of silt, algae, plants, stumps, and rocks. There should be no sudden drops or grade changes.
3. If water levels vary due to tides or rainfall and the swimming area is extended outward during periods of low water, swimmers may find themselves over sudden drop-offs, potholes, stumps, or other hazards that were not a factor before the area was extended. This should be considered when selecting a site for a waterfront camp or public beach.
4. The entire swimming area should be enclosed by a combination of docks and colored buoy lines. The greater the portion of the swimming area enclosed by docks, the greater the safety.
5. Docks, and especially diving platforms, should be assembled with bolts rather than nails. Docks and piers should be at least four feet wide.
6. Planks should be splinter-free and spaced one-half inch apart to permit drainage and ventilation.
7. Since creosoted lumber will "bleed" in hot weather, and because creosote can cause severe skin burns, creosoted lumber should not be used in the construction of docks and piers.
8. There should be a minimum of cross-bracing under piers and docks to minimize the possibility of swimmers being trapped underneath. Further, there should be an air space of at least one foot under a dock or pier.

9. Bathhouses should have adequate light and should be ventilated. The floors should be adequately drained and constructed of, or covered with, nonskid material.
10. The first aid room should be well supplied. Equipment should include a mechanical or manual resuscitator, since camps and public beaches are often located some distance from hospitals and fire departments.
11. All public beaches and camps with large waterfront areas should have a boat. A johnboat equipped with a small outboard motor is most practical for inland waters. For ocean waters, surfboats of the double-ended dory type are the most practical.
12. Torpedo buoys, heaving lines, ring buoys, surfboards, and grappling irons should be on hand.
13. At summer camps, classification tests should be utilized to determine the swimming areas in which campers are permitted. Before campers are allowed in deep water, they should be required to demonstrate an ability to swim twice the length of the swimming area and an ability to float and/or tread water for one minute.
14. If the director's cabin has a good view of the waterfront area, some protection is afforded during the night and at other periods when swimming instructors or lifeguards are not on duty.
15. It is standard practice to provide one lifeguard for every twenty campers during free swimming. A larger number of lifeguards should be provided for nonswimmers and beginners.
16. The swimming area should be divided into sections according to swimming ability. Campers should be restricted to the area for which they have passed the required test.
17. At large public beaches, lifeguards should be equipped with two-way radios to facilitate communication between the several lifeguard posts and headquarters. A portable, battery-powered megaphone is helpful to lifeguards when the noise level is high due to wind, surf, or large crowds.
18. Animals and pets should not be permitted on the beach.
19. Swimming instruction and other aquatic activities for groups should be conducted only with the written approval of the person in charge.
20. Swimming should be prohibited when a lifeguard is not on duty.

/ 9 /

First Aid and Athletic Training

Coaches and physical educators are expected by the courts to provide first aid treatment in life-threatening situations. However, they are not expected to possess the knowledge and skill of physicians and, in fact, are cautioned against exceeding the limits of first aid. The American Red Cross defines first aid as the immediate and temporary treatment given the victim of an accident or illness until the services of a physician can be secured. Coaches and physical educators must resist the temptation to go beyond these limits.

Previous sections defined *tort* as a legal wrong for which a court will provide a remedy in the form of damages. A legal wrong may result from an act of omission, in which the defendant failed to carry out a legal duty. It may also result from an act of commission, in which the defendant committed an act that is not legally his to perform. Failure by a teacher or coach to provide first aid could constitute an act of omission; exceeding the limits of first aid treatment could constitute an act of commission. The criterion for measuring the actions of a defendant is: were the actions those of a person of reasonable and ordinary prudence?

Final decisions regarding medical diagnosis are the exclusive domain of the physician. But, admittedly, it is often the case that the first aider must quickly evaluate the nature of a trauma or physiological problem before administering first aid. Obviously, the preceding two statements imply a fine line between recognition of an injury and its diagnosis. They also point out the advisability for coaches and physical educators, given an absence of an athletic trainer, nurse, or physician, to have undergone training in first aid.

Only 270 U.S. high schools, out of a total of 25,000, employ a certified athletic trainer. Others use student trainers, who must be closely supervised. The athletic trainer who holds certification in physical therapy is in stronger legal position with regard to limits of treatment, since he is trained in the use of various modalities.

Athletic trainers should never use equipment that they know to be dangerous or faulty. Conversely, they should never state that a piece of equipment is absolutely safe or foolproof because if its use leads to injury an implied warranty liability could result.

GAME INJURIES

The athletic trainer, coach, team physician, and athletic director should prepare a policy for handling injuries that occur during games and contests. This policy should be checked by the local district attorney's office to ensure that the policy complies with all legal requirements. The policy should be sound from both the therapeutic and legal standpoints. In the absence of a physician, the policy should call for at least the following:

1. Make an immediate preliminary examination to ascertain the type and extent of the injury.
2. If the injury is recognized as being beyond the scope of your ability, send for the physician immediately.
3. Give first aid if it is indicated.
4. Should the condition of the player be such that he requires removal from the area, determine whether he is in a condition that would warrant medical sanction before attempting to move him. If the player is unconscious or is unable to move under his own power with assistance, use a stretcher. The trainer and his assistants should know the proper methods of transporting injured persons.
5. For some contact sports, particularly football, an ambulance should be on call for all games. Some trainers feel that the presence of an ambulance on or near the field has a negative psychological effect on the players. Thus it is wise if the ambulance is available but out of view of both spectators and players. (The attendants should be inconspicuously seated where they can be summoned quickly.)
6. Use a standard accident report form upon which all pertinent information may be recorded (see Figure 9.1 for a sample form). Such a form should contain:
   a. Names, addresses, and telephone numbers of persons involved.
   b. Date, time, and place of the accident.
   c. Sport being played.
   d. Nature and extent of the injuries.
   e. Brief description of how the injuries occurred.
   f. Emergency procedures followed and final disposition of the injuries.
   g. Names, addresses, telephone numbers, and, if possible, signatures of at least two witnesses.

Figure 9.1

THE UNIVERSITY OF CONNECTICUT
School of Physical Education
Injury Report

Date _____

_____   _____
Student's Name   P. E. Class & Sec.

Was Injured _____ _____ _____
                    Date   Time   Place

While participating in: activity_____

during _____ class _____ intramurals_____ free play

other_____

Number of participants in the same activity was_____

Nature of Injury _____

_____

_____

Exact disposition of case: (First Aid Given _____)

_____

_____

_____

Witnesses (2) _____

                                              _____
                                              Instructor

Klafs and Arnheim offer the following suggestions for athletic trainers to avoid legal liability, while still protecting the health and welfare of student athletes:[1]

1. Establish and maintain qualified and adequate supervision of the training room, its environs, facilities, and equipment.
2. Exercise extreme caution in the distribution of medications. In interscholastic situations, age is a definite factor, inasmuch as the athlete is a minor. Obtain proper clearance for dispensing pharmaceuticals of any kind.
3. Use only those therapeutic methods for which you are qualified. Certain modalities, by law, must be used only under the direction or supervision of a physician.
4. Do not prescribe beyond the limits of your own training and limitations.
5. Do not use, or permit the use of, faulty or hazardous equipment.
6. Work cooperatively with the coach and the team physician in selecting protective equipment, and insist that the best be obtained.
7. Do not permit injured players to participate unless cleared by the team physician. Players suffering a head injury should not be permitted to reenter the game. (In some states, a player who has suffered a concussion may not continue in the sport for the balance of the season.)
8. Do not, under any circumstances, give a local anesthetic to enable an injured player to continue participation. It is dangerous as well as unethical.
9. Develop an understanding with the coaches that an injured athlete will not be allowed to reenter competition until, in the opinion of the team physician or the trainer, he is mentally and physically able. Do not permit yourself to be pressured to clear an athlete until he is fully able to resume competition.
10. Follow the express orders of the team physician at all times.
11. Make it a point to become familiar with the health and medical histories of the athletes under your care, such that you will be aware of particular problems that could present a need for additional care or caution on your part.
12. Use common sense.

PHYSICAL EXAMINATIONS AND RECORDS

The athletic trainer should file health appraisal records and medical histories for all athletes (unless these functions are performed by the school health services department). (See Figure 9.2 a, b, c for a sample form.) These records should be kept up-to-date and should include any accident report forms. Such records are useful in lawsuits and in settling insurance claims, which may not come to the attention of the athletic trainer until several years after the injury.

---

[1]Carl E. Klafs and Daniel D. Arnheim, *Modern Principles of Athletic Training*, 5th ed. (St. Louis: C.V. Mosby Co., 1981), p. 42.

Figure 9.2a

SUGGESTED HEALTH EXAMINATION FORM

(Cooperatively prepared by the National Federation of State High School Athletic Associations and the Committee on Medical Aspects of Sports of the American Medical Association.) Health examination for athletes should be rendered after August 1 preceding school year concerned.

_____

    (Please Print)   Name of Student   City and School

Grade _____ Age _____ Height _____ Weight _____ Blood Pressure _____

Significant Past Illness or Injury_____

_____

Eyes _____ R 20/ :L20/ Ears _____ Hearing R /15; L /15

Respiratory _____

Cardiovascular _____

Liver _____ Spleen _____ Hernia _____

Musculoskeletal _____ Skin _____

Neurological _____ Genitalia _____

Laboratory Urinalysis _____ Other: _____

Comments _____

Completed Immunizations: Polio _____ Tetanus _____
                            Date   Date

Instructions for use of card   Other_____

"I certify that I have on this date examined this student and that, on the basis of the examination requested by the school authorities and the student's medical history as furnished to me, I have found no reason which would make it medically inadvisable for this student to compete in supervised athletic activities, EXCEPT THOSE CROSSED OUT BELOW."

BASEBALL	FOOTBALL	ROWING	SOFTBALL	TRACK
BASKETBALL	HOCKEY	SKATING	SPEEDBALL	VOLLEYBALL
CROSS COUNTRY	GOLF	SKIING	SWIMMING	WRESTLING
FIELD HOCKEY	GYMNASTICS	SOCCER	TENNIS	OTHERS _____

*Estimated desirable weight level: _____ pounds.

Date of Examination: _____ Signed: _____

Physician's Address _____ Telephone _____

STUDENT PARTICIPATION AND PARENTAL APPROVAL FORM

Name of student: _____ Name of School: _____
              First   Last   Middle Initial

Date: _____ Date of Birth: _____ Place of Birth: _____

This application to compete in interscholastic athletics for the above high school is entirely voluntary on my part and is made with the understanding that I have not violated any of the eligibility rules and regulations of the State Association.

Instructions for use of card   Signature of Student:_____

PARENT'S OR GUARDIAN'S PERMISSION

"I hereby give my consent for the above named student (1) to represent his school in athletic activities, except those crossed out on this form by the examining physician, provided that such athletic activities are approved by the State Association, (2) to accompany any school team of which he is a member on any of its local or out-of-town trips. I authorize the school to obtain, through a physician of its own choice, any emergency medical care that may become reasonably necessary for the student in the course of such athletic activities or such travel. I also agree not to hold the school or anyone acting in its behalf responsible for any injury occurring to the above named student in the course of such athletic activities or such travel."

                    Signature of Parent or Guardian:_____

Date: _____ Address: _____
                  (Street)   (City or Town)

NOTE: This form is to be filled out completely and filed in the office of the high school principal or superintendent of schools before student is allowed to practice and/or compete.

Figure 9.2a   (continued)

Special tests as indicated

X-ray _____

_____

Urine (Albumin) _____ (Specific gravity) _____ (Sugar) _____ (Microscopic) _____

Blood (Red) _____ (White) _____ (Hemoglobin) _____

This page to be sent to school. Use space at bottom for remarks.

PHYSICIAN'S REPORT TO SCHOOL
Significant findings of medical examination

Name of athlete _____

School _____ Grade _____

Name of parent _____

Address _____ Phone _____

Physical findings which are of significance to the school:_____

_____

_____

_____

_____

Recommendations to the school: _____

_____

_____

_____

_____

_____

Is athlete capable of sports competition? Yes _____   No _____

Should there be restrictions?   Yes _____   No _____

Remarks:

_____ M.D.
(Signature of examining physician)

Date   _____

Address _____

Phone _____

Figure 9.2b   Suggested Medical Record for High School Athletes

Fill in each space. This part to be retained in physician's office.

HEALTH HISTORY

Identification

Name_____   Address _____

School _____   Grade _____   Date _____

Birthplace _____   Date of birth _____   Sex _____

Father's name_____   Business address _____

Home phone _____   Business phone_____

Date of last dental examination or treatment _____

Date last attended by family physician_____

Name of family physician _____

Physician's address_____   Phone _____

Family history: (If living, state present health; if deceased, cause of death.)

Father _____   Mother _____

Brothers _____   Sisters _____

_____

_____

_____

_____

Record of illness (Check those which occurred at any time; star illness of past 5 years.)

Frequent colds _____	Diphtheria_____	Hernia _____
Influenza _____	Measles _____	Chorea _____
Bronchitis _____	Mumps _____	Rheumatic fever _____
Pneumonia _____	Whooping cough _____	Bone & joint disease ____
Tuberculosis _____	Scarlet fever _____	Skin disease (name) _____
Allergies _____	Poliomyelitis _____	Diabetes _____
Chickenpox _____	Appendicitis _____	Kidney disease _____

Other: (Specify) _____

Source: Committee on the medical aspects of sports: A guide for medical evaluation of candidates for school sports, Chicago, 1965, the American Medical Association, pp. 2–3.

Figure 9.2c

MEDICAL EXAMINATION

Body type and general appearance_____

_____

Skin _____

Scalp _____

Eyes _____

Vision without glasses   R_____   L_____

Vision with glasses   R_____   L_____

Nasopharynx _____

Tonsils _____

Ears _____

Hearing   R_____   L_____

Nasal obstruction _____

Mouth _____

Teeth _____

Thyroid _____

Lymph glands _____

Other _____

Chest _____

Lungs _____

Observation of posture _____

_____

Heart _____

_____

Blood pressure _____

Pulse _____

Abdomen _____

_____

_____

Hernia _____

Genitalia _____

Nervous system _____

_____

Reflexes _____

_____

Emotional problems _____

_____

All students participating in interscholastic or intercollegiate sports should undergo a physical examination conducted by a physician far enough in advance of the season to allow for any necessary consultation, diagnosis, and treatment. Although the American Medical Association suggests that the student athlete's personal physician conduct the examination, since he is familiar with the student's health history, there are a great many student athletes whose parents are unable to afford a family physician. For this reason, it is advisable that the school retain a team physician for this purpose also.

The team physician should be familiar with the physical demands and stresses of all sports sponsored by the school. The team physician can provide uniformity in interpreting the results of physical examinations and, further, it is probable that the team physician will be more objective in interpreting the results.

The physician must evaluate the student's health status in relation to the demands of the sport. A history of concussions may not preclude participation in tennis or swimming, but almost certainly would rule out football or ice hockey. Similarly, the physician should check the knees of football players and skiers more closely than those of golfers.

A cardiac condition does not necessarily preclude participation in athletics. The physician must consider the severity of the condition and the athlete's response to activity, as related to the demands of the sport. Sports medicine has become a complex medical specialty, and a team physician is obviously more likely to become knowledgeable in sports medicine than is a general practitioner.

Periodic physical examinations are conducted at given intervals, usually once each year. A referral examination is given when a need is recognized. An athlete may be referred for an examination when (1) significant illness or injury is suffered; (2) the athlete undergoes surgery or therapy; or (3) the athlete has not been under direct observation of physical education or coaching staff for a significant period of time. Point (3) indicates that candidates for fall sports should undergo physical examinations in, say, August rather than in the spring, since coaches usually do not have an opportunity to observe them during the summer months.

An athlete should be referred for an examination if he complains of any of the following: recurrent headaches, dizziness, interrupted sleep, uneven heartbeat or undue pounding, digestive upsets, pain unrelated to a known injury, unusual fatigue, muscle twitching, or shakiness. Likewise, the athlete should undergo a physical if he shows evidence of excessive breathlessness, blue lips, pale or clammy skin, fainting, disorientation, or personality change.

Not only schools, but all agencies that sponsor athletic programs should require from the physician and from the participant's parents written certification that the athlete may participate in the program. Sponsors of athletic programs should know that parents cannot waive the legal rights of a child under the age of legal majority (usually eighteen, sometimes twenty-one) because when the child reaches legal age such releases are null and void as applied to the child (although they still bind the adult parents). Sponsors should make no guarantee that participants will not be injured.

ACCIDENT DATA SYSTEMS

The gathering of data, nationwide, on sports injuries is important for several reasons. First, decision-makers can utilize the information to formulate policies that enhance the safety of participants in sports. This information also can be helpful to others: manufacturers of sporting goods, rules-making bodies, architects of sports facilities, athletic directors, recreation leaders, physical education department chairpersons, coaches, physical education teachers, and recreation leaders.

Information on the relative incidence of injuries tells the administrator which sport most requires his time and the resources available for prevention of injuries. Information regarding the most frequently injured parts of the body tells the coach where protection is most needed, in terms of both equipment and conditioning programs. Injury information can be used by manufacturers to enhance the protective qualities of, for example, football helmets. As a concrete example of the value of such data, it is noted that the increase in vertebral injuries in football led to rules prohibiting spearing.

Damron provides an illustration of how such data were used by one large school system to decrease the incidence of injuries:[2]

> The safety coordinator in a large school system was reviewing the monthly summary chart [of injuries]. He noted a disproportionately high number of accidents . . . in the team sports sponsored under school jurisdiction. The fact became evident from the tabulations recorded for the chart item "Activity by Classification of Accident." The highest incidence was in varsity football. He then summarized the football accidents by: (a) status of the activity; (b) nature of injury and parts of the body injured; (c) agency involved; (d) unsafe physical condition; (e) unsafe act; and (f) unsafe personal factor.
>
> In investigating further he found that most of the incidents were broken teeth and mouth damage and that no mouthguards were being used. The problem was discussed with the safety coordinator, coaching staff, physical education teachers, and school administrators. This led to a request for the local dental association to assist in developing corrective measures. An experimental mouthpiece was developed that could be fitted individually for each football player. The chief school administrator approved the funding to purchase mouthguards for participants. The coaches agreed to require all players to wear them, and the safety coordinator agreed to evaluate the results. During the next football season no tooth damage incidence was reported.

---

[2]C. Frazier Damron, *Accident Surveillance Systems for Sports, Monograph #2*, Sports Safety Series, American School and Community Safety Association, American Alliance for Health, Physical Education, Recreation, and Dance (1977), p. 5.

When an institution is a member of a national accident reporting system, it demonstrates its concern for the safety and welfare of its athletes. As a result of completing forms and participating in discussions about decreasing injuries, sports program personnel are also motivated toward greater efforts to prevent accidents.

National Safety Council

The National Safety Council (NSC) was one of the first organizations to report on injuries nationwide. (The NSC primarily serves elementary and secondary schools.) A standard student accident report form, monthly student accident summary forms (for both girls and boys), and annual student accident summary forms (for boys and girls) have been developed. (A sample of the form is provided in Figure 9.3.)

For additional information or to participate in the NSC program, write:

> National Safety Council
> School and College Department
> 425 North Michigan Avenue
> Chicago, Illinois

National Electronic Injury Surveillance System (NEISS)

NEISS collects data on the nature and scope of product injuries to consumers. It is administered through the U.S. Consumer Product Safety Commission, a regulatory agency of the federal government, whose address is:

> U.S. Consumer Product Safety Commission
> 1750 K Street, N.W.
> Washington, D.C.

NEISS has authority to make rules designed to reduce the risk of injury to consumers, including consumers using products related to competitive and recreational sports. This agency may ban or seize "imminently hazardous products" and may impose mandatory standards to reduce injuries due to products deemed "unreasonably" risky. In other cases, the commission may rely on voluntary compliance.

The commission also conducts research designed to determine the causes of, and means of preventing, product-related injuries. Further, it has the authority to inspect the records of companies, as these records relate to the safety of the company's products. NEISS is the only system in the world that provides for continuous monitoring of product-related injuries.

The NEISS system is truly national in scope. Data on all emergency room patients with product-related injuries are transmitted electronically every twenty-four hours to a central computer in Washington, D.C. Consequently, NEISS can provide up-to-date information on the safety record of recently introduced products. Information gathered through this system is disseminated through a monthly periodical, *NEISS NEWS,* which contains

Figure 9.3

(check one) ☐ School Jurisdictional ☐ Non-School Jurisdictional.	**RECOMMENDED** **STANDARD STUDENT ACCIDENT REPORT** (See instructions on reverse side)	(check one) Recordable Reportable Only

School District:
City, State:

<table>
<tr><td rowspan="4" style="writing-mode:vertical">General</td><td colspan="2">1. Name</td><td colspan="3">2. Address</td></tr>
<tr><td colspan="2">3. School</td><td>4. Sex   ☐ Male
       ☐ Female</td><td>5. Age</td><td>6. Grade/Special Program</td></tr>
<tr><td colspan="5">7. Time Accident Occurred
       Date: Day of Week: Exact Time: AM / PM</td></tr>
</table>

Injury	8. Nature of Injury
	9. Part of Body Injured
	10. Degree of Injury (check one) Death ☐ Permanent ☐ Temporary (lost time) ☐ Non-Disabling (no lost time) ☐
	11. Days Lost From School: From Activities Other Than School: Total:
	12. Cause of Injury

Accident

13. Accident Jurisdiction (check one)
     School: Grounds ☐   Building ☐   To and From ☐
     Non-School: Home ☐   Other ☐   Other Activities Not on School Property

14. Location of Accident (be specific)	15. Activity of Person (be specific)
16. Status of Activity	17. Supervision (if yes, give title & name of supervisor) Yes ☐ No ☐
18. Agency Involved	19. Unsafe Act
20. Unsafe Mechanical/Physical Condition	21. Unsafe Personal Factor

22. Corrective Action Taken or Recommended

23. Property Damage
     School $ Non-School $ Total $

24. Description (Give a word picture of the accident, explaining who, what, when, why and how)

Signature	25. Date of Report
	27. Principal's Signature

26. Report Prepared by (signature & title)

This form is recommended for securing data for accident prevention and safety education. School districts may reproduce this form, adding space for optional data. Reference: *Student Accident Reporting Guidebook*, National Safety Council, 425 N. Michigan Avenue, Chicago, Illinois 60611. 1966. 34 pages.

short articles on product safety and data on a number of products. Periodically, information also is released to the news media.

A primary objective of NEISS is the development of standards for sports products. The Consumer Products Safety Act (which established the U.S. Consumer Product Safety Commission, which administers NEISS) leaves it to the public to establish a standard in the first instance. However, if the public makes no such move, the Commission may do so.

The first step in writing a standard is to determine whether use of a product constitutes an unreasonable risk. Unreasonable risk is determined by the following:

1. The number and severity of accidents involving the product.
2. The contributing role of the product in the accidents.
3. Whether the hazards the product presents can be eliminated through technically feasible measures.
4. What expense would be involved in required modifications.
5. Whether the risk to the user is assumed knowingly or unknowingly (voluntarily or involuntarily).
6. The uniqueness of the function the product serves.
7. Public exposure to the product.

Athletic, recreation, and physical education departments can utilize the findings of NEISS in their injury control programs.

Occupational Safety and Health System

The Occupational Safety and Health Act of 1970 established a system for recording work-related injuries and illnesses, to be administered under the Bureau of Labor Statistics of the Department of Health, Education, and Welfare. While the system does not cover amateur sports, it does cover professional sports and workers in physical education, athletics, and recreation (as well as all others in an employment relationship). The Bureau of Labor Statistics does not publish accident data information about individual professional sports or about professional sports as a whole.

National Athletic Injury Reporting System (NAIRS)

NAIRS is designed to collect injury and illness data specifically on varsity sports at educational institutions. It is a practical means for collecting and interpreting data on injuries to both male and female athletes in a uniform manner. The system makes it possible to assess trends and patterns of athletic injuries on a nationwide basis. This in turn facilitates decision-making regarding corrective measures.

The system operates on the basis of ten geographic districts. A principal investigator is the chief administrator and is responsible for interpreting the data. A coordinator supervises the data collection process. An athletic trainer certified by the National Athletic Trainers Association serves as the district coordinator in each of the ten districts. Cluster coordinators supervise the use of NAIRS in particular localities. A recorder completes NAIRS forms in each participating institution. Athletic directors at the member institutions supervise the institution's participation in NAIRS. Finally, a national advisory board contributes to the formulation of policies.

Forms for reporting injuries (called "case abstracts") define injuries in a specific manner to avoid the necessity of analyzing nuisance injuries. Illnesses and injuries reported include:

1. Brain concussion, if the athlete must be observed before being permitted to return to play.
2. Dental injuries requiring the attention of a dentist.
3. Injuries that cause athletes to miss practice on the day following the injury.
4. Injuries that require substantive medical attention.

NAIRS uses several forms, all of which are coded to facilitate scoring and interpretation by the computer. The forms used include: (1) a participant abstract; (2) a case abstract; (3) a weekly transmittal abstract; (4) abstracts for selected sports; and (5) a seasonal summary. (Samples of two of the NAIRS forms are presented as Figures 9.4 and 9.5.)

As a result of the forms, injury rates can be determined and expressed epidemiologically in terms of squad size; number of games or practices; types of players (substitute, regular, star); age; height; weight; and other variables. Further, injury rates to athletes participating in a given sport, using a certain sports product, or playing a particular position can be quickly analyzed. Characteristics of the coach and school size are also reported and may be utilized in drawing conclusions from the data.

Complete confidentiality is observed with regard to NAIRS data. Only an athlete's code number is indicated on injury reports submitted to NAIRS headquarters, and injury records of one school or agency are never released to other schools or agencies. It has been estimated that when NAIRS is completely operational (that is, when there is a full complement of subscribers and grant funds have stabilized), the annual subscription cost will be fifty dollars. Additional information may be secured by writing to:

> National Athletic Trainers Association
> 3315 South Street
> Lafayette, Indiana

Athletic Association Surveys

Since 1931, the National Collegiate Athletic Association, the American Football Coaches Association, and the National Federation of State High

Figure 9.4   NAIRS Abstract Form for Reporting Details of Reportable Injuries

CODE 0 OR 00 IF "UNKNOWN" CHECK OR PRINT CODES THAT APPLY

1. INSTITUTION

2. PARTICIPANT

Sport   Athlete   Episode

NAIRS—I
75—76
CASE ABSTRACT

3. ONSET
Date   Month

4. TIME
[1] AM (Before Noon)
[2] Aft (Noon-6pm)
[3] Eve (After 6pm)

5. RETURN
Date   Month

6. DIAGNOSIS
Principal   Other

If Extremity
[1] Rt
[2] Lt

REMARKS:

7. OCCASION

10 Not Sport-Related
  [11] Residence
  [12] Vehicle, Passenger
  [13] Vehicle, Pedestrian
  [14] School, not sport/phys ed
  [15] Job
  [16] Public, Other

2* Varsity Sports
  [20] Competition, Home
  [21] Competition, Away
  [22] Competition, Warmup
  [23] Team Travel, Vehicle
  [24] Team Travel, Other
  [25] Locker/Shower/Training Room
  [26] Between Lockerroom/Arena
  [27] Practice/Skill Training
  [28] Practice/Conditioning
  [29] Practice/Competition

3* Sub-Varsity Sports
4* Club Sports
5* Intramural Sports
6* Physical Education
7* Community Recreation
8* Other Varsity Sport
90 Other: _____

*for second digit, refer to
 Varsity Sport subheadings

WHEN STRICKEN:
9. POSITION
10. ACTIVITY
11. SITUATION
12. SURFACE

13. SURFACE CONDITION
[1] Normal
[2] Icy
[3] Snow-covered
[4] Wet
[5] Slippery, not wet
[6] Muddy
[7] Baked/Hard
[8] Irregular

14. PROTECTION OF INJURED BODY PART
[1] None
[2] Taped
[3] Wrapped
[4] Specially padded
[5] Customary uniform
[6] Bandaged
[7] Brace
[8] Cast

15. EQUIPMENT INVOLVED

Type   Brand   Vintage

Code for Vintage
1 New this season
2 New previous season
3 Used previous
  season
4 Reconditioned for
  this season
5 Reconditioned previous season(s)

16. NATURE OF INJURY/ILLNESS

[1] New Problem, this season and last
[2] Recurrence, this sport, this season
[3] Recurrence, this sport, last season
[4] Recurrence, other sport, since last season
[5] Complication, this sport, this season:

EPISODE

[6] Complication, other sport, since last season

17. ACTION TAKEN

[1] Not hospitalized, not confined to bed
[2] Hospitalized overnight or less and released
[3] Hospitalized at least two days
[4] Confined, other, at least two days

18. PRINCIPAL MANAGEMENT OF INJURY/ILLNESS

[1] Surgery
[2] Superficial debridement, minor suturing, etc.
[3] Nonsurgical immobilization
[4] Formal physical therapy
[5] Prescription drug therapy
[6] Proprietary management (aspirin, butterfly bandage)
[7] Rest
[8] Post-season surgery scheduled (returned to play)

8. SOURCE OF DIAGNOSIS

Physician   OR   Non-Physician

[1] Team Physician,
    Institution Staff
[2] Team Physician,
    Community based
[3] Clinic/Hospital Staff
[4] Community Physician
[5] Other: _____

Also Code:
[1] M.D.   [3] D.C.
[2] D.O.   [4] Other: _____

[71] Athletic Trainer,
     NATA Certified Member
[72] Athletic Trainer,
     NATA Associate Member
[73] Athletic Trainer, Other
[74] Coaching Staff
[75] Student Trainer
[76] School Nurse
[77] Emergency Care Personnel
[78] Parent
[79] Other: _____

19. RESEARCH
(1)   (2)   (3)   (4)

Figure 9.5   Sample Form of Nairs Sports Season Closeout Abstract

CODE 0 OR 00 IF "UNKNOWN" CHECK OR PRINT CODES THAT APPLY

NAIRS—I
75—76
SPORT SEASON
CLOSEOUT
ABSTRACT

1. INSTITUTION   ⬚⬚⬚⬚⬚⬚⬚   **2. SPORT** ⬚⬚

3. PRIMARY PHYSICIAN SUPERVISION
[1] Team Physician(s), Institution Staff
[2] Team Physician(s), Community based
[3] Clinic/Hospital
[4] Community Physicians as needed
[5] Other
   Also Code:
   [1] M.D.   [3] D.C.
   [2] D.O.   [4] Other

4. PRIMARY NON-PHYSICIAN SUPERVISION
[71] Athletic Trainer, NATA Certified Member
[72] Athletic Trainer, NATA Associate Member
[73] Athletic Trainer, Other
[74] Coaching Staff   [77] Emergency Care Personnel
[75] Student   [78] Parent
[76] School Nurse   [79] Other _____

5. COACHING STAFF SIZE ⬚⬚

6. HEAD COACH

Sex
[1] Male
[2] Female

Education
[1] Bacc. Degree, PE major or minor
[2] Bacc. Degree, other
[3] Masters Degree, PE major or minor, undergrad or grad
[4] Masters Degree, other
[5] Doctorate, PE major or minor, undergrad or grad
[6] Doctorate, other
[7] No college degree

Experience Coaching This Sport
[1] 1—2 years
[2] 3—5 years
[3] 6—10 years
[4] 10 + years

Experience Playing This Sport
[1] 1—2 years, h.s. only
[2] 1—2 years, college only
[3] 3—6 years, h.s. only
[4] 3—6 years, college only
[5] 3—6 years, h.s. and college
[6] 3—6 years, college and post college
[7] 6 + years, college and post college
[8] None

7. COACHING PREFERENCES*

	1—Yes	
	Pre-Season	In Season
Isometrics	☐	☐
Endurance Training	☐	☐
Weight Training	☐	☐
Flexibility Training	☐	☐
Taped Ankles	☐	☐
Wrapped Ankle	☐	

*Record yes if prescribed routinely for squad

8. PRESEASON MEDICAL EXAM
[1] Required only for athlete's first sport of year
[2] Required for each sport
[3] Required only for athlete's first sport in institution
[4] Not required

9. FACILITIES*

		Surface
Primary Practice Arena	☐	☐
Home Contest	☐	☐

*See item 12 in Code Book under the respective sport.

10. EQUIPMENT*

		Type	Brand	% of Squad	Vintage
HEADGEAR:	1	☐☐	☐☐	☐☐	☐
	2	☐☐	☐☐	☐☐	☐
	3	☐☐	☐☐	☐☐	☐
	4	☐☐	☐☐	☐☐	☐
DENTAL GUARD:	1	☐☐	☐☐	☐☐	
	2	☐☐	☐☐	☐☐	
SHOES,	1	☐☐	☐☐	☐☐	
Natural Surface:	2	☐☐	☐☐	☐☐	
	3	☐☐	☐☐	☐☐	
	4	☐☐	☐☐	☐☐	
SHOES,	1	☐☐	☐☐	☐☐	
Artificial Surface:	2	☐☐	☐☐	☐☐	
	3	☐☐	☐☐	☐☐	
	4	☐☐	☐☐	☐☐	
_____		☐☐	☐☐	☐☐	☐
_____		☐☐	☐☐	☐☐	☐
_____		☐☐	☐☐	☐☐	☐
		☐☐	☐☐	☐☐	

Code for Vintage

1—New this season
2—New previous season
3—Used previous season
4—Reconditioned for this season
5—Reconditioned previous season(s)

*See item 15 in Code Book under the respective sport

11. PURCHASE OF PERSONAL EQUIPMENT (shoes, helmets, etc.)
[1] Institute responsibility
[2] Athlete responsibility
[3] Shared, primarily institution
[4] Shared, primarily athlete

12. WIN/LOSS RECORD
[1] Won at least two-thirds of contests
[2] Won between one-third and two-thirds of contests
[3] Won less than one-third of contests

RESEARCH   (1) ☐☐   (2) ☐☐   (3) ☐☐   (4) ☐☐

School Associations have cooperatively conducted a national survey of football fatalities. The data collected through this survey have been used to support rules changes, such as: (1) requiring players to wear mouth guards; (2) requiring that during the first three days of practice players practice in shorts to facilitate acclimatization to vigorous activity conducted in the heat; and (3) regulating the number of days of practice permitted before the first game.

/ 10 /

Special Problems

School administrators of physical education, athletic, and recreation programs are sometimes faced with a variety of special situations that call for an understanding of relevant laws and court interpretations of these laws. These special situations include homosexual or deviant sexual behavior of teachers or students, drug abuse, and objections to school activities or procedures on the basis of religious beliefs, as well as issues concerning freedom of speech and assembly, corporal punishment, and other aspects of the legal rights of students and faculty.

SEXUAL BEHAVIOR

Recent years have witnessed an increase in the number of court cases dealing with dismissal of public school teachers for "immorality," "moral turpitude," or "unfitness to teach." Communities in all parts of the country have become embroiled in heated debates. Efforts have been made to pass laws to prohibit the hiring and require the firing of anyone in the public schools advocating, soliciting, imposing, encouraging, or promoting private or public sexual acts defined in the penal code between persons of the same sex in a manner likely to come to the attention of other employees or students, or publicly or indiscreetly engaging in said actions.

Due to the subjectivity involved, terms such as "immorality" and "immoral conduct" are difficult to define. Nevertheless, in 1920 the Supreme Court of Minnesota held that immoral conduct included "such acts and practices as are inconsistent with decency, good order, and propriety of personal conduct."[1] In 1933, the Supreme Court of Oklahoma defined im-

---

[1] *Paust v. Georgian*, 179 N.W. 735 (1920).

247

moral conduct as that which is "willful, flagrant, or shameless, and which shows a moral indifference to the opinions of the good and respectable members of the community."[2]

Today, however, the courts tend to relate immorality to unfitness to teach.

Flygare presented an illustration of the thinking of the courts in an article in the *Phi Delta Kappan*.[3] In the case illustrated, a former student reported to the vice-principal that a teacher had told him that he (the teacher) was "deeply involved" with a man who had run an advertisement in the newspaper of the Dorian Society, a homosexual group. The vice-principal advised the teacher of the student's statement, charges were pressed, and after a hearing, the school board discharged the teacher.

The teacher challenged his dismissal in state court. The court upheld the firing, stating that the school board had sustained its finding of immorality. The teacher appealed to the Washington State Supreme Court, which returned the case to the lower court for further findings, holding that the lower court had given special weight to the testimony of school officials. The lower court reaffirmed its earlier findings, stating that although there was no evidence of overt homosexual acts committed by the teacher, he had admitted to being a homosexual, and that "sexual gratification with a member of one's own sex is implicit in the term homosexual."[4]

Since such sexual gratification would presumably involve the crimes of sodomy and lewdness (cohabitation with someone other than a spouse), it could be concluded that the teacher had engaged in immoral activity. The court reasoned that this immorality impaired the teacher's effectiveness and that the school was injured after it became publicly known because of parental concern, fear, and suspicion engendered by the knowledge that the teacher was an admitted homosexual.

The teacher again appealed to the Washington State Supreme Court, which supported the lower court's ruling by a vote of six to two. The majority expressed the view that although the teacher may have been a latent homosexual and had never engaged in sexual acts with other men, he should have said so during his trial. The majority concluded: "Homosexuality is widely condemned as immoral and was so condemned as immoral during biblical times."[5]

The court went on to state that since homosexuality is an "acquired orientation," the teacher "made a voluntary choice for which he must be held morally responsible." Since the teacher had concealed his homosexuality until the point of his discharge, he was aware of the serious consequences of same.

---

[2]*Warkentin* v. *Kleinwacter*, 27 P. 2d 160 (1933).

[3]Thomas J. Flygare, "Schools and the Law," *Phi Delta Kappan*, March 1978, pp. 482–83.

[4]*Gaylord* v. *Tacoma School District 10*, 85 Wn. 2d 348, 535 P. 2d 804 (1975).

[5]*Gaylord* v. *Tacoma School District 10*, Docket No. 44078, 155CC H, Employment Practices Decisions, Par. 7857 (Wash. S. Ct., January 20, 1977).

Five years after the issue first arose, the teacher appealed to the U.S. Supreme Court, which refused to hear the case.

In another *Phi Delta Kappan* article, Frances and Stacey reported on other court cases involving homosexuality.[6] In one case, a public school teacher was arrested and charged with having engaged in oral copulation with another man. Criminal charges were lodged, and he was tried but acquitted on a technicality. Ten months prior to adjudication of the criminal charges, he was given a compulsory leave of absence. The teacher demanded that he be permitted to resume teaching and that he receive back pay for the period of his forced leave. The court rejected the argument that acquittal on the criminal charges should permit him to resume teaching.

In another case, a teacher was arrested for engaging in oral copulation in a doorless toilet stall in a public restroom. The school board dismissed him, and he appealed to the courts. The court refused to reinstate him, declaring that: "The law has long recognized in many ways that children are entitled to special protection. This is especially true during the process and period of their compulsory education."[7]

The dismissal of still another teacher for homosexual behavior was overturned by the California Supreme Court, which established a legal test for cases involving dismissal of teachers for immorality. The elements of the test were:[8]

1. Effects of the conduct on students and teachers.
2. Recency of the conduct.
3. Type of teaching certificate held by the accused.
4. Presence or absence of extenuating circumstances.
5. Likelihood of recurrence.
6. Possible "chilling" effect of punishment on the teacher's Constitutional rights.

The public expects teachers to observe the moral code of the community and to project an image of rectitude. The courts generally reinforce the public in this regard.

PROFANITY IN THE CLASSROOM

A California teacher reproduced and distributed to her students materials that they had prepared. The material contained vulgar references to the male and female sexual organs and to the sex act. The teacher contended that her economically and culturally disadvantaged students were well ac-

---

[6]Samuel N. Francis and Charles E. Stacey, "Law and the Sensual Teacher," *Phi Delta Kappan*, October 1977, pp. 98–102.

[7]*Board of Education* v. *Calderon*, 110 Cal. Rptr. 916 (1973).

[8]*Morrison* v. *State Board of Education*, 82 Cal. Rptr. 175 (1969).

quainted with these words. She was dismissed and the trial court upheld her dismissal.[9]

Another teacher was dismissed (and the court upheld her dismissal) for distributing to her eighth grade class copies of a poem entitled "Getting Together." The poem advocated rejection of the discipline of home life, the use of LSD and marijuana, public nudity, and sexual promiscuity.[10]

In another case, a teacher wrote a four-letter word for fornication on the blackboard in his eleventh grade class during a discussion of taboo words. In his suit to win reinstatement to his teaching position, the federal court held that students in an eleventh grade class are sophisticated enough to deal with this word. The court declared: "The Fourteenth Amendment recognizes that a public school teacher has not only a civic right to freedom of speech both inside and outside the schoolhouse, but also some measure of academic freedom as to his in-classroom teaching."[11]

BIZARRE BEHAVIOR

A teacher was witnessed several times on his own property dressing and undressing a mannequin in female attire, caressing its breasts, engaging in lewd and suggestive actions, and engaging in a form of masturbation. The U.S. District Court of Massachusetts did not accept the plaintiff's claim that he had a right to privacy on his own property. Further, it reasoned that his effectiveness in teaching and his relationship within the school system were impaired, due to the certainty that some notoriety would result.

It should be noted that the court upheld the teacher's dismissal primarily because of the effect of his behavior upon his effectiveness as a teacher, rather than for reasons of morality.[12]

"SWINGING"

A California teacher was arrested and charged with a felony when she performed fellatio with two men, neither of whom was her husband, at a "swingers" party. Two years later, her teaching credentials were revoked. She and her husband had appeared on a nationally syndicated television show on which they promoted "swinging." She appealed the revocation of her teaching certificate, but the California Supreme Court upheld the revocation, citing her action as not only criminal, but also semipublic in nature.[13]

---

[9]*Oakland Unified School District* v. *Olicker,* 102 Cal. Rptr. 421 (1972).

[10]*Brubaker* v. *Board of Education,* 502 F. 2d 973 (7th Cir. 1974).

[11]*Mailloux* v. *Kiley,* 323 F. Supp. 1387 (D. Mass. 1971).

[12]*Wishart* v. *McDonald,* 36 F. Supp. 530 (D. Mass. 1973).

[13]*Pettit* v. *State Board of Education,* 513 P. 2d 889 (1973).

Another teacher, who had been married for less than one month and was eight and one-half months pregnant, was dismissed for immorality. Both the trial court and the appellate court reversed the action of the school board, ruling that immorality is sufficient cause for dismissal "only where the record shows harm to pupils, faculty, or the school itself."[14] It had been brought out during the hearing that neither parents nor students complained about the teacher, nor had there been any damage to her teaching effectiveness or her relationships with her colleagues or to the school.

SHOPLIFTING

A guidance counselor was arrested and charged with petty larceny as a result of shoplifting. The school board dismissed the teacher, even though testimony failed to substantiate the charge that the incident impaired his effectiveness as a counselor. The New York Supreme Court, Appellate Division, upheld the decision, noting that the counselor had a reputation in the community of being a shoplifter. The court reasoned that although this behavior was not directly related to his work as a guidance counselor, it was clearly conduct unbecoming a teacher.[15]

MARIJUANA

Two California teachers were arrested and convicted for possession of marijuana. The first teacher's teaching credentials were revoked by the state board of education for immoral conduct. The second teacher was dismissed from his teaching position. (The two situations were separate and unrelated.)

In each case, the appellant argued that marijuana had been found to be medically harmless and in common use. The court rejected this argument, since it was based on the faulty premise that a criminal act cannot be characterized as immoral if it is medically harmless and frequently committed.

The court also stated, however, that a school board or other administrative agency cannot characterize a teacher's behavior as immoral unless that behavior indicates unfitness to teach, as supported by evidence that (a) the teacher's conduct demonstrated a potential for harmful school relationships, or (b) the behavior received enough bad publicity to be harmful to the school.

The court reinstated the first teacher's credentials, but in the second case the court affirmed the teacher's dismissal on the grounds that his arrest and conviction were reported in the local newspaper.

---

[14]*Reinhardt* v. *Board of Education,* 311 N.E. 2d 710 (1974).

[15]*Caravello* v. *Board of Education, Norwich City,* 369 N.Y.S. 2d 829 (1975).

TITLE IX AND EQUAL RIGHTS

Title IX of the Educational Amendments Act of 1972 prohibits sex discrimination in recruiting and admissions, financial aid, athletics, textbooks, curriculum, housing facilities, career counseling, insurance and health care, single-sex groups and programs, extracurricular activities, and employment. It specifies that no person in the United States shall be excluded on the basis of sex from participation in, be denied the benefits of, or be subjected to, discrimination under any educational program or activity receiving federal funds.

This law requires that the institution conduct a self-study to ascertain if there are any discriminatory practices, to modify any such practices found, to provide "assurance of compliance," and to assign one person responsibility for compliance with Title IX provisions, including the establishment of procedures for handling grievances by students and employees.

Exemptions from Compliance

A number of different groups are exempt from compliance with Title IX. These include social fraternities and sororities, YMCAs and YWCAs, the Boy Scouts, the Girl Scouts, Campfire Girls, military and religious schools, father-son and mother-daughter events (providing that, if an event is held for one sex, a comparable event is held for the other), scholarships for beauty pageants, and scholarships awarded to one sex only and established by a foreign government, a will, or a trust.

Scholarship may be provided for members of only one sex on separate athletic teams, but the total number of such scholarships must be in proportion to the number of students of each sex participating in the entire interscholastic or intercollegiate athletic program.

Practices such as sexual quotas, awarding of athletic scholarships to males only, use of different criteria in assessing the financial needs of males and females, prohibiting males from enrolling in women's studies courses, treatment of pregnancy as other than a temporary disability, and unequal dormitory facilities, have all been ruled violations.[16]

A case arose in 1972, in which two girls brought suit against the Illinois High School Athletic Association because its rules prohibited them from participating on the boys' interscholastic swimming team. (The girls' high school did not have a separate swimming team.) The Illinois court pointed out that in the Olympic Games the performances of men are, in almost every instance, better than those of women. The court further pointed out that experts in athletics deplore the mixing of the sexes in athletic competi-

---

[16]Patricia A. Hollander, *Legal Handbook for Educators* (Boulder, Colorado: Westview Press, 1978), p. 232.

tion and believe that male domination of the sports will result from such mixing. The court ruled for the defendant.

In a related case, the Michigan High School Athletic Association had a rule prohibiting girls from competing when one or both of the competing teams was composed of boys. A girl sued the Michigan State Board of Education, contending that the rule violated her right of equal protection, as guaranteed by the Fourteenth Amendment. The district court judge issued an injunction against the association's rule that prohibited athletes from competition on the basis of sex.[17]

The case was appealed by the association, but the United States Court of Appeals agreed with the district court, except that it added the word "noncontact," indicating that it believed that girls should not compete against boys in contact sports.

Since 1970, female participation in high school athletic programs has increased 600 percent, while female enrollments dropped five percent. At the college level, female participation in intramural and intercollegiate sports has increased by over 100 percent since 1971. This increased participation by females cannot be attributed entirely to Title IX, since the trend began before passage of that law. Further, the federal Department of Health, Education, and Welfare (HEW) has received complaints of discrimination against only sixty-two institutions of higher education.

The History of Title IX

The law requires that all HEW (now the Department of Education) Title IX regulations be approved by the President. But to circumvent the necessity of presidential approval, the Department of Education (DE) has issued "policy interpretations" which it considers binding legal requirements upon schools and colleges. In this way, DE enacted law through administrative fiat without following the procedures prescribed by law.

When Title IX was enacted by Congress in 1972, the federal departments were authorized to write public regulations enforcing the law. These regulations would have the force of law after receiving presidential approval. However, after two years, DE still had not published regulations. Consequently, Congress passed a law in 1974 ordering the department (then HEW) to publish Title IX regulations within thirty days, "which shall include with respect to intercollegiate athletic activities reasonable provisions considering the nature of particular sports."

In 1975, President Ford signed the Title IX regulations. These regulations mandated equal athletic opportunities for both sexes but stated that "unequal aggregate expenditures for members of each sex . . . will not constitute noncompliance with this section. . . ."

---

[17]*Morris* v. *Michigan State Board of Education,* 472 F. 2d 1207 (6th Cir. 1973).

Many questions have been raised, and are being raised, concerning the applicability of Title IX regulations to revenue-producing sports. Although a 1978 HEW policy interpretation addressed the problems of insufficient financial resources devoted to women's intercollegiate sports and the effort to encourage a greater number of women to participate, it indicated that discrepancies in average expenditures would be ignored by HEW if they were the result of "nondiscriminatory factors," such as the "nature and level of competition" of a particular sport, variations in cost of equipment and supplies, cost of travel, and cost of publicity. The unique nature of collegiate football was admittedly a consideration in determining the wording of this policy interpretation.

In a recent ruling, former HEW Secretary Joseph Califano issued the policy interpretation that Title IX does not prohibit a school from offering six-player, half-court basketball for girls. He also stated: "The regulation does not require that any particular sport be offered or that the same sports be offered to boys and girls. It does not require schools to offer identical versions of the same sport."

As the law is presently interpreted, a school may limit participation in a contact sport exclusively to members of one sex. In noncontact sports, the school may provide separate teams for boys and girls, or it may have only one team, with membership open to either sex based solely on ability.

The Colorado High School Activities Association excluded females from participation in interscholastic soccer on the basis that it is a dangerous sport for girls. The federal district court invalidated this practice because of the potential contribution of athletic participation to the social and physical development of children, and because the exclusion was stated as being based on sex. This court offered three alternatives: (1) discontinue the interscholastic soccer program; (2) field separate boys and girls soccer teams; or (3) permit girls to try out for the team.[18]

Federal district courts in Ohio and Wisconsin have invalidated rules excluding females from participation in contact sports.[19] The New Jersey Department of Education ruled that high school girls must be permitted to compete against boys for positions on contact sport teams. In 1977, New York approved the exclusion of girls in football, basketball, and wrestling but permitted them to try out for limited contact sports such as baseball.

HEW's Final Interpretation

Congress passed Title IX in 1972, and in 1975 HEW issued regulations for implementation of Title IX. Although all colleges were to comply with the provisions of Title IX by 1978, almost no college did so. Considerable confu-

---

[18]Colorado High School Activities Association, Rule XXI, Section 3.

[19]*Yellow Springs Exempted Village School Dist. Bd. of Ed.* v. *Ohio High School Athletic Association,* 443 F. Supp. 753 (S.D. Ohio W.D. 1978).

sion existed concerning the requirements. Tacit resistance to the requirements was also a likely factor. Consequently, HEW felt it advisable to publish policy interpretations, which it did in 1979.

As the Title IX successor to HEW, the Department of Education will now determine whether a school's athletic program is in compliance by assessing three aspects of the program. These are as follows:

1. *Financial assistance to athletes.* The total dollar amount of scholarships awarded to female athletes, relative to the total scholarship fund, must be proportional to the percentage of female athletes. If $200,000 is the total amount of the scholarship fund, and if there are 140 male and 60 female athletes, female athletes must receive a total of at least $60,000, while male athletes can receive a total of $140,000.
2. *Athletic benefits and opportunities.* Services available to, benefits for, and treatment of, male and female athletes must be "equivalent." DE will assess a number of areas to determine whether equal athletic opportunity is provided, for example:
   a. Equipment and supplies.
   b. Practice and game schedule.
   c. Salaries paid to coaches and tutors.
   d. Housing and dining services.
   e. Amount of publicity.
   f. Travel and per diem costs.
   g. Opportunities to receive coaching and tutoring.
   h. Quality and quantity of locker rooms and other facilities.
   i. Medical and training services.
   j. Recruitment.
   k. Other support services.
   Identical benefits, opportunities, or treatment are *not* required, provided the overall effect of any differences is negligible.
3. *Accommodation of student interest and abilities.* DE will determine whether schools are providing equal opportunity in the selection of sports and levels of competition available to members of both sexes by examining the following factors: the variety of sports offered, the levels of competition available, and the athletic interests and abilities of the students. DE must periodically select several schools and conduct investigations to determine whether they are in compliance with Title IX requirements. In addition to these compliance reviews, DE must investigate complaints alleging sex discrimination.

To expedite resolution of the backlog of cases, as well as to prevent future backlogs, DE has established a timetable. After receipt of a complaint, DE has ninety days to conduct an investigation and to inform the school of its findings. Within another ninety days, it must resolve violations by obtaining a voluntary compliance agreement from the school. If a school is found in noncompliance, and if voluntary compliance attempts are unsuccessful, a formal process is initiated to terminate the school's federal funding.

TITLE IX AND SALARIES

Title IX's involvement in faculty discrimination has been challenged in the courts. Consequently, the Office of Civil Rights has indicated it will investigate an employment complaint only if it can be shown that the employment discrimination has a direct impact upon students.

Sections of Title IX that discuss coaches are concerned with the effect of coaching discrimination on student athletes. Therefore, those who plan to file a complaint under Title IX are advised to show that inequitable salaries result in inequities to female athletes. Such inequities should be documented in the complaint. If a case cannot be made showing a relationship between inequitable salaries and inequities in the girls' athletic program, DE will either refer the complaint to the Equal Employment Opportunity Commission or inform the complainant to do so.

Many women's organizations have been organized to counsel and assist women with complaints about pay inequities. One of these organizations is the Project on Equal Education Rights (PEER), an arm of the Legal Defense and Education Fund of the National Organization for Women (NOW). PEER's mission is to monitor enforcement of federal laws prohibiting sex discrimination in education. PEER has published *Anyone's Guide to Filing a Title IX Complaint.* Most of the suggestions on the following pages have been taken from this publication.

Any individual, whether a student, citizen, or school employee, and any group can file a complaint. The abovementioned guide suggests that those who fear harassment as a result of filing a complaint may solicit organizations such as NOW, the American Civil Liberties Union, or the Women's Equity Action League to press the case. And since harassment itself is a violation of Title IX, that charge should be added to the complaint.

A Title IX complaint generally must be filed within 180 days after the discrimination occurs. However, in the case of ongoing discrimination, the complaint may be filed at any time. Usually a letter is sufficient, although DE may mail the complainant a form to ensure that the basic information necessary for the investigation is provided. Complaints should be directed to:

Project Director
1029 Vermont Ave., NW, Suite 800
Washington, D.C. 20005

Complaints should include the following information:

1. Name and address of the school district, college, or other institution allegedly discriminating by sex.
2. A general description of the person or persons suffering from discrimination. (Complaints need not give names or addresses, although if there are only one or two victims of specific acts of discrimination, it would be helpful to include this information.)
3. The approximate date the discrimination occurred or indication that the discrimination is an ongoing problem.
4. The complainant's name, address and, if possible, a telephone number for daytime use.
5. Sufficient information about the discrimination for DE to understand what happened.
6. Names, addresses, and telephone numbers of people who can provide additional information about the charge. (The complainant should explain why DE should interview these people.)
7. Copies of relevant documents (such as student or employee manuals or school board budget documents) to reinforce the charges.
8. References to any imminent firings or suspensions (that is, indication that action must be taken quickly by DE).
9. Requests to withhold the name of the complainant, if so desired.
10. Indications of any pattern of discrimination throughout the school district or college, if applicable.

DE is required to provide the complainant with a copy of its formal letter of findings, which is directed to the defendant institution. If the complainant so requests, DE must also provide copies of any correspondence with the institution.

The EEOC and Salaries

As indicated earlier, where inequities in salaries do not contribute to inequities in athletic or educational programs, complaints are best made to the Equal Employment Opportunity Commission (EEOC), rather than to DE under Title IX. The Equal Pay Act of 1963 prohibits discrimination in salaries and almost all fringe benefits on the basis of sex. This law requires employers to provide equal pay for substantially equal work within the institution.

The four criteria to determine whether different jobs involve substantially equal work are: (1) the level of skill required; (2) the degree of effort required; (3) level of responsibility; and (4) working conditions. *SPRINT*, a publication for information on sex equity in sports and an arm of the Women's Equity Action League (WEAL), points out that if a defendant institution cites a male team's longer season, greater number of games, or greater public pressure to justify a higher salary for the male coach, the institution is probably in violation of Title IX, since the institution is then discriminating against girls in its athletic programs.[20]

Complaints alleging equal pay violations can be filed with the EEOC district or area office in the complainant's locale. The address can be found in the telephone book under U.S. Government. The *SPRINT* article advises the complainant to indicate that the female coach's work is "substantially equal" to that of the male coach by comparing the work of the two coaches in the same sport or in similar sports (field hockey and soccer, for example). The letter should indicate exactly what the two jobs entail in terms of the nature of the games, the number of players supervised, the length of practices and playing seasons, the amount of travel required, and any additional responsibilities. To prove unequal pay, it is necessary to indicate the difference in salaries, the anticipated employer argument against the complaint, and the complainant's rebuttal to the anticipated employer's argument.

The *SPRINT* article goes on to offer the following advice:

1. File as early as possible.
2. Seek the support of the teachers' and/or coaches' union.
3. If the union refuses to help, contact both an attorney and a teachers' rights specialist at the National Education Association.
4. If the complainant is harassed, a charge of harassment should be added to the complaint.
5. If the EEOC accepts the case, they will pay the cost of processing and prosecuting the case.
6. An employer found guilty is required to equalize salaries, may be liable for two or three years of back pay, and will be required to pay legal costs.

In another *SPRINT* article, those who believe their athletic rights have been violated are advised to look into state laws. Many states have passed equal rights amendments. Information on such laws can be secured by writing to the public information office of the state attorney general. Those who wish to consult an attorney familiar with sex discrimination laws are advised to contact the state or local office of the American Civil Liberties Union (ACLU), the Women's Rights Project of the ACLU (located at 22 East 40th Street, New York, N.Y. 10016), or the Women's Legal Defense Fund (1010 Vermont Ave., N.W., Suite 210, Washington, D.C. 20005).

An article in *In the Running,* another publication of WEAL's Educational and Legal Defense Fund, suggests using human relations commissions of the various states to press for salary equity for female coaches. The Pennsylvania

---

[20]"The Equal Pay Act," *SPRINT* (WEAL Fund, Suite 82, 805 15th St., N.W., Washington, D.C. 20005).

Human Relations Commission won salary equity and back pay for Linda Richards of the Millcreek School District. Harriet Ehrlich, head of this commission's Affirmative Enforcement Division, stated: "We're sending a letter to all 505 school districts in the state, telling them about the Millcreek decision, and that equal pay is the law of the land. They'll have to clean up their act or face a lot of back pay." Women coaches are increasingly turning to these human rights commissions in complaints concerning equal pay.

(The reader is referred to the Appendix for the complete text of an article from the WEAL fund. This article is reprinted in its entirety because of the difficulty of abstracting it without diminishing its effectiveness, and because of its potential helpfulness to those who wish to work for sex equity in athletics and administration.)

There can be little doubt that the intent of the Title IX regulations is admirable, in that they are designed to promote equity and freedom, which are hallmarks of a democratic society. Statistical evidence indicates that efforts to promote equity in athletic programs is long overdue.

A *Reader's Digest* article reported on HEW efforts to enforce Title IX compliance by Grove City College (Pennsylvania).[21] The president of the college refused to execute a routine HEW "assurance of compliance" form. This refusal would result in the college's losing federal funding. The college is a Presbyterian-oriented institution, whose original dedication was "instilling Christian truth and values and an appreciation of a free market economy." President Charles S. MacKenzie feared that governmental intrusion would "secularize and neutralize" that mission. In conformance with that ideal, the college has repeatedly rejected the nearly $300,000 a year that Pennsylvania offers in subsidies.

The president and board of trustees stated that since the college received no federal funds, it need not sign the form. The president received increasingly stern phone calls from HEW. "The callers kept telling me that we had better sign, that they had ways of making us sign," said MacKenzie. He also stated: "When I asked the callers to put their statements — some of which were threatening to the point of intimidation — in writing, all refused."

Since Grove City receives no federal funds, HEW could not withhold any funds. So the officers of HEW decided to exert pressure by threatening to cut off aid to students. (Some 700 of the college's 2200 students were receiving Basic Educational Opportunity Grants or guaranteed student loans from banks.) Such action would have punished the students.

Governmental agencies can make laws by administrative fiat, and DE also has its own administrative courts. Grove City College was summoned to such a court by the Secretary of HEW and was ordered to show why the student grants and loans should not be terminated. Although the judge

---

[21]William J. Miller, "A Little School Against the Big Bureaucracy," *Reader's Digest*, August 1980, p. 159.

ruled against the college, he wrote that while under the existing law he had no power to find any HEW regulations illegal, "there is very clearly given to the director of the Office of Civil Rights a total and unbridled discretion to require any certification of compliance that he may desire, reasonable or unreasonable. There are no guidelines."

Grove City College filed suit in Pittsburgh's federal court, claiming that the department's regulations were illegal and unconstitutional because they exceeded the scope of the law and violated constitutional rights, among which was a student's right to due process of law. The judge ruled that the college did not have to sign the form, that HEW could not cut off guaranteed student loans, and that the Basic Educational Opportunity Grants could not be cut off unless HEW proved the college was guilty of sexual discrimination (and then only if it provided hearings for each student involved).

In September 1981, the American Alliance for Health, Physical Education, Recreation, and Dance, in its publication *Update*, reported that the Reagan administration was trying to dismantle or severely diminish the effectiveness of Title IX. The principal attack was being made by means of Senator Orrin Hatch's amendment to Title IX, which would:

1. Curtail coverage of teachers, administrators, and other staff.
2. Require that the particular program or activity in which discrimination was alleged *directly* receive federal funds in order to be covered by Title IX, rather than simply be a part of an institution that received federal funding for any purpose, related or unrelated to the area of discrimination.
3. Exclude most federally financed student aid for higher education in defining federal financial assistance.

Senator Hatch feels that Title IX gave the federal government dictatorial powers in areas covered by the act, whereas it should serve as a facilitator of educational programs.

PROGRAMS FOR THE HANDICAPPED

Federal law P.L. 94-142, the Education for All Handicapped Children Act, requires that all handicapped children, ages three to twenty-one, receive a free and appropriate education in the least restrictive educational environment. This law covers handicapped children in public and private care facilities, as well as public and private schools. Handicapped children who can learn in regular classes with the use of supplementary aids and services are to be educated with children who are not handicapped.

Public schools must locate, identify, and evaluate all handicapped students and those suspected of having a disability. Locating these students is thus the first step for the school administrator. (Parents have been known to hide physically impaired or retarded children.) In this regard, the school administrator should make use of local media to issue announcements and notices. He should utilize various local agencies to assist in making phone calls and mailing letters.

After the students have been located and identified, they must be evaluated. The law requires that an individualized education program (IEP) be prepared for each child before any action is taken with respect to initial placement.

Individualized Education Programs

The IEP must include a statement of (1) the child's present level of functioning; (2) annual goals for the child, including short-term, measurable objectives that contribute toward long-term goals; (3) the educational services to be provided; (4) the degree to which the child will be able to participate in the regular program; and (5) the evaluative procedures and objective criteria that will be used in annual reviews of instructional objectives.

The IEP must be developed by a representative of the local educational agency (usually the building principal), the teacher, the parents or guardians, and when appropriate, the handicapped child himself.

In evaluating the child's present level of functioning, it is important to gather appropriate assessment data. These might include measures of intellectual development, social development, and physical capacities (such as the use of legs, arms, eyes, ears, and speech). These measures are important in establishing goals, as are data regarding the child's age, grade, level of learning, general health, special talents, and mode of learning most effective for him in particular.

Planners of the IEP should use the above evaluations, measures, and observations, as well as the amount of time available for instruction, to establish realistic goals. Planners must decide whether the goals can be met within the regular program, or whether supplementary instruction or additional hours with a specialist are necessary. Where the services of additional support personnel are required, this need should be documented and the persons responsible for this support should be listed in the IEP.

Alternative Placement

If the nature or severity of the child's handicap is such that he cannot achieve satisfactorily in a regular classroom, special classes, separate schooling, or some other educational environment should be selected. (See section 612 (5) (B) of P.L. 94-142.) This implies that school districts provide a continuum of alternative placements, including instruction in regular classes, special classes, and special schools, as well as home instruction and instruction in hospitals or institutions.

The act also requires that supplementary services be provided, such as a resource room for itinerant instruction, in conjunction with regular class work. Severely handicapped children sometimes display unpleasant behavior or behavior defects (language, social interaction, motor behavior) that are extremely difficult and time-consuming to correct. When the handicapped child is so disruptive in a regular classroom that the education of other students is significantly impaired, or when the needs of the handicapped child cannot be met in that environment, placement in regular classes is obviously inappropriate. (See section 12a, 552(c), (d) of P.L. 94-142.)

Extracurricular Activities

The law requires that nonacademic services or extracurricular activities, such as meals, recess periods, athletics, and clubs, should be arranged in such a way that children with handicaps may participate with nonhandicapped children to the extent appropriate. (See section 12a, 553.) The law also requires modifications in school facilities, such as ramps, special toilet facilities, and crash-bar doors, to accommodate students in wheelchairs and those who suffer sensory defects. The child must be given access to all aspects of the school program normally provided for the nonhandicapped, including art, music, physical education, library science, and other special subjects or services.

Testing Programs

Further, the regulations state that teachers should not "put undue reliance" on tests that may discriminate against those with below-average sensory, manual, or visual skills. Parents or legal guardians must be informed in advance of any placement decision. This probably requires that parents be consulted with regard to "social promotion" (promoting a child to the next grade even though he has not satisfactorily mastered the previous grade). If the parents disagree with the placement decision, they may appeal at a formal hearing.

School officials must assure the confidentiality of all data and information regarding the child, and access to the child's records must always be made immediately available to the child's parents.

It should be obvious that P.L. 94-142 has thoroughly prepared the ground for future litigation. School administrators are advised to become thoroughly familiar with this law and to institute procedures and practices to decrease the likelihood of legal action.

P.L. 94-142 and Athletics

Handicapped students may not be denied the opportunity to compete on athletic teams or to participate in physical education, intramurals, or club activities due to their handicaps. The handicapped student can be denied participation only if he does not meet basic prerequisites for an activity. Denial of admission into the activity must be on the same basis as for students without handicaps.

A due process violation may be deemed to have occurred if a child is classified as handicapped when he actually is not, or if the child is improperly classified. A charge of misclassification may be made if the court rules that the criteria utilized are invalid. Some courts have accepted the argument that intelligence tests bear little relationship to intelligence if they are administered in a language other than the child's native language, or within a cultural context with which the child is not familiar.[22]

Athletic Scholarships

If college athletic scholarships are awarded in a given sport, individuals may not be denied such scholarships due to handicaps. A handicapped athlete can only be denied a scholarship if the decision is based on skills and abilities, as compared to other candidates for scholarships in the particular sport in question. However, section 504 neither states nor implies that scholarships must be awarded in specific sports. For an athletic team sponsored entirely for handicapped students, such as wheelchair basketball, it is not necessary to award scholarships just because they are given to participants in regular basketball.

Handicapped students who have not reached their majority, whether they are in high school or college, may be required to obtain parental consent (and in the case of contact sports, a physician's approval) in order to participate. If a student has reached majority age, the student himself must provide signed consent.

In writing a handicapped student's IEP, it is not only permissible, but highly desirable, to list physical or motor fitness outcomes as goals. Recent research from the Paralyzed Veterans of America shows that individuals confined to wheelchairs due to paraplegia, quadriplegia, or leg amputations have significantly higher incidences of fatal cardiac, cardiorespiratory, and cardiovascular dysfunctions. Similar findings have been reported for people with other types of handicaps. Programs to reduce obesity and improve physical fitness of handicapped students would satisfy a realistic need.

Special Services for the Handicapped

A U.S. district court has ruled that the state of Pennsylvania must provide special education in excess of the usual 180-day school year to any handi-

---

[22]*Hobson* v. *Hanson,* 369 F. Supp. 401, 514 (D.D.C. 1967), aff'd sub. nom. *Smuch* v. *Hobson,* 408 F. 2d 1975 (D.C. Cir. 1969); *Larry P.* v. *Riles, Jr.* 10; *Diana* v. *State Board of Education,* Cir. No. C-70-37, R.F.P. (N.D. Col. January 7, 1970 and June 18, 1973); *Mattie, T.* v. *Holladay,* Cir. No. D.C. 75-31-5 (N.D. Miss., filed April 25, 1975); *Diana* v. *Bd.,* fn. 13; *Guadalupe Oeg.* v. *Tempe,* Civ. Act. No. 71-435 (D. Ariz. 1972); *Serna* v. *Portales,* 449 F. 2d 1147 (10th Cir. 1974).

capped child who requires such a program. If children with severe handicaps would regress as a result of interruptions of their special education program over weekends or the summer months, the school district must provide for such need.

If handicapped students wish to play wheelchair basketball, but their number is insufficient to form a full team, the local education agency must make efforts to provide this program. Although the individual school would be unable to provide the program, the school district should make efforts to organize a system-wide team with members from several schools, or cooperative efforts could be undertaken with the city recreation department or through participation in the National Wheelchair Basketball Association.

If games can be modified to enable the handicapped to participate, without placing other participants at a disadvantage, the physical educator, intramural director, or recreation director must do so. (For example, a ball might be painted other than its usual color to increase its visibility for partially or legally blind players.) Many adjustments are possible to enable the handicapped to participate in physical education and intramurals. A few of these are use of the buddy system (in which a handicapped child is paired with a nonhandicapped child), peer tutoring, team teaching with a regular and a special physical education teacher, extra classes for the handicapped to supplement (but not replace) the regular physical education class, utilization of student squad leaders or gym captains, and the use of teaching stations.

The American Alliance for Health, Physical Education, Recreation, and Dance has answered a number of questions concerning implications of P.L. 94-142 and Section 504 for the conduct of physical education programs.[23] The alliance points out that, for example, students unable to enter the water unassisted could be lifted from their wheelchairs and placed into the pool, or could be carried into the water on a stretcher, which is removed afterward. However, these procedures could be utilized only from the date of passage of the law until June 3, 1980. This "transition period" was written into the law to give schools time to adapt the physical characteristics of their facilities and grounds. After June 3, 1980, schools were expected to have made it possible to achieve program accessibility in more appropriate and acceptable ways.

At the present time, the use of a stretcher may or may not be a violation, as determined on a case-by-case basis. With individuals who are so severely handicapped that mobility can only be achieved through use of a stretcher, the above procedure is acceptable. However, for individuals with greater mobility, use of the procedure to circumvent making the swimming pool accessible would be a violation of the spirit and letter of Section 504, its policies and interpretations.

If a student majoring in physical education has a condition that prohibits meeting a specific course requirement, such as swimming, the student may not be expelled from the overall program. Rather, other requirements must

---

[23]American Alliance for Health, Physical Education, Recreation, and Dance, *Update,* November 1979, p. 12; June 1979, pp. 12–13.

be substituted. The rationale for this is that not all physical education teachers are expected to teach swimming, just as not all physicians are required to perform surgery (and, therefore, blind students cannot be denied entrance into medical schools).

The case of an applicant for a registered nursing program, who was denied admission because of a hearing impairment, may have some implications for possible future court decisions.[24] Frances Davis successfully completed the prerequisites for admission to the nursing program at Southeastern Community College in North Carolina, but during a routine admissions interview it became evident that she suffered from a hearing disability. After examination, an audiologist reported that even with an improved hearing aid, Frances Davis could not understand normal speech. College officers consulted the executive director of the North Carolina Board of Nursing, who stated that Davis's disability would make it impossible for her to participate safely in the normal clinical training program or to practice as a registered nurse. The conclusion was that it would not be possible to make modifications in the training program to accommodate Davis without destroying the benefits of the program.

Davis's suit in federal district court, based on Section 504, was lost because her disability would prevent her from performing "sufficiently" in the program. Davis then appealed to the U.S. Court of Appeals, which held that her application should have been considered on the basis of her academic and technical qualifications, without regard to her hearing ability. The case was next taken to the Supreme Court, where it was determined that "Section 504 does not compel educational institutions to disregard the disabilities of handicapped individuals or to make substantial modifications in their programs to allow disabled persons to participate."[25]

Flygare points out that the Davis decision is a momentous one because the court emphasized that Section 504 does not require affirmative action, but rather imposes the lesser obligation that institutions avoid discrimination against handicapped persons.[26] This ruling may nullify such requirements of the Department of Education as the use of supplementary aids and services to "mainstream" handicapped students into regular school programs, payment by school districts for a public or private residential program (including nonmedical care and room and board, when necessary), or the making of costly structural alterations.

It is a violation of Section 504 to deny handicapped students instruction from trained and certified teachers of physical education on the basis that their special education teachers are carrying out the student's IEP. Under these circumstances, handicapped students are being discriminated against,

---

[24]*Davis* v. *Southeastern Community College,* 424 F. Supp. 1341 (E.D.N.C. 1976); 584 F. 2d 1158 (4th Cir. 1978).

[25]47 U.S.L.W. 4689.

[26]Thomas J. Flygare, "Schools and the Law," *Phi Delta Kappan,* February 1979, pp. 456–57; September 1979, pp. 63–64.

since they are not receiving the services of physical education specialists to the same degree as are non-special-education students.

Reimbursement for Handicapped Students

The law authorizes a payment to each state of thirty percent of the average per-pupil expenditure in U.S. elementary and secondary schools, multiplied by the number of handicapped children ages three to twenty-one who are receiving special education and related services. By 1982, the reimbursement will be forty percent, for a maximum payment of $31.6 billion. The local education agency receives seventy-five percent of the funds, while the state education department receives twenty-five percent.

P.L. 94-142 and Lawsuits

P.L. 94-142 is pregnant with possibilities for lawsuits. There may be litigation contending bias in evaluation and placement procedures. Or the tests themselves or the manner in which they are administered or interpreted may be cause for litigation. If a test is represented as having been validated for a specific purpose, and if the validation is later shown to be defective, both the producer of the test and the user may be held liable.

Placement decisions that rely heavily on teacher assessments that consider cultural background and adaptive behavior may be challenged. A student with learning disabilities could allege that his placement in a regular class forced him to compete with students who were not learning disabled, and that he suffered severe emotional and psychic injury as a result. Parents may feel that they have not been adequately included in the decision-making process or in the preparation of the IEP.

Although the regulations state that a teacher or other school employee is not to be held liable for the child's failure to achieve the objectives of the IEP, it is certain that liability will arise if school personnel: (1) fail to furnish a handicapped child with an IEP, do not require the IEP to be developed by the required group of persons, or make no efforts to involve the child's parents; (2) exclude a child from the IEP conference if he could contribute to it; (3) write IEPs that assure only minimum projections of short-term goals and long-term objectives; or (4) fail to furnish, or do not make good faith efforts to secure, all the services necessary for the child.

Because of the number of people involved in the construction of an IEP, confidentiality of records will pose a problem. Transportation of students with a variety of handicaps will increase the probability of an accident that could lead to litigation. School administrators should check with their insurance agents regarding coverage for these situations.

Prudent school administrators and teachers should take all the necessary steps when dealing with parents to prevent direct confrontation and litigation. An adversary relationship between school personnel and parents must be avoided.

/ 11 /

Transportation

As Edmund E. Reutter put it: "The transportation of pupils is one of the most hazardous activities engaged in by school boards today."[1] The stakes are high, in terms of money, the value of human life, and physical well-being. But it is not a danger that is limited solely to school boards. It extends to all drivers and pedestrians.

If A loans his car to his son so he can drive to a basketball game, what happens if he is in an accident? What happens if someone he picked up is injured? And does it make any difference if he was specifically told not to pick up riders? What if a teacher loans his car to a student to do an errand? If there is an accident, is the teacher liable?

With the advent of shorter work weeks and more leisure time, the shape of education will also change. Instead of simply developing the mind, education will develop the body as well. And since most schools will not have proper facilities for this phase of education, schools will be assuming even greater roles in the area of transportation.

Education is a dynamic process. Stimulation of an individual's desire to learn has been recognized as an important goal. What better way to awaken the desire to learn than to use the resources available in the community? But to reach these resources, transportation must be provided. And as field trips increase, so does the likelihood of injury.

Another consideration is the U.S. Constitution. Equal protection requires equal treatment for all persons. The courts have begun to actively enforce this mandate. The Constitution is the supreme law of the land, but our democratic right to privacy cushions its effect on private organizations.

---

[1] Edmund S. Reutter, *Schools and the Law*, 3rd ed., Legal Almanac Series No. 17 (Dobbs Ferry, N.Y.: Oceana Publications, Inc., 1970), p. 87.

STATE ACTION AND TRANSPORTATION

Private schools that receive governmental assistance fall directly under the injunction not to discriminate, just as do all public institutions. This touchstone of governmental aid, which allows the federal law to directly affect a private entity, is called *state action*.

With respect to private institutions and athletic activities, if the school is in a conference composed solely of private schools, or if it is not part of a conference, it is not strictly under the control of state action. However, a private institution that is part of a conference with public schools does fall under the umbrella of state action. One day, of course, state action may be expanded to include all schools.

There is an affirmative duty to provide equal opportunities for both men and women. To aid in determination of whether or not there actually is equality for both sexes, the Department of Education has stated that it will examine a number of factors. Among these will be per diem expenses and transportation.[2] This will most likely mean that more transportation will be provided through the schools.

According to the Supreme Court, the Constitution does not bar the use of public funds for transportation of children to nonpublic schools.[3] Thus we foresee "public" transportation used in conjunction with new and varied activities.

As the availability of transportation increases, so do opportunities for legal liability on the part of those who provide the transportation.

STATUTES AND STANDARDS OF CARE

Statutes are particularly important in the area of transportation. It is through statutes that legal authorities set the standard of care to be applied. Without specified standards parents would have no way of complaining that a school board used unsafe equipment or employed careless drivers.[4] The importance of checking all applicable statutes on driver and vehicle eligibility requirements cannot be overemphasized.[5]

Since 1900, almost all the states have enacted legislation relating to school transportation: who is allowed to be carried, where and when, safety

---

[2]Philip R. Hochberg, chairman, representing professional and college sports teams and leagues, Practicing Law Institute, Patents, Copyrights, Trademarks, and Literary Property Course Handbook Series, No. 84 (New York: 1977), p. 379, C.F.R. 86.41 cc.

[3]Reutter, *Schools and Law*, p. 87.

[4]Madeline Kinter Remmlein and Martha L. Ware, *School Law*, 3rd ed. (Danville, Ill.: The Interstate Printers and Publishers, Inc., 1970), p. 258.

[5]Herb Appenzeller, *From the Gym to the Jury* (Charlottesville, Va.: Education Division, The Michie Co., 1970), p. 147.

standards for drivers, and insurance requirements.[6] Besides checking state-wide legislation, it is also important to check individual school board rules and regulations, since these have the effect of laws.

Generally speaking, the courts have been much less liberal in interpreting transportation statutes than they have been in construing other statutory powers of local school boards. For example, a statute that allowed transportation to be provided to and from school would not be interpreted to include extracurricular activities, such as school-related field trips and transportation to athletic contests.[7]

When there are rules or regulations governing student conduct on school buses, they can be enforced by the drivers, since the drivers are among those sought to be aided by the enactment of such laws.[8]

TRANSPORTATION AS A GOVERNMENTAL OR PROPRIETARY FUNCTION

Since governments are generally immune from suit, it is very important to determine whether transportation was made available as a governmental function or as a proprietary function. (As the reader will recall, the former connotes a discretionary function performed by the government through its employees; the latter connotes a business activity in which the government is the owner, similar to an independent businessman.)

As an example, a female minor was injured by a school bus that was owned by the school district and negligently operated by one of its employees. The victim was unable to recover because the Pennsylvania law said that the school district was immune from tort liability, since the operation of school buses was deemed a governmental function. Had the tort arisen from some performance of a proprietary act, the school district would have been a possible defendant.[9]

Some jurisdictions have not yet ruled whether transportation of pupils is a governmental or a proprietary act. Where it is not specifically stated to be the latter, immunity is presumed.

Unless there is a statute expressly stating otherwise, a school district may not be sued for the wrongful acts of its officers, employees, or agents when they are engaged in a purely governmental function. Transportation of pupils to school is usually considered a governmental function.

An employee of the government is not necessarily protected by the veil of governmental immunity for damages resulting from negligent operation

---

[6]Reuter, *Schools and Law,* p. 83.

[7]Ibid., pp. 84–85.

[8]Ibid., p. 88.

[9]*Meyerhoffer* v. *East Hanover Township School District,* 280 F. Supp. 81 (Penna. 1968).

of a motor vehicle, even though the negligent operation occurred during the course of his employment. For example, Henry Strueland was negligently driving a school bus when he struck a Ms. Anderson's car at an intersection. Ms. Anderson sued both Strueland and the school district.

At the time and in the jurisdiction where the accident occurred, there was no statute waiving governmental immunity, but there was a statute providing for the purchase of a limited amount of liability insurance. Thus Ms. Anderson could not sue the school district but was able to recover from the driver of the school bus. The court reasoned that the one who commits a tort, or wrongful act, violates a duty owed to the injured party. Thus Strueland was liable, even though he was engaged in a governmental function and his employer was exempt.[10]

SCHOOL DISTRICTS AS PLAINTIFFS

When a party is unable to sue a school district, the school district may still sue for damages to its own property. Consider a bus, operated by a school district employee, which is involved in a collision with an automobile in the course of the driver's employment. In this situation, the driver of the car might be prevented from bringing suit against the school district, but the school district could sue the car driver for damages to the bus. The driver of the car could raise the defense of the bus driver's own negligence and thereby prevent the school district from recovering. But the car driver could not recover for the damages he sustained as a result of the collision.

When nothing is expressly stated, immunity is presumed, although such strict immunity may be circumvented where there is a law that relates to transportation or recovery for a transportation-related injury. The mere existence of the law could imply that compensation should be given to the injured party.[11] For example, statutes requiring the purchase of auto insurance for bodily injury and liability could enable an injured party to recover up to the amount of insurance authorized or actually purchased.[12]

INSURANCE RIDERS

The importance of securing an insurance rider to cover passengers in a personal vehicle cannot be overemphasized. As a case in point, Forest Nag-

---

[10]*Anderson* v. *Calamus Community School District, Clinton County,* 174 N.W. 2d 643 (Iowa 1970).

[11]*Independent School District No. 16 of Payne County* v. *Reed,* 503 P. 2d 1265 (Oklahoma 1972).

[12]Reutter, *Schools and Law,* p. 88; *Longpre* v. *Joint School District No. 2,* 443 P. 2d 1 (Montana 1968).

gle was hired by a school district as a teacher and coach. With the permission of school officials and at their expense, Mr. Naggle drove his own car to a basketball tournament. He took with him two student participants — Darlene and his own child, Lanny. On the return trip, there was a serious accident. Mr. Naggle was killed and the two students were injured. Mrs. Naggle sued for death benefits for her husband and for medical benefits for Lanny. Darlene's father also sought medical benefits for her.

The relevant insurance policy and rider specifically covered the school's ten buses and allowed for a substitute auto to be included whenever one of the buses was not used (for whatever reason). Since this was an officially approved athletic event , Mr. Naggle's car was covered by the insurance. Lanny and Darlene's medical expenses were covered by the policy. However, the insurance rider had a specifically worded disclaimer of coverage for the owner of the substitute auto. Thus Mrs. Naggle was unable to collect any benefits from the school as a result of the loss of her husband.[13]

It is recommended that the school board's attorney or insurance agent make certain that the school's policy cover personal cars as follows:

1. When a personal car is loaned out for a school or business errand.
2. Coverage if the car owner is injured when the car is in use for school business.
3. Coverage of passengers when the car is used for school business.
4. Coverage not only for medical bills, but for liability (in the event of a suit arising out of an accident occurring when the car is on school business).
5. Coverage when the car is carrying another teacher.
6. Coverage when carrying guests (parents, students, spectators) *at no charge*.
7. Coverage for passengers who are being charged (for example, pitching in for gas, buying a meal, or supplying other compensation for the ride).

GUESTS AND AUTO LIABILITY

Consider the case of Clark, who offered to drive some cheerleaders to an away game. Father Studer, the athletic director, gave his consent but gave Clark no directions or instructions. Clark was to receive no compensation for his services.

As Clark was cruising along, at about fifty-five mph, he approached the intersection at which he was supposed to turn. Realizing that he was not going to be able to make the turn in time, he started to drive on. At that

[13]*Southern Farm Bureau* v. *Naggle,* 437 S.W. 2d 215 (Arkansas 1969).

instant, some of the five cheerleaders yelled "Turn!" In a panic, Clark turned. He thought he could make the turn, but he was wrong. Rosemary was one of the cheerleaders injured in the ensuing accident.

The applicable law required proof of wanton or willful misconduct or recklessness on the part of the operator before a "guest" could recover for injuries. This level of conduct is similar to an intentional act of negligence. The court found that this incident entailed only simple negligence, not the recklessness required by the statute.

A passenger is not a "guest," within the meaning of the statute, when the owner of the motor vehicle receives some benefit from transporting the passenger. However, benefits that are derived from hospitality, companionship, or good fellowship are not included; they are considered insufficient to render a passenger not a guest. (A passenger who is not a guest, within the meaning of the statute, has an easier task of showing that the owner or operator simply failed to use ordinary care, or that the owner or operator simply was negligent.)

Clark's benefit in driving the cheerleaders to the game was of the abstract type and was insufficient to render his passengers nonguests. No additional compensation was given to him. He simply offered to drive the cheerleaders to an away game, with the athletic director's approval.

Since Rosemary was considered a guest, she had to show that Clark exercised gross negligence. But the court found nothing more than simple negligence, and Clark was not held liable for the injuries.[14]

CAR OWNER'S LIABILITY

Although the operator of an automobile is always held primarily liable for negligent operation in the event of an accident, in many states the owner may be held liable even though he was not driving at the time of the accident. The owner in most states is not liable for injuries to a guest in his vehicle unless the driver was found to be grossly negligent. "Guest statutes" generally state that a person who is the guest of another in his vehicle, without compensation, may not sue the owner or operator for injury, death, or loss in case of an accident, unless that accident was caused by the willful or wanton misconduct of the owner or operator.

The rationale for the differing treatment of guests and nonguests in this context can be seen in its history: one of the reasons guest statutes were originally enacted was to prevent collusion between owners and operators of motor vehicles and their friends (guests) against newly formed insurance companies.

---

[14]*Fessenden v. Smith,* 124 N.W. 2d 554 (Iowa 1964).

Teachers, coaches, and athletic directors should determine whether their state has a guest statute before transporting athletes in private or school-owned vehicles.

PRINCIPAL-AGENT RELATIONSHIP

In determining liability for injuries sustained in a transportation-related accident, it is important to establish who is responsible for the transportation. For example, is the driver an agent for someone else, or is he an independent contractor? The doctrine of *vicarious liability* imputes the agent's acts to the principal, if the agent was acting within the scope of his job or duty. In a principal-agent relationship, the former will only be responsible for the agent's acts if he has somehow consented to them with knowledge of all material facts.

In a relevant case, an automobile dealer, Oxford Motors, contracted with a county school superintendent to loan a car for use in the driver education program. Due to abuses in the use of the driver education car the previous year, and due to the reluctance with which it was loaned in the subject year, a letter was circulated to all school principals notifying them that use of the car was restricted to the driver education program.

Mr. Strickland, a school principal and basketball coach, told Mr. Frazier, the driver education teacher, that he (Strickland) had the dealer's permission to use the car for school-related errands. One of these errands consisted of driving to another city to arrange for participation in a basketball tournament. While en route, there was an accident in which both Strickland and a student passenger were fatally injured.

Strickland was not a driver education instructor, nor did he have the school board's authority to use the driver education car. The court ruled that whether the dealer and Mr. Frazier knew the school principal was using the car for other school-related errands was not important, since it did not equate this knowledge with knowledge on the part of the county board of education. Without this knowledge on the part of the board of education, the county could not be held liable for the death of the student passenger. It had neither authorized nor consented to such use of the car by its agent, the high school.[15]

There are several theories that come to bear in the principal-agent relationship. Since the principal hires the agent, he is responsible for selecting a competent agent. It is the principal who has the power to set an activity in motion by hiring an agent to perform certain acts. The principal also has power to set standards by which the agent operates. Thus, the principal has control over the agent's activities. The principal receives the benefit and,

---

[15]*Sumter County* v. *Pritchett,* 186 S.E. 2d 798 (Georgia 1971).

therefore, should also be responsible for damages resulting from the agent's acts. Of course, the principal is much more apt to carry insurance than is the agent or employee. And the principal is in a much better position to distribute the cost of a loss due to an employee's negligence to all beneficiaries of a service.

For example, if a child is run over by a bus driven by an employee of a school district, and if the school district is required to pay a certain amount for the child's wrongful death, the school district would be able to raise transportation costs to pay the court's order and to compensate for increased insurance expenses.

In another case, Coach Russ needed a car to transport some players to a football game. A fellow teacher volunteered the use of her car, with the specification that only Coach Russ drive it. Her compensation was limited to reimbursement for gas by the school district.

The coach died as a result of taking an abrupt curve at too great a speed. Rick, a passenger and team member, was among the injured. As incredible as it may seem, the teacher who lent her car had to bear the cost of the accident. The court ruled that since she was the owner, a prima facie case was established that the coach was her agent. Since no mention was made of her *lending* the car, or of the coach *borrowing* the car, the evidence showed her to be the principal and, therefore, in control of the agent.

As for the team members in the car, the court found that they, in turn, were under the coach's control. Thus the principal, or owner of the car, was also responsible for Rick's injuries.[16]

INDEPENDENT CONTRACTORS

By definition, an *independent contractor* is not his employer's agent but is in control of his own work, usually having independent financial responsibility. An employer will not be liable for the negligent acts of an independent contractor.

There is frequently a fine line between agents and independent contractors, and the courts are not reluctant to look beyond the form of the agreement (that is, to the substance of the employment) in establishing the type of relationship that actually existed.

The case of Cumberland (Wisconsin) High School (previously discussed in Chapter 4) bears reexamination. When the high school won the right to participate in a state basketball tournament, the school's principal arranged for three buses to transport students and chaperones. He did this by polling students, faculty, and parents to determine how many buses to hire. After a

---

[16]*Gorton* v. *Doty*, 69 P. 2d 136 (Idaho 1937).

multi-vehicle collision in which one of the buses rammed into a faculty member's car, the question of liability arose: who was responsible, the bus company or the school?

Among the evidence the court used in arriving at its decision was the state's statute dealing with school transportation. The statute read that a school district "may provide transportation" for extracurricular activities. The court interpreted this to mean that although the school district did not have to provide such transportatlon, it might choose to through a contract with a common carrier, provided that the company had sufficient insurance. (Only minimal amounts of insurance were specified.)

The court ruled that whether the trip involved a contract carrier or a common carrier, the overall designation of the transportation company as a common carrier was not altered in this case. This is important in determining liability for injuries sustained. If the transportation company were found to have been hired by the school, it is considered an independent contractor and is liable for its own acts. If it is found to have been employed by the school, subject to the school's *control*, the transportation company would be considered a mere agent of the school, and the school would be responsible for the accident. To determine such an important matter, the court had to decide who had the right to control the details of the work.

The school principal had signed a "commercial charter coach order," which stated the departure and arrival times for the trip. The route was also designated. Although the high school activity fund issued a check for the trip, the expense was ultimately paid for by collecting from the passengers.

The court ruled that had anything been left out, one would have to question whether a contract existed at all: the driver was not specially picked, the manner of driving was not specified, nor was the specific bus chosen. All significant factors that could possibly give rise to liability were left to the transportation company.

The general rule is that one who contracts for services of an independent contractor is not liable to others for the acts of the independent contractor. The exception is where contracted services involve inherent danger or special risks. Driving on the highway does not fall within this exception.

CHARTERED V. LEASED VEHICLES

A chartered vehicle is distinguished from one that is rented or leased. The amount of control the user exercises over each is different, and the courts have so held.[17]

There are situations in which an employer who hires an independent contractor could be liable for injuries caused by the latter's acts. If the employer knows of dangerous practices and allows them to continue, he

---

[17]*Averette v. Traveler's Insurance,* 174 So. 2d 881 (La. App. 1965).

will be considered negligent. If the employer is negligent in either giving directions or in providing equipment to the independent contractor, he may also be liable. There is a rule of law that no one can delegate liability by delegating inherently dangerous work or work involving a special risk.

Common carriers or public transporters also cannot delegate the duty imposed by law to keep their passengers free from even ordinary negligence. The rationale for this is that they warrant to the public that they shall provide good, comfortable, and reasonably safe transportation. This establishes a duty and if they fail in this duty, with resulting injuries, they will be held liable.

JOINT VENTURES AND SHARED LIABILITY

It is often the case that a manager, say, a club manager, may befriend a young member who is anxious to learn more about the operation. This young "colleague" hangs around and offers to help with general odd jobs. He "volunteers" to tag along, to keep the manager company while running errands. Similarly, a coach frequently brings a player with him when he goes to pick up or drop off equipment. Or a group of people may get together for a camping trip during spring break.

Consider what these situations have in common: more than one person is involved, and each situation involves transportation of property belonging to one or more participants.

If the driver of a car used in such an activity is negligent in causing injury, it is possible that *all those accompanying him could be equally liable* for the damage done. When this happens, the situation is termed a *joint venture*.

In such a situation, the negligence of one participant is imputed to the others (unless it is an action of one against another). Joint venture usually applies to, but is not limited to, commercial activities. The following four characteristics should be present to constitute a joint venture: (1) express or implied agreement among the joint venturers to participate; (2) a common group purpose; (3) a community of pecuniary interest in the group (to make money); and (4) an equal right of control or voice in the group's operation.

With the school principal's permission, Everett J. Mullins, a janitor, got five volunteers from the eighth grade to help load a drag onto his truck so that he could return it to its owner. Though nothing was said about the volunteers accompanying Mullins, they jumped on the back of the truck. At a curve in a gravel road, there was a small incline about twenty-seven inches high and at an angle of about seventy degrees. At the top of the incline was a train, which was backing up at about forty-five to fifty mph.

The train crashed into Mullins's truck, and all six were killed. Testimony revealed that although the locomotive did not brake until it was within a few feet of the truck, it appeared to all that Mullins would stop at any second and that he never looked either way, only straight ahead. Since no negligence was shown on the part of the railroad, it was dismissed as a defendant.

The court ruled that the volunteers were not joint venturers with Mullins — they were not acting with a common business purpose, with mutual interest in the trip itself as part of that purpose. Each was not responsible for the manner in which the truck was operated. The boys were only performing a requested service, solely for the benefit of a school employee and for the school district.

The court also said that the five volunteers were not guests. Therefore there was no need to show willful or wanton misconduct in order to recover. The benefit received by Mullins was more than incidental to hospitality and companionship. It was primarily for a specific objective. Therefore, the five passengers were not considered guests within the meaning of the guest statute. A new trial was ordered on the grounds of ordinary negligence, with the school district and Mullins's estate as defendants.

In a suit seeking wrongful death and funeral expenses, the jury determined that there was no negligence by the school district in requesting its students to perform services for it.[18]

DUE CARE

The law imposes on all persons the duty to use due care under the circumstances. That is, the law is not looking for "super teacher" or "super driver," but merely requires that each person exercise the standard of care that an average prudent person would exercise in the same or similar circumstances. This duty to use due care naturally varies with the age and maturity of the individual involved.

Modern principles define duty in terms of foreseeability. If, given a certain situation, injury or loss could reasonably have been foreseen, there exists a duty to avoid the injury or loss.

On June 3, 1965, LeRoy Patten was pulling a bus into the half-circle driveway to take his regular riders home from school. To reach the proper loading point, Patten had to pull out and around two buses that had arrived before he did. Although the driveway was nineteen feet wide, Patten's left wheels went off the edge as he pulled around. Going about fifteen mph, Patten applied his brakes when he saw a six-year-old child run out in front of the bus to retrieve a shoe. Skidding some twelve feet, Patten did not stop until he was about even with the bus he was attempting to pass. The left calf muscle of the child was severely torn as the bus skidded over his leg.

The court ruled that Patten did not act as a reasonably prudent person would have acted in the same or similar circumstances. It was negligence to operate a school bus on school grounds in close proximity to young children in the manner in which Patten did.[19]

---

[18]*Enlow* v. *Illinois Central Railroad Company,* 243 N.E. 2d 847 (Illinois 1969).

[19]*Crawford* v. *Wayne County Board of Education,* 168 S.E. 2d 33 (North Carolina 1969).

In another case, a boy just under thirteen years of age was killed by a bus that backed up on a playground. The jury found that the driver was not negligent. This means that he must have driven the bus with due care in the vicinity of school children. Some recovery was allowed for the boy's parents. The school district was brought in as a second defendant under the theory that it had failed to provide supervision of the students while they awaited the buses, and that it had failed to promulgate and enforce rules and regulations for the children's safety while they waited.[20]

Yet another case involved a university van loaded with equipment and soccer players. It proceeded as part of a small convoy for a game in Philadelphia. The coach's car led the way as they left the campus and cruised along the highway. As they approached an intersection, the light turned to yellow and the coach, Mr. Kline, suddenly stopped his car. The student who was driving the van, Gary Adams, applied his brakes, but it did no apparent good. The van crashed into Coach Kline's car, and Adams was hurt.

The reason for Adams's injury was that the van was overloaded, which prevented the brakes from working effectively. The van was carrying between 1300 and 1400 pounds in equipment and passengers, but its carrying capacity was only about 900 pounds. In this case, since there was no prior warning that the brakes were defective, the duty to exercise due care in the circumstances did not include a duty on the part of the coach or university to test the brakes or to examine the vehicle. Had they known, or should they have known, that something was amiss, such a duty would have arisen.

But the court found that Adams, the injured van driver, did have a valid personal claim against Coach Kline. The theory under which Adams could sue was that Kline provided the university van and knew, or should have known, that when he allowed the overloading the van would not be able to stop as quickly. Thus it was foreseeable that an injury could occur.

The court stated: "If a teacher allows his pupil to use an instrument of equipment which is under the control of the teacher and which the teacher knows, or should know, is unsuitable for such use and could foreseeably cause harm, the teacher is liable for any harm proximately resulting from the pupil's use of the unsuitable equipment or instrument."[21]

To return to the case of school bus drivers, reasonable care would include safe exit from the bus to the sidewalk, although this does not make the driver an insurer of the child's absolute safety. In a relevant case, seven-year-old Lorraine Pratt alighted from a school bus with her two older brothers. Eight children regularly used this stop, and all eight had to cross a busy intersection in order to reach home, the same intersection that the bus passed en route to the next stop. (The facts of the case are unclear as to

---

[20]*Barth* v. *Central School District No. 1,* 102 N.Y.S. 2d 263 (New York 1951).

[21]*Adams* v. *Kline,* 239 A. 2d 230 (Delaware 1968), p. 231.

whether this was a regular route or part of a detour.) On the day in question, the bus attendant was absent and no one took his place.

Together the three youngsters crossed the intersecting streets, but by the time the boys reached the third intersection, Lorraine was lagging behind. Mr. and Mrs. Pratt had instructed the boys to take their sister's hand when crossing. On this occasion they did not. The bus driver watched the boys cross the busy intersection and saw an oncoming truck. Seeing that the bus was obstructing Lorraine's view, the driver blew his horn in an effort to warn her. It did not help, and she was hit by the truck.

Lorraine and her parents sued the city, the school district, and the bus company. But the court did not allow any recovery for the substantial bodily injuries she received. Negligence on the part of the school district (in locating the bus stop blocks away from a dangerous intersection that the children had to pass) could only be found if there was a duty of the school district to transport the students to a location from which they could walk home without crossing any dangerous streets. Such a duty could arise through statutes enacted by the state legislature, which imposed an obligation to consider the relative hazards in the paths of different children in routing school transportation. However, most statutes deal with distances and not hazards.

The court explained that the school's duty to the students arose from having actual physical custody of them, limited to the time the children were in its charge, and that when threatened by the negligence of a third party, the school had to use reasonable efforts to anticipate harm. This duty, according to a bare majority of the court, ceased when the parent was free to assume control over the child's protection.

A minority of the court argued that the duty once undertaken continued or resulted in a new duty to transport the students in a reasonably prudent manner. Attempts had been made to change the bus stop location. Since routes are flexible and since it would not have cost much in time or money, the majority believed that reasonable minds could have differed as to whether or not a duty existed, and whether a breach of duty occurred. Therefore, the majority contended, the issue should have gone to a jury to determine if there was negligence in not relocating the bus stop. If duty is to be defined in terms of foreseeability, then the school district did have a duty. According to the minority, a parent telling young brothers to watch out for their sister can never be a replacement for the duty of the school district.[22]

The court's decision in the case was a close one. This could indicate an impending change in the way the courts view the legal duty required of those who undertake the responsibility of transporting youngsters and athletes.

---

[22]*Pratt v. Robinson*, 349 N.E. 2d 849 (New York 1976).

Circumstances vary with each situation. No two cases need necessarily result in the same conclusion because no two situations are identical.

FACTORS DETERMINING DEGREE OF CARE

In examining the circumstances of a case, the court will consider each individual's knowledge of the situation and whether instructions or rules were given and followed as required by applicable laws. The law considers the different reactions one would have in an emergency situation and in a nonemergency situation. Likewise, circumstances will vary with the physical capacity, age, and maturity of individuals. The court weighs all factors carefully before determining liability for injuries.

Consider the following case. At the intersection of Robinhood Road and Shady Bluff Drive, children waited for a bus to take them to school. Although it was 8:05 A.M. and early in February, the weather was fair in North Carolina, and the children were already at play. Since there was no sidewalk at the intersection, the children were in the street, and:

> As the defendant's driver approached the stop he saw the children, who were divided into two groups . . . standing at the side of the road; the children were pushing and shoving; as the defendant's driver approached these groups he slowed the bus and pulled somewhat to the left of the curb, was traveling about two miles per hour, looking over the right front fender. The boys started to pound on the door before the bus stopped, and just before the bus came to a complete stop, the driver saw the plaintiff's head disappear under the right front fender, the bus moving approximately five feet after plaintiff's head disappeared under the right front fender."[23]

The child was knocked down and the right front wheel of the bus rolled over her.

The negligence of the driver, which was the proximate cause of the injury, consisted of approaching the children at the intersection without the high degree of care and caution occasioned by the circumstances.

Another aspect of liability in school bus accidents is illustrated by the case of a school bus that was crossing a narrow bridge. The bus was wider than the lane, so it jutted over the solid yellow line in the center of the road. When about halfway across the bridge, the driver saw a car coming toward him. But if he pulled to the right, the driver would risk colliding with a railing. The driver stayed where he was, jutting over the median, thus having made his choice between two risks, neither of which was of his own making. For the accident that ensued, should the driver be considered negligent and, therefore, liable?

---

[23]*Bin* v. *Charlotte Mechlenberg,* 1535 E. 2d 335 (North Carolina 1967), p. 528.

To determine whether taking a risk is negligent, the court looks to the probability of harm, the severity of possible harm, and the burden of taking precautions. If the first two are great and the third is less so, taking the risk is considered unreasonably negligent. In the case above, the driver was not negligent in choosing between the two risks, neither of which was of his making. The likelihood and severity of harm would be high had he chosen to hug the railing any closer. Thus the burden of taking that precaution at that point would have been considrable.[24]

PROXIMATE CAUSE AND ZONE OF DANGER

To again define legal negligence, recall that one must have failed in his duty to use due care in the circumstances, which failure proximately caused injury. To *proximately cause* an injury, the act must have been a substantial factor in inducing the result. There must be an unbroken chain between the act and the injury. A defendant, no matter who he is, may be found liable for more than just the immediate injury if a court or jury finds proximate cause to be present.

In a New Hampshire case, six-year-old Terri-Lee climbed down from the school bus, which had stopped opposite her home. From a neighbor's yard, her mother watched as she crossed the street and "when Terri reached the middle of the road, saw her struck by defendant's truck, thrown on its fender, then underneath the truck, rolling and tossing as the truck was going down; and finally she flew out from under the truck way up.[25]

Allegedly, Terri-Lee was crushed to death under the wheels of the truck. The mother's anguish and physical sickness can only be imagined. But there was no compensation for the mother! Why?

At one time, there could be no recovery for apprehension of negligently caused danger or injury for a third party who was outside the "zone of danger." The rationale was based on the idea that liability had to stop somewhere; it could not be permitted to extend indefinitely. A mother would be permitted to recover if she was, herself, so close to the collision that she feared for her own well-being. Since Terri's mother was in a distant yard, there is no way she could have feared for her own safety.

Today, courts are finally beginning to see the fallacy of the *impact rule* (physically touching), or *zone of danger rule*. To deny liability in the absence of contemporaneous impact, or because a plaintiff parent was outside the zone of physical danger, is to betray the theorem that liability should follow negligence.[26]

---

[24]*Bates* v. *Escondido Union High School District,* 24 P. 2d 884, aff'd 48 P. 2d 728 (California 1935).

[25]*Jelley* v. *La Flame,* 238 A. 2d 728 (N.H. 1968), p. 729.

[26]23 ATLA L. Rep. 58.

The same jurisdiction, in a subsequent case, dispensed with the zone of danger rule, which also limited recovery to close relatives. In the latter case, neither parent witnessed the accident, but both were on the scene within seconds and the mother had heard the terrible thud.[27]

Another jurisdiction allowed recovery for negligent infliction of mental distress when there was a definite, objective physical injury to the parent.[28] Still another jurisdiction, which set aside the impact rule criteria, did not continue to limit recovery only to family members.[29]

So the trend is away from the zone of danger rule and toward recovery for any injury that could reasonably have been foreseen to result from another's negligent act, regardless of the relationship to the actual victim.

* * * * *

As previously discussed, the principal (in the legal sense) will not be liable for failure to foresee and guard against intentional acts of his agents. Common carriers, such as airlines and bus companies, represent an exception to this rule. They would be liable for intentional acts done to their passengers that were foreseeable.

A case in point involved Thomas Hankinson, who for twenty years had a contract with the school board to use his own bus to transport elementary school children. During the course of his employment, he regularly helped to discipline his travelers by using his mirror to spot troublemakers or by assigning them seats near himself. Mr. Hankinson was also assigned two student patrol boys, who monitored conduct on the bus.

On June 5, 1963, the children began a spitball and rubber band fight. Two days later, on the homeward bound bus, the same kind of rowdiness continued. Mr. Hankinson and one of the patrol boys (the other was absent) succeeded in taking the rubber bands away from several students, but not from all of them.

The antics continued, causing thirteen-year-old Ralph Jackson, Jr. to bend over his seat. When Ralph thought it was safe, he looked up toward the back of the bus. Suddenly, something metal struck him in the eye. Ralph lost all sight in one eye, probably due to a paper clip shot from a rubber band by a fellow student.

Neither the teachers nor Mr. Hankinson had been instructed to keep rubber bands and paper clips away from children who might take them from the classroom. Although the teachers were warned of the hazards of flying objects in the classroom, Mr. Hankinson did not receive even this precautionary instruction.

---

[27]*Corso* v. *Merrill,* 406 A. 2d 300 (N.H. 1979).

[28]*Toms* v. *McConnell,* 207 N.W. 2d 140 (Michigan 1973).

[29]*Leong* v. *Takasaki,* 520 P. 2d 758 (Hawaii 1974).

Mr. Hankinson was an independent contract businessman. As such, he had the duty to exercise reasonable care for the safety of the children, and the jury found that he had properly discharged that duty.

The school board, however, was not as fortunate. The court emphasized that the relationship between students and school authorities is not voluntary but is compelled by law. School authorities are obligated to take reasonable precautions for student safety and well-being in return for their attendance at school. This obligation continues during the course of transportation, if the schools provide transportation. When they negligently discharge a duty, with injury resulting, the school authorities should be held accountable in the same manner as other tortfeasors (wrongdoers). Since municipal entities are held accountable according to the ordinary principles of negligence, it is easier for the victim to show a causal relationship between his injury and the school board's negligence in their duty of "reasonable supervisory care" for student safety.

Left for the jury to determine in the above case were the following questions: (1) whether the school board knew or should have known of the propensity of thirteen-year-old children to throw objects that could endanger eyesight; (2) whether the board failed to take necessary precautions to prevent the students from obtaining rubber bands and paper clips from the teacher's desk before boarding the bus; and (3) whether the assumption of responsibility by the school board's representatives for pupil safety on buses was adequately implemented by reasonably effective methods of supervision.[30]

INTENTIONAL V. NEGLIGENT TORTS

Intentional torts are distinguished from negligent torts. An intentional tort that occurs with some regularity in the area of transportation is false imprisonment. The occasion for such false imprisonment is often student misconduct, as illustrated in the following.

On June 20, 1967, Mr. Mooney began his regular route at about 12:15 P.M., picking up between sixty-five and seventy children in a city bus used as a school bus. On this particular day, the children persisted in their rowdiness to the point of causing damage to the bus. Mr. Mooney finally said that he was not making any more stops, but was proceeding directly to the police station.

One of the junior high school boys, Justin, watched as six other youngsters successfully escaped through a bus window. Justin decided to try it. As the bus slowed to turn a corner, it ran over the curb. Justin was jarred, fell, or jumped from the window. With its right rear wheels, the bus ran over him and Justin was crippled for life.

---

[30]*Jackson* v. *Hankinson*, 238 A. 2d 685 (New Jersey 1968); 229 A. 2d 267 (1967).

Mr. Mooney falsely imprisoned the children on the bus. Such conscious confinement is said in the law to invite escape. The court reasoned that the child's fear of his parents' reaction, as well as his fear of involvement with police, could be found to encourage escape through the window, and that it was foreseeable, especially after one or more other children succeeded in the same endeavor.

The court determined that Mr. Mooney must have known about some of the preceding escapes, and that it was foreseeable that some kind of injury would result. It was not deemed important that the type of injury that resulted was not what would normally be expected. Since Mr. Mooney was acting within the scope of his authority, both he and the city transit authority were held liable. The defense of his having been justified was denied, since it was not timely made.

Damages awarded to Justin were $500,000 for mental suffering and $75,000 for physical suffering. His father was awarded $75,000 for loss of services and $5,797.85 for medical expenses.[31]

GUIDELINES FOR SCHOOL BUS PROGRAMS

National statistics show that school buses are the safest form of transportation — they are twelve times safer than private cars. The major credit for this goes to the drivers, who must not only drive but also must serve as baby-sitters for up to fifty children (with their backs turned to the children). Children are naturally restless and often rowdy, but bus drivers have little authority to enforce good conduct and, consequently, must utilize persuasion and psychology. They must also depend upon the education of students concerning behavior on the bus. Such an educational program can be carried out only by parents and teachers.

The heavy responsibility placed upon school bus drivers mandates that they be carefully selected and that they undergo a continuing training program. The following criteria should be used in selecting drivers:

1. *Age.* Drivers should possess the judgment that comes with maturity as well as the physical capacities characteristic of young adults. Young parents often make excellent bus drivers.
2. *Experience.* The driver should have extensive and accident-free driving experience, as well as an understanding of the mechanics involved.
3. *Attitude.* Drivers must possess a sense of responsibility and self-discipline.
4. *Emotional stability.* Drivers must be patient, calm, and understanding.

---

[31]*Hanson* v. *Reedley Joint Union High School District,* 111 P. 2d 415 (California 1941); *Childs* v. *Dowdy,* 188 S.E. 2d 638 (N.C. 1972).

5. *Knowledge and skill.* Drivers should know all the local and state vehicle regulations, as demonstrated through a written test. They should also be required to demonstrate a satisfactory level of skill in driving a school bus, as demonstrated through an on-the-road test.

Drivers should be required to satisfactorily complete a basic course of instruction. Recommendations for a complete instructional program are contained in a publication of the National Commission on Safety Education, entitled *Selection, Instruction, and Supervision of School Bus Drivers.* School boards and superintendents are advised to initiate such a course. Seaton, Stack, and Loft summarize the contents of such a course as follows:[32]

1. Policies and procedures.
2. Traffic accident problems.
3. Human consideration in driving.
4. Natural laws and their relationship to driving.
5. Traffic rules and regulations.
6. A job analysis for the school bus driver.
7. Responding to emergency driving situations and providing first aid to injured passengers.
8. Proper care and maintenance of the school bus.
9. Record keeping and required reports.

The practical part of such a course, that is, actual driving instruction, should emphasize the following:

1. Basic driving skills, including experiences in starting the engine, shifting gear ratios, stopping, turning, backing, and parking.
2. Training in traffic, including a variety of situations requiring the application of defensive driving techniques.

The length of the training program will depend upon the individual needs of the drivers.

Continuing Bus Driver Education

Programs for school bus drivers should be planned and scheduled in advance, as a phase of the total instructional program. This arrangement would provide for:

1. Regular monthly meetings.
2. Meetings designated to consider special problems.

---

[32]Don C. Seaton, Herbert J. Stack, and Bernard I. Loft, *Administration and Supervision of Safety Education* (New York: The Macmillan Co., 1969), pp. 150–51.

3. Literature and pertinent instructional information.
4. Individual driver sessions with the transportation supervisor.
5. Periodic recognition meetings to present awards for accident-free driving records.
6. Informing the public of efforts to increase the efficiency of school bus transportation by sponsoring driver education.

* * * * *

School buses should always carry a fully stocked first aid kit. It is the responsibility of the driver to ensure that the kit is adequately supplied. Further, the driver must be knowledgeable regarding first aid procedures.

School bus programs must be well organized. Buses must be carefully selected and regularly inspected and maintained. Routes and stops must be carefully selected and monitored. Accurate records on drivers, equipment, violations, and accidents, as well as any letters of commendation or complaint, should be kept.

The often shocking behavior of students on school buses makes it essential that parents and children be made aware of their responsibilities in this regard. Parents should be required to pay for damage done by their children. They will then be more likely to impress on the children the importance of respecting the rights of others. Perhaps, after due process, offenders should be denied the privilege of riding the bus after a second report of unacceptable behavior. This would force parents to transport their own children, which would motivate most parents to assume responsibility for their children's behavior. Although writing of reports and securing witnesses would entail use of the bus driver's time, the long-term results would be very effective in helping solve a problem that has become troublesome, and even dangerous, in recent years.

Bus Program Supervisors

The school bus program should be under the direction of a qualified supervisor. This person would be responsible for:

1. Purchase of school buses.
2. Supervision of bus maintenance.
3. Selection and screening of drivers.
4. Instructional programs for drivers.
5. Routing and scheduling.
6. Accident investigation and analysis.
7. Solicitation of teacher and parent cooperation with regard to the bus program.
8. Arranging for instructional programs in first aid for drivers.

Guidelines for Drivers

The following guidelines are taken in large part from a publication issued by the Illinois Office of the Superintendent of Public Instruction.[33] The publication recommends that all drivers observe the following rules and regulations when operating a school bus.

1. Check the condition of the bus daily before starting out. Make certain that the windshield, lenses of all lights, rear windows, and interior of the bus are cleaned daily, and that the exterior is washed as often as necessary. In weekly inspections, check for loose nuts, loose glass, and broken or damaged seats, as well as for the proper functioning of emergency doors, batteries, radiators, brakes, and fire extinguishers.
2. Observe all rules of the road, signs, signals, and courtesies due others. Drive on the right side of the road; never stop on the left side of the road. When it is necessary to overtake a slower vehicle, be sure no third vehicle is approaching from any direction. Never pass another vehicle on a curve or upgrade.
3. Never turn or swerve suddenly. Go slowly over bumps and rough spots. Avoid jerky starts and sudden stops.
4. When carrying children, do not drive faster than fifty-five mph on the best concrete roads, and drive more slowly when required by heavy traffic, bad weather, poor roads, or other conditions. Observe the speed limits for different parts of your route. When weather conditions warrant, attach chains to bus tires. Never drive your bus within 100 feet of an automobile that you are following, except when passing, or within 300 feet of a larger vehicle.
5. Be sure that all doors are closed at all times when the bus is in motion. The emergency door must be used only in case of emergency.
6. Never leave the bus with the motor running.
7. Never coast with the clutch disengaged or the gears in neutral. Avoid changing gears on a hill; make necessary changes before starting up the hill.
8. Never operate a school bus with a trailer attached.
9. Never fill the gas tank while there are children in the bus or while the motor is running.
10. At railroad crossings, stop between ten and fifty feet from the nearest rail; open the door to the right and listen for any possible warning signal; look in both directions. When it is possible to see a sufficient distance up and down the tracks to determine that no train is coming, proceed completely across in low gear. If the nature of the crossing is such that you cannot see far enough in either direction to assure a safe crossing, the senior patrol boy or girl should get out, go to the tracks,

---

[33]Illinois School Bus Transportation Circular, ser. A., no. 171 (Office of Superintendent of Public Instruction, Springfield, Ill., 1965).

look both ways, signal the bus to come on, and walk beyond the tracks for thirty to forty feet, where the bus will stop for him. Do not open the door for a patrol boy until the bus has come to a full stop.

11. Support the patrol in its efforts to see that all children obey the rules of safe conduct and to maintain order (in going to and from the bus, boarding and alighting, and while the bus is in motion). The bus driver is always fully responsible for the safety of both bus and passengers.

12. Bus drivers must give complete attention to their driving duties and to supervision of children. Children should not be permitted to carry on any unnecessary conversation with the driver and should always be seated when the bus is in motion.

13. Drivers should park buses at the school loading point before children leave their classrooms. Buses should not be backed while pupils are in the vicinity, unless an assistant or a bus patrol member is present to guide the bus driver and to see that no children are endangered.

14. When the children are picked up in the morning and must cross a road (if the patrol is not used), the driver should beckon them to cross when it is safe to do so. The children must be instructed to await the signal that it is safe to cross. Students should be instructed to be ready when the bus arrives.

15. To discharge students, either the bus should be driven onto the school grounds or the students should be discharged where they will not have to cross a road to reach the school. It is permissible to stop a school bus on the paved portion of a roadway to load or unload.

    At all discharge points where it is necessary for students to cross a highway, it is recommended that a patrol accompany those who must cross, going at least ten feet in front of the bus to a point where traffic in both directions may be observed. The patrol and the pupils crossing the highway must receive the permission of the driver before the patrol permits the crossing to be made. When no pupil patrol is used, the driver should direct the children to a distance some ten feet in front of the bus on the shoulder of the highway. The children should remain there until a signal is given by the driver for the pupils to cross.

16. See that pupils sit in assigned seats, if this procedure is authorized by the school principal. Drivers should not put children off the bus along the route for a breach of discipline. If the breach of discipline is not corrected after a warning, and if it is of such serious nature as to warrant suspension or expulsion from school, the superintendent or principal should be notified and such pupils should not be transported until the suspension or expulsion ends.

17. Instruct pupils at least twice during the school year in (a) the use of the emergency door; (b) the safe operation of the windows; (c) the proper use of fire extinguishers; (d) the safety rule of sitting back in their seats; and (e) the safety rule of not extending hands, arms, or head through the bus windows.

18. Allow no one other than regularly assigned school officials and pupils to ride in your bus.
19. Transport no animals with school children.
20. Permit no loaded weapon or explosive of any kind on the bus.
21. In the event of an accident or breakdown while the bus is transporting children, do not leave the bus to summon help. Rather, send two of the patrol or other responsible persons to the nearest house. In case an accident causes personal injury that cannot be properly treated by the driver, a doctor should be contacted immediately. In any case of accident, notify the superintendent, principal, or other person directly in charge of transportation. Also, *notify proper police officials at once. Immediately report all school bus accidents to the office of the superintendent of schools.*
22. When stalled on the highway or shoulder of a highway, place signals (flares or red reflectors) upon the highway, one approximately 100 feet in front, one approximately 100 feet to the rear of the vehicle, and a third on the roadway side of the vehicle. This procedure applies to the period between sunset and sunrise. At other times, red warning flres are to be placed at distances of approximately 200 feet.
23. Never drive the bus with the "School Bus" signs displayed if it is not in use for official transportation.
24. Make proper use of the semaphore "Stop" arm. This arm should be swung to a stop position only when loading or unloading school children, and then only after the vehicle comes to a complete stop. The sign should be swung back before starting out again. This signal is not to be used when turning, stopping at railroad crossings, or at other stops created by traffic conditions. Do not misuse the "Stop" arm.

School Bus Patrols

Students transported on each bus should select the members of their bus patrol. They are more likely to follow instructions and commands of patrol members who were elected by them. Each bus should have a front and a rear guard. The duties of the bus patrol are to:

1. Make sure all riders are seated before the bus starts.
2. Ensure that all objects such as books and lunch boxes are properly stored.
3. Enforce the rule that children keep their heads and hands inside the bus.
4. Prohibit inconsiderate and rowdy behavior.
5. Assist younger children in getting on and off the bus.
6. Assist the driver in making attendance checks.
7. Assist in emergency situations.
8. Assist the driver by observing traffic at railroad crossings and dangerous intersections.

Patrol leaders should be drilled in procedures to be followed in emergency stops. The forward patrol leader's responsibilities in an accident are as follows:

1. If the driver is not injured:
   a. Locate injured students, if any.
   b. Assist the driver in first aid procedures.
   c. Go to the nearest phone and call for assistance.
2. If the driver is injured:
   a. Stop the bus, if it is moving.
   b. Turn off the motor and put on the hand brake.
   c. Phone for assistance.

In any emergency stop, the forward patrol leader should position flares or flags at the proper distances from the front and rear of the bus. The rear patrol leader opens the emergency door when so instructed by the driver. Both patrol leaders assist students in getting off the bus and direct them to a safe location (seventy-five to one hundred feet from the bus and off the highway). They should know how to use the fire extinguishers and be capable of helping the physically handicapped. A school bus emergency evacuation plan should be familiar to everyone riding the bus. Such a plan, however, can be effective only if periodic drills are held.

Selection, Inspection, and Maintenance of Buses

States should adopt uniform standards for school buses, and periodic inspections should be made of all buses. Drivers should report any malfunctions as soon as they become evident.

Buses must be maintained at optimum efficiency. The frame and sides of the bus must be of sufficient strength. Cheaply constructed buses can be very expensive in terms of loss of life and injury to children in the event of an accident. The *Uniform Vehicle Code* devoted several pages to regulations for school buses. Each state should adopt these codes, and schools should conform to them in all regards, that is, bus selection, maintenance, and operation. School districts should purchase an insurance policy that covers the occupants of the bus and the driver (for both liability and property damage).

Coaches, athletic directors, and directors of recreation programs, all of whom transport children on buses, are cautioned to check that the procedures described in this section are followed. If they have not been followed and an accident occurs, negligence may be proven in a lawsuit.

AIR TRAVEL

How often we have been amazed at the large leaps and bounds taken in the field of travel. More so today than ever before, we are living in a small world. With the cry for three- and four-day work weeks, there is more leisure time than ever before imagined. The general public is no longer content to sit and watch sporting events on television; the public is ready for action.

Education is keeping in step with the demands of the public, and schools are participating in world-wide competition. For example, Notre Dame's football team traveled to play in Tokyo. And far from being a trip reserved for athletes, the band joined the team.

The legal aspects in this area are not limited to the athlete-traveler. In December 1977, shortly after an NFL football game, Donald Kriner crashed a small plane into the Baltimore stadium that was the site of the game. That should make even land-glued observers and their loved ones stop and think.

One of the earliest of air disasters involving sports of which the authors are aware was in March 1931, when Knute Rockne was killed. News of his death was considered the biggest sports news story of the year according to an Associated Press poll of sports experts. The cause of that accident was finally determined to be the weather, which caused a wing to become heavily iced and to break off. There were those who contended that the pilot should have landed or turned back when weather conditions created such a low ceiling, rather than attempting to climb above the clouds.

Knute Rockne became a hero, and a movie was made portraying his life and death. He did not become a hero for dying in a plane crash, nor did the seven other passengers. Rockne was on his way to California, where he was to make a movie. After his death, the project was completed. Rockne was already famous for being responsible for the forward pass, for the offensive shift, and for changing the shape of the line in football. (He took the larger linemen and used them as interference, and he used the small, fast men in the backfield.)

There has not yet been a fatal crash involving an American professional team, but individual athletes have been killed in air accidents. Among the list are Ken Hubbs, second baseman for the Chicago Cubs; Wendell Ladner of the New York Nets basketball team; and Thurman Munson of the New York Yankees.

The National Transportation Safety Board reports statistics from 1972 to 1976 revealing that small aircraft accounted for 17,312 accidents, which took 4,806 lives.

* * * * *

Leased airplanes are not bound by the same safety standards as regularly scheduled commercial or chartered flights. This fact was revealed by the General Accounting Office, an investigative arm of Congress, to a House of Representatives subcommittee. While airline owners are actually running charters, they will use subterfuges to appear to lease the planes.[34] The 1979

---

[34]*New York Times,* August 29, 1978, p. 92; supplementary material from the New York Times News Service and the Associated Press, by Jeffrey Mills, AP writer.

Wichita State University crash, which involved twenty-eight members of the football team, was an example of this practice.

Although there is no assurance that higher safety standards would prevent other fatal crashes, a study in the Miami area found a crash rate three times as high for leased aircraft as for commercial airlines. There are vast differences between safety regulations for private and commercial aircraft, even for the same type of plane. The different safety standards apply not only to plane maintenance programs, but also to pilot experience. In essence, once an airline determines that a plane's maintenance costs are prohibitive, they may sell the plane to a new owner, who could then lease it without undertaking the extensive maintenance measures required.

Another method used to avoid commercial safety regulations is to have a third party provide a flight crew, while the owner provides the aircraft to a lessee (for example, a school). It is less costly to conform to the private regulations than it is to conform to the commercial requirements.

In time, technology will do much to improve the safety conditions of flying. It has already been alleged that, statistically, it is safer to fly than to ride in a car.

Collision-avoidance systems are one example of the advancements being made. Once a plane is airborne, such a mechanism is used to detect obstacles in the flight pattern and to change an aircraft's course, thus avoiding collision. Unfortunately, collision-avoidance systems are not yet sufficiently developed for congested areas, such as the vicinities of airports.

On December 13, 1977, the University of Evansville had a charter plane scheduled to leave from Indianapolis for Nashville. Accompanying the five crew members and twelve basketball players were a sportscaster, the sports information director, the assistant athletic director, an assistant business manager, three student managers, the president of the charter service, and the coach, Bobby Watson.

Due to bad weather, the flight was delayed for two hours. They were finally allowed to take off and were not airborne long before they crashed. All were killed. But the reason for the crash was not the weather. As it turned out, although the luggage and equipment were within the weight limits, the distribution was off-balance and caused control problems.

Other air disasters have claimed the lives of athletes from California Polytechnic Institute, Wichita State University, and Marshall University. In addition, a chartered jet crashed on February 15, 1961, en route to the World Figure Skating Championships in Prague, Czechoslovakia. All eighteen members of the United States team were among the sixty-one passengers killed. And in 1968, when Lamar University (Beaumont, Texas) was still known as Lamar Tech, four members of its track team died in a crash of a return flight from the Drake Relays in Iowa. Most of the team members from Lamar did not even participate in the relays.

The real tragedy of these disasters is the loss of life, but it does not stop there. The effects are compounded by the enduring memories of the disasters, as well as the monetary loss due to cancellation of the seasons. Following the Evansville crash, two damage suits were filed. Each asked for $7 million.

Professional organizations struck with disasters, wiping out nearly all members of a team, have contingency plans to combat the devastating losses and to help the team get back on its feet. The four major professional athletic organizations in the United States — the National Football League, the National Hockey League, the National Basketball Association, and Major League Baseball — have developed such contingency plans. Although the plans vary, all are similar in that they specify a manner for creating new professional expansion teams. This is accomplished when all teams within the league place players in a pool, from which the victimized team may select new players to complete its roster.

Colleges, on the other hand, must begin to build a new team from incoming freshmen. According to the athletic director at Marshall University, the process of rebuilding a good team took about three years. Thus smaller conferences and independent schools should consider some type of contingency plan, especially in light of the fact that, on the average, air disasters that kill an entire team or nearly an entire team occur every three years.

/ 12 /

Alternatives to Litigation

Litigation is filing a lawsuit or defending one. It is "going to court." Litigation is also expensive and time-consuming. But there are alternatives.

WORKMEN'S COMPENSATION

Workmen's compensation is insurance carried by an employer to cover employees injured within the scope of their employment. The employee gives up his right to sue for full damages, but in return he need not prove negligence on the part of the employer and cannot be held guilty of contributory negligence or assumption of risk. In order to recover under workmen's compensation, an employee need only prove that he was injured by an unusual event that occurred within the scope of his employment.

Workmen's compensation laws for most states and the nation as a whole require employers with several employees (the number varies from state to state) to carry workmen's compensation insurance. As stated above, when an employee is covered by workmen's compensation, he receives a small amount of compensation for his injury and waives the right to sue his employer for negligence. But when one has a claim under workmen's compensation, it is still wise to consult a lawyer to determine whether an additional claim against a third party can be made, whereby full damages for pain, suffering, disability, and disfigurement might be recovered.

Private schools, public schools, and athletic businesses should carry liability insurance to protect employees in the event of a claim for injuries made against them.

ARBITRATION

Professionals, including teachers and coaches, are subject to suits for possible malpractice, just as physicians are. This is also true of the new entrepreneur who opens up a racket ball court or a health spa. In each of these cases, arbitration should be considered as an alternative to lawsuits.

This can best be accomplished by having each person involved enter into a contract to arbitrate any claims arising out of injuries. This could take the form of an agreement signed before participating, just as a parent's consent form is used. The agreement would require that if anyone were injured on the premises, he would submit his claim to arbitration pursuant to the rules of the American Arbitration Association. The arbitrators' decision would be just as binding as a court decision. The arbitration procedure is already used in the medical profession, whereby malpractice suits are submitted to arbitration in some states, if the patient agrees to this procedure.

Those involved in sports (professional, commercial, or private), whether they operate a health spa or a roller skating rink, or whether they teach in the schools, might get their professional associations to lobby through a law requiring that cases involving sports injuries be submitted to a panel of professionals, rather than to a lay jury. To be fair, it might be well if the panel included some persons from occupations other than sports and physical education.

Arbitration is the submission of a disagreement to one or more impartial persons, with the understanding that the parties will abide by the arbitrators' decision. Arbitration differs from the usual judicial proceeding in a courtroom in several respects. Usually, arbitrators are selected who have a particular expertise within the field (rather than using a permanent tribunal for all disputes).

The general principles of law are not necessarily followed in arbitration, nor are arbitrators bound by the rules of evidence. The proceedings are conducted in private and usually without a recorded transcript. Reasons need not be given in support of decisions. The proceedings are usually expeditious and relatively inexpensive. Any award by the arbitrators is subject to limited appellate review. Arbitration is generally governed by rules established by the American Arbitration Association for the purpose of guaranteeing each side a fair hearing and a just decision.

As mentioned, arbitration usually comes about by contract. Such contracts may be made in advance of any dispute by including a future arbitration clause. The authors recommend this procedure for health spas, tennis clubs, country clubs, racket ball clubs, and any other contemporary commercial sports undertakings.

The American Arbitration Association recommends future arbitration clauses in contracts. The authors recommend such clauses in contracts

signed by customers when they sign up to use facilities, worded along the
following lines:

> Any controversy or claim arising out of, or relating to, this contract, or
> any breach thereof, or any injury on our premises, or arising out of the use
> of our equipment, or any other injury or dispute arising between the parties
> hereto, shall be settled in accordance with the rules of the American Arbi-
> tration Association, and judgment upon the award may be entered in any
> court having jurisdiction thereof.

A few states permit arbitration for breach of contract but do not allow it
for sports injuries allegedly due to negligence.

At this writing, there is a bill pending before the United States Senate,
the Amateur Sports Act, suggesting the American Arbitration Association
serve to settle any controversies among the various national amateur sports
organizations that seek recognition as the sole governing body of a sport.

In recent years, the medical profession has been plagued by a large
number of lawsuits, usually for large sums of money. The cost of malpractice
insurance has become almost prohibitive, thereby increasing the costs of
medical services. Further, malpractice insurance has become increasingly
difficult to obtain because fewer and fewer insurance companies are willing
to offer such policies.

The problem has caused great consternation among physicians, resulting
in extensive study by the legislative department of the American Medical
Association (AMA). The studies conducted by the AMA in this area may
have implications for the American Alliance of Health, Physical Education,
Recreation, and Dance, for associations of coaches and physical educators,
for associations of manufacturers of sporting goods, and for associations of
commercial sports facilities operators.

The experiences of the medical profession in cases involving the consti-
tutionality of arbitration statutes in various states may provide some
guidelines for those in athletics, physical education, and recreation who
might wish to initiate arbitration procedures.

A Pennsylvania trial court held that the compulsory arbitration system
provided by the Pennsylvania Health Care Services Malpractice Act is constitutional, but that the arbitrators' award is not admissible at a later trial. The
California supreme court held that a governmental entity, acting as the
bargaining agent for state employees, can enter into an agreement providing
that all medical malpractice claims arising under the group medical services
plan be submitted to binding arbitration, and that such agreement is binding
upon each covered state employee.

AMA efforts to hold down the costs of litigation have taken two approaches. In addition to arbitration, the AMA has also looked into pretrial
screening procedures. Both approaches are currently in the process of
refinement and, consequently, have encountered legal opposition in some

states while having been declared constitutional in other states. Through its pioneering efforts, the AMA could be breaking the ground for future efforts by those involved in sports, physical education, and recreation.

PRETRIAL HEARINGS

The mandatory pretrial screening procedure, as followed in Nebraska, requires a claimant to file his complaint with the medical review panel, which consists of three physicians and one nonvoting attorney (prior to commencement of court action). The panel expresses its expert opinion as to whether the evidence warrants court action. The Nebraska supreme court stated that this procedure eliminates nonmeritorious malpractice claims and limits the amount of recovery in claims found to have merit.

In Maryland, on the other hand, where the panel consisted of one attorney, one health care provider, and a member of the general public, a trial court held that the pretrial screening procedure was unconstitutional. The panel was to hear evidence, determine liability, and award damages and court costs. Either party would have been able to petition a court for modification of a panel decision, and either party would have been able to reject the panel's decision by filing an action in court. The Maryland court, however, held that these panels were unconstitutional for the following reasons:

1. They unconstitutionally usurped the power delegated to the judiciary.
2. They inhibited a claimant from reasonable access to the courts and to a trial by jury.
3. The panel procedure would result in a significant increase in the time necessary to achieve a final judicial resolution.

The Florida supreme court, in reversing a lower court, upheld that state's mandatory pretrial screening procedure. The court held that the procedure, which provided mandatory submission of malpractice claims to a pretrial panel, did not violate the patient's rights to due process and equal protection, nor did it deny free access to the state courts as guaranteed by the Florida constitution.

In New York, a pretrial panel consists of one physician, one attorney, and one justice of the state supreme court. The appellate division of the supreme court held that the mandatory pretrial screening procedure is constitutional, if all three members concur on the question of liability, and if the panel's recommendation is admissible at a later trial.

The Arizona supreme court upheld all of the Arizona medical review panel statute except a provision requiring the posting of a $2,000 bond prior to initiating court action. The court held that this provision violated the plaintiff's constitutional right of access to the courts. The court further held that while the panel findings were admissible into evidence in the event of a court trial, they were essentially an expert opinion that the jury could either accept or reject. Unlike review panel statutes in some other states that have been declared unconstitutional (as invasions of the judicial function of the courts), under the Arizona statute, a judgment cannot be entered upon a decision of the panel. The panel's actions are advisory.

The authors believe that those involved in sports and athletics — whether in teaching, coaching, administration, provision of facilities and equipment, or manufacture and sales of equipment — could benefit from the groundwork laid by the AMA. Pretrial panels are a means for decreasing the high cost of litigation.

In medical malpractice suits, multi-defendants are often named. These may include the hospital, the surgeon, the anesthesiologist, the nurses, and the residents. Similarly, in sports, the coach or teacher, the administrator, and the manufacturer of the equipment in use at the time of the accident may be named as defendants. This situation duplicates the cost of investigation and defense. It may also create unnecessary adversary relationships among the defendants. In such situations, the authors recommend that sports associations (AAHPERD, ACSM, AAU, NCPEA, NCAA, or others) provide guidelines for sharing the cost of defense actions.

In the situation suggested, prior to participation in physical education, recreation, or sports programs, or upon payment of the fee at health spas, ski resorts, or camps, children and their parents would be asked if they would like to sign an agreement to submit to a pretrial panel in the event of an injury or other claim of tortuous action. It should be made clear that the findings of the panel cannot result in a legal judgment, nor can they eliminate the possibility of a later jury trial. Rather, utilization of the pretrial panel could considerably reduce legal expenses for both parties.

Pretrial panels could be composed of an attorney, a judge, a physical educator or coach, a physician, and a lay person.

WHAT TO DO AFTER THE ACCIDENT

An accident has happened, and a student has been injured. What do you do now to avoid liability?

First and foremost, do not move the patient. The reasons for this are not only medical and humanitarian, but also legal. The best way to avoid liability is not to move the patient. There have been many suits involving liability for moving a patient, which action aggravated the injury. Further, don't start practicing medicine without a license by asking the patient to wiggle his toes or move his head. He might try too hard and injure himself further.

The second point is to retain control over the situation, starting with yourself. This is, keep calm and take charge of the situation. Don't let anyone else touch or move the patient because you are in charge and responsible for that patient until medical personnel arrive. "Control" means the type of control that an insurance adjuster is taught to exercise over a claim he is handling. The best way to retain control is to show your genuine concern for the patient through your actions.

It may be necessary to stop the game or get a substitute to take over supervision, so that you can personally go with the patient to the hospital. If you cannot leave, go to the hospital as soon as you are able. At the hospital, talk to the patient, if he is able to communicate. Talk to the parents if they are there; if not, try to contact them immediately and help to set them at ease. If you cannot reach them immediately, don't give up. The best way you can keep control of a case, in terms of keeping it away from a lawyer, is to maintain a good personal relationship between you and the patient and his parents.

When talking to the parents and expressing your deep concern, do not make any statements regarding liability. Do not say the school will pay the bills. When you say you are sorry that it happened, do not imply that it was your fault.

To retain control, return to the hospital that evening or the next morning to show your continuing concern. Continue to check back at least once a day with the student or his parents. As tort lawyers will attest, people hardly ever sue a teacher or coach whom they are fond of and who they felt had a genuine concern for the child's welfare.

If you saw the accident happen and are asked about it by the parents, give them a simple statement of how their child was injured. They are entitled to that. Most importantly, do it with courtesy and sympathy. If the parents or anyone else persists in asking you further questions, don't be afraid to repeat the simple statement that you previously gave on how the accident happened.

If the parents want to know who is going to pay the hospital bill, tell them that you will assist them in checking the school's insurance coverage. Don't make statements such as "The school will take care of everything," or "The school will pay the bills." Statements such as these can often be misinterpreted as an admission of liability on your part. Simply state that the school probably has insurance, and that you will help check into the matter. (You should contact school authorities immediately after an accident, so that an insurance adjuster will be on the case as quickly as possible.)

Do not play doctor and do not play lawyer. Don't try to be helpful by telling the parents what their legal position is or what their legal rights are. Don't suggest that they see an attorney.

Most schools carry insurance that will pay the medical bills, much as your car insurance includes coverage for the medical bills of passengers injured in your car, regardless of who caused the accident. Most schools also have liability insurance to cover a claim that might be your fault, much like the liability insurance on your automobile.

It would be well to check the school's insurance now, rather than waiting until after an accident has occurred. You might also check the various teacher organizations to see if they offer insurance that would cover teachers for liability. (The American Alliance for Health, Physical Education, Recreation, and Dance does have such a policy available for a small fee.)

Most lawsuits can be avoided, even following serious injury, if the teacher — the potential defendant — continues to visit the patient daily, keeps in constant touch with the parents, and continues to express his concern. The teacher should follow this practice even if there has been mention of involving an attorney. There have been many instances of persons authorizing their attorneys to sue the school board or school officials but specifically refusing to sue the teacher or coach.

If the family is out of town at the time of an accident, place daily long distance calls to keep them informed. This may be the best and cheapest insurance you can buy. Most people who come into a lawyer's office about a claim arising out of an injury do so because the school, coach, teacher, or others have shunned them, told them nothing, and left them to struggle with the bills by themselves. They had received no help, counsel, or comfort from any source.

Many coaches try to develop a macho attitude in their students, to encourage them to ignore pain. Some coaches teach students to ignore pain and continue to play when they are injured. But pain is a means of protecting the body. A real injury is the occasion not for machismo, but for sympathetic comfort and caring.

KNOWLEDGE OF LEGAL PROCEDURES

Attorneys would be well advised to read this book, as well as have their expert witnesses read the book, so that everyone knows what is coming and what is expected of him. This would also give the expert witnesses opportunity to review the safety standards offered in previous chapters, and the attorney could then ask expert witnesses to testify as to reasonable standards of conduct. If expert witnesses testify that the defendant failed to comply with reasonable safety standards, the case will have been aided greatly.

The plaintiff and defendant should also read this book, so that they will overcome some of the fears of a lawsuit, and so that they will know what is coming and what is expected of them. They can then be more at ease in the courtroom and can concentrate on their testimony.

The authors have advised the coach or teacher, as a possible defendant, to avoid mention of consultation with an attorney to the injured party. This is sound legal advice to a possible defendant. Conversely, the proper legal advice to a possible plaintiff is, yes, do consult an attorney. If your next door neighbors were injured in an accident, would you tell them, "Don't see a lawyer; I will handle the case for you." If you would not handle their case, you should not handle your own. Go see your lawyer.

This rule applies to teachers and other employees, as well as students. Injury cases are usually handled on a contingent fee basis (that is, the attorney receives a percentage of the recovery). Therefore, there is no attorney's fee if there is no recovery, although the plaintiff is usually expected to pay any out-of-pocket expenses.

PROFESSIONAL STANDARDS

It has long been time for professional associations of coaches and physical educators to set standards similar to those of the accounting, legal, and medical professions. The standards set out in this book might serve as a starting point. These associations should involve themselves in the continuing education of their professionals, not only for their edification, but for the safety and improvement of the persons served by the professionals.

Most other professions require licensing or certification. Coaches and others involved in athletics should also be licensed. It is the collective social duty of physical education and related fields to establish qualifications and board certification of their specialists.

We are dealing here with lobbying efforts to obtain laws and governmental inspections and requirements. The authors suggest that organized professional associations establish controls, certification, continuing education, and other procedures. If an association of professionals does not assume this responsibility, what is to prevent a lawsuit against such association for not discharging its responsibility to act as a reasonably prudent organization, as has occurred in other professions?

AVOIDING LITIGATION THROUGH PRECAUTIONS

The mere happening of an accident does not constitute negligence, and every injury is not a basis for a lawsuit. The only possible basis for a lawsuit is negligence on the part of a teacher, the school, or some other party. The best alternative to litigation is, of course, the avoidance of injuries through the use of precautions.

The precautionary guidelines offered throughout this book apply equally to the school setting and to commercial settings (ski areas, racket ball clubs, the YMCA, skating rinks, and health spas, for example). All institutions and companies involved in athletic activities should be more aware that they will be held to a high standard of care by virtue of their greater knowledge and awareness of the hazards involved in these activities. For example, a mother teaching her Cub Scouts to play ball would not be held to the same degree of care as a professionally trained coach or athletic supervisor. And there is greater awareness of this fact on the part of the general public, which will result in increased probability of lawsuits.

Teachers work in close proximity with students who are injured and consequently are more commonly sued. School administrators, school boards, and school corporations are usually sued as legal principals for the negligence of their agent-teachers. Sometimes school boards are sued because of their own negligence (for example, in providing faulty equipment, defective grounds or buildings, improper rules and regulations, or inadequate enforcement of regulations).

Safety Consciousness

The most basic precaution for avoiding liability is to be patient when you have the lives and well-being of students or customers in your control. With the right to control goes the corresponding duty to teach, assist, and most importantly, to protect. The best way to protect is to practice safety, teach safety by your example, and preach safety. Make others around you safety-conscious by being so yourself.

Supervision

Schools frequently permit the use of their premises for meetings, activities, and athletic events. Schools also sponsor intramural sports and interscholastic athletics, which create areas of exposure to liability, as well as opportunities for practicing safety.

When a school event is scheduled, if you are the principal and therefore in control and legally responsible for the activity, don't leave it to chance that some good-hearted teachers will volunteer to stay after work in order to supervise. It is your responsibility to see to it that adequate supervision is furnished. There is no law against paying overtime, and sometimes it is the cheapest insurance you can buy.

Different rules apply when the premises are rented out. When the persons coming onto the premises buy a ticket, they become business invitees. Your duty is to furnish them a reasonably safe place. This is the time to pay overtime in order to make certain that adequate supervision is present and that the custodian has cleaned up, policed the area, and locked up.

Adequate Insurance Coverage

Before any accident occurs, and before any lawsuit is filed, check to make certain that the school has insurance to cover you in the event that you become a party defendant in a suit. It would be well to make this check immediately, since it is the type of chore that is easily deferred and then forgotten. It might be well to check with your insurance company to make certain that your policy will cover you while transporting students or others in the course of your employment, as well as on your own time as a volunteer.

Save Harmless Statutes

As additional legal advice, the authors recommend a check to ascertain whether your state has a *save harmless statute*, which would provide that a board of education assume liability for damages arising out of a teacher's alleged negligence occurring within the scope of his employment. If your state does not have such a statute, it is recommended that the teacher's association begin lobbying to obtain one.

Physical Prerequisites for Athletics

Contact sports such as football are fine, but like everything else, they have their place. Do contact sports belong in elementary schools? The authors think not.

Children of such tender years are more susceptible to permanent and disabling injuries. For example, injury to the growth areas of bones can result in a cessation of growth, resulting in a shortened limb. Children of elementary school age would be better involved in team sports such as soccer or flag football.

It is the duty of the school, whether an elementary school or a university, to ensure that each participant is physically fit for the particular sport in question. Likewise, it is the duty of the school to provide qualified referees, who should look out for the physical well-being of the participants, as well as rules infractions.

Safe Premises

There are several different areas in which an owner of premises must be cautious in order to avoid liability. Product liability, advertising, consumer risks, and premises liability are a few. In any discussion of safety precautions as an alternative to litigation, the safety of premises must play an important part. And in any treatment of premises, it should be pointed out that bleachers and other seating arrangements are very prominent occasions for spectator litigation.

A typical case involved a woman who was injured at a wrestling meet when she attempted to escape a fracas. A crowd had gathered to witness a dispute between the contestants and the referee. The area in which the plaintiff was standing was so crowded that she got up on her chair, intending to walk over the other chairs to reach the aisle and escape the commotion. As the crowd surged back, the portable chairs collapsed. The plaintiff was allowed to recover for her injuries from the owner of the premises. (*Camp* v. *Rex, Inc.*, 24 NE Reporter, 2d, p. 4.)

SCHOOL REGULATIONS

Since many lawsuits have concerned school regulations, it follows that proper formulation and enforcement of school regulations will help the school avoid litigation.

For every right there is a corresponding duty. Schools have the right to govern students; they also have the corresponding duty to recognize the rights of students. Students have the right to a public education; they also have the corresponding duty to submit to the lawful rules and regulations prescribed by school authorities.

The family's right to govern its children gives way at the school premises, where the school's right to govern takes over. By the same token, the school's right to govern, generally speaking, ceases when the children leave the school premises.

School authorities are invested with the power to govern students and to discipline them. The courts usually will not interfere, unless the school violates the law or the individual rights of students.

Schools have wide latitude in establishing regulations for the maintenance of order and discipline within the educational system. If severe punishment is involved, the school must have established a rule that reasonably informs the student of the specific conduct proscribed. And the school has a right to reasonably govern recreational and social activities of students.

Participation in interscholastic athletics is not a right but a privilege, and it is governed by the regulations of the school, conference, or association under which the program operates. Reasonable rules, such as limitations on transfer students or prohibiting students from accepting awards, have been held to be reasonable.

The courts have ruled that participation in athletics is a privilege; thus such participation is not derived from, nor protected by, the U.S. Constitution. However, the acts of interscholastic athletic associations do come under the Constitution, due to the part they play in public education.

As long as girls have athletic programs that are comparable to those for boys, the courts have been unwilling to find any violation of the equal protection clause of the Fourteenth Amendment. The courts have held that separation of the sexes is permissible where the sport involves physical contact. Since there are physical differences between the sexes, regulations can be tailored to fit each sex without violating the equal protection clause.

Massachusetts held that schools cannot bar females and males from participating jointly in wrestling and football solely on the basis of sex.

(1977, Mass. 371 NE 2d, 426.) And the court of the state of Washington decided that the school districts could not deny qualified high school students permission to play interscholastic football simply because they were girls. (540 Pacific 2d, 882.) The same court held that denying girls the right to play football on interscholastic teams violated the equal protection clauses of the state and federal constitutions.

Court decisions have also addressed questions regarding the equal treatment of public school and private school students in interscholastic athletics, and the rights of vision-impaired students to participate in contact sports. Still another court decision addressed a school's right to ban married students from extracurricular activities. (In this case, the court said it was reasonable in order to discourage early student marriages and to discourage dropping out.)

Similarly, schools have been upheld in penalizing students for membership in certain organizations, fraternities, sororities, or secret organizations. Conversely, a court held that the school did not have the right to prohibit membership in secret societies.

Schools have the right to forbid leaving the school grounds during school hours, even for midday meals. And school regulations limiting the use of automobiles by students during school hours have been enforced by the courts. Schools may establish dress codes, as long as (a) they are not unduly restrictive and do have a rational relationship to the orderly conduct of the educational process; (b) they are not arbitrary; and (c) the teachers had not permitted violations of such regulations without discipline.

The criterion for judging school regulations is their *reasonableness.* Schools are well advised to make only reasonable regulations and to check court rulings that apply to their particular locality.

/ 13 /

Legal Liability in the Future

The role of prophet is best played by a fool or an egomaniac. Yet it is necessary to attempt to foresee the future in order to plan with greater wisdom and accuracy. Fortunately, by observing current trends in sports and in lawsuits, it is possible to make some enlightened progoses about the future.

In the future, those involved in sports and recreation will be working with a greater variety of people. For example, more older people will be participating in athletics and fitness programs. People are living longer and maintaining a higher level of physical activity through more advanced years. A greater proportion of middle-aged and elderly people are participating in sports and fitness programs.

The need and capabilities of older people differ from those of students and young adults: their bones are more brittle; the cartilage between bones does not cushion as well; and there is less elasticity and strength in the muscles, tendons, and ligaments. Further, there are decreases in reaction time, in visual and auditory acuity, in cardiovascular-respiratory endurance, and in muscular strength. Yet, if those on the downhill side of peak physiological function are to maintain optimal health, they must keep physically active.

Leaders in sports and other forms of human movement will be expected to understand these differences in the capacities of youth, the middle-aged, and the elderly. Thus they will have to keep up with research findings. This means that even after graduation from college, they will have to set aside time for learning throughout their working lives, just as physicians and attorneys must do. More research is published in one year today than was published in fifty years prior to 1900. The output of research has increased geometrically. The rate of progress and change is constantly accelerating. Nevertheless, professional people responsible for the health and welfare of others will be held responsible for injuries to those under their direction.

For example, if a fifty-year-old member of a fitness class were instructed to lift a barbell with the knees extended, resulting in damage to the lumbar area, the instructor would very likely be held liable. Similarly, he would probably be held liable if he imposed an excessive cardiac load on an elderly person that resulted in cardiac failure.

Physicians are held responsible for inept practice due to lack of knowledge. There is no valid reason why coaches, physical educators, and recreation leaders should not be held equally liable for faulty leadership, resulting from lack of knowledge, which leads to physical harm.

By virtue of the increased hazard of legal liability (due to the need for greater knowledge coupled with a greater popular disposition to bring suit), the days of the generalist may come to an end. It is a rare individual who can be knowledgeable in the myriad of sports and physical activities. If only specialists can be employed, however, the cost of programs will increase due to the necessity of employing more people and more competent people. Schools and colleges that are unable or unwilling to meet these added expenditures will have to limit the variety of their offerings.

The number of females participating in sports will continue to increase, and they will be striving to reach higher levels of performance. Some females will insist upon competing against males in contact sports. If the activity leader permits this competition, and the female is injured, he may be sued for permitting competition between physically unequal competitors. If he prohibits the competition, he may be sued under Title IX.

It will become necessary for professional associations to establish guidelines and standards for competition between the sexes. This is difficult at the present time due to a certain militancy on the distaff side. However, as the pendulum of popular trends swings back toward more rational thinking, the anatomic and physiologic differences between males and females will be accepted more gracefully. At that time, such standards and guidelines will also be accepted. Consequently, leaders in sports and recreational activities will have to know the differences in the physical capacities of males and females. Again, this implies the necessity of keeping up with advancing knowledge.

Obviously, if the general public expects leaders in human movement to accumulate a large body of knowledge and to be as responsible as physicians, they will have to pay them commensurately. Higher standards of performance demand greater compensation. This is necessary not only from the standpoint of achieving equity, but from a practical point of view. If the most able young people are to be attracted to the professions dealing with human movement, the financial rewards must be competitive with other professions. Conversely, the paying public will be unwilling to pay salaries on a par with other professions unless the human movement professions attract the most able young people; require them to undergo rigorous preparation; provide ample opportunities for practitioners to keep up-to-date (through clinics, symposia, and dissemination of research); and weed out the inept, unscrupulous, or lazy practitioners.

With more leisure time and broader media dissemination of knowledge regarding human movement, people will be more able to distinguish between safe and unsafe leadership techniques in sports. And they will bring this knowledge to the jury box. Even today, the media disseminate information that ten years ago was found only in physical education textbooks. Coaches and physical educators who follow hazardous procedures or disseminate incorrect information will be readily identified. This could well result in an increase in both the incidence of injuries and lawsuits.

With greater enlightenment and a higher cultural level, it is very probable that more people will abhor violence in sports. There is ample evidence that unnecessary violence in sports is already being rejected: bills are being proposed in Congress, and cases charging unnecessary violence are being brought to court.

As an increasing number of athletics professionals and program administrators are brought to court due to negligence (either their own or of their employees), they will select their coaches, physical educators, and other employees with greater care. They will insist that those they hire have at least a minor or an area of concentration in coaching. Skilled athletic performance or ability to diagram a play will no longer be the sole criterion for employment as a coach. Coaches will be expected to possess a knowledge of human physiology and anatomy, first aid, athletic training, kinesiology, the physiology of exercise, group dynamics, the principles of physical education, safety procedures, and law and liability in athletics. They will be expected to understand the effects of exercise on the human body, the potentials and limitations of the body, and the potentials and limitations of those with various forms of physical anomalies, as well as those of various age groups. They will be expected to use sports as a means to achieve educational objectives, not merely to post a good win-loss record.

There seems to be a trend toward more organized athletic and leisure activities. We have gone from sandlot ball to Little League, from walking to organized jogging, from the swimming hole to the health spa. With the advent of neighborhood recreation parks comes a greater responsibility for supervision on behalf of paid employees and volunteers.

* * * * *

The foregoing predictions may make some readers uneasy. Those who are unwilling to measure up to the criteria above *should* transfer to some less demanding work, so that those who are more able can receive the level of compensation they deserve.

Greater Variety and Complexity of Equipment

The future will bring different equipment for weight control and reducing exercises. Thus there will be new machines in the health spas that will require supervision, and physical educators will also be responsible for the maintenance of, and proper instruction regarding, new forms of equipment.

Recreation centers will be open to all types of people. As a precautionary measure, recreation directors would be well advised to have medical personnel on call during open hours. Where contact sports are involved, there should be an emergency medical squad present (but out of sight).

Homes are becoming leisure centers. In the future, more yards will contain swimming pools, deck tennis courts, universal gyms, and other exercise equipment. Like the doctor of yesterday, the physical educator will be making house calls to examine this new equipment and to train the family in its proper use. It is probable that in the future it will be the physical and recreation educator's responsibility to make recommendations regarding the environment within which athletic activities are conducted.

Teacher Malpractice

"Teacher malpractice" will become a much more common term in the future. As teachers become more professional as a result of upgrading of college programs and an increase in the number of degrees completed, they are going to be held to a higher standard of care.

We have already seen a rash of lawsuits against teachers for the use of excessive discipline. Currently we are seeing teacher malpractice suits brought by parents who feel that their children have been undertrained. Social promotion is increasingly coming under criticism.

Just as doctors are sued for failure to obtain informed consent (a failure to adequately inform a patient before a procedure is undertaken), teachers may be sued in the near future for failure to obtain informed consent from the parent for social promotion and similar practices. One way to avoid such liability might consist of adequately informing the parents of the situation and letting them make the decision regarding their child's promotion.

SOCIETAL ROLE OF LAWSUITS

Laws regulate the conduct of persons who are in close contact with one another in our civilized society. The threat of a lawsuit is one method employed to ensure that laws are obeyed. Lawsuits, in addition to establishing liability, also serve to right a wrong by attempting to put the victim in as good a condition as he was prior to the incident.

Aside from enforcing our laws, lawsuits also provide for enforcement of safety procedures that render the environment safer. The idea of holding one responsible for his own acts serves as a deterrent to negligent conduct in our society. Damage suits also serve, in a manner of speaking, to police the environment, since the threat of a lawsuit increases the sense of responsibility to make the environment safer. Lawsuits also put pressure on leagues and other organizations to regulate and police themselves.

Lawsuits bring disagreements off the street and into a forum where they can be patiently adjudicated and fairly settled. The days of settling disputes out in the back alley, of exacting an eye for an eye, have been replaced with courts, judges, and juries. This is merely an expansion of the principle of a third party arbitrating between two disagreeing parties.

In our society, we would prefer to have an injured student sue the coach, or an injured coach sue the student or administrator, rather than have them take the law into their own hands and seek revenge. We believe it is better for the provider of a defective football helmet, for example, or for the one who negligently fails to give adequate instruction, to pay for the loss or injury, rather than for the innocent victim to bear the costs alone.

The authors hope that this book will contribute to the worthwhile societal goal of making the environment in which athletic activities are conducted a safer one.

The physical educator, recreationist, or coach who receives a subpoena informing him that he is being sued usually feels anger, anxiety, and frustration. He probably also feels that a rank injustice is being perpetrated because he has dedicated himself to the service of humanity. Those of us in the profession, upon hearing about lawsuits against our colleagues, feel that opportunists are taking advantage of our vulnerability, and we worry that valuable activities that contain an element of risk will be eliminated from programs. We also feel anger at attorneys, who seem to get a slice of every pie — divorce, death, house closings, torts, traffic accidents, and many others. However, it can be easily argued that suits for negligent behavior or unequal treatment play an important and necessary societal role.

The primary purpose of a legal system is to ensure equity. Equity is perceived differently by different people, and even by the same people in different situations. For these reasons, laws are usually based on majority opinion. A jury of peers reaches a decision based on the weight of the evidence. In our society, man has the fundamental right to be free from the wrongful acts of others. Secure families can have their hopes, desires, security, and their entire lives rearranged as a result of an injury in sports. As a result of an accident, they may become a financial burden upon society, and they suffer pain and anguish. Whereas cancer and heart disease usually cripple or kill those in their later years, injuries in sports most often strike young people, who should have many years of productive life remaining to be enjoyed.

Professional people such as physicians, dentists, physical therapists, teachers, and coaches are expected to possess a higher level of knowledge in the areas of their expertise than others. Because of this knowledge, they are in a position to take advantage of others when working in the area of their expertise. They could take shortcuts in their services or use inferior materials. And because of their knowledge and skills, they are generally compensated at a higher rate than laborers or tradesmen, who have not had as extensive preparation for their work.

If professionals do not possess the requisite knowledge and skills, they are misrepresenting themselves. Recipients of their services have a right to expect that these professionals do, in fact, possess the requisite knowledge and skills. When the recipients of professional services suffer injury because the professional did not possess the knowledge, or because of his negligence, they are entitled to compensation for the wrong done to them. Our system of law will determine whether a wrong was done, as well as the amount of compensation.

Laws reflect the currently prevailing value system. In the year 1800, the general public was not ready for the Title IX provisions of the Education Amendments of 1972. In 1900, it was not ready for the Civil Rights Act of 1964. In 1925, it was not ready for the provisions of Public Law 94-142 (mainstreaming of the handicapped). The majority of the general public today perceives these laws as ensuring equity to segments of the population. The system of law in a democracy prevents anarchy.

Appendix A

SPORTSMANSHIP CODE

To consider all athletic opponents as guests and treat them with all the courtesy due friends and guests.

Accept all decisions of officials without question.

Never hiss or boo a player or an official.

Never utter abusive or irritating remarks from the sidelines.

Applaud opponents who make good plays or show good sportsmanship.

Never attempt to rattle an opposing player, such as a player attempting a free throw.

Seek to win by fair and lawful means, according to the rules.

Do unto others as we would have them do unto us.

Try to win without boasting and lose without excuse.

Ask that every player and fan in the arena do his level best throughout the game to cooperate with us in living up to this code.

And may the best club win!

Appendix B

What Price Prudence?

Terry W. Parsons

Tort, product liability, assumption of risk, discriminatory behavior, contributory negligence--all these concepts and countless more comprise the contemporary "sue syndrome." The long-term proposition that governmental agencies (the schools) and their employees are magically immune from liability persecution is rapidly vanishing. Today teachers, coaches, and administrators serving in programs involving great potential risks for participants can no longer hide behind the concept of sovereign immunity and be immune from legal prosecution. This change, plus a nationwide growth in the concern for individual rights, places each administrator in a position of awesome responsibility and never-ending concern.

However, overzealous protectionism in a profession which by its nature is invigorated by risk-taking necessities may result in a "milk toast and pablum" experience for participants. When predetermined fear of possible consequence assures noncommital behaviors, little achievement of any consequence can be expected. Excessive caution manifested by administrators in physical education programming may provide a stifling effect upon the teacher/coach when the vital moment of decision arrives as to degree of risk-taking to be permitted--much less encouraged--for the student performer.

What constitutes severe degrees of risk-taking? Where does the administrator cease encouraging vigilance of safety standards and begin promoting increased degrees of risk-taking? Each administrator in each setting must ultimately make that final determination, but certainly our charge must be that of "prudent vigilance." We must consistently exercise judicious foresight with resultant behavior aimed at prevention of injurious incidents--without deterring the implementation of the "fear-hope chanciness" inherent in the dynamic physical education experience. Holding of extensive appropriate professional liability insurance is an essential corollary!

The following exercise should provide personal guidance for the administrator as to the establishment of an appropriate degree of prudence commensurate with the professional, as well as legal, responsibility of the contemporary administrator in physical education and/or athletics.

While it is certainly difficult to determine what constitutes a passing mark for the administrator on the above rating scale, failure in any one of the above responsibilities carries the potential for personal and legal tragedy. Thoughtful response culminating in a check mark in the "never" or "rarely" columns should provoke a sufficient degree of concern to result in immediate detailed investigation and subsequent remedial behavior. A consistent series of red marks in the "always" column stimulates a sense of professional well-being yet should not result in administrative complacency. If indeed "eternal vigilance is the price of liberty" then "eternal prudent vigilance is the ongoing price of legally sane physical education programs."

What price prudence? Administrative policy must provide assurance that activity programs will be conducted according to proper guidelines--without squelching the spirit of adventure presented by the "hope for success vs. fear of failure" wagering occurring in any vibrant physical education experience.

Degree of Compliance

The prudent administrator:

	Always	Frequently	Rarely	Never
1. Seeks to prohibit the situation which may lead to litigation through constant foresight and care inherent in the professional role he/she holds.	___	___	___	___
2. Assigns instructional and supervisory duties concerning an activity to only those people who are qualified for that particular activity.	___	___	___	___
3. Conducts regular inspections of all equipment used and insists on full repair of faulty items prior to use.	___	___	___	___
4. Establishes procedures and enforces rules concerning safe use of equipment and proper fitting of all uniforms and protective gear.	___	___	___	___
5. Has written plans with adequate review procedures to assure that participants do not progress too rapidly into areas of skill performance beyond their present skill level.	___	___	___	___
6. Selects opponents for each participant/team with care to avoid potentially dangerous mismatching.	___	___	___	___
7. Establishes and scrupulously enforces rules regarding reporting of illness or injury, to include compilation of written records and names and addresses of witnesses.	___	___	___	___
8. Does not treat injuries unless professionally prepared and certified to do so.	___	___	___	___
9. Regularly updates first aid and emergency medical care credentials.	___	___	___	___
10. Does not permit participation in any activity without medical approval following serious illness or injury.	___	___	___	___
11. Readily recognizes the presence of any attractive nuisance, and initiates firm control measures.	___	___	___	___
12. Posts safety rules for use of facilities, then orients students and colleagues to danger areas in activities, facilities, and personal conduct.	___	___	___	___
13. Does not place the activity area in the control of nonqualified personnel for *any* reason.	___	___	___	___
14. Relies on waiver forms not as a negation for responsibility for injury only as a means of assuring that parents/guardians recognize students' intent to participate.	___	___	___	___
15. Does not permit zeal for accomplishment or emotion of the moment to suppress rational behavior.	___	___	___	___
16. Provides in letter and spirit nondiscriminatory programs for all students.	___	___	___	___
17. Cancels transportation plans if unable to be thoroughly convinced of the personal and prudent reliability of drivers, means of transportation and adequacy of insurance coverage.	___	___	___	___
18. Does not conduct a class/or practice/or contest without a plan for medical assistance in the event of injury regardless of the setting.	___	___	___	___
19. Holds professional liability insurance of significant dollar dimensions and pertinent applicability to professional pursuits involving physical activity.	___	___	___	___
20. Does not permit excessive concern about legal liability to prohibit the development of a challenging and accountable physical education experience for each participant.	___	___	___	___

Source: Parsons, Terry W. "What Price Prudence?" *Journal of Physical Education and Recreation* 50 (January, 1979) p. 45.

Appendix C

STANDARD METHOD OF IMPACT TEST AND
PERFORMANCE REQUIREMENTS FOR FOOTBALL HELMETS

Prepared by

NATIONAL OPERATING COMMITTEE
ON STANDARDS FOR ATHLETIC EQUIPMENT

Revised September 1973
Revised September 1977
Revised October 1978
Revised January 1980

P R E F A C E

In an effort to minimize head injuries in football, the National Operating Committee on Standards for Athletic Equipment (NOCSAE) has developed a procedure for testing football helmets and the minimum requirements to be met under each test. It is believed safer helmets and fewer head injuries will be incurred provided the following conditions are met:

a) Manufacturer adherence to the testing of new helmets under the NOCSAE Test Standard.

b) Manufacturer implementation of an effective Quality Assurance Program.

c) Consumer adherence to a program of periodically having used helmets retested under the NOCSAE Recertification Program.

d) Reconditioners' adherence to the testing of reconditioned helmets under the NOCSAE Test Standard for recertification.

The methods of test and performance required are based on research begun in 1971 at Wayne State University, Department of Neurosurgery Biomechanics Laboratory.

NOCSAE recognizes the difficulty of formulating a laboratory standard to control head injury in a game in which the injury incidence is relatively low and no tolerable index is available for hemorrhagic injuries and subdural hematomas which are the primary cause of death and permanent injury in football. This Standard is a recommended procedure for helmet manufacturers and reconditioners which if followed will produce safer helmets and thereby aid in the reduction of concussions in the future. Since the testing requirements and certification of manufacturers models are based on new helmets, it is recommended that a Recertification Program be maintained by the consumer. It is recognized the Standard should be continuously reviewed in the light of progress in injury reporting, research and manufacturing techniques and suggestions for improvement by interested parties. In instances where changes affect any of the following critical test parameters, the effective date of the revised Standard will be the time of issuance plus six months.

a) headform characteristics
b) drop heights
c) environmental conditions
d) anvil and/or impact surface characteristics
e) Severity Index (SI)

---

[1]
NOCSAE membership established 1969: American College Health Association - Sporting Goods Manufacturers Association - National Athletic Trainers Association - National Collegiate Athletic Association - National Federation of State High School Associations - National Junior College Athletic Association and The Sports Foundation. The National Athletic Equipment Reconditioners Association was accepted into membership on July 21, 1975. The National Association of Intercollegiate Athletics was accepted into membership on January 12, 1977.

      f)   number of drops
      g)   impact location
      h)   instrumentation

No procedural changes will be made to the Standard other than those written into the Standard as a revision.

1.   SCOPE

This Standard establishes methods of test and performance requirements for new football helmets as supplied by manufacturers and recertification procedures for reconditioners.

2.   PURPOSE

To test new football helmets to determine their shock absorption properties under various conditions of temperature and humidity, and to establish methods and procedures for recertification by reconditioners.

3.   REQUIREMENTS

3.1 With respect to helmets manufactured or reconditioned from time of issuance of this document plus six months, when an impact attenuation test is conducted in accordance with 5, 4, the Severity Index defined as of $\int {}^T A^{2.5} dt$ shall not exceed 1500^2. A is the resultant acceleration expressed as a multiple of G (acceleration of gravity), t - time, seconds and the integration is carried out over the essential duration (T) of the acceleration pulse.

3.2 Labeling

Each helmet shall be permanently and legibly labeled in a manner such that the following information can be easily read without removing padding or any other permanent part.

      (1) Name of manufacturer
      (2) Model designation
      (3) Size
      (4) Month and year of manufacture
      (5) Meets NOCSAE Standard

4.   PRELIMINARY TEST PROCEDURES

Before subjecting a helmet to the test series, prepare it according to the following procedures:

4.1 Helmet Positioning

Prior to each drop, fix the helmet on the test head from such that the ear holes are approximately concentric with the model ear index

---

[2]Gadd recommends SI = 1500 as concussion threshold for non-contact impact (9).

APPENDIX C

holes and the front rim is located with the nose gage. Secure the helmet with the chin strap so that it does not shift position prior to impact during testing.

4.2 Face Masks

Helmets shall be tested without a face mask.

4.3 Conditioning

Immediately prior to the testing sequence, specified in 5.4, condition the helmet in accordance with the following procedures:

a. High Temperature - Exposed to a temperature of 120°F for at least four hours.

b. Ambient Conditions - Exposed to laboratory conditions for at least four hours.

c. Record temperature and humidity. If, during testing, the time out of the conditioning environment exceeds five minutes, return the sample to the conditioning environment for a minimum of three minutes for each minute out of the conditioning environment or four hours, whichever is less, prior to resumption of testing.

5. TEST CONDITIONS

5.1 Head Model

Physical properties of the NOCSAE-WSU head models to be used in these tests are given in Figure 1 - Table 1.

5.2 Mechanical Test System

A diagram of the helmet drop test system to be used in these tests is shown in Figure 2.

5.3 Instrumentation

A triaxial accelerometer is mounted at the center of gravity of the head model with the positive X-axis pointing in the posterior-anterior direction. The signal from the transducer is conditioned and recorded by equipment illustrated in Figure 3.

5.4 Impact Attenuation Test

Impact attenuation is measured by determining the head model resultant center of gravity acceleration - time history when it is dropped in guided free fall onto a flat, rigid anvil padded with a 1/2 inch thick, 6 inch diameter, 30 shore A durometer natural rubber surface. Drop tests for initial certification shall be conducted on a separate helmet of each model for each environmental condition. One helmet of each model is to be tested in each of the following sizes, 6 5/8, 7 1/4 and 7 5/8. All sizes must pass the test in order for model certification. Time interval between drops in a single location will be 75 seconds $\pm$ 15.

LOCATION[3] - DROP HEIGHT (INCHES)

	(1)	(2)	(3)	(4)	(5)	(6)
	FR	SIDE	F.BOSS	R.BOSS	REAR	TOP
Ambient						
Temperature	36	36	60	60	60	60
	48	48	60	60	60	60
	60	60				
	60	60				

High
Temperature   60   NOTE: The high temperature
                                    60   conditions may be done after
                                                the ambient tests.

For calibration purposes, two drops of the head model without helmet will be conducted into the right frontal boss from a height of eighteen inches.[4] This procedure will be repeated at the beginning and end of each environmental condition.

6. RECERTIFICATION PROCEDURE

6.1 Firms that recondition football helmets may conduct a recertification test on only those helmets which have been previously NOCSAE listed. The recertification procedure is as follows:

6.2 Test procedures and conditions will be followed as described in Sections 4.1, 4.2, 4.3, 5.1-2-3 and a partial Impact Attenuation Test as follows:

a. One of each model year from each school will be tested by conducting two 60-inch drops at the front location.

b. Test one of each model year from each school (different from the helmet tested in 6.2a), by conducting two 60-inch drops on one of the alternate five locations described in Figure 4. The alternate locations will be changed frequently, such as daily or as the production schedule allows, to give equal numbers of tests to each location.

---

[3]See Figure 4 for impact location details. For front, side front boss, rear boss and rear impacts, the pedestal shall be clamped to the bedplate between the guide wires with the pedestal center 7 1/2 inches from the left side. For the top position it shall be clamped 13 in from the left side.

[4]Average of before and after head model 18 inch calibration drop test results must agree within $\pm$ 7% for validation of test results.

c. If helmets fail in either tests 6.2a and/or 6.2b, those helmets and no other helmet of that model year belonging to the school shall be recertified until all are reconditioned in order that upon retesting on the site(s) that failed they now fall within the maximum allowable 1500 Severity Index.

6.3 A Severity Index exceeding 1500 on the second 60-inch drop will constitute failure of a helmet to be recertified.

6.4 For calibration purposes, two drops of the head model without helmet will be conducted onto the right frontal boss from a height of eighteen inches. This procedure will be followed before and after each day's testing. Records will be kept of these calibration values. Average of before and after head model 18 inch calibration drop test results must agree within $\pm$ 7% for validation of test results.

6.5 Helmets that are recertified will have attached to the inside of the shell a recertification seal that will include the name of the firm and the date of recertification. This seal will supplant the original certification seal and read as follows: "This helmet has been recertified according to procedures established to meet the NOCSAE Standard."

TABLE 1

MEASUREMENTS OF NOCSAE HEAD MODELS*

(SEE FIGURE 1)

POINTS OF MEASUREMENT	HEAD MODEL SIZES		
	6 5/8	7 1/4	7 5/8
1 Head Breadth	5.75	6.00	6.59
2 Maximum brow width (frontal diameter)	4.68	5.06	5.62
3 Earhole to earhole (bitragion diameter)	5.50	5.68	6.00
4 Maximum jew width (bigonial diameter)	4.68	4.75	4.75
5 Head length (glabella landmark to back of head)	7.31	7.81	8.34
6 Outside eye corner (external canthus) to back of head	6.68	6.87	6.87
7 Earhole (tragion) to back of head	3.62	3.75	3.93
8 Earhole to outside corner of eye (tragion to external canthus)	3.06	2.93	2.93
9 Earhole to top of head (tragion to vertex)	4.34	4.75.	5.28
10 Eye pupil to top of head	3.56	4.25	4.65
11 Earhole to jaw angle (tragion to gonion)**	3.00	3.25	3.62
12 Bottom of nose to point of chin (subnasal to menton)	2.31	2.42	2.50
13 Top of nose to point of chin (nasion to menton)	4.25	4.50	4.75
14 Head circumference	20.87	22.62	24.12
15 Head weight including neck	8.3 lbs.	9.8 lbs.	11.7 lbs.

**The right ear of each model must be removed flush with the skin surface.

* The anthropometric measurements are based upon the following references:
1. Churchill, E., et. al: Anthropometry Research Project Yellow Springs, OH December 1971; Anthropometry of U.S. Army Aviators-1970; National Technical Information Service; U.S. Dept. of Commerce; 5285 Port Ridge; Springfield, VA 22151; December 1971.
2. Claus, W.D., et. al: Development of Headforms for Sizing Infantry Helmets; Technical Report 75-23-CEMEL Project Ref. 1 T662713DJ90 Series: CEMEL-131; Clothing, Equipment, and Materials Engineering Laboratory; U.S. Army Natick Laboratories; Natick, MA 01760.

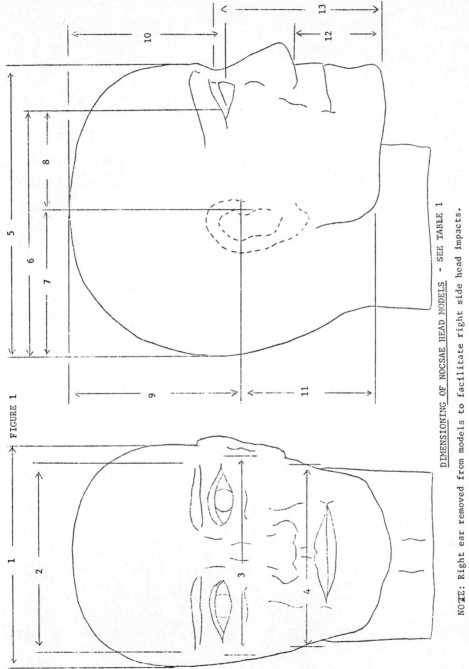

FIGURE 1

DIMENSIONING OF NOCSAE HEAD MODELS - SEE TABLE 1

NOTE: Right ear removed from models to facilitate right side head impacts.

FIGURE 2

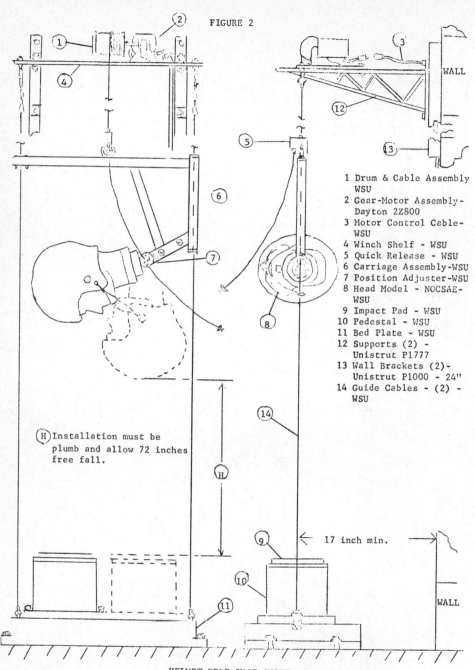

1 Drum & Cable Assembly
   WSU
2 Gear-Motor Assembly-
   Dayton 2Z800
3 Motor Control Cable-
   WSU
4 Winch Shelf - WSU
5 Quick Release - WSU
6 Carriage Assembly-WSU
7 Position Adjuster-WSU
8 Head Model - NOCSAE-
   WSU
9 Impact Pad - WSU
10 Pedestal - WSU
11 Bed Plate - WSU
12 Supports (2) -
   Unistrut P1777
13 Wall Brackets (2)-
   Unistrut P1000 - 24"
14 Guide Cables - (2) -
   WSU

(H) Installation must be
    plumb and allow 72 inches
    free fall.

WALL

17 inch min.

WALL

HELMET DROP TEST SYSTEM

TRANSDUCER AND SIGNAL CONDITIONING FOR MEASURING

HEAD MODEL IMPACT ACCELERATIONS

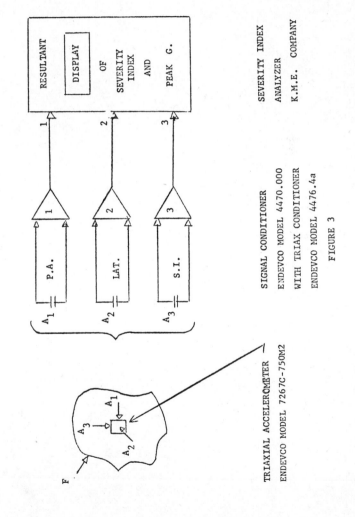

RESULTANT

DISPLAY

OF

SEVERITY
INDEX

AND

PEAK G.

SEVERITY INDEX

ANALYZER

K.M.E. COMPANY

SIGNAL CONDITIONER
ENDEVCO MODEL 4470.000
WITH TRIAX CONDITIONER
ENDEVCO MODEL 4476.4a

FIGURE 3

TRIAXIAL ACCELEROMETER
ENDEVCO MODEL 7267C-750M2

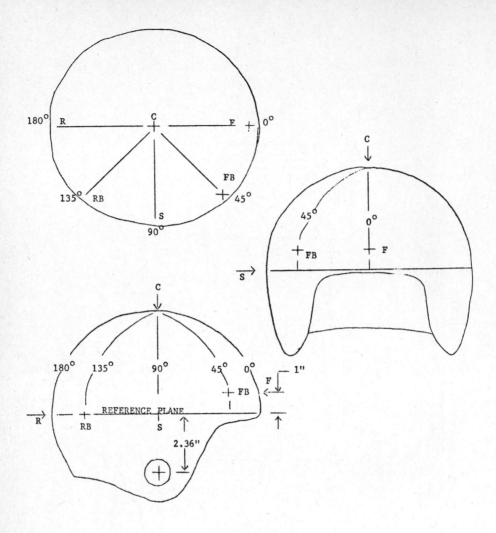

IMPACT LOCATIONS

FIGURE 4

R E F E R E N C E S

1. Strength and Response of the Human Neck (710855), Mertz, H. J., Patrick, L. M.: Proceedings of <u>Fifteen Stapp Car Crash Conference</u>, November 17-19, 1971. SAE, Incorporated, Two Pennsylvania Plaza, New York, New York 10001.

2. CSA Standard D230-1970. Safety Helmets for Motorcycle Riders. 178 Rexdale Boulevard, Rexdale 603, Ontario, Canada.

3. NETSA (49 CFR Part 571 - Docket Notice 72-6: Notice 1). Motorcycle Helmets. Proposed MVSS, Federal Regulations, Volume 37, No. 98, May 19, 1972.

4. Use of a Weighted - Impulse Criterion for Estimating Injury Hazard. Gadd, C. W. (600793), Proceedings of the <u>Tenth Stapp Car Crash Conference</u>, November 8-9, 1966. SAE, Incorporated, Two Pennsylvania Plaza, New York, New York 10001.

5. Biomechanical Study of Football Head Impacts Using a Human Cadaver. Hodgson, V. R., Thomas, L. M., January 1972, Final Report, prepared for National Operating Committee on Standards for Athletic Equipment.

6. Biomechanical Study of Football Head Impacts Using a Human Head Model. Hodgson, V. R., Thomas, L. M., April 19, 1973, Final Report prepared for National Operating Committee on Standards for Athletic Equipment.

7. Comparison of Head Acceleration Injury Indices in Cadaver Skull Fracture. Hodgson, V. R., Thomas, L. M., SAE Transactions, Volume 80 (1971), paper 710854.

8. Effect of Long-Duration Impact on Head. Hodgson, V. R., Thomas, L. M., Proceedings of the <u>Sixteenth Stapp Car Crash Conference</u>, November 8-10, 1972. SAE, Incorporated, Two Pennsylvania Plaza, New York, New York 10001.

9. Report to SAE Performance Criteria Subcommittee. Gadd, C. W., Vehicle Research Department, General Motors Research Laboratories, G. M. Technical Center, Warren, Michigan 48090, March 8, 1972.

Appendix D

That this Act may be cited as the ''Sports Violence Act of 1980''.   (H.R. 7903)

   SEC. 2. Chapter 7 of title 18 of the United States Code is amended by adding at the end the following:
''§115. Excessive violence during professional sports
         events

   ''(a) Whoever, as a player in a professional sports event, knowingly uses excessive physical force and thereby causes a risk of significant bodily injury to another person involved in that event shall be fined not more than $5,000 or imprisoned not more than one year, or both.

   ''(b) As used in this section, the term--

      ''(1) 'excessive physical force' means physical force that--

         ''(A) has no reasonable relationship to the competitive goals of the sport;

         ''(B) is unreasonably violent; and

         ''(C) could not be reasonably forseen, or was not consented to, by the injured person, as a normal hazard of such person's involvement in such sports event; and

      ''(2) 'professional sports event' means a paid-admission contest, in or affecting interstate or foreign commerce, of players paid for their participation.''
SEC. 3. The table of sections for chapter 7 of title 18 of the United States Code is amended by adding at the end the following new item:

''115. Excessive violence during professional sports
        events.''

CONGRESSIONAL RECORD—*Extensions of Remarks*

July 31, 1980

SPORTS VIOLENCE ACT OF 1980

HON. RONALD M. MOTTL

OF OHIO

IN THE HOUSE OF REPRESENTATIVES

Thursday, July 31, 1980

● Mr. MOTTL. Mr. Speaker, today I am introducing the Sports Violence Act of 1980, a bill intended to deter and punish through criminal penalties the episodes of excessive violence that are increasingly characterizing professional sports.

The bill would make it a Federal crime for professional athletes to engage in excessive violence in the course of a sports event.

This measure is not directed at, and will not affect, the kinds of natural physical contact that are a normal part of rugged physical sports, such as football, hockey, and boxing. Instead, this bill is directed toward the kinds of vicious, dangerous contact that a civilized society should brand as criminal whether it occurs inside or outside the sports arena—conduct in which a player actually steps outside the role of athlete and sportsman.

It is difficult to draw a clear line between the contact that we all agree is part of the game, and needlessly violent, dangerous conduct that creates a risk of injury while having no reasonable relationship to a particular sport. The job is made more difficult when prosecutors take a hands-off attitude toward sports violence that each year sends players to the hospital, and when professional sports organizations make it clear that sports violence should be handled within the family and not in the courts.

I believe, however, that a line can be drawn to serve notice on the professional sports world that extreme acts of excessive violence on the field are as repugnant as street corner muggings, and will be punished accordingly. When a hockey player slams his stick over the head of an opponent, or a basketball player smashes the face of an opponent with his fist, it is not sport. Players, team organizations, fans. and sports themselves would all benefit from a statute making it clear that you can play rough and hard, but you cannot play to deliberately or recklessly hurt someone.

My bill states in relevant part that a professional player who "knowingly uses excessive physical force and thereby causes a risk of significant bodily injury to another person involved in that event shall be fined not more than $5,000 or imprisoned not more than 1 year, or both.

Excessive physical force is specifically defined by the bill as force that has no reasonable relationship to the competitive goals of the sport, is unreasonably violent, and could not be reasonably foreseen or consented to by the person affected.

The criminal sanctions in the bill would apply to players in any professional sport. The bill does not supercede the application of State and local assault and battery criminal statutes by local authorities. Because of the inconsistent application of these laws to professional sports, and because of the interstate nature of modern professional sports, it is felt that a Federal criminal statute would be complementary to existing State and local laws.

I am indebted in the drafting of this legislation to Richard B. Horrow, a recent Harvard Law School graduate who authored the book, "Sports Violence: The Interaction Between Private Lawmaking and the Criminal Law" (copyright 1980, Carrollton Press, Arlington, Va.). It is Mr. Horrow's careful research and analysis that have both documented the need for a Federal sports violence statute, and suggested the form such a statute should take. Mr. Horrow counts many figures within the sports world as supporters and sympathizers for his efforts in this area.

Mr. Horrow's research reveals how State and local assault and battery laws have traditionally had little usefulness in the area of professional sports violence. These laws and the judicial cases interpreting them have focused on ordinary street crime, and have proven almost irrelevant to the special circumstances of mayhem on the field, ice, or court.

I believe this proposed statute would have a deterrent effect, making professional sports safer for all participants, and would also help players know the outer limits of acceptable conduct while reducing peer and management pressure to use excessive violence to injure or intimidate opposing players.

As an avid sports fan and participant myself, I want American sports to remain clean, fun, and healthy. For those benefits to be preserved, however, law enforcement cannot stop at the ticket gate.

Following is an article providing background on the issue of sports violence:

[From the Fort Lauderdale News and Sun-Sentinel, July 20, 1980]

SPORTS, THE COURTS AND VIOLENCE: THE PROBLEM IS DRAWING THE LINE

(By John Meyer)

"The premium the NHL puts (on fighting) was reestablished every time I talked to a team on behalf of a draft choice. Invariably, the interview would get around to how well my client could fight . . . To my endless amazement, the clubs—if they got the impression the boy wasn't tough—frequently offered to enroll him in boxing classes."

—sports agent Bob Woolf

Sparky Anderson must have been living in a dream world.

Two plain-clothes Chicago detectives were attempting to arrest Tigers outfielder Al Cowens, who earlier in the evening had assaulted White Sox pitcher Ed Farmer. "Take your time," one told Cowens as he dressed, "but you're coming with us."

Whoa, said Sparky. "You'll take him over my dead body," Anderson blustered. "Get out of here. This is my clubhouse and you have no jurisdiction."

The cops left, perhaps to arrest Cowens another day, but to suggest the clubhouse provided some sort of medieval sanctuary from the law was patently absurd. Athletic immunity is a myth, without the slightest legal basis, but it is a de facto shield because athletes and prosecutors have traditionally respected it as valid.

That seems likely to change. And Rick Horrow is one of the people trying to make it happen.

Horrow grew up in Miami, and had season tickets to the Dolphins when they were worse than bad. At Harvard Law School, Horrow turned his sports addiction to a positive use, spending three years investigating the issue of sports violence and its relationship to the law. He has published his findings in a legal tract, *Sports Violence: The interaction between private law-making*

and the criminal law, and he proposed federal legislation to turn what is a very gray legal dilemma into some black and white guidelines for the courts.

Rep. Jack Kemp, the former AFL quarterback who very nearly became Ronald Reagan's running mate last week, is interested in Horrow's work. Should he sponsor such legislation this summer, Horrow is confident that Sen. Bill Bradley, a former member of the New York Knicks, will co-sponsor the bill.

"The athlete sees the law as ineffective," Horrow says, "and he translates that as accepting violent behavior. They say, 'We have our own law.' We're not saying, 'Haul everyone into court,' but we have to say certain extreme acts will not be tolerated."

The problem that bedevils the courts is where to draw the line—where "legal" violence stops, in the context of the game, and where criminal conduct begins—and that is what Horrow is trying to correct. There is, as Steelers coach Chuck Noll once testified in court, a "criminal element" in pro football. That may soon be taken literally, but in the absence of laws to define what is criminal and what is sporting, courts all over the land are being forced to make their own law. When Jack Tatum paralyzed Darryl Stingley for life, by all accounts the hit—however vicious—was "legal."

Boobie Clark's attack on Dale Hackbart was not.

(Psychological preparation before a football game should be) "designed to generate an emotional equivalent to that . . . experienced by a father whose family had been endangered by another driver who attempted to force the car off the edge of a mountain road. The precise pitch of motivation . . . should be the feeling of that father when, after overtaking and stopping the offending vehicle, (the father) is about to open the door and take revenge upon the other driver."

—former Denver coach John Ralston testifying in the Hackbart case

In a 1973 game, Dale Hackbart was kneeling near the sideline, five seconds after the play was blown dead, when Boobie Clark hit him from behind with a forearm smash to the neck. Neither Clark nor Hackbart were involved in the play, but Clark was venting the frustration of losing the game. Hackbart suffered three broken vertebrae, causing muscular atrophy in one arm, a shoulder and his back.

Hackbart filed suit for $1 million in damages two years later. A lower court ruled against him, holding that Hackbart took an implied risk by playing a violent game, and anything that happened to him between the sidelines was part of that risk. But that decision was overturned on appeal, on the grounds that Hackbart had no reason to expect an assault fully five seconds after a play is blown dead. The case was sent back to the lower court, where it is still outstanding, and the Supreme Court's refusal to hear the case last fall, in effect, ratified the notion that Hackbart had grounds to sue.

The confusion over the Hackbart case is just another indication that the courts really don't have a clue when, and how they should involve themselves in sports violence cases. That is what Horrow is trying to clarify with a federal law. To some, that may be another invitation for the federal government to meddle in something that's none of its business, but the simple fact is that it must get involved. Otherwise the courts will continue to stumble from case to case, making law as they go along.

In summary, Horrow's bill would draw the line with players who deliberately and recklessly injure another player, outside the rules of the sport, in an act that "bears no reasonable relationship to the competitive goals of the particular sport." Like Clark vs. Hackbart.

"A lot of people are paranoid about getting the federal government's big, powerful hand in every single play," say Horrow. "But we're not talking about creating a government sports agency. We're talking about a law that would be a deterrent, and would apply in only the most egregious situations.

"I've talked to (former Dolphins) Nick Buoniconti, who is a lawyer, and Dick Anderson, who is a legislator. They say if there had been a law like this when they played, it would have changed the way they played. They argue that if you make somebody afraid to hit someone hard, it's a sissy game. But that's just a smoke-screen for people who don't want any intervention."

"The big wheels of the NHL figure they have to have blood to fill the arenas. I refereed for five years, and that was all they were interested in."
      —former NHL ref Jack Mehlenbacher

Deliberate violence in sport, particularly in football and hockey, is often an instrument of strategy. It's called "intimidation," and it is indoctrinated into the athlete from an early age. Woody Hayes loved Tatum because he was already a vicious hitter when he came to Ohio State. The Oakland Raiders nearly intimidated Lynn Swann out of football five years ago, when they put him to sleep in the AFC championship game.

"I almost retired," said Swann. "It wasn't the intimidation, it was the unnecessary brutality. I couldn't see playing a game and risking my life."

It is no difference in hockey. Former Bruins coach Don Cherry loves a good fight, and once gave "enforcer" John Wensink a back-handed compliment for scoring a few out-of-character goals. "I just hope he doesn't forget what got him there," said Cherry. "I mean the goals are nice. I was happy he got the hat trick the other night, but not so happy as I've been when he's won

some big fights for us. I know I shouldn't say that, but that's the honest truth."

Cherry once longed for an "enforcer" who could stand up to Stan Mikita. "I only wish I had one man I could have sent after Mikita," said Cherry, "to send him back to Czechoslovakia in a coffin."

For everything, there is a purpose, including violent behavior in sport. It has certainly helped to sell football—the NFL denies it, but don't believe it—and in hockey, there are those who say it helps sell the game to American fans who don't understand it.

"The large numbers of people who are being exposed to the game now are often not aware of the skills and finesse that give the game its real appeal," Retired hockey star Brian Conacher wrote in "Hockey in Canada the Way It Is,". "But brawling is something they do understand . . . If there is a little blood, so much the better for people with color sets."

Basketball certainly isn't immune, but its acts of violence are easier to separate from the game itself, since it is supposed to be a noncontact sport. Thus it was possible to convince a jury to side with Rudy Tomjanovich of the Houston Rockets after Kermit Washington "maliciously" attacked him in 1977. Tomjanovich's jaw was broken, his skull fractured, and he still talks with a discomfiting nasal twang. For this, Commissioner Larry O'Brien fined Washington $10,000, and suspended him 60 days.

The jury awarded $3.3 million—$600,000 more than Tomjanovich sought—but it was Washington's club—the Lakers—who would pay. Rocket's general manager Ray Patterson called it "a landmark decision," and predicted it would "do a great deal to make the club responsible for its players." And an NBA spokesman admitted, "if the first case can be won, the second seems much more winnable."

"The mere act of putting on a uniform and entering a sports arena should not serve as a license to engage in behavior which would constitute a crime if committed elsewhere. If (a player) is allowed to feel immune . . . maiming and serious bodily injury may well become the order of the day."
      —Prosecutor Gary Flakne,
      State vs. Dave Forbes.

The decision-makers of professional sports don't want the interference. They prefer to "keep it in the family." Horrow's research documents the pressures brought to bear on a victim to let the league handle any discipline, rather than seeking justice from the courts. But the light sentences passed out by commissioners—who functioned as judge, jury and executioner—do little to discourage violent behavior. When Dave Forbes of the Bruins clobbered Minnesota's Henry Boucha in 1975 with his stick, and finished the job by pounding Boucha into the ice until subdued by another player, Forbes was "punished" with a three-game suspension. Boucha required surgery to repair a fracture in the floor of his right eye socket, and it took 25 stitches to close the wounds in his head.

"Obviously, the same act, had it occurred outside the arena, would yield certain criminal prosecution," said Gary Flakne, the Minnesota prosecutor who filed criminal charges against Forbes. "Since it receives only a token penalty inside the arena, there is no real compelling force to curtail that type of conduct." The jury could not reach a verdict in the Forbes case.

So the hits keep on coming. Last December, several Bruins climbed into the stands for a tag-team bout with fans of the New York Rangers. Fines of more than $30,000 and 20 games of suspension were ordered by the league, which then-coach Fred Creighton called "far, far too severe." Four spectators filed a $7 million damage suit against nine Bruins, both teams, the NHL and the city of New York. That may become another "landmark case," because—even without the statutorial guidelines Horrow proposes—there's little doubt that a fight eight rows from the rink isn't "part of the game."

Neither was Cowens vs. Farmer, Washington vs. Tomjanovich, or Clark vs. Hackbart for that matter. If Congress doesn't remove the myth of immunity in sports, there will almost certainly be more incidents of extra-curricular violence. And one day, someone may have to deliver a eulogy.●

Appendix E

STATEMENT OF CONGRESSMAN RONALD M. MOTTL
SUBCOMMITTEE ON CRIME
SEPT. 30, 1980

MR. CHAIRMAN, THANK YOU FOR CALLING THIS HEARING TODAY AND FOR PERMITTING ME TO APPEAR BEFORE THE SUBCOMMITTEE. I AM CONFIDENT THAT UNDER YOUR ABLE LEADERSHIP, THE SUBCOMMITTEE WILL EXAMINE FAIRLY AND FULLY THE SERIOUS PROBLEM OF EXCESSIVE SPORTS VIOLENCE.

ON JULY 31, 1980, I INTRODUCED IN CONGRESS H.R. 7903, THE SPORTS VIOLENCE ACT OF 1980. TO MY KNOWLEDGE, THIS BILL IS THE FIRST SERIOUS ATTEMPT IN CONGRESS TO CURB THE EPISODES OF EXCESSIVE VIOLENCE THAT INCREASINGLY CHARACTERIZE PROFESSIONAL SPORTS.

MY BILL WOULD MAKE IT A FEDERAL CRIME FOR PROFESSIONAL PLAYERS TO USE EXCESSIVE DURING-THE-GAME FORCE THAT CREATES A SIGNIFICANT RISK OF INJURY, WHEN THAT FORCE HAS NO REASONABLE RELATIONSHIP TO THE COMPETITIVE GOALS OF THE SPORT, IS UNREASONABLY VIOLENT, AND COULD NOT BE REASONABLY FORESEEN OR CONSENTED TO BY THE INTENDED VICTIM.

IT IS DIFFICULT AT TIMES TO DRAW A CLEAR LINE BETWEEN CONTACT THAT WE ALL AGREE IS PART OF ANY RUGGED, PHYSICAL GAME, AND NEEDLESSLY VIOLENT, VICIOUS AND DANGEROUS CONTACT THAT HAS NO PLACE ON OR OFF THE FIELD.

BUT FOR THE GOOD OF SPORTS, PLAYERS AND FANS, IT IS TIME WE BLEW THE WHISTLE ON CONDUCT THAT WOULD BE PROSECUTED IF IT HAPPENED ON THE STREET BUT WHICH HAS TOO OFTEN BEEN OVERLOOKED IN THE ARENA.

LET ME BE SPECIFIC ABOUT THE KINDS OF CONDUCT MY BILL IS INTENDED TO PENALIZE.

IT IS DIRECTED TO THE PLAYER WHO SMASHES A HOCKEY STICK OVER THE HEAD OF AN OPPONENT. THIS IS NOT SPORT.

IT IS DIRECTED TO THE BASEBALL PLAYER WHO DROPS HIS BAT OR GLOVE AND RAISES HIS FISTS. THIS IS NOT SPORT.

It is directed to the basketball player who crushes the face of another with his fist. This is not sport.

It is directed to the lineman who deliberately slams into and injures the opposing quarterback long after the play is dead. This is not sport.

When we are looking at these extreme kinds of actions, I have no doubt whatsoever that a carefully drawn federal statute can preserve the health and vitality of professional sports, while serving notice on pro athletes that they have no license to commit televised assault and battery.

A statute marking out the line between normal and accepted aggressive behavior in sports, and excessively violent and repugnant conduct, would yield a number of important benefits.

First, the threat of criminal prosecution would deter most extreme acts and make each game safer for all participants.

Second, a player who stays on the safe side of the line need never worry about prosecution.

Third, legislation will symbolically confirm that fundamental law and order do not stop at the ticket gate.

Finally, and in my book most importantly, I believe that incidents of excessive during-the-game violence must be punished when countless young people look to professional sports figures as role models for their own behavior on and off the field.

Recently in my own city of Cleveland, a pro basketball player in a local summer league became angered and reportedly struck a young referee in the face. The injury later required an eye operation, but that wasn't the major concern of this young referee who himself was a college athlete.

The referee later said, "What hurts me the most is that the young kids in the stands will think, 'Hey, he did it. I can to it too'."

Yes, I've received my share of mail calling sports violence a phony issue, describing my bill as the latest example of needless Big Government meddling, and asking why I haven't single-handedly solved inflation if I have so much time on my hands.

I send my correspondents some comments on this issue from figures who

HAVE ATTAINED MORE PROMINENCE IN THE SPORTS WORLD THAN I ACHIEVED AS A NOTRE DAME PITCHER AND ONE-SEASON MINOR LEAGUER.

JOSEPH ROBBIE, AN OWNER OF THE MIAMI DOLPHINS, HAS STATED: "I PERCEIVE THAT ONE OF THE GREATEST THREATS TO THE FUTURE OF PROFESSIONAL SPORTS OF EVERY KIND, HERE AND ABROAD, IS MAYHEM ON THE FIELD AND CROWD VIOLENCE. WE NEED TO TAKE STERN AND STRICT MEASURES FOR ADEQUATE CONTROL IN EACH INSTANCE. FOOTBALL AND HOCKEY ARE GAMES OF CONTROLLED VIOLENCE, AND ANY DELIBERATE ACT WHICH WOULD CONSTITUTE CRIMINAL ASSAULT SHOULD BE HANDLED IN THE SAME MANNER AS ANY SIMILAR ACT OFF THE FIELD."

VETERAN SPORTS COMMENTATOR AND ANALYST HOWARD COSELL HAS COMMENTED: "IN MY OPINION, EXCESSIVE VIOLENCE IN PROFESSIONAL SPORTS IS A SERIOUS PROBLEM THAT HASN'T GOTTEN ENOUGH ATTENTION FROM THOSE IN A POSITION TO DO SOMETHING ABOUT IT. THE OPERATION OF LAW SHOULD NOT STOP AT THE TICKET GATE OF ANY SPORTING EVENT. IF LEAGUE OFFICIALS AND LOCAL PROSECUTORS WON'T ACT TO CLEAN UP PROFESSIONAL SPORTS, THEY MAY BE LEAVING CONGRESS NO CHOICE BUT TO FILL THE VACUUM."

IN DRAFTING THIS BILL, I HAVE HAD THE INVALUABLE ASSISTANCE OF RICHARD B. HORROW, A LEGAL EXPERT AND AUTHOR ON SPORTS VIOLENCE. THE SPORTING NEWS EDITORIALIZED RECENTLY THAT THE PRODUCT OF OUR WORK "IS NOT A RANDOM SWING AT VIOLENCE, BUT A THOROUGHLY ANALYZED AND RESEARCHED PROPOSAL."

THE ATTORNEY FOR DARRYL STINGLEY, A FORMER NEW ENGLAND PATRIOT FOOTBALL PLAYER WHO IS PARALYZED FROM A PLAYING FIELD COLLISION, IS O. JACKSON SANDS OF BOSTON. SANDS HAS STATED: "IT APPEARS THAT THE UNITED STATES CONGRESS IS THE ONLY FORUM AVAILABLE TO THOSE OF US WHO ARE GRAVELY CONCERNED ABOUT THE INCREASED VIOLENCE IN PROFESSIONAL SPORTS. IT IS APPARENT THAT THE LEAGUES THEMSELVES ARE UNWILLING TO TAKE THE NECESSARY CORRECTIVE MEASURES. FURTHERMORE, IT SEEMS UNMANAGEABLE FOR THE VARIOUS STATE COURTS TO INTERVENE AS WE COULD HAVE FIFTY DIFFERENT RULES OF CONDUCT IN PROFESSIONAL SPORTS."

MR. CHAIRMAN, I BELIEVE THAT PRO ORGANIZATIONS HAVE NOT DEALT SWIFTLY AND EFFECTIVELY WITH EXCESSIVE VIOLENCE IN THEIR SPORTS, EVEN THOUGH THEY PREFER TO KEEP THIS MATTER WITHIN THE FAMILY. YET THE PERFORMANCE OF OUR FINE OLYMPIC HOCKEY TEAM AGAINST THE SOVIETS THIS YEAR GAVE LIE TO THE NOTION

THAT YOU CAN'T PLAY GOOD, TOUGH, CROWD-PLEASING HOCKEY WITHOUT FISTFIGHTS EVERY FIVE MINUTES. WHAT DO WE SEE IN NEARLY EVERY NATIONAL HOCKEY LEAGUE GAME? A BARROOM BRAWL ON SKATES.

LOCAL PROSECUTION FOR ASSAULT AND BATTERY, WHILE ATTEMPTED INCREASINGLY BY CONCERNED LOCAL OFFICIALS, HAS BEEN INCONSISTENT AND INEFFECTIVE.

CONGRESS, THEREFORE, MAY INDEED BE THE ONLY FORUM AVAILABLE FOR THE PROTECTION OF THE PUBLIC INTEREST AS A WHOLE.

THIS IS NOT A NEW ISSUE FOR CONGRESSIONAL INTEREST. I WAS A MEMBER OF THE SELECT COMMITTEE ON SPORTS IN THE 94TH CONGRESS. THE MORE WE LOOKED INTO PROFESSIONAL SPORTS VIOLENCE, THE MORE CONCERNED WE BECAME.

WE CONCLUDED IN OUR FINAL REPORT THAT "ESCALATING SPORTS VIOLENCE WILL FORCE LOCAL PROSECUTORS TO SEEK CRIMINAL SANCTIONS TO CONTAIN THE LEVEL OF VIOLENCE IN THE PUBLIC INTEREST." AND WE FOUND THAT "THE PROFESSIONAL SPORTS INDUSTRY AS A WHOLE COULD REDUCE OR ELIMINATE VIOLENCE IN A VERY SHORT TIME BY MAKING IT PERFECTLY CLEAR THAT SUCH ACTS WILL NOT BE TOLERATED."

IF WE HAD SEEN APPRECIABLE IMPROVEMENT SINCE THIS 1977 REPORT, I WOULD NOT BE SITTING HERE TODAY. BUT I HAVE BECOME CONVINCED THAT TO CURB THIS PROBLEM WHILE PRESERVING THE SPORTS THEMSELVES, A NATIONAL STANDARD FOR UNACCEPTABLE DURING-THE-GAME CONDUCT IS NECESSARY.

A WEEK AGO SUNDAY, WASHINGTON QUARTERBACK JOE THEISMANN WENT THROUGH A BRUISING GAME AGAINST OAKLAND. HE CAME OUT COMPLAINING OF LATE HITS AND CHEAP SHOTS, INCLUDING ONE EPISODE IN WHICH HE WAS LITERALLY PICKED UP AND SLAMMED DOWN ON HIS SHOULDER BY A LINEMAN WHO DREW AN UNNECESSARY ROUGHNESS PENALTY.

THEISMANN'S COMMENTS TO THE WASHINGTON POST SAY IT ALL:

"THIS HAS NO PLACE IN THE GAME OF FOOTBALL, AND IT SHOULD BE DEALT WITH ACCORDINGLY. IT STILL GOES ON AND YOU DON'T SEE ANY REAL MAJOR PUNISHMENTS, OR FINES, OR SUSPENSIONS. WHAT ARE THEY WAITING FOR? SOMEBODY TO GET KILLED, AND THEN THEY'RE GOING TO DO SOMETHING? THERE'S GOT TO BE A DETERRENT IN SOME WAY, SHAPE OR FORM. AND UNTIL THEY PUT A HEAVY ENOUGH DETERRENT ON IT, IT'S GOING TO HAPPEN."

YET, WHAT IS THE NFL NOW FINING PLAYERS FOR? BAGGY SOCKS! EVEN MORE IRONIC, THE RATIONALE FOR SOCKING IT TO SEVERAL CINCINNATI BENGALS IS THAT

SUCH SLOPPINESS HARMS PRO FOOTBALL'S PUBLIC IMAGE, AND THAT YOUNG PEOPLE EMULATE WHAT THEY SEE ON TELEVISION!

So, Mr. Chairman, for the league officials who follow me to this table, I'll repeat Joe Theismann's question: What are you waiting for?

Thank You.

Appendix F

Rick Horrow
Chambers of the Hon. George L. Hart, Jr.
4335 United States District Court for the
    District of Columbia
Third & Constitution, NW
Washington, D.C. 20001
(202) 426-7258

after 10/1980: Paul & Thomson
1300 Southeast First National Bank Building
Miami, Florida 33131
(305) 371-2000

15 September, 1980

THE SPORTS VIOLENCE ACT OF 1980: A JUSTIFICATION

  Thank you for allowing me to discuss the Sports Violence Act of 1980.
The bill, which I researched and drafted for Congressman Ronald M. Mottl
(D. Ohio), would make it a criminal offense for professional players to
engage in excessive violence meeting specific criteria. Under H.R. 7903,
players can be punished for knowingly using excessive physical force that
could cause injury and which bears no reasonable relationship to the
competitive goals of the sport, is unreasonably violent, and could not
be reasonably forseen and consented to.

  The violent incidents of the past year are symptomatic of the alarming
trend toward excessive violence in all professional sports. In one recent
National Hockey League season, for example, penalties totalled a record
22,329 minutes, a 25 percent increase over the preceeding year. Football
is no better. In 1905, President Theodore Roosevelt threatened to abolish the
game by Executive Order unless it could be made less violent. Sixty nine
years later, however, 1,638 National Football League players missed two or
more games with "serious injuries," and studies have revealed that football
is so physically debilitating that a pro's life span is significantly
shorter than that of most males. With basketball players throwing elbows and
baseball players knocking down batters and sliding in with their spikes flailing,
excessive violence becomes an issue in what the casual fan would consider
"non-contact" sports. As athletes become more competitive, and as the pressures
to succeed become stronger, the possibility of violent conduct during the game
increases.

  While most "during the game" sports violence is rightfully considered
"just part of the game," many exceptionally severe acts must be dealt with by
the league and -- if the league fails -- by the courts. In my book, Sports
Violence: The Interaction Between Private Lawmaking and the Criminal Law
[Carrollton Press; Arlington, Va.], I attempt to explore all aspects of this
increasingly serious and significant problem. The book's conclusions are based
on surveys sent to 1490 professional athletes, coaches, owners, general managers,

and prosecuting attorneys. A number of disturbingly clear findings emerge: (A) Excessive violence will continue to increase as long as the pressures and incentives to be violent remain; (B) The leagues and their players, coaches, owners, general managers, and commissioners cannot be left unsupervised to adequately police themselves; (C) The courts cannot resolve the problem until the line separating legitimate, aggressive play from excessive, illegal contact is clearly drawn.

Clearly, the criminal law must be used only as a last resort. Presently, courts apply traditional assault and battery statutes to all sports violence situations. Too often, this results in inter-jurisdictional confusion, and, most importantly, the creation of an attitude that all athletes are implicitly immune from the courts. In short, the rampant ambiguities and line drawing problems suggest that the criminal justice system is attempting to meet a specific problem with a set of statutes that have, at best, only partial application. The Sports Violence Act of 1980 suggests a more cohesive and rational approach to this problem.

In his letter to the Sports Lawyers' Association, Congressman Mottl discussed the basic premises supporting our proposal. It is important, however, to reiterate the advantages of H.R. 7903 in the context of the most significant opposition arguments:

1. The bill, because of its inability to draw a clear line separating acceptable from unacceptable conduct, will inject "uncertainty" into hard hitting professional sports and, thus, "reduce the competitiveness of the game." This argument demonstrates a misunderstanding of H.R. 7903. The bill is carefully targeted at only the most outrageous kinds of conduct, such as a deliberate attempt to injure. This bill seeks to draw a line between the kinds of natural physical contact that are normal in any rugged sport and the kinds of conduct that society should brand as criminal wherever it occurs -- conduct in which a player actually steps outside the role of athlete and sportsman. As such, since any conduct which does not come within the statute is implicitly "legal," a player who observes the rules need never worry about criminal prosecution.

2. If criminal prosecution is indeed appropriate, local assault and battery laws provide the present remedy. Theoretically, an act of excessive sports violence may satisfy technical assault and battery criteria. However, because of the interstate nature of modern professional sports and the diversity and inconsistency of enforcement of state and local assault and battery laws, a federal sports violence law would be important symbolically as a national standard for unacceptable sports behavior. State and local assault and battery laws have traditionally had little usefulness in the area of professional sports violence. These laws and the cases interpreting them have focused on ordinary street crime, and have proven almost irrelevant to the special circumstances of mayhem on the field, ice, or court. However, the bill does not supercede the application of state and local assault and battery statutes by local authorities. It is hoped that this federal law could become a model for state legislation. Attorney O. Jackson Sands, counsel for paralyzed former New England Patriot Darryl Stingley summarized this argument: "It seems unmanageable to allow the fifty states to create a minimum standard for unacceptable sports behavior. It appears that the United States Congress is the only forum available to those of us who are gravely concerned about the increased violence in professional sports."

3. The respective sports leagues can adequately handle the problem "within the family." There is an unfortunate attitude within much of the professional sports world that law enforcement stops at the ticket gate,

and that violent outbreaks by players should be handled within the family."
For most acts, admittedly, internal league disciplinary mechanisms are
quite satisfactory. For exceptionally severe acts of sports violence,
however, league fines and suspensions are inherently inadequate, regardless
of any good faith intentions that each commissioner may possess. As Hennepin
County Prosecutor Gary Flakne noted after litigating State v. David Forbes,
"The mere act of putting on a uniform should not serve as a license to
engage in behavior which would constitute a crime if committed elsewhere.
If (a player) is allowed to feel immune...maiming and serious bodily
injury may well become the order of the day." Legislation [even if only
rarely used to prosecute] will symbolically confirm that no segment of
society can be licensed to break the law with impunity; and that the
operation of law does not stop at the ticket gate of any sporting event.

4. Professional sports violence is only an insignificant portion of the entire
sports violence problem. Though the criminal sanctions would apply to
players in any professional sport, the deterrent effect of a symbolic
federal statement on the problem will "trickle down" to the youth and
amateur levels of each sport. Research that I have compiled and codified
through the Institute of Sport and Social Analysis confirms that the
"lower levels" of sports will "follow the lead" of the professionals. This
is also the basic thesis of the January 3, 1977 Final Report of the House
Select Committee on Professional Sports. Steve Jacobson of Newsday suggests
the problem: "If there is an exciting brawl on a hockey telecast, the next
day juvenile hockey players will be quick to drop their gloves or swing
their sticks. If intimidation is a concept of the pros, it will be taught
as a concept of the amateurs..." If the professionals become less violent,
the amateurs and little leaguers will soon follow.

This issue is an extremely important and significant one. My work with
The Institute of Sport and Social Analysis convinces me that the problem
is not merely limited to the rink or field; rather, its implications effect
all levels of society. I am attempting to develop permanent vehicles through
which to explore sports violence. I am Chairman of a Sports Violence Task
Force for the American Bar Association Sports Forum Committee. I am also
planning to coordinate the creation of a similar committee under the auspices
of The Sports Lawyers' Association.

The Sporting News editorialized recently that The Sports Violence Act
"is not a random swing at violence, but a thoroughly researched and
analyzed proposal." In Hackbart v. Cincinnati Bengals, Inc., 435 F. Supp.
352 (D.Colo. 1977), Judge Matsch noted that, as in the areas of coal mining
and railroad safety, the rapidity and specificity of legislative action is
required in "industries of extreme danger." For the professional sports
industry, the time for The Sports Violence Act of 1980 has come.

Most sincerely,

Rick Horrow

Rick Horrow

Testimony on the subject of the Sports Violence Act of 1980

Stanley Cheren, M.D.
Associate Professor of Psychiatry
Boston University School of Medicine
824 Boylston Street
Brookline, Massachusetts 02167
(617) 277-9630

Mr. Chairman, there are strong psychological reasons for
societal limits on the free reign of violent aggression
independent of the damage done to the victim. The range
of psychological effects is such that society needs the
benefit of both clear definition of the limits of acceptable
behavior and clear sanction against the violation of these
limits. The problem of controlling violence in sports is a
problem belonging not only to the governing agents of the
sports, but to society as a whole, because the free
sanctioned play of acts of vicious attack participates in
elevating the level of violence in society in general.
Sports function as an acceptable outlet for aggression, but
vicious, violent behavior in sports or elsewhere stimulates
more violence, rather than serving as an outlet.

There are three psychological approaches to the phenomenon
of aggression. One is to view it as an instinct. A second
is to view it as a drive stimulated by frustration of efforts
to attain a goal. And the third is to view it as learned
social behavior. A major task of psychological maturation
is the development of increasingly effective, safe, and
adaptively progressive styles of handling aggression.
Athletics function in this process as a prototype of socially
acceptable and rewarded behavior in which aggression is
stripped of its dangerous, damaging potential, and rendered
safe but still able to be expressed. Athletics teach that
an individual can discharge aggressive impulses and still
maintain regard for the bodies and lives of others.

In fact, many institutions in society work on the project of
limiting and modifying aggressive forces in its members.
The reason for this is that aggressive forces are indeed very
difficult to channel and to control. Some people develop
internalized regulatory agents, processes generally called
"the conscience," which allow them to adjust and regulate

their aggression with relative ease and without much help
from external reminders. Their internal sense of the limits
of acceptable behavior is sufficiently firm, that they are
relatively independent of group pressure. More commonly,
however, individuals fall somewhere on a continuum of greater
or lesser dependence on external controls to maintain their
sense of the limits of appropriateness of aggression (conscience.)

Context greatly influences the conscience. We have seen
dramatic demonstrations of this phenomenon in certain Viet
Nam veterans suffering from post traumatic stress syndrome
who, upon returning to civilian life, become horrified by the
memory of things they had done in Viet Nam which could be
acceptable to their consciences only so long as they remained
in Viet Nam. When they returned to their normal context,
the normal limits again returned, and they were unable to
reconcile their acts with those limits. This was one of the
themes captured in the film "Apocalypse Now."

Aggression as an instinct was postulated by Sigmund Freud
and then by Konrad Lorenz. Modern psychology accepts the
instinctual aggressive drive as a substrate upon which
experiential influences operate. The operation of these
external influences is what is most relevant to the subject
at hand. One influence is the development of an effective
conscience. A second is the maintenance of social supports
to that conscience. A third is the provocation of increased
levels of aggressive feeling by exposure to aggressive models.
And the fourth is a phenomenon of habituation, of jadedness,
which requires escalation of levels of stimulation.

Empathy is one of the influences which help to develop an
effectively working conscience. It has been demonstrated
experimentally, as well as frequently perceived experientially,
that when people recognize that someone is being hurt, both
aggressive feelings and aggressive behavior are reduced.
Signs of pain on the face of a victim, cries of pain,
begging for mercy, are all generally responded to by a
reduction of aggressive feeling and behavior in people around
the victim. (Baron, R.A., "Magnitude of Victim's Pain Cues
and Level of Prior Anger Arousal as Determinants of Adult
Aggressive Behavior," <u>Journal of Personality and Social</u>

Psychology, Volume 17, page 236, 1971.)   Conversely,
contexts in which aggressive behavior is rewarded materially
and/or socially tend to reduce the operation of the conscience
as an inhibiting agent. Often the way this is done is that
the aggressor simply views the victim as sufficiently
different from the self as to be outside the realm of
empathic response. It is curious how the conscience works
in this regard because, even in situations where people
experience frustration and disappointment which, under
certain circumstances in agreement with the drive theory
mentioned above, would increase aggressive feeling, they
in fact show diminished aggressive responses when they
feel that the frustration that they experience is justified,
i.e. consonant with their consciences. (Worchel, S., "The
Effect of Three Types of Arbitrary Thwarting on the
Instigation to Aggression," Journal of Personality, Volume 42,
page 301, 1974.)

While people generally rely on external cues and supports
to maintain a sense of conscience,
and while the conscience of normal people is subject to
strong social influence, more angry people have a still
more tenuous hold on aggressive behavior. People who arrive
at provocative situations with an existing load of anger
as part of their psychological baggage are far more readily
provoked to a point where they do not heed the influences of
conscience. It takes less provocation. One of the powerful
provoking experiences able to overwhelm an internal sense
of control in people with predisposing angry tendencies is
simple exposure to aggressive, violent behavior in others.
Violent behavior is then seen as both possible and
acceptable. Baron has studied the question of exposure to
live aggressive models and the role played by that exposure
in the spread of collective violence. He has amassed a large
body of research that indicates that the presence of people
who behave in a highly aggressive way stimulates similar
aggressive action in people witnessing this behavior.
(Baron, R.A., "Aggression as a Function of Victim's Pain Cues,
Level of Prior Anger Arousal, and Exposure to an Aggressive
Model," Journal of Personality and Social Psychology,
Volume 29, page 117, 1974.)

Violence in the media has been shown to have a powerful
influence on aggressive behavior in children. Children
who are not exposed to adults modeling aggressive behavior
tend to be far less aggressive than children who are
exposed to adults engaged in aggressive behavior.
Conversely, children who witness aggressive behavior become
more aggressive than they were prior to that exposure.
In addition, children adopt the specific violent behaviors
to which they are exposed. (Liebert, R.M. and Baron, R.A.,
"Some Immediate Effects of Televised Violence on Children's
Behavior," Developmental Psychology, Volume 6, page 469, 1972.)
Children seem to learn the specific types of aggressive
behavior styles from what they witness, and employ them
in the service of their increased level of violent behavior
and feeling. They seem to learn new ways of inflicting
harm on others through this exposure. They have also been
noted to be less responsive to pain cues in suffering
persons than children not exposed to violence. That is,
they become desensitized to the empathic cues which normally
serve as some amount of check on aggressive impulse.
Thomas has been particularly impressed with this process.
(Thomas, M.H., Horton, R.W., Lippincott, E.C., and
Drabman, R.S., "Desensitization to Portrayal of Real Life
Aggression as a Function of Exposure to Television Violence,"
Journal of Personality and Social Psychology, Volume 35,
page 450, 1977.)

Physicians understand this process particularly well. I
would imagine that people in other professions exposing them
to great horror are also aware of it. As one becomes more
experienced in witnessing gruesome, horrible scenes, one
becomes less intensely moved by them. Physicians frequently
talk about their early experiences in medicine and the
shock that they felt on their first exposure to some of the
horrible conditions that can occur to people in order to
revive in themselves the sense of upset. Without that kind
of reminder, without attention to stirring up such feelings,
they gradually diminish, and it takes more extreme experiences
to stir them up.

However, violence is not only a source of disquieting
experiences, it is also a source of excitement and

stimulation. The popularity of contact sports is in part
related to this fact. The popularity of increasing amounts
of viciousness in such sports also testifies to this fact.
For some time psychology thought that the interest in
watching contact sports was that they provided some
catharsis for aggressive feelings within the viewer. As
far as we can tell, however, this hypothesis is not entirely
true. Research on that subject not only has failed to
demonstrate that watching aggressive behavior discharges
aggressive drive; rather, as I indicated above, it has
demonstrated the opposite.

As the population becomes more experienced with violence,
the need for more extreme violence to satisfy the wish
for violent stimulation grows. In our daily life, we see
traffic slow to a standstill as passing motorists stop to
see the victims of an accident. And people pay fortunes
to see other people get hurt. A few weeks ago, a crowd
crushed a wall in its eagerness to get a better look at
Gary Wells' body bouncing on the pavement of a Las Vegas
hotel. People were indeed injured in their frenzied push
actually to see the man hurt. It escalates as people become
jaded. In the 1930's it was shocking to see James Cagney
slap a woman on the screen. Now far more serious acts of
violence are demanded for excitement. A cycle of brutalization
is established, wherein individual acts of violence
contribute to a general atmosphere of violence, which
in turn allows for and stimulates more individual acts of
violence.

Sociologists have indicated a variety of forces which
together create the increasing violence in our society.
Poverty, inflation, crowding, urbanization, noise, and
ambient temperatures all seem to have influences.
However, root-causes notwithstanding, the mechanism of
violence provoking violence is clear. In the context
of spreading and increasingly severe acts of violence
within our society, there are psychological grounds for
seeking clear definitions of what is and is not acceptable
aggressive behavior in all social contexts, especially
those involving live human behavior as opposed to fiction
or fantasy.

Deterrants to aggressive behavior that have been demonstrated
to be effective are few. However, an outstanding one which
has demonstrated effectiveness is punishment, when the
punishment is appropriate to the magnitude of the misbehavior
and is not itself vicious and cruel. Threats of punishment
may be ineffective in situations where the likelihood of
punishment is small and the likelihood of gain through
aggression is great. Punishment is an effective deterrant
only when the likelihood of its being carried out is high,
and when the aggressor has relatively little to gain from
his aggressive behavior.

STATEMENT OF HENRY C. BOUCHA

BEFORE THE SUBCOMMITTEE ON CRIME

OF THE HOUSE JUDICIARY COMMITTEE

ON H. R. 7903, THE SPORTS VIOLENCE ACT OF 1980

My name is Henry C. Boucha. I was born on June 1, 1951 in
Warroad, Minnesota. At a very early age I began playing ice
hockey. As i progressed, I was told by various persons including
coaches that if I worked hard enough at developing my skills
someday I might qualify to play in the National Hockey League.

Developing my skills as a player took up much of my childhood
time. While other children were doing the things most young
children do to enjoy themselves, I was working to improve my
hockey skills. For instance, I would play in as many leagues
as possible and this required me to travel. I had to learn to
do many conditioning exercises and between school and hockey,
I had no other time.

I am of American Indian ancestry and as such I felt an
obligation to do as well as I could financially in order to
improve my family's well-being. My mother and father have had
to work hard all their lives for what little they have.

As part of my development as a young hockey player I was told repeatedly that in order to play professional hockey I would have to learn to be aggressive and to fight both offensively and defensively. This always bothered me because by nature I am not an aggressive person.

I did very well in hockey and led my High School team to the State of Minnesota finals in 1969. Upon graduation from high school I had a career decision to make. I was offered hockey scholarships to various Universities and Colleges. I was also offered a chance to play with various Junior "A" Clubs. This type of hockey is an overall Junior Hockey System in Canada which is the most important supplier of talent to the NHL. Playing Junior Hockey is like working. It is very demanding and essentially is a 100% committment to hockey. On the other hand, most of the players in the NHL are products of this system. I decided to play for Winnipeg and forego the college scholarships.

I played 1 year for Winnipeg and did well enough to qualify for the United States National Team. I would like to point out that I was shocked by the emphasis put on physical intimidation and violence in the Junior Hockey program. I was repeatedly advised to improve my skills as a fighter because I already had the proper skating ability and coordination. Of course, I tried my best because I knew that NHL scouts attended most of our games.

When I was in the U.S. Army, 1970-72, I was fortunate to play for the U.S. National Team. We traveled extensively and competed in the 1972 Winter Olympics in Sapporo, Japan. I did very well and was drafted by the Detroit Red Wings of the NHL.

I signed with the Wings in 1972 and joined them at the end of the 1971-72 season. I was amazed at the amount of intimidation and violence in the game played at the NHL level. I was disgusted with the fact that some players who didn't have the talent were playing only because they could intimidate better players with different acts of violence in order to win. I was traded to the

Minnesota North Stars in the summer before the 1974-75 season.
The North Stars were a team noted for their lack of physical,
aggressive play. Other clubs knew this and exploited this fact.

In a game played at Bloomington Minnesota, January 4, 1975,
my career was for all intents and purposes ended when I was struck
in the eye by a player for the Boston Bruins. After surgery, I
attempted to continue playing but was finally terminated by the
Colorado Rockies Hockey Club in 1976 because my eye injury had
prevented me from being able to compete on the NHL level.

I believe that there are no effective means currently in effect
in the National Hockey League to prevent incidents such as happened
to me from occurring again. I believe that the Board of Governors
of the National Hockey League has not done enough to insure that
the game of professional hockey will be played in a reasonably
safe manner. In my opinion, they will do nothing that may affect
their ability to sell tickets. Unless laws like H. R. 7903 are
passed persons will continue to suffer serious injuries and loss
of livelihoods and perhaps even lives.

Mr. Chairman, I appreciate your invitation to join you
today and am prepared to answer any questions you or the other
Members may have.

LAW OFFICES
BRIAN M. SMITH AND ASSOCIATES
PROFESSIONAL CORPORATION
1441 EAST MAPLE ROAD, SUITE 307
TROY, MICHIGAN 48084

BRIAN M. SMITH
JOHN J. MALLON
MATT W. ZEIGLER
MICHAEL J. RINKEL

TELEPHONE
(313) 524-1404

My name is Brian M. Smith. I have been a practicing attorney in the State of Michigan since 1970. I am a 1960 graduate of the University of Notre Dame with a Bachelor of Science Degree in Civil Engineering. In 1962 I received a Masters in Business Administration from Western New England College. In 1970 I graduated from the University of Detroit School of Law. My firm specializes in the area of corporate law with the emphasis on labor law, along with the representation of professional athletes. I have represented professional athletes who have played in all major professional leagues in baseball, football and hockey. I have also represented hockey players who have played hockey in Europe. I have been involved in major litigation involving the reserve clauses in professional hockey and also in several cases arising out of violent incidents in professional sports. I have three children and all of them have competed in amateur sports. My law firm is one of several firms located around the United States designated by the National Football League Players Association to advise professional football players with respect to their legal rights in cases where the player has been injured.

During the past five years, I have personally been involved in two major injury litigation cases involving professional and amateur hockey. In addition, I have given counsel to two other professional hockey players who were the victims of violent incidents occurring during the course of hockey games. I have had the opportunity to know the persons who were the victims of these incidents on a personal basis and accordingly feel that I am qualified to speak, not only with respect to the legal issues involved, but also the personal hardship caused by these cases. The four situations to which I refer, above, involved Henry Boucha, a professional hockey player employed by the Minnesota

North Stars; John Kellogg, a linesman or game official employed by the International Hockey League; Greg Neeld, an "amateur" who was playing hockey in the Ontario Hockey Association in Ontario, Canada; and Dennis Polonich, a professional hockey player employed by the Detroit Red Wings.

GREG NEELD

Greg Neeld was a young, amateur hockey player injured during a scheduled hockey game in the Ontario Hockey Association in Ontario, Canada. The Ontario Hockey Association is known to be one of the biggest suppliers of hockey talent to the National Hockey League. National Hockey League scouts attend OHA games regularly to scout future NHL players. Neeld was involved in a violent incident whereby an opposing player struck him in the face with his stick causing the loss of Neeld's eye. Neeld had been rated by the NHL scouting system as an outstanding prospect. Neeld, despite his loss of an eye was drafted by the Buffalo Sabres Hockey Club. At this point, the National Hockey League enforced By-Law 12.6 of the National Hockey League By-Laws to prevent the Sabres from signing Neeld. By-Law 12.6, in short, states that persons with vision in only one eye will not be eligible to play for any of the member clubs of the National Hockey League. Greg Neeld's career was effectively terminated and 11 years of effort on the part of Neeld in preparing himself for a professional career was wasted. It is ironic that there were not sufficient safeguards in effect in the Ontario Hockey Association to protect Neeld from the attack he sustained, yet, there were rules and regulations in effect at the National Hockey League level which precluded him from competing after he was injured.

DENNIS POLONICH

In a professional hockey game between the Colorado Rockies and the Detroit Red Wings played at Olympia Stadium in Detroit, Michigan on October 25, 1978, Wilf Paiement of the Colorado Rockies attacked Dennis Polonich of the Red Wings with his stick. Paiement struck Polonich across the face with his hockey stick in a manner described by Referee John McCauley as a "baseball type swing". Polonich sustained severe nasal fractures, multiple lacerations to the face and a concussion. If the blow had struck Polonich an inch higher on his face, he could well have lost the sight of one or both eyes. Polonich had no recollection of the events for several hours after the injury. As a result of the attack, Paiement was suspended for 15 games by the National Hockey League. He was fined the maximum amount allowed permitted under the rule - Five Hundred Dollars ($500.00). The Wayne County Prosecutor's Office investigated the incident and decided not to prosecute Paiement. However, Prosecutor William L. Cahalan stated "The operation of the law does not stop at the ticket gates of any sports event in my jurisdiction. Even though this specific incident will not result in a criminal prosecution, every one concerned should understand that criminal violence occurring during any sporting event will, if supported by fact of law, be prosecuted."

Polonich is my client and I can assure you that his ability to play professional hockey has been severely impaired as a result of this injury. It is my judgment that the penalty and fine assessed against Paiement was too little and too late to deter such future acts of violence.

JOHN KELLOGG

John Kellogg, a 27 year old father of three children, was viciously attacked while officiating an International Hockey League playoff game in 1975. After calling a play off side, one of the players of the Saginaw Gears jumped off the bench and brutally attacked Kellogg from behind, knocking him into the goal post. Kellogg not only suffered serious physical injury, but the traumatic effect of the attack caused him severe psychological damage. According to medical testimony from doctors employed by the League and from Kellogg's own doctors, the incident resulted in severe psychological damage to Kellogg. Kellogg has been unemployed since the incident.

Kellogg and his wife presented themself at my office in late 1975. The Kelloggs , at that point, had little or no income to support their family, let alone pay the medical bills required for proper treatment. I contacted the International Hockey League concerning Kellogg's right to collect Michigan Workmen's Compensation. I was advised by the League that Kellogg, and other game officials were considered to be independent contractors and, therefore, not eligible for benefits under the Workmen's Compensation statute. At that point, Kellogg filed a petition for Workmen's Compensation benefits and after four years of delay and frustration, Kellogg received his compensation benefits. One fortunate by-product of this case was that game officials employed by the International Hockey League are now eligible for Workmen's Compensation benefits in Michigan. However, it should be noted that this League also operates franchises in Ohio, Indiana and Wisconsin. I am not sure whether the Workmen's Compensation statutes in those states apply to game officials employed by the International Hockey League.

I would like to point out that the individual who attacked Kellogg during the game in 1975 was employed by the Saginaw Gears, in my opinion, because of his reputation as an intimidator. This player, Reggie Fleming, had made a reputation for himself in the National Hockey League as an aggressive and belligerent player who engaged in many fights on the ice. The message is clear - Fleming by virtue of his reputation and style would help the Saginaw Gears to sell more tickets.

HENRY BOUCHA

Mr. Boucha has been my client for 8 years and is here today to testify at these hearings. His case has been well documented. Again, he was the victim of a vicious attack during a National Hockey League game in Bloomington, Minnesota in 1975. The attack resulted in the prosecution of the player involved, David Forbes, by the Hennepin County Prosecutor's Office. Mr. Boucha instituted civil litigation against the National Hockey League, the Boston Bruins and David Forbes in 1975. Because of the crowded Wayne County, Michigan dockets, a trial date was not fixed until a few months ago. Mr. Boucha's litigation was settled out of court, but the aftermath of the incident has had and will continue to have a profound effect on his life.

It is my opinion that the type of conduct which is allowed to exist today in professional hockey is the cause of incidents similar to the four recited above. I have been involved in all of the above cases and have had first hand experience in dealing with the victims of these attacks. These four cases are but a small part of the total number of cases which occur on a regular basis each hockey season. The continued existence of this situation requires that this committee give H.R. 7903 fullest consideration.

For the purposes of this appearance, I will limit my comments to need for legislation such as H.R. 7903 with respect to the sport of hockey.

My expereience as a hockey fan, amateur player, and sports attorney has lead me to conclude that based on the situation as it exists today in the National Hockey League, there are compelling reasons for the passage of H.R. 7903.

At the outset, I would like to state, that I have had the opportunity to represent several hockey players from Sweden. In Sweden, the government exercises a great deal of control over all major sports. There are stringent penalties in effect in European hockey which result in permanent suspension of flagrant violators. Swedish and European hockey players are well aware that if they flagrantly foul an opponent such as by viciously using their stick as an offensive weapon, they will be dealt with harshly. Consequently, to my knowledge, there are few, if any, reported cases of serious injury resulting from blatant attacks by other players in European hockey. It is my considered opinion that there is no need for this kind of conduct in professional hockey in

Canada and the United States in order to make the sport commercially successful.
One need only to harken back to the recent 1980 Olympic competition at Lake
Placid, New York to realize that clean, fast hockey (played European style)
can capture the interest of the public. Unfortunately, based on my experience
over the past 6 or 7 years, it is my opinion that the owners or the people that
control professional hockey in Canada and the United States believe that the
admixture of intimidation, aggression, hostility and brutal attacks helps to
sell tickets. I have visited many hockey arenas and witnessed many hockey
games. One need only to take a random sampling of programs sold at these
arenas to realize that the persons responsible for publishing the programs
highlight with vivid pictures and stories incidents of violence occurring in
previous games.

The committee should take note that for many years, professional
hockey existed in the United States and Canada as a six team sport including
teams in Montreal, Toronto, Chicago, New York, Boston and Detroit. In
the late 1960's, based in large part on marketing surveys, the Board of Governors
of the National Hockey League went from the six original teams to eighteen
teams. In short, the number of franchises trebled in one year. Of course,
this expansion opened up new markets where hockey had to be promoted.
Included among the new urban areas where professional hockey would be
displayed were: Atlanta, Georgia; Philadelphia, Pennsylvania; Kansas City,
Missouri; St. Louis, Missouri; Oakland, California; Los Angeles, California;
Pittsburgh, Pennsylvania and Washington, D.C. Although there may have been
a small nucleus of knowledgeable fans in these cities, I believe a reasonable
person would agree that these were not centers of keen hockey interest as
compared to Detroit, Boston, Toronto and Montreal. An obvious by-product of
the marketing in hockey in these areas was the introduction of blatant violence
based on the belief that fan interest would be heightened. When I speak of violence,
I do not mean the normal physical aspect of the game of hockey, because it is

a contact sport, but I speak rather of outraeous violations which result in serious injury and could perhaps result in a needless death.

The tragedy of the situation as it exists today is that not enough has been done by the parties responsible to control this violence. Hockey operates according to a set of rules adopted by the Board of Governors of the National Hockey League and ratified by the National Hockey League Players Association. These rules as currently constituted do not deter the violent incidents that continue to plague professional and amateur hockey. Although I am not a psychologist or a sociologist, it is clear from the many expert studies written on the subject that young hockey players today are trained and instructed by their coaches beginning at age six or seven that intimidation and aggressive play (including injuring an opponent, if necessary) are the qualities that will impress the scouts at a major league level.

Going back for a moment to the recent evolution of professional hockey beginning with the expansion period of the late 1960s, one can note that at that time the Boston Bruins were known generally as the most aggressive hockey team in the league. In the early 1970s the Philadelphia Flyers introduced a new style of play in the National Hockey League which adopted the Bruins' methods and perfected them. Philadelphia introduced the "designated Goon" to professional hockey. This was the player designated to attack the better player on the opposing team. Fighting and violence became their trademark. Unfortunately for the public, their methods succeeded. The Flyers won hockey games. The cases of violence involving the Philadelphia Flyers are too numerous to be recounted at this hearing. Suffice it to say, that they were a hockey team during the middle 1970s, which were fully capable of playing fast, clean and positional hockey without resorting to illegal and violent tactics. Because of the success of the Flyers both at the box office and with respect to won-loss percentage, other teams in the National Hockey League began to imitate their strategy. The result has created the situation today.

As I mentioned earlier, I have practiced both as a sports attorney and a labor lawyer. I believe in the concept of collective bargaining. I feel very strongly that the process of collective bargaining, should have and would have worked if the NHL Players Association and the Board of Governors had come to grips with the problem at its early stages. I think that the Player's Association has succumbed to the usual temptation of negotiating economic issues to the detriment of health and safety issues. The owners consider the adoption and enforcement of rules and regulations of hockey to be part of their sole domain. It is part of their "management rights". Furthermore, I believe the Association feels that it is put in a compromising position by agreeing to the adoption of more restrictive and more severe suspensions and punishments because this could have an adverse effect on certain of their dues paying membership. I believe a similar situation existed in collective bargaining between industry and labor in the United States which lead to the enactment of the Occupational Safety and Health Act a few years ago. As a matter of public policy, the people of the United States felt that the government should step in, as a last resort, to protect the health and safety of the American citizens where their own unions and companies were unable to do so. This is similar to the situation we face today in the United States with respect to our major professional sports.

The rules and system of penalties currently in effect in the National Hockey League do not serve as a deterrent to frequent incidents of violent conduct. My comments this morning have been limited to cases involving players or officials. A recent phenomena is the advent of player and crowd involvement. Spectators engaging in fights with players possibly leading to riots. I believe this is a natural extension of the failure to adequately control violence between players.

Finally, if I have any criticism of H.R. 7903 it would be because the bill does not go far enough in assessing blame and punishing the persons who are responsible. As noted above, I believe the power structure of professional hockey has the authority to correct the current situation but has chosen not to do so. Their motives for failing to act are not the point. The board of Governors has not taken appropriate remedial action. Some sort of fine or criminal penalty should be assessed against the individual clubs who promote or encourage their players to engage in the type of conduct prohibited by H.R. 7903. Certainly, if the clubs were required by the National Hockey League to pay substantial fines when their players are involved in violent situations, the ownership would deal with the problem. I venture to say that if the fines or penalties were severe enough in nature, the clubs would exercise more control over the activities of their players. To simply place the entire blame on the players involved ignores the fact that they are motivated by their employers to play in an overly aggressive manner. If a crime exists, should not the persons who planned it be punished as well as the persons who carried it out?

Appendix G

Your Nissen equipment is the finest high quality equipment in the field. But even the finest car is safety checked periodically. For the safety of your gymnasts, make it a point to safety check your gymnastic equipment, too.

This safety check should be done approximately once every two months and just before the heavy use of equipment that occurs during a meet or an exhibition. However, the habit of conscientious inspection whenever gymnasts are using the equipment should be the goal of instructors, and they should develop this habit in their pupils. Develop the habit of everyday vigilance for loose fastenings and improperly adjusted equipment.

To assist your inspection when there is more than one piece of equipment, assign it a unit number on this sheet and paint or stamp the same number on the apparatus to which it refers. When you make your inspection, enter a check mark for OK or an "R" for repair or replacement. Act immediately on the "R" items and always take such equipment out of the program until repairs are completed.

NISSEN CORPORATION
Cedar Rapids, Iowa

UNIT NUMBER

Item	#1	#2	#3	#4	#5
1. Location of equipment (should be suitable distance from wall, sharp corners on chairs, benches, etc.) Keep in mind that a man landing off balance may take a few steps and then fall.					
A. Rings					
B. Horizontal Bar					
C. Side Horse					
D. Parallel Bar					
E. Tumbling Mats					
F. Free Exercise Area					
G. Long Horse					
H. Trampoline					
I. Climbing Ropes					
J. Mats placed to eliminate Crevices					
K. Mini-Tramp					
L. Buck or Vaulting Box					
M. Miscellaneous					
2. Safety Equipment					
A. Hand Belts					
1. Condition of main body of belt					
2. Condition of all stitching-- buckle to belt, sliding pad to webbing					
3. Condition of webbing where ring to rope contacts webbing					
4. Rope snaps and rope attachment to snap					

	UNIT NUMBER				
ITEM	#1	#2	#3	#4	#5
B. Overhead spotting suspension					
1. Girder clamp--bolts tight_____					
2. If a traveling suspension, metal-to-metal wear of hooks, turnbuckle, and cable_____					
3. Condition of pulleys--grease pully wheel axles_____					
4. Condition of rope_____					
5. Belt (see 2-A)_____					
3. Horizontal Bar					
A. Examine Bar for evidence of a "set"-downward bend of the bar. Test with the bar UNMOUNTED by using a straight edge or tightly stretched chalk line. If permanent set is more than 1/2", bar should be replaced. Under no circumstances should you reverse the bar.					
B. If bar is adjustable, examine efficiency of pin for height adjustment and knob for tightening height adjustment pin_____					
C. Fastening of Horizontal Bar to vertical supports (examine pins or bolts)_____					
D. Fastening of cables to uprights_____					
E. Condition of cables (and chain), look for cable damage_____					
F. Fastening of cables to end hardware (turnbuckles)_____					
G. Condition of hooks and turnbuckles_____					
H. Floor Plates (watch during workout for any signs of loosening)_____					
4. Rings					
A. Test clamps which are fastened to girders (tight, no play)_____					

UNIT NUMBER

ITEM	#1	#2	#3	#4	#5
B. Examine all hardware between girder and rings.					
C. Examine cable for wear and ropes for fraying (replace ropes that show aging--old fibers are easily torn)					
D. Condition of webbing and buckles and hooks on rings					
E. If adjustable Rings:					
1. Examine wall fastening bolts (no play)					
2. Examine fastening for chain					
3. Examine chain					
4. Condition of chain to rope fastening and rope itself					
5. Pulleys--oil axles, examine all parts for wear and all fastenings to wall or ceiling					
5. Climbing Rope					
A. Clamp to girder or beam; all fastenings and entire unit solid (no play)					
B. Examine carefully all hardware between clamp to girder and the rope					
C. Examine rope carefully at hardware contact points					
D. Examine length of rope for fraying and old age					
6. Trampoline					
A. Examine all parts of frame for firm bracing and evidence of play					
B. See that safety pads are firmly in place on the frame					
C. Examine shock cords and springs and rotate cables periodically to prevent wear by sliding around through ring of hooks					

ITEM	UNIT NUMBER				
	#1	#2	#3	#4	#5
D. Examine bed for need for sewing and condition of loops around the edge					
E. Review proper folding and unfolding by referring to Owner's Manual					
7. Parallel Bars					
A. Note condition of wooden bars. If cracking occurs, rub in boiled linseed oil, wipe off excess, allow to dry 3 days (weekend) then lightly sand and chalk bar					
B. Note especially metal fastenings to wooden bar (no play)					
C. Examine height and width adjustment					
D. All nuts, bolts, and screws (tight and no play)					
E. Rollers free of lint, easily raised and lowered (if built into base); lightly grease caster swivel for ease of movement					
F. Examine pads under base to prevent slipping and to protect floor					
8. Mats					
Check all edges, handles, tufting, sewing and note wear					
9. Side Horse					
A. Check pommel surfaces					
B. Check fasteners which hold pommels tight					
C. Condition of body of Horse					
D. Fasteners of body to base					
E. Height adjustment mechanism					
F. Rubber base pads					
10. Buck					
A. Condition of body					

	UNIT NUMBER				
ITEM	#1	#2	#3	#4	#5
B. Fasteners of body to base					
C. Height adjustment mechanism					
D. Rubber base pads					
11. Springboard					
A. Condition of wood--any splits or breaks					
B. Take-off surface rough enough to prevent slipping					
C. Examine all fastenings					
12. Mini-Tramp					
A. Condition of Frame					
B. Condition of bed					
C. Condition of cables and fastenings					
D. Frame pads intact					
E. Frame floor pads solid					
13. Vaulting Box					
A. Top surface firm and intact					
B. Examine joints for solidity, wood surface for splits or breaks					
14. Physical Educator					
A. Ropes and webbing sound					
B. Examine for metal to metal wear					
C. Tighten all nuts and bolts and screws					
15. Physical Exerciser					
A. Examine all parts for solidity of support					

Appendix H

96TH CONGRESS
1ST SESSION
S. 583

To provide for the development and implementation of programs for children and youth camp safety.

IN THE SENATE OF THE UNITED STATES

MARCH 8, (legislative day, FEBRUARY 22), 1979

Mr. RIBICOFF (for himself, Mr. WEICKER, Mr. McGOVERN, Mr. SARBANES, Mr. RIEGLE, and Mr. MAGNUSON) introduced the following bill; which was read twice and referred to the Committee on Labor and Human Resources

---

A BILL

To provide for the development and implementation of programs for children and youth camp safety.

1   *Be it enacted by the Senate and House of Representa-*

2 *tives of the United States of America in Congress assembled,*

3 That this Act may be cited as the "Children and Youth

4 Camp Safety Act".

5   STATEMENT OF PURPOSE

6   SEC. 2. (a) It is the purpose of this Act to protect and

7 safeguard the health and well-being of the youth of the

8 Nation attending day camps, residential camps, short-term

    II—E

1 group camps, travel camps, trip camps, primitive or outpost

2 camps, and Federal recreational youth camps, by providing

3 for establishment of Federal standards for safe operation of

4 youth camps, to provide Federal financial and technical as-

5 sistance to the States in order to encourage them to develop

6 programs and plans for implementing safety standards for

7 youth camps, and to provide for the Federal implementation

8 of safety standards for youth camps in States which do not

9 implement such standards and for Federal recreational youth

10 camps, thereby providing assurance to parents and interested

11 citizens that youth camps and Federal recreational youth

12 camps meet minimum safety standards.

13   (b) In order to protect and safeguard adequately the

14 health and well-being of the children and youth of the Nation

15 attending camps, it is the purpose of this Act that youth

16 camp safety standards be applicable to intrastate as well as

17 interstate youth camp operators.

18   CONGRESSIONAL INTENT REGARDING STATE

19   INVOLVEMENT

20   SEC. 3. It is the intent of Congress that the State

21 assume responsibility for the development and enforcement of

22 effective youth camp safety standards. The Secretary shall

23 provide, in addition to financial and technical assistance, con-

24 sultative services necessary to assist in the development and

25 implementation of State youth camp safety standards.

1   DEFINITIONS

2   SEC. 4. For purposes of this Act—

3   (1) The term "youth camp" means any residential

4 camp, day camp, short-term group camp, troop camp, travel

5 camp, trip camp, primitive or outpost camp, or Federal recre-

6 ational youth camp located on private or public land,

7 which—

8   (a) is conducted as a youth camp for the same ten

9   or more or more campers under eighteen years of age;

10   (b) may include activities promoted or advertised

11   as something other than a youth camp, but offers

12   youth camp activities;

13   (c) may include any site or facility primarily de-

14   signed for other purposes, such as, but not limited to,

15   any school, playground, resort, or wilderness area; and

16   (d) may include any site or facility advertised as a

17   "camp" for youth regardless of activities offered.

18   (2) The term "youth camp activities" includes, but is

19 not limited to, such waterfront activities as swimming,

20 diving, boating, lifesaving, canoeing, sailing, and skindiving;

21 such other activities as archery, riflery, horseback riding,

22 hiking, and mountain climbing, and other sports and athlet-

23 ics; and campcraft and nature study activities, under the aus-

24 pices of a youth camp operator. The term does not include—

1   (a) the activities of a family and its guests carried

2   out as a purely social activity;

3   (b) regularly scheduled meetings of voluntary or-

4   ganizations such as the Girl Scouts or Boy Scouts that

5   do not involve camping experience:

6   (c) regularly scheduled athletic events that do not

7   involve camping experience;

8   (d) bona fide extracurricular activities conducted

9   under the auspices of the schools;

10   (e) learning experiences in the arts and drama or

11   conferences of forums; and

12   (f) activities carried on in private homes.

13   (3) The term "permanent campsite" means a camp-

14   ground which is continuously or periodically used for camp-

15   ing purposes for a portion of a day by a youth camp operator,

16   which may or may not include temporary or permanent

17   structures and installed facilities.

18   (4) The term "residential camp" means a youth camp

19   operating on a permanent campsite for four or more consecu-

20   tive twenty-four-hour days.

21   (5) The term "day camp" means a youth camp operated

22   on a permanent campsite for all or part of the day but less

23   than twenty-four hours a day and which is conducted for at

24   least five days during a two-week period, but does not in-

25   clude—

1   (a) swimming facilities operated by a public

2   agency or by a private organization on a membership

3   basis, except where that private organization utilizes

4   such facilities as part of a youth camp;

5   (b) a day care center except where the center op-

6   erates a day camp; or

7   (c) playgrounds and other recreation facilities pro-

8   vided for neighborhood use by local public agencies.

9   (6) The term "troop camp" means a youth camp which

10   provides youth camp activities conducted for not less than

11   twenty-four hours a day for organized groups of campers

12   sponsored by a voluntary organization serving children and

13   youth.

14   (7) The term "short-term group camp" means an orga-

15   nized camping activity of more than twenty-four but less than

16   a ninety-six-hour period for groups, clubs, and troops of

17   campers sponsored by an organization or person.

18   (8) The term "travel camp" means a youth camp which

19   provides youth camp activities conducted for not less than

20   twenty-four hours a day and which uses motorized transpor-

21   tation to move campers as a group from one site to another

22   over a period of two or more days.

23   (9) The term "trip camp" means a youth camp which

24   provides youth camp activities conducted for not less than

25   twenty-four hours a day which moves campers under their

1 own power or by a transportation mode permitting individual

2 guidance of a vehicle or animal from one site to another.

3   (10) The term "primitive or outpost camp" means a

4 portion of the permanent camp premises or other site, under

5 the control of the youth camp operator at which the basic

6 needs for camp operation, such as places of abode, water

7 supply systems, and permanent toilet and cooking facilities

8 are not usually provided.

9   (11) The term "Federal recreation camp" means a camp

10 or campground which is operated by, or under contract with,

11 a Federal agency to provide opportunities for recreational

12 camping to campers.

13   (12) The term "camper" means any child under eigh-

14 teen years of age, who is attending a youth camp or engaged

15 in youth camp activities.

16   (13) The term "youth camp operator" means any pri-

17 vate or public agency, organization, or person, and any indi-

18 vidual, who operates, owns, or controls, a youth camp,

19 whether such camp is operated for profit or not for profit.

20   (14) The term "youth camp staff" means any person or

21 persons employed by a youth camp operator, whether for

22 compensation or not, to supervise, direct, or control youth

23 camp activities.

24   (15) The term "youth camp director" means the individ-

25 ual on the premises of any youth camp who has the primary

1 responsibility for the administration of program operations

2 and supportive services for such youth camp and for the su-

3 pervision of the youth camp staff of such camp.

4   (16) The term "youth camp safety standards" means

5 criteria issued by the Secretary designed to provide to each

6 camper safe and healthful conditions, facilities, and equip-

7 ment which are free from hazards that are causing, or are

8 likely to cause, death, serious illness, or serious physical

9 harm, including adequate supervision to prevent injury or ac-

10 cident, and safety instruction by properly qualified personnel,

11 wherever or however such camp activities are conducted and

12 with due consideration to the type of camp involved and to

13 conditions existing in nature. The criteria shall be directed

14 toward areas including—but not limited to—personnel quali-

15 fications for director and staff; ratio of staff to campers; sani-

16 tation and public health; personal health, first aid and medi-

17 cal services; food handling, mass feeding and cleanliness;

18 water supply and waste disposal, water safety; including use

19 of lakes and rivers; swimming and boating equipment and

20 practices; firearms safety; vehicle condition and operation;

21 building and site design; equipment; and condition and densi-

22 ty of use.

23   (17) The term "Secretary" means the Secretary of

24 Health, Education, and Welfare.

1   (18) The term "State" includes each of the several
2 States, the District of Columbia, Puerto Rico, American
3 Samoa, Guam, the Virgin Islands, and the Trust Territories
4 of the Pacific.

5   (19) The term "serious violation" means any violation
6 in a youth camp if there is substantial probability that death
7 or serious physical harm could result, unless the operator did
8 not, and could not, with the exercise of reasonable diligence
9 know of the presence of the violation.

10   (20) The term "consultative services" means advice on
11 the interpretation of applicability of the general duty under
12 section 5; of the general duty under State law required by
13 section 8(b)(2); or of youth camp safety standards, and advice
14 on the most effective methods of complying with such duty
15 and such standards.

16   GENERAL DUTY

17   SEC. 5. Each youth camp operator shall provide to each
18 camper—

19   (1) safe and healthful conditions, facilities, and
20   equipment which are free from recognized hazards
21   which cause, or are likely to cause, death, serious ill-
22   ness, or serious physical harm, and

23   (2) adequate and qualified instruction and supervi-
24   sion of youth camp activities at all times, wherever or

1   however such youth camp activities are conducted and

2   with due consideration existing in nature.

3   DIRECTOR OF YOUTH CAMP SAFETY

4   SEC. 6. (a) There is established in the office of the Sec-

5   retary an Office of Youth Camp Safety which shall be headed

6   by a Director of Youth Camp Safety (hereinafter referred to

7   as the "Director"). In the performance of his functions under

8   this Act, the Director shall be directly responsible to the Sec-

9   retary.

10   (b) The Director shall be appointed by the Secretary.

11   (c) The Director shall report to the President and to the

12   Congress, on or before January 1 of each year, on the activi-

13   ties carried out under this Act, including the statistics sub-

14   mitted to and compiled by the Director under section 11(c),

15   and such report shall include the certification required under

16   section 8(d).

17   PROMULGATION OF YOUTH CAMP SAFETY STANDARDS

18   SEC. 7. (a) The Director shall develop, with the ap-

19   proval of the Secretary, and shall by rule, promulgate,

20   modify, or revoke youth camp safety standards. In develop-

21   ing such standards, the Director shall consult with the Feder-

22   al Advisory Council on Youth Camp Safety established under

23   section 15, with State officials, and with representatives of

24   appropriate public and private organizations, and shall con-

25   sider existing State regulations and standards, and standards

S. 583——2

1 developed by private organizations which are applicable to

2 youth camp safety, and shall make such suitable distinctions

3 in such standards as are necessary and appropriate in order

4 to recognize the differences in conditions and operations

5 among residential camps, day camps, short-term group

6 camps, travel camps, trip camps, primitive or outpost camps,

7 or Federal recreational youth camps. The Director shall pro-

8 mulgate the standards required by this section within one

9 year after the effective day of this Act. Such standards shall

10 take effect in each State at the completion of the first regular

11 legislative session of such State which begins after the date

12 on which such standards are promulgated.

13   (b) Notwithstanding any other provision of law, the Di-

14 rector shall, before promulgating any standard under subsec-

15 tion (a) or any rule or regulation under any other provision of

16 this Act, transmit such proposed standard, rule, or regulation

17 to each House of the Congress. No such proposed standard,

18 rule, or regulation may take effect if either House of the

19 Congress adopts a resolution, within sixty legislative days of

20 continuous session of the Congress after such proposed stand-

21 ard, rule, or regulation is transmitted by the Director, which

22 disapproves such proposed standard, rule, or regulation. Any

23 such resolution shall void the proposed standard, rule, or reg-

24 ulation involved. The failure of either House of the Congress

25 to adopt any such resolution shall not be considered to be an

1 expression by the Congress that the standard, rule, or regula-
2 tion involved is within the scope of authority delegated to the
3 Director by this Act.

4 STATE JURISDICTION AND STATE PLANS

5 SEC. 8. (a) During the two-year period after the initial
6 promulgation of Federal standards and annually thereafter
7 any State which, at any time, desires to assume responsibili-
8 ty for development and enforcement of comprehensive youth
9 camp safety standards applicable to youth camps therein
10 (other than Federal recreational youth camps operated by a
11 Federal agency) shall submit a State plan for the develop-
12 ment of such standards and their enforcement.

13 (b) The Director shall approve a plan submitted by a
14 State under subsection (a), or any modification thereof, if
15 such plan in his judgment—

16   (1) designates a State agency as the agency re-
17   sponsible for administering the plan throughout the
18   State,

19   (2) provides that each youth camp operator shall
20   have the same general duty under State law as is pro-
21   vided under section 5,

22   (3) provides, after consultation with youth camp
23   operators and other interested parties in that State, for
24   adoption and enforcement of comprehensive youth
25   camp safety standards which standards (and the en-

1   forcement of such standards) are or will be at least as

2   effective in providing safe operation of youth camps in

3   the State as the standards promulgated under section

4   7, and provides that where penalties are not employed

5   as a method of enforcement of such standards, a

6   system of licensing and loss of license is in effect which

7   is at least as effective as penalties,

8   (4) provides for the enforcement of the standards

9   developed under paragraph (3) in all youth camps in

10   the State which are operated by the State or its politi-

11   cal subdivisions,

12   (5) provides a procedure whereby the State

13   agency may petition the appropriate State court to

14   seek injunctive relief to restrain any conditions or prac-

15   tices in any youth camp or any place where camp ac-

16   tivities are conducted which are such that a danger

17   exists which would reasonably be expected to cause

18   death or immediate serious physical harm, or before

19   the imminence of such danger can be eliminated

20   through the enforcement procedures otherwise provided

21   by State law or regulation, which is at least as effec-

22   tive as that provided in section 13,

23   (6) provides for a procedure for the issuance of

24   variances from standards developed under paragraph

25   (3) upon application by a youth camp operator showing

1   extraordinary circumstances or undue hardship, on

2   terms and conditions at least as effective as that pro-

3   vided in section 14,

4   (7) provides for consultative services to youth

5   camps in the State with respect to the general duty

6   and comprehensive youth camp safety standards under

7   such State plan,

8   (8) provides for an inspection of each such youth

9   camp at least once a year during a period that camp is

10   in operation,

11   (9) provides for a State youth camp advisory com-

12   mittee, to advise the State agency on the general

13   policy involved in inspection and licensing procedures

14   under the State plan, which committee shall include

15   among its members representatives of other State

16   agencies concerned with camping or programs related

17   thereto; persons representative of professional or civic

18   or other public or nonprofit private agencies, organiza-

19   tion, or groups concerned with organized camping; and

20   members of the general public having a special interest

21   in youth camps,

22   (10) provides for a right of entry and inspection of

23   all such youth camps which is at least as effective as

24   that provided in section 11,

1   (11) contain satisfactory assurances that such

2   State agency has or will have the legal authority and

3   qualified personnel necessary for the enforcement of

4   such standards,

5   (12) gives satisfactory assurances that such State

6   will devote adequate funds to the administration and

7   enforcement of such standards,

8   (13) provides that such State shall coordinate the

9   inspection efforts of such State agency so that undue

10   burdens are not placed on camp operators with multi-

11   ple inspections,

12   (14) provides that such State agency will make

13   such reports in such form and containing such informa-

14   tion as the Director may reasonably require,

15   (15) provides assurances that State funds will be

16   available to meet the portions of the cost of carrying

17   out the plan which are not met by Federal funds, and

18   (16) provides such fiscal control and fund account-

19   ing procedures as may be necessary to assure proper

20   disbursement of and accounting of funds received under

21   this Act.

22   (c) The Director shall approve any State plan which

23   meets the requirements of subsection (b), but shall not finally

24   disapprove any such plan, or any modification thereof, with-

1 out affording the State agency reasonable notice and an op-
2 portunity for a hearing.

3   (d)(1) The Director shall review annually each of the
4 State plans which he has approved, and the enforcement
5 thereof, and shall certify that each such plan is administered
6 so as to comply with the provisions of such plan and any
7 assurances contained therein, and report such certification to
8 the Congress in the annual report required under section 6(c).

9   (2) Whenever the Director finds, after affording due
10 notice and opportunity for a hearing, that in the administra-
11 tion of the State plan there is a failure to comply substantial-
12 ly with any provision of the State plan (or any assurance
13 contained therein), and such failure would result in the failure
14 to meet the standards developed by the Director under sec-
15 tion 7, he shall (A) notify the State agency of his withdrawal
16 of approval of such plan and upon receipt of such notice such
17 plan shall cease to be in effect, but the State may retain
18 jurisdiction in any case commenced before the withdrawal of
19 the plan in order to enforce standards under the plan when-
20 ever the issues involved do not relate to the reasons for the
21 withdrawal of the plan; and (B) shall notify such State
22 agency that no further payments will be made to the State
23 under this Act (or in his discretion, that further payments to
24 the State will be limited to programs or portions of the State

1 plan not affected by such failure), until he is satisfied that

2 there will no longer be any failure to comply. Until he is so

3 satisfied, no further payments may be made to such State

4 under this Act (or payment shall be limited to programs or

5 portions of the State plan not affected by such failure). Any

6 such failure of a State to comply with any provision of the

7 State plan shall not in any way impede any youth camp

8 therein pending action by the Secretary under this section.

9 (e) The State may obtain a review of a decision of the

10 Director withdrawing approval of or rejecting its plan by the

11 United States court of appeals for the circuit in which the

12 State is located by filing in such court within thirty days

13 following receipt of notice of such decision a petition to

14 modify or set aside in whole or in part the action of the

15 Director. A copy of such petition shall forthwith be served

16 upon the Director and thereupon the Director shall certify

17 and file in the court the record upon which the decision com-

18 plained of was issued as provided in section 2112 of title 28,

19 United States Code. Unless the court finds that the Direc-

20 tor's decision in rejecting a proposed State plan or withdraw-

21 ing his approval of such plan is not supported by substantial

22 evidence the court shall affirm the Director's decision. The

23 judgment of the court shall be subject to review by the Su-

24 preme Court of the United States as provided in section 1254

25 of title 28, United States Code.

1   (f)(1) The Secretary, at the request of the Director, is

2 authorized to make personnel from the Department of

3 Health, Education, and Welfare, who have the necessary ex-

4 pertise, available to States to assist in developing State

5 plans, and in training State inspectors and other personnel

6 associated with youth camps. The Director may call upon the

7 expertise of organized camping groups for such assistance to

8 Federal and State personnel.

9   (2) The Secretary, at the request of the Director, shall

10 provide technical assistance and consultative services neces-

11 sary to assist in the development and implementation of the

12 plan.

13   GRANTS TO STATES

14   SEC. 9. (a) The Director shall make grants to the States

15 for the development of State youth camp safety plans in ac-

16 cordance with section 8; to States which have in effect plans

17 approved under section 8; to assist such States with plan

18 initiation and training costs; and to States for the early oper-

19 ation and improvement of youth camp safety programs. Any

20 grant made under this section shall be based upon objective

21 criteria which shall be established under regulations promul-

22 gated by the Secretary in order to insure equitable distribu-

23 tion. No such grant may exceed 80 per centum of the cost of

24 developing and carrying out the State plan.

1   (b) Payments under this section may be made in install-

2   ments and in advance or by way of reimbursement with nec-

3   essary adjustments on account of underpayments or overpay-

4   ments.

5   CONSULTATIVE SERVICES AND ENFORCEMENT

6   SEC. 10. (a) Upon the request of any youth camp opera-

7   tor or director, or during any inspection under section 11(a),

8   the Director shall provide consultative services to youth

9   camps in States which do not have in effect a State plan

10 approved under section 8. No citations shall be issued nor

11 shall any civil penalties (except penalties for repeated viola-

12 tions under section 12(b)) be proposed by the Director upon

13 any inspection or visit at which consultative services are ren-

14 dered, but if, during such inspection or visit, an apparent se-

15 rious violation of the duty imposed by section 5, of any stand-

16 ard, rule, or order provided pursuant to section 7, or of any

17 regulations prescribed pursuant to this Act is discovered, the

18 Director shall issue a written notice to the youth camp opera-

19 tor describing with particularity the nature of the violation,

20 and the action which must be taken within a reasonable

21 period of time specified by the Director for the abatement of

22 the violation. Where a youth camp operator fails to comply

23 with the abatement instructions within the prescribed period,

24 a citation may be issued as provided in subsection (b) or a

25 civil penalty under section 12 may be assessed. Nothing in

1 this subsection shall affect in any manner any provision of

2 this Act the purpose of which is to eliminate imminent dan-

3 gers.

4   (b) The Director shall issue regulations and procedures

5 providing for citations to youth camp operators in States

6 which do not have in effect a State plan approved under sec-

7 tion 8 for any violation of the duty imposed by section 5, of

8 any standard, rule or order promulgated pursuant to section

9 7, or of any regulations prescribed pursuant to this Act. Each

10 citation shall fix a reasonable time for abatement of the viola-

11 tion. The Director may prescribe procedures for the issuance

12 of a notice in lieu of a citation with respect to minor viola-

13 tions which have no direct or immediate or serious relation-

14 ship to safety or health.

15   (c) The Director shall afford an opportunity for a hear-

16 ing in accordance with section 554 of title 5, United States

17 Code, to any youth camp operator issued a citation under

18 procedures promulgated pursuant to subsection (b) of subject

19 to penalties under section 12, or under any other procedure

20 applying enforcement by the Director under this Act. Any

21 youth camp operator adversely affected by the decision of the

22 Director after such hearing may obtain a review of such deci-

23 sion in the United States court of appeals for the circuit in

24 which the youth camp in question is located or in which the

25 youth camp has its principal office by filing in such court

1 within thirty days following receipt of notice of such decision

2 a petition to modify or set aside in whole or in part such

3 decision. A copy of the petition shall forthwith be served

4 upon the Director, and thereupon the Director shall certify

5 and file in the court the record upon which the decision com-

6 plained of was issued as provided in section 2112 of title 28,

7 United States Code. Such decision, if supported by substan-

8 tial evidence, shall be affirmed by the court. The judgement

9 of the court shall be subject to review by the Supreme Court

10 of the United States, as provided in section 1254 of title 28,

11 United States Code.

12 INSPECTIONS, INVESTIGATIONS, AND RECORDS

13 SEC. 11. (a) In order to carry out his duties under this

14 Act, the Director may enter and inspect any youth camp and

15 its records in States which do not have in effect a State plan

16 approved under section 8, may question employees privately,

17 and may investigate facts, conditions, practices, or matters to

18 the extent he deems it necessary or appropriate. The Direc-

19 tor shall inspect each such youth camp at least once a year

20 during the period the camp is in operation.

21 (b) In making his inspections and investigations under

22 this Act the Director may require the attendance and testi-

23 mony of witnesses and the production of evidence under oath.

24 Witnesses shall be paid the same fees and mileage that are

25 paid witnesses in the courts of the United States. In case of a

1 contumacy, failure, or refusal of any person to obey such an
2 order, any district court of the United States, or the United
3 States courts of any territory or possession, within the juris-
4 diction of which such person is found, or resides, or transacts
5 business, upon the application by the Secretary, shall have
6 jurisdiction to issue to such person an order requiring such
7 person to appear to produce evidence if, as, and when so
8 ordered, and to give testimony relating to the matter under
9 investigation or in question, and any failure to obey such
10 order of the court may be punished by said court as a con-
11 tempt thereof.

12   (c) To determine the areas in which safety standards are
13 necessary and to aid in promulgating meaningful regulations,
14 camps subject to the provisions of this Act shall be required
15 to report annually, on the date prescribed by the Director, all
16 accidents resulting in death, injury, and serious illness, other
17 than minor injuries which require only first aid treatment,
18 and which do not require the services of a physician, or in-
19 volve loss of consciousness, restriction of activity or motion,
20 or premature termination of the camper's term at the camp.
21 Camps operating solely within a State which has in effect a
22 State plan approved under section 8 shall file their reports
23 directly with that State, and the State shall promptly forward
24 such reports on to the Director. All other camps shall file
25 their reports directly with the Director. The Director shall

1 compile the statistics reported and include summaries thereof

2 in his annual report required under section 6(c).

3   (d) Any information obtained by the Director, or his au-

4 thorized representative, under this Act shall be obtained with

5 a minimum burden upon the youth camp operator and with

6 full protection of the rights of youth camp staff members.

7 Unnecessary duplication of efforts in obtaining information

8 shall be reduced to the maximum extent feasible.

9   (e) A representative of the youth camp staff director and

10 a representative authorized by the youth camp staff shall be

11 given an opportunity to accompany the Director or his au-

12 thorized representative during the inspection. Where there is

13 no authorized youth camp staff representative, the Director

14 shall consult with a reasonable number of youth camp staff

15 members concerning the matters of health and safety.

16   PENALTIES

17   SEC. 12. (a) Any youth camp operator who fails to cor-

18 rect a violation for which a citation has been issued under

19 section 10(b) or for which a notice has been issued under

20 section 10(a) within the period permitted for its correction

21 may be assessed a civil penalty of not more than $500 for

22 each day during which such failure or violation continues,

23 until the camp closes in its normal course of business.

24   (b) Any youth camp operator who willfully or repeatedly

25 violates the requirements of section 5, of any standard, rule,

1 or order promulgated pursuant to section 7, or of any regula-

2 tions prescribed pursuant to this Act may be assessed a civil

3 penalty of up to $1,000 for each day during which such viola-

4 tion continues, until the camp closes in its normal course of

5 business.

6   (c) Civil penalties assessed under this Act shall be paid

7 to the Director for deposit into the Treasury of the United

8 States and shall accrue to the United States and may be

9 recovered in a civil action in the name of the United States

10 brought in the United States district court for the district in

11 which the violation is alleged to have occurred or in which

12 the operator has his principal office.

13 PROCEDURES TO COUNTERACT IMMINENT DANGERS

14   SEC. 13. (a) The United States district courts shall have

15 jurisdiction, upon petition of the Director, to restrain any

16 conditions or practices in any youth camp, or in any place

17 where camp activities are conducted in States which do not

18 have in effect a State plan approved under section 8, which

19 are such that a danger exists which could reasonably be ex-

20 pected to cause death or immediate serious physical harm or

21 before the imminence of such danger can be eliminated

22 through the enforcement procedures otherwise provided by

23 this Act. Any order issued under this section may require

24 such steps to be taken as may be necessary to avoid, correct,

25 or remove such imminent danger and prohibit the presence of

1 any individual in locations or under conditions where such

2 imminent danger exists except individuals whose presence is

3 necessary to avoid, correct, or remove such imminent danger.

4   (b) Upon the filing of any such petition, the district court

5 shall have jurisdiction to grant such injunctive relief or tem-

6 porary restraining order pending the outcome of an enforce-

7 ment proceeding pursuant to this Act.

8   (c) Whenever and as soon as an inspector concludes that

9 conditions or practices described in subsection (a) exist in any

10 campsite or place of camp activity, he shall inform parents or

11 guardians, camp owners, and camp supervisory personnel

12 and shall assure that all affected campers are so informed of

13 the danger and that he is recommending to the Director that

14 relief be sought.

15   VARIANCES

16   SEC. 14. The Director, in States which do not have in

17 effect a State plan approved under section 8, upon applica-

18 tion by a youth camp operator showing extraordinary circum-

19 stances or undue hardship, and upon the determination by a

20 field inspector, after inspection of the affected premises and

21 facilities, that the conditions, practices, or activities proposed

22 to be used are as safe and healthful as those which would

23 prevail if the youth camp operator complied with the stand-

24 ard, may exempt such camp or activity from specific require-

25 ments of this Act, but the terms of such exemption shall re-

1 quire appropriate notice thereof to parents or other relatives

2 of affected campers. Such notice shall be given at least annu-

3 ally. Nothing in this Act shall allow the operation of a sub-

4 standard camp.

5   FEDERAL ADVISORY COUNCIL ON YOUTH CAMP SAFETY

6   SEC. 15. (a) The Director shall establish in the Depart-

7 ment of Health, Education, and Welfare a Federal Advisory

8 Council on Youth Camp Safety to advise and consult on

9 policy matters relating to youth camp safety, particularly the

10 promulgation of youth camp safety standards. The Council

11 shall consist of the Director, who shall be chairman, and fif-

12 teen members appointed by him, without regard to the civil

13 service laws, from persons who are specially qualified by ex-

14 perience and competence to render such service and shall

15 include one representative from the Department of the Interi-

16 or, the Department of Health, Education, and Welfare, and

17 the Department of Agriculture and the Department of Labor.

18 There shall be eight such members so appointed from appro-

19 priate associations representing organized camping. There

20 shall be appointed three members from the general public

21 who have a special interest in youth camps.

22   (b) The Director may appoint such special advisory and

23 technical experts and consultants as may be necessary in car-

24 rying out the functions of the Council.

1   (c) Members of the Advisory Council, while serving on

2 business of the Advisory Council, shall receive compensation

3 at a rate to be fixed by the Director but not exceeding $100

4 per day; including traveltime; and while so serving away

5 from their homes or regular places of business, they may be

6 allowed travel expenses, including per diem in lieu of subsist-

7 ence, as authorized by section 5703 of title 5, United States

8 Code, for persons in the Government service employed inter-

9 mittently.

10   ADMINISTRATION AND AUDIT

11   SEC. 16. (a) The Director is authorized to request di-

12 rectly from any department or agency of the Federal Govern-

13 ment information, suggestions, estimates, and statistics

14 needed to carry out his functions under this Act; and such

15 department or agency is authorized to furnish such informa-

16 tion, suggestions, estimates, and statistics directly to the Di-

17 rector.

18   (b) The Director shall prepare and submit to the Presi-

19 dent for transmittal to the Congress at least once in each

20 fiscal year a comprehensive and detailed report on the admin-

21 istration of this Act.

22   (c) The Director and the Comptroller General of the

23 United States, or any of their duly authorized representa-

24 tives, shall have access for the purpose of audit and examina-

1 tion to any books, documents, papers, and records of States

2 receiving assistance under this Act.

3   NONINTERFERENCE

4   SEC. 17. (a) Nothing in this Act or regulations issued

5 hereunder shall authorize the Director, a State agency, or

6 any official acting under this Act, to prescribe, determine, or

7 influence the curriculum, admissions policy, program, or min-

8 istry of any youth camp.

9   (b) Nothing in this Act or regulations issued hereunder

10 shall be construed to control, limit, or interfere with either

11 the religious affiliation of any camp, camper, or camp staff

12 member, or the free exercise of religion of any youth camp

13 which is operated by a church, association, or convention of

14 churches, or their agencies.

15   (c) Nothing in this Act or regulations issued hereunder

16 shall authorize the Director, a State agency, or any official

17 acting under this Act, to require or authorize medical treat-

18 ment for a person who objects (or, in the case of a child,

19 whose parent or guardian objects) thereto on religious

20 grounds; nor shall examination or immunization of such

21 person be authorized or required except during an epidemic

22 or threat of an epidemic of a contagious disease.

23   AUTHORIZATION

24   SEC. 18. There are authorized to be appropriated

25 $7,500,000 for the fiscal year ending September 30, 1980,

1 and for each of the four succeding fiscal years, to carry out

2 the provisions of this Act.

3   EFFECT ON EXISTING LAWS

4   SEC. 19. (a) Nothing in this Act shall be construed to

5 supersede or to enlarge or diminish or affect in any other

6 manner the common law or statutory rights, duties, or liabil-

7 ities of youth camp operators and campers under any law

8 with respect to injuries, diseases, or death of campers arising

9 out of, or in the course of, participation in youth camp activi-

10 ties covered by this Act.

11   (b) Notwithstanding the provisions of this Act, no State

12 law which provides youth camp health and safety standards

13 equal to or superior to those promulgated under the provi-

14 sions of this Act shall be superseded thereby.

Appendix I

Athletic Training Practice Act of the State
of New Jersey
as proposed by the New Jersey Athletic Trainers
Association

Section 1. Title

This act shall be known and may be cited as the Athletic Training Practice Act of the State of New Jersey.

Section 2. Definitions

As used in this act unless the context otherwise requires, the following words shall have the following meaning:

A. Board - shall mean the Board of Medical Examiners which shall enforce and administer the provisions of this act.

B. Advisory Committee - means the Athletic Training Advisory Committee as described in Section 5 of this act.

C. Athletic Training - shall mean and include the treatment of athletes by the use of various techniques and physical agents of heat, cold, massage, sound, water, electricity, air, radiant energy, conditioning and reconditioning exercises, education for the purpose of preventing athletic injury from occurring, providing emergency care for an injured athlete, and to provide support for any athletic activity.

D. Athletic Trainer - shall mean a person who practices athletic training with a school, college, university, professional team, or a bona fide amateur athletic organization under the direction of a licensed physician.

Section 3. Limitations

No person shall practice, nor hold himself out to be able to practice Athletic Training in this state unless he is licensed in accordance with the provisions of this act.

Section 4. Duties of Board

The Board (after consultation with the Athletic Training Advisory Committee) shall establish rules and regulations for the administration of this act.

Section 5. Duties of Advisory Committee

There is hereby created in the Division of Consumer Affairs of the Department of Law and Public Safety, under the State Board of Medical Examiners, an Athletic Training

Section 5.(continued)

Advisory Committee. The committee shall consist of five members, four of whom shall be licensed athletic trainers of this state having at least 5 years experience in the practice of athletic training in the State of New Jersey immediately prior to appointment. The members of the committee shall be appointed for terms of 3 years. Each member shall hold office after the expiration of his term until his successor shall be duly appointed and qualified. A vacancy in the office of any member shall be filled for the unexpired term only.

The Advisory Committee shall meet at least twice a year and shall also meet upon the call of the Board or of the Attorney General. The Advisory Committee shall carry out the responsibilities assigned to it under this act and such matters as the Board may require. The Attorney General shall provide the Advisory Committee with such facilities and personnel as shall be required for the proper conduct of its business.

The Board, with approval of the Attorney General, may authorize reimbursement of the members of the Advisory Committee for their actual expenses incurred in connection with the performance of their duties as members of the Advisory Committee.

Section 6. Limitations of Practice

From and after one year from the effective date of this act, it shall be unlawful for any person to practice or hold himself out as being able to practice athletic training in this State unless he is trained and licensed in accordance with the provisions of this act. Nothing in this act, however, shall prohibit any person trained and licensed to practice in this State under any other law, from engaging in the practice for which he is trained and licensed.

A. Supportive Personnel

This act shall not prohibit students who are enrolled in schools or educational programs of athletic training by the Board, from performing acts of athletic training as is incidental to their course of study; nor shall it prevent any student in an educational program in the healing arts approved or accredited under the laws of New Jersey in carrying out prescribed courses of study Nothing in this act shall apply to any person employed by an agency, bureau, or division of the federal government while in the discharge of official duties, however, if such individual engages in the practice of athletic training outside the scope of official duty, he must be trained and licensed as herein provided. The provisions of this act are not intended to limit

Section 6. (continued)

the activities of persons legitimately engaged in the nontherapeutic administration of baths, massage and normal exercise.

B. Exceptions to Limitations

In the absence of standards established by the Board, nothing in this act shall be construed as to prohibit services and acts relating to athletic training rendered by an athletic trainer assistant or supportive personnel if such services and acts are rendered under the direction or supervision of a licensed athletic trainer who is acting with accordance to the provisions of this act.

Section 7. Qualifications for Licensure

An applicant for licensure as an athletic trainer shall submit to the Board evidence, in such form as the Board may prescribe, that the applicant (1) has attained his or her 18th birthday, (2) is of good moral character and is not addicted to the habitual use of alcohol, narcotics or other habit forming drugs, (3) is a graduate of a high school approved by the New Jersey Department of Education or has obtained equivalent education acceptable to the Board, (4) hold a degree in physical therapy and have spent two academic years working under the direct supervision of a licensed athletic trainer or have met the athletic training curriculum requirements of a college or university approved by the Board and give proof of graduation.

The Board, in establishing, altering or amending the standards for approving such programs that grant degrees in instruction of athletic training, shall consult with the Athletic Training Advisory Committee and may take into consideration the standards suggested by the National Athletic Trainers Association.

Section 8. Examination for Licensure

The Board shall give an examination to applicants who comply with the qualifications for licensure. The examination shall include a written and oral-practical examination which shall test the applicants knowledge of the basic and clinical sciences that are pertinent to athletic training, emergency care of the injured athlete, and principles of injury evaluation and conditioning including the selection and use of various physical modalities and exercise techniques.

The examination shall be administered within the State of New Jersey in January of each year. The deadline for making application for examination shall be sixty (60) days prior to the date of the administration of the test. The applicant will be notified of the Board's decision

Section 8. (continued)

regarding the applicant's eligibility for examination thirty (30) days prior to the administration of the examination.

A. Reexamination

In the case of failure of the first examination, the applicant for licensure shall have, after the expiration of six months, but within two years, the privilege of a second examination. In case of failure of the second examination, an applicant may, at the discretion of the Board, be granted the privilege of further examination provided the applicant makes new application and qualifies for examination under the conditions in force at the time of said re-application.

Section 9. Licensure Without Examination

On payment to the Board the application fee as provided for in Section 12, and upon approval of a written application on forms provided by the Board, the Board shall issue without examination a license to: (a) any person who applies for such licensure within one year after the act takes effect, and who meets qualifications 1 and 2 in Section 7 and who presents to the Board evidence of having provided athletic training services as defined in Section 2 of this act, for five (5) years or more as a major responsibility of his/her employment in the State of New Jersey prior to the date this act was approved; or as a resident of the State of New Jersey presents evidence of being certified by the National Athletic Trainers Association; or (b) any person who is licensed or otherwise registered as an athletic trainer in any other state or territory of the United States or the District of Columbia, if the requirements for license or registration satisfy the equivalence of the requirements of this act at the date of application for license. The equivalence of said requirements shall be determined by the Board, who shall consult with the Athletic Training Advisory Committee.

Section 10. Issuance of License

The applicant is entitled to an athletic trainer license if he possesses the qualifications enumerated in Section 7 herein, and (a) has satisfactorily completed the examination administered by the Board, or (b) if the applicant is so entitled under the provisions in Section 9 of this act. Any person who holds a license pursuant to the section may use the words "athletic trainer" or "licensed athletic trainer" and may use the letters "L.A.T." in connection with his name to denote his licensure hereunder.

Section 11. Temporary License

Upon submission of a written application on forms provided by it, the Board shall issue a temporary license to a person who has applied for licensure under the provisions of Section 12 of the act, and who is, in the judgment of the Board, eligible to take the examination provided for in Section 8 of the act. Such temporary license shall be available to an applicant only with respect to his first application for license under Section 12 and such license shall expire when the Board makes a final determination with respect to said application.

Section 12. Application Procedure

Each initial application under this act shall be accompanied by a fee of $50.00. Licenses under this act shall expire annually on January 31 and shall be renewed upon application and payment of a fee of $10.00. If said fee is not paid by that date, the license shall automatically expire. A license which has thus expired may within 3 years of its expiration date, be renewed on the payment to the Board the sum of $10.00 for each year or part thereof during which the license was ineffective and the restoration fee of $10.00. After said 3 year period such license may be renewed only by complying with the provisions herein relating to the issuance of an original license.

Section 13. Fees and Revenues

All fees and revenues collected under the provisions of the act shall be paid into _____
for the use of _____.

Section 14. Services Under the Direction of a Physician

Any person licensed under this act as an athletic trainer shall not treat human ailments by athletic training except under the direction of a physician licensed to practice medicine and surgery in this state. Nothing in this act shall be construed as authorization for an athletic trainer to practice any branch of athletic training except as described in this act. Any person violating the provisions of this act shall be guilty of a misdemeanor as described in Section 17.

Section 15. Refusal, Suspension or Revocation of License

The Board shall have the power to refuse to issue a license to any person and after notice and hearing in accordance with rules and regulations, may suspend or revoke the license of any person who has:

    A. practiced athletic training independently of the direction of a duly licensed physician,

    B. attempted to or obtained licensure by fraud or misrepresentation,

Section 15. (continued)

    C.   committed repeated acts of negligence or in-
competence in the practice of athletic training,

    D.   been convicted of a felony in the courts of this
state or any other state, territory or country.
Conviction as used in this paragraph shall include
a finding or verdict of guilt, an admission of
guilt or a plea of nole contendre,

    E.   habitually indulged in the use of narcotics or
other habit forms of drugs, or excessively
indulged in the use of alcoholic liquors,

    F.   been guilty of unprofessional conduct. Unpro-
fessional conduct shall include any departure
from or the failure to conform to the minimal
standards of acceptable and prevailing athletic
training practice in which preceding actual
injury to an athlete need not be established,

    G.   been judged mentally incompetent by a court of
competent jurisdiction,

    H.   treated or undertaken to treat human ailments
otherwise than by athletic training as defined
in this act,

    I.   had his license to practice athletic training
revoked or suspended or having other disciplinary actions taken, or his application for license
revoked or suspended by the proper licensing
authority of another state, territory or country,

    J.   violated the provisions of this act or the rules
or regulations adopted hereunder.

All actions of the Board shall be taken subject to the
right of notice, hearing and adjudication and the right
of appeal therefrom in accordance with the provisions of
The Penalty Enforcement Law (N.J.S. 2A:58-1).

Section 16. Appropriation of Administrative Fees

There is hereby appropriated to the Department of Law
and Public Safety, for the purpose of administering this
act, all fees and revenues received by the Board from the
effective date of this act until_____.
The expenditure of such appropriation shall be authorized
by the Attorney General with the approval of the Director
of the Division of Budget and Accounting.

Section 17. Penalties: Violations and Perjury of Application

Any person who violates any provisions of this act shall
be guilty of a misdemeanor, as herein set forth, and upon
conviction shall be punished by a fine of not less than
$100 nor more than $500, or by imprisonment for not less

Section 17. (continued)

than 30 days nor more than 90 days, or both; each additional offense shall be subject to a fine of not less than $500 and imprisonment of not less than 6 months nor more than 12 months, at the discretion of the court. Any person who knowingly makes a false statement in his application for a license under this act or in response to an inquiry of the Board is guilty of a misdemeanor and upon conviction is punishable by a fine of not less than $50 nor more than $100, or imprisonment for not less than 60 days, or both.

Section 18. Injunctive Relief

The Board, may in the name of the people of the State of New Jersey, through the Office of the Attorney General, apply for injunctive relief in any court of competent jurisdiction to enjoin any person from committing any act that is in violation of this Act. Such injunctive proceedings shall be in addition to, and in lieu of, all penalties and other remedies of this Act.

Section 19. Repealer

All laws and parts of laws in conflict with this Act are hereby repealed.

Appendix J

POLICY STATEMENT REGARDING THE USE OF HUMAN SUBJECTS AND INFORMED CONSENT

By law, any experimental subject or clinical patient who is exposed to possible physical, psychological, or social injury must give informed consent prior to participating in a proposed project. Informed consent can be defined as the knowing consent of an individual or his legally authorized representative so situated as to be able to exercise free power of choice without undue inducement or any element of force, fraud, deceit, duress, or other form of constraint or coercion.

The Editorial Board of MEDICINE AND SCIENCE IN SPORTS requires that all appropriate steps be taken in obtaining the informed consent of any and all human subjects employed by investigators submitting manuscripts for review and possible publication. In most cases, informed consent should be obtained by having the subject read a document (an Informed Consent Form) presenting all information pertinent to the investigation or project and affixing a signature indicating that the document has been read and consent given to participation under the conditions described therein. The document should be so written as to be easily understandable to the subjects and provided in a language in which the subject is fluent.

Investigators are requested to consider the following items for inclusion in an Informed Consent Form as appropriate to the particular project:

1. A general statement of the background of the project and the project objectives.
2. A fair explanation of the procedures to be followed and their purposes, identification of any procedures which are experimental, and description of any and all risks attendant to the procedures.
3. A description of any benefits reasonably to be expected and, in the case of treatment, disclosure of any appropriate alternative procedures that might be advantageous for the subject.
4. An offer to answer any queries of the subject concerning procedures or other aspects of the project.
5. An instruction that the subject is free to withdraw consent and to discontinue participation in the project or activity at any time without prejudice to the subject.
6. An instruction that, in the case of questionnaires and interviews, the subject is free to deny answer to specific items or questions.
7. An instruction that, if services or treatment are involved in the setting or context of the project, neither will they be enhanced nor diminished as a result of the subject's decision to volunteer or not to volunteer participation in the project.
8. An explanation of the procedures to be taken to insure the confidentiality of the data and information to be derived from the subject. If subjects are to be identified by name in the manuscript, permission for same should be included in the Informed Consent Form or obtained in writing at a later date.

If the subject is to be videotaped or photographed in any manner, this must be disclosed in the Informed Consent Form. The subject must be advised as to who will have custody of such videotapes or photographs, who will have access to the tapes or photographs, how the tapes or photographs are to be used, and what will be done with them when the study is completed.

The informed consent document must not contain any exculpatory language or any other waiver of legal rights releasing, or appearing to release, an investigator, project director, or institution from liability. At the bottom of the form, provision should be made for the signature of the subject (and date signed) and/or a legally authorized representative. It is generally advisable to precede this with a statement to the effect that the subject and/or representative have read the statement and do understand. In the case of minors, one or both parents should sign as appropriate. For minors of sufficient maturity, signatures should be obtained from the subject and the parent(s).

The Editorial Board endorses the Declaration of Helsinki of the World Medical Association as regards the conduct of clinical research. Physicians are expected to comply with the principles set forth in this declaration when research involves the use of patients. In the case of psychological research, investigators will be expected to comply with the principles established by the American Psychological Association. These principles are presented in the publication, "Ethical Principles in the Conduct of Research with Human Subjects" (American Psychological Association, Washington, D.C., 1973).

It will not be necessary for an author to describe in the manuscript the specific steps that were taken to obtain informed consent, to insure confidentiality of results, or to protect the privacy rights of participating subjects. It will be satisfactory for the author to indicate by a phrase that, "Informed consent was obtained from the subjects," or similar. It will be understood by the editors that such a statement indicates the author's guarantee of compliance with the directives presented above.

Appendix K

INJURED PERSON

1. NAME (Last, First, Middle Initial)

2. ADDRESS AT COLLEGE   ☐ On campus   ☐ Off campus
Address and name of dorm or house

THE PURPOSE OF THIS REPORT is to provide information which can be used in preventing similar accidents in the future, hence every accidental injury severe enough to require first aid or medical treatment should be reported. See reverse side for instructions and additional space for explanations. Record file number; cut at dotted line for confidential study purposes.

FILE NO.

3. AGE _____ years   4. SEX ☐ Female ☐ Male

5. STUDENT CLASSIFICATION ☐ Freshman ☐ Junior ☐ Graduate ☐ Sophomore ☐ Senior ☐ Special

6. ENROLLMENT AT this college _____ years

FILE NO.

ACCIDENT

7. Date, day, and hour of accident

8. Estimate of Severity ☐ Non-disabling (loss of less than a full day from normal activity) ☐ Disabling (loss of one or more full days from normal) ☐ Fatal

9. College (or school) in which enrolled

10. School or department supervising activity at time of accident

15. Activity at time of accident (e.g. driving auto, diving from low board, lifting crate)

11. Was student an employee at time of injury?   ☐ Yes   ☐ No

16. Details of accident (Describe fully events, conditions including environmental, physical and emotional personal factors, which contributed to the injury. Use reverse side or additional sheets if needed)

12. JURISDICTION
☐ On or in college property, or in college conducted or supervised activity
☐ Off campus in non-college conducted activity

13. TYPE OF FACILITY
☐ Athletic or physical education
☐ Recreation or entertainment
☐ Instruction
☐ Housing
☐ Exterior walk or sidewalk
☐ Street or highway
☐ Commerce or industry
☐ Service or maintenance
☐ Undeveloped area

14. SPECIFIC LOCATION
☐ Gymnasium
☐ Sports arena or play field
☐ Swimming pool
☐ Pub. recreation or entertain
☐ Pvt. recreation or entertain
☐ Bath, shower or locker room
☐ Interior stair or ramp
☐ Interior corridor or hall
☐ Classroom or lecture hall
☐ Auditorium or library
☐ Laboratory
☐ Other, specify_____
☐ Shop (mechanical)
☐ Home economics
☐ Storeroom
☐ Food preparation or service
☐ Eating place
☐ Public transportation
☐ Private transportation
☐ Bldg. exterior or grounds
☐ Water area
☐ Farm, field or woods
☐ Retail shop or professional office

17. Action to prevent similar accidents (Indicate if taken or recommended)

INJURY

18. NATURE OF INJURY
☐ Amputation
☐ Bruise, contusion
☐ Burn, scald
☐ Concussion
☐ Cuts, open wounds
☐ Dermatitis, infection
☐ Other, specify_____
☐ Exposure, frostbite
☐ Fracture
☐ Foreign body
☐ Heat exhaustion sunstroke
☐ Inhalation - dust, fumes, gases
☐ Internal injury
☐ Poisoning, internal
☐ Shock, electrical
☐ Shock, fainting
☐ Sprains, strains, dislocation
☐ Suffocation, drowning, strangulation
☐ Rupture, hernia

19. PART OF BODY INJURED
☐ Generalized
☐ Skull or scalp
☐ Eye
☐ Nose
☐ Mouth
☐ Jaw
☐ Other head
☐ Other, specify_____
☐ Neck
☐ Spine
☐ Chest
☐ Abdomen
☐ Back
☐ Pelvis
☐ Other trunk
☐ Shoulder
☐ Upper arm
☐ Elbow
☐ Forearm
☐ Wrist
☐ Hand
☐ Finger
☐ Hip
☐ Thigh
☐ Knee
☐ Lower leg
☐ Ankle
☐ Foot
☐ Toe

20. WITNESSES AND THEIR ADDRESSES

TREATMENT

21. EMERGENCY CARE & PATIENT STATUS
☐ First Aid only, not at hospital or by doctor
☐ Treatment at College Health Service or hospital or by medical personnel
☐ Confinement at College Health Service, hospital, or in residence
☐ Other specify_____

22. This report prepared by (Signature)_____ Date_____
Title or Status_____
Address_____

PREPARATION AND DISTRIBUTION OF STANDARD ACCIDENTAL INJURY REPORT, FORM COLLEGE 1, STUDENT

All injuries severe enough to require first aid or medical treatment shall be reported, preferably within 24 hours following the accident. Because of familiarity with the facilities, activities and operations which were related to the incident, it is advantageous that the report be initiated by the person supervising or responsible for the area in which it occurred. In some instances it may be completed at the health service; or if the accident occurred away from the college, by the injured student, or by a witness.

In preparing the report, avoid non-specifics or generalities. Information provided may help other departments in preventing similar accidents. Use Form 2 for administrative, faculty, and operational staff member accidents. A student injured while employed by the college shall be reported on Form 2. Conversely, a staff member injured while attending class as a part-time student shall have injury reported on this form. In case of multiple injuries, or those involving more than one body part, check all boxes for which the condition was significant.

SUPPLEMENTARY INFORMATION ON INJURIES SUSTAINED IN PHYSICAL EDUCATION AND ATHLETICS

1. **Activity or sport:**_____ . Check appropriate block on following items, except No. 3 (yes or no, each block), and No. 9 (give as complete an explanation as necessary.)

2. **Organization**	3. **Supervision**	Yes	No	4. **Psychological factors**	5. **Weather**
☐ Varsity	Instr./Supv. present	☐	☐	☐ Calm, normal	☐ Clear, cloudy
☐ Intramural	Officiated	☐	☐	☐ Angry	☐ Rain, fog
☐ Phys. Ed. Class	Rules understood	☐	☐	☐ Excited	☐ Snow, sleet
☐ Unorganized	Rules enforced	☐	☐	☐ Overly agressive	6. **Temperature**
8. **Pers. Protect.**	Med. Pers. Present	☐	☐	☐ Fearful	☐ Hot
☐ Not needed	Phys. Exam. in 6 mo.	☐	☐	☐ Inattentive	☐ Av., normal
☐ Needed, unused	Adequate condition	☐	☐	☐ Overly daring	☐ Cold
☐ Used	Suffic. experience	☐	☐	☐ Fatigued	7. **Surface**
9. Action or movement leading to injury:				☐ Ill	☐ Even, level
					☐ Bumps, holes
					☐ Slippery, wet
					☐ Obstructed

_____

_____

Appendix L

Tuesday
December 11, 1979

DEPARTMENT OF HEALTH, EDUCATION, AND WELFARE

Office for Civil Rights

Office of the Secretary

■

Intercollegiate Athletics: Sex Discrimination
HEW/Secretary/Civil Rights Office issues policy
interpretation of Title IX Education Amendments of
1972; effective 12-11-79

DEPARTMENT OF HEALTH, EDUCATION, AND WELFARE

Office for Civil Rights

Office of the Secretary

45 CFR Part 86

Title IX of the Education Amendments of 1972; a Policy Interpretation; Title IX and Intercollegiate Athletics

AGENCY: Office for Civil Rights, Office of the Secretary, HEW.

ACTION: Policy interpretation.

SUMMARY: The following Policy Interpretation represents the Department of Health, Education, and Welfare's interpretation of the intercollegiate athletic provisions of Title IX of the Education Amendments of 1972 and its implementing regulation. Title IX prohibits educational programs and institutions funded or otherwise supported by the Department from discriminating on the basis of sex. The Department published a proposed Policy Interpretation for public comment on December 11, 1978. Over 700 comments reflecting a broad range of opinion were received. In addition, HEW staff visited eight universities during June and July, 1979, to see how the proposed policy and other suggested alternatives would apply in actual practice at individual campuses. The final Policy Interpretation reflects the many comments HEW received and the results of the individual campus visits.

EFFECTIVE DATE: December 11, 1979

FOR FURTHER INFORMATION CONTACT: Colleen O'Connor, 330 Independence Avenue, Washington, D.C. (202) 245–6671

SUPPLEMENTARY INFORMATION:

I. Legal Background

A. The Statute

Section 901(a) of Title IX of the Education Amendments of 1972 provides:

No person in the United States shall, on the basis of sex, be excluded from participation, in, be denied the benefits of, or be subjected to discrimination under any education program or activity receiving Federal financial assistance.

Section 844 of the Education Amendments of 1974 further provides:

The Secretary of (of HEW) shall prepare and publish * * * proposed regulations implementing the provisions of Title IX of the Education Amendments of 1972 relating to the prohibition of sex discrimination in federally assisted education programs which shall include with respect to intercollegiate athletic activities reasonable provisions considering the nature of particular sports.

Congress passed Section 844 after the Conference Committee deleted a Senate floor amendment that would have exempted revenue-producing athletics from the jurisdiction of Title IX.

B. The Regulation

The regulation implementing Title IX is set forth, in pertinent part, in the Policy Interpretation below. It was signed by President Ford on May 27, 1975, and submitted to the Congress for review pursuant to Section 431(d)(1) of the General Education Provisions Act (GEPA).

During this review, the House Subcommittee on Postsecondary Education held hearings on a resolution disapproving the regulation. The Congress did not disapprove the regulation within the 45 days allowed under GEPA, and it therefore became effective on July 21, 1975.

Subsequent hearings were held in the Senate Subcommittee on Education on a bill to exclude revenues produced by sports to the extent they are used to pay the costs of those sports. The Committee, however, took no action on this bill.

The regulation established a three year transition period to give institutions time to comply with its equal athletic opportunity requirements. That transition period expired on July 21, 1978.

II. Purpose of Policy Interpretation

By the end of July 1978, the Department had received nearly 100 complaints alleging discrimination in athletics against more than 50 institutions of higher education. In attempting to investigate these complaints, and to answer questions from the university community, the Department determined that it should provide further guidance on what constitutes compliance with the law. Accordingly, this Policy Interpretation explains the regulation so as to provide a framework within which the complaints can be resolved, and to provide institutions of higher education with additional guidance on the requirements for compliance with Title IX in intercollegiate athletic programs.

III. Scope of Application

This Policy Interpretation is designed specifically for intercollegiate athletics. However, its general principles will often apply to club, intramural, and interscholastic athletic programs, which are also covered by regulation.[1] Accordingly, the Policy Interpretation may be used for guidance by the administrators of such programs when appropriate.

This policy interpretation applies to any public or private institution, person or other entity that operates an educational program or activity which receives or benefits from financial assistance authorized or extended under a law administered by the Department. This includes educational institutions whose students participate in HEW funded or guaranteed student loan or assistance programs. For further information see definition of "recipient" in Section 86.2 of the Title IX regulation.

IV. Summary of Final Policy Interpretation

The final Policy Interpretation clarifies the meaning of "equal opportunity" in intercollegiate athletics. It explains the factors and standards set out in the law and regulation which the Department will consider in determining whether an institution's intercollegiate athletics program complies with the law and regulations. It also provides guidance to assist institutions in determining whether any disparities which may exist between men's and women's programs are justifiable and nondiscriminatory. The Policy Interpretation is divided into three sections:

• *Compliance in Financial Assistance (Scholarships) Based on Athletic Ability:* Pursuant to the regulation, the governing principle in this area is that all such assistance should be available on a substantially proportional basis to the number of male and female participants in the institution's athletic program.

• *Compliance in Other Program Areas (Equipment and supplies; games and practice times; travel and per diem; coaching and academic tutoring; assignment and compensation of coaches and tutors; locker rooms, and practice and competitive facilities; medical and training facilities; housing and dining facilities; publicity; recruitment; and support services):* Pursuant to the regulation, the governing principle is that male and female athletes should receive equivalent treatment, benefits, and opportunities.

• *Compliance in Meeting the*

Interests and Abilities of Male and Female Students: Pursuant to the regulation, the governing principle in this area is that the athletic interests and abilities of male and female students must be equally effectively accommodated.

V. Major Changes to Proposed Policy Interpretation

The final Policy Interpretation has been revised from the one published in proposed form on December 11, 1978. The proposed Policy Interpretation was based on a two-part approach. Part I addressed equal opportunity for participants in athletic programs. It required the elimination of discrimination in financial support and other benefits and opportunities in an institution's existing athletic program. Institutions could establish a presumption of compliance if they could demonstrate that:

• "Average per capita" expenditures for male and female athletes were substantially equal in the area of "readily financially measurable" benefits and opportunities or, if not, that any disparities were the result of nondiscriminatory factors, and

• Benefits and opportunities for male and female athletes, in areas which are not financially measurable, "were comparable."

Part II of the proposed Policy Interpretation addressed an institution's obligation to accommodate effectively the athletic interests and abilities of women as well as men on a continuing basis. It required an institution either:

• To follow a policy of development of its women's athletic program to provide the participation and competition opportunities needed to accommodate the growing interests and abilities of women, or

• To demonstrate that it was effectively (and equally) accommodating the athletic interests and abilities of students, particularly as the interests and abilities of women students developed.

While the basic considerations of equal opportunity remain, the final Policy Interpretation sets forth the factors that will be examined to determine an institution's actual, as opposed to presumed, compliance with Title IX in the area of intercollegiate athletics.

The final Policy Interpretation does not contain a separate section on institutions' future responsibilities. However, institutions remain obligated by the Title IX regulation to accommodate effectively the interests and abilities of male and female

---

[1] The regulation specifically refers to club sports separately from intercollegiate athletics. Accordingly, under this Policy Interpretation, club teams will not be considered to be intercollegiate teams except in those instances where they regularly participate in varsity competition.

students with regard to the selection of sports and levels of competition available. In most cases, this will entail development of athletic programs that substantially expand opportunities for women to participate and compete at all levels.

The major reasons for the change in approach are as follows:

(1) Institutions and representatives of athletic program participants expressed a need for more definitive guidance on what constituted compliance than the discussion of a presumption of compliance provided. Consequently the final Policy Interpretation explains the meaning of "equal athletic opportunity" in such a way as to facilities an assessment of compliance.

(2) Many comments reflected a serious misunderstanding of the presumption of compliance. Most institutions based objections to the proposed Policy Interpretation in part on the assumption that failure to provide compelling justifications for disparities in per capita expenditures would have automatically resulted in a finding of noncompliance. In fact, such a failure would only have deprived an institution of the benefit of the presumption that it was in compliance with the law. The Department would still have had the burden of demonstrating that the institution was actually engaged in unlawful discrimination. Since the purpose of issuing a policy interpretation was to clarify the regulation, the Department has determined that the approach of stating actual compliance factors would be more useful to all concerned.

(3) The Department has concluded that purely financial measures such as the per capita test do not in themselves offer conclusive documentation of discrimination, except where the benefit or opportunity under review, like a scholarship, is itself financial in nature. Consequently, in the final Policy Interpretation, the Department has detailed the factors to be considered in assessing actual compliance. While per capita breakdowns and other devices to examine expenditures patterns will be used as tools of analysis in the Department's investigative process, it is achievement of "equal opportunity" for which recipients are responsible and to which the final Policy Interpretation is addressed.

A description of the comments received, and other information/ obtained through the comment/ consultation process, with a description of Departmental action in response to the major points raised, is set forth at Appendix "B" to this document.

VI. Historic Patterns of Intercollegiate Athletics Program Development and Operations

In its proposed Policy Interpretation of December 11, 1978, the Department published a summary of historic patterns affecting the relative status of men's and women's athletic programs. The Department has modified that summary to reflect additional information obtained during the comment and consultation process. The summary is set forth at Appendix A to this document.

VII. The Policy Interpretation

This Policy Interpretation clarifies the obligations which recipients of Federal aid have under Title IX to provide equal opportunities in athletic programs. In particular, this Policy Interpretation provides a means to assess an institution's compliance with the equal opportunity requirements of the regulation which are set forth at 45 CFR 86.37(c) and 86.41(c).

A. Athletic Financial Assistance (Scholarships)

1. *The Regulation*—Section 86.37(c) of the regulation provides:

[Institutions] must provide reasonable opportunities for such award [of financial assistance] for members of each sex in proportion to the number of students of each sex participating in * * * inter-collegiate athletics.[2]

2. *The Policy*—The Department will examine compliance with this provision of the regulation primarily by means of a financial comparison to determine whether proportionately equal amounts of financial assistance (scholarship aid) are available to men's and women's athletic programs. The Department will measure compliance with this standard by dividing the amounts of aid available for the members of each sex by the numbers of male or female participants in the athletic program and comparing the results. Institutions may be found in compliance if this comparison results in substantially equal amounts or if a resulting disparity can be explained by adjustments to take into account legitimate, nondiscriminatory factors. Two such factors are:

a. At public institutions, the higher costs of tuition for students from out-of-state may in some years be unevenly distributed between men's and women's programs. These differences will be considered nondiscriminatory if they are not the result of policies or practices which disproportionately limit the

---

[2] See also § 86.37(a) of the regulation.

availability of out-of-state scholarships to either men or women.

b. An institution may make reasonable professional decisions concerning the awards most appropriate for program development. For example, team development initially may require spreading scholarships over as much as a full generation (four years) of student athletes. This may result in the award of fewer scholarships in the first few years than would be necessary to create proportionality between male and female athletes.

3. *Application of the Policy*—a. This section does not require a proportionate number of scholarships for men and women or individual scholarships of equal dollar value. It does mean that the total amount of scholarship aid made available to men and women must be substantially proportionate to their participation rates.

b. When financial assistance is provided in forms other than grants, the distribution of non-grant assistance will also be compared to determine whether equivalent benefits are proportionately available to male and female athletes. A disproportionate amount of work-related aid or loans in the assistance made available to the members of one sex, for example, could constitute a violation of Title IX.

4. *Definition*—For purposes of examining compliance with this Section, the participants will be defined as those athletes:

a. Who are receiving the institutionally-sponsored support normally provided to athletes competing at the institution involved, e.g., coaching, equipment, medical and training room services, on a regular basis during a sport's season; and

b. Who are participating in organized practice sessions and other team meetings and activities on a regular basis during a sport's season; and

c. Who are listed on the eligibility or squad lists maintained for each sport, or

d. Who, because of injury, cannot meet a, b, or c above but continue to receive financial aid on the basis of athletic ability.

B. Equivalence in Other Athletic Benefits and Opportunities

1. *The Regulation*—The Regulation requires that recipients that operate or sponsor interscholastic, intercollegiate, club, or intramural athletics, "provide equal athletic opportunities for members of both sexes." In determining whether an institution is providing equal opportunity in intercollegiate athletics, the regulation requires the Department

to consider, among others, the following factors:

(1) [3]

(2) Provision and maintenance of equipment and supplies;

(3) Scheduling of games and practice times;

(4) Travel and per diem expenses;

(5) Opportunity to receive coaching and academic tutoring;

(6) Assignment and compensation of coaches and tutors;

(7) Provision of locker rooms, practice and competitive facilities;

(8) Provision of medical and training services and facilities;

(9) Provision of housing and dining services and facilities; and

(10) Publicity

Section 86.41(c) also permits the Director of the Office for Civil Rights to consider other factors in the determination of equal opportunity. Accordingly, this Section also addresses recruitment of student athletes and provision of support services.

This list is not exhaustive. Under the regulation, it may be expanded as necessary at the discretion of the Director of the Office for Civil Rights. [4]

2. *The Policy*—The Department will assess compliance with both the recruitment and the general athletic program requirements of the regulation by comparing the availability, quality and kinds of benefits, opportunities, and treatment afforded members of both sexes. Institutions will be in compliance if the compared program components are equivalent, that is, equal or equal in effect. Under this standard, identical benefits, opportunities, or treatment are not required, provided the overall effect of any differences is negligible.

If comparisons of program components reveal that treatment, benefits, or opportunities are not equivalent in kind, quality or availability, a finding of compliance may still be justified if the differences are the result of nondiscriminatory factors. Some of the factors that may justify these differences are as follows:

a. Some aspects of athletic programs may not be equivalent for men and women because of unique aspects of particular sports or athletic activities. This type of distinction was called for by the "Javits' Amendment" [5] to Title IX, which instructed HEW to make

---

[3] 86.41(c) (1) on the accommodation of student interests and abilities, is covered in detail in the following Section C of this policy Interpretation.

[4] See also § 86.41(a) and (b) of the regulation.

[5] Section 844 of the Education Amendments of 1974, Pub. L. 93–380, Title VIII, (August 21, 1974) 88 Stat. 612.

"reasonable (regulatory) provisions considering the nature of particular sports" in intercollegiate athletics.

Generally, these differences will be the result of factors that are inherent to the basic operation of specific sports. Such factors may include rules of play, nature/replacement of equipment, rates of injury resulting from participation, nature of facilities required for competition, and the maintenance/upkeep requirements of those facilities. For the most part, differences involving such factors will occur in programs offering football, and consequently these differences will favor men. If sport-specific needs are met equivalently in both men's and women's programs, however, differences in particular program components will be found to be justifiable.

b. Some aspects of athletic programs may not be equivalent for men and women because of legitimately sex-neutral factors related to special circumstances of a temporary nature. For example, large disparities in recruitment activity for any particular year may be the result of annual fluctuations in team needs for first-year athletes. Such diferences are justifiable to the extent that they do not reduce overall equality of opportunity.

c. The activities directly associated with the operation of a competitive event in a single-sex sport may, under some circumstances, create unique demands or imbalances in particular program components. Provided any special demands associated with the activities of sports involving participants of the other sex are met to an equivalent degree, the resulting differences may be found nondiscriminatory. At many schools, for example, certain sports—notably football and men's basketball—traditionally draw large crowds. Since the costs of managing an athletic event increase with crowd size, the overall support made available for event management to men's and women's programs may differ in degree and kind. These differences would not violate Title IX if the recipient does not limit the potential for women's athletic events to rise in spectator appeal and if the levels of event management support available to both programs are based on sex-neutral criteria (e.g., facilities used, projected attendance, and staffing needs).

d. Some aspects of athletic programs may not be equivalent for men and women because institutions are undertaking voluntary affirmative actions to overcome effects of historical conditions that have limited participation in athletics by the members of one sex. This is authorized at § 86.3(b) of the regulation.

3. *Application of the Policy—General Athletic Program Components*—a. *Equipment and Supplies (§ 86.41(c)(2)).* Equipment and supplies include but are not limited to uniforms, other apparel, sport-specific equipment and supplies, general equipment and supplies, instructional devices, and conditioning and weight training equipment.

Compliance will be assessed by examining, among other factors, the equivalence for men and women of:

(1) The quality of equipment and supplies;

(2) The amount of equipment and supplies;

(3) The suitability of equipment and supplies;

(4) The maintenance and replacement of the equipment and supplies; and

(5) The availability of equipment and supplies.

b. *Scheduling of Games and Practice Times (§ 86.41(c)(3)).* Compliance will be assessed by examining, among other factors, the equivalence for men and women of:

(1) The number of competitive events per sport;

(2) The number and length of practice opportunities;

(3) The time of day competitive events are scheduled;

(4) The time of day practice opportunities are scheduled; and

(5) The opportunities to engage in available pre-season and post-season competition.

c. *Travel and Per Diem Allowances (§ 86.41(c)(4)).* Compliance will be assessed by examining, among other factors, the equivalence for men and women of:

(1) Modes of transportation;

(2) Housing furnished during travel;

(3) Length of stay before and after competitive events;

(4) Per diem allowances; and

(5) Dining arrangements.

d. *Opportunity to Receive Coaching and Academic Tutoring (§ 86.41(c)(5)).* (1) Coaching—Compliance will be assessed by examining, among other factors:

(a) Relative availability of full-time coaches;

(b) Relative availability of part-time and assistant coaches; and

(c) Relative availability of graduate assistants.

(2) Academic tutoring—Compliance will be assessed by examining, among other factors, the equivalence for men and women of:

(a) The availability of tutoring; and

(b) Procedures and criteria for obtaining tutorial assistance.

e. *Assignment and Compensation of Coaches and Tutors (§ 86.41(c)(6)).* [6] In general, a violation of Section 86.41(c)(6) will be found only where compensation or assignment policies or practices deny male and female athletes coaching of equivalent quality, nature, or availability.

Nondiscriminatory factors can affect the compensation of coaches. In determining whether differences are caused by permissible factors, the range and nature of duties, the experience of individual coaches, the number of participants for particular sports, the number of assistant coaches supervised, and the level of competition will be considered.

Where these or similar factors represent valid differences in skill, effort, responsibility or working conditions they may, in specific circumstances, justify differences in compensation. Similarly, there may be unique situations in which a particular person may possess such an outstanding record of achievement as to justify an abnormally high salary.

(1) Assignment of Coaches—Compliance will be assessed by examining, among other factors, the equivalence for men's and women's coaches of:

(a) Training, experience, and other professional qualifications;

(b) Professional standing.

(2) Assignment of Tutors—Compliance will be assessed by examining, among other factors, the equivalence for men's and women's tutors of:

(a) Tutor qualifications;

(b) Training, experience, and other qualifications.

(3) Compensation of Coaches—Compliance will be assessed by examining, among other factors, the equivalence for men's and women's coaches of:

(a) Rate of compensation (per sport, per season);

(b) Duration of contracts;

(c) Conditions relating to contract renewal;

(d) Experience;

(e) Nature of coaching duties performed;

(f) Working conditions; and

(g) Other terms and conditions of employment.

(4) Compensation of Tutors—Compliance will be assessed by examining, among other factors, the equivalence for men's and women's tutors of:

(a) Hourly rate of payment by nature of subjects tutored;

(b) Pupil loads per tutoring season;

(c) Tutor qualifications;

(d) Experience;

(e) Other terms and conditions of employment.

f. *Provision of Locker Rooms, Practice and Competitive Facilities (§ 86.41(c)(7)).* Compliance will be assessed by examining, among other factors, the equivalence for men and women of:

(1) Quality and availability of the facilities provided for practice and competitive events;

(2) Exclusivity of use of facilities provided for practice and competitive events;

(3) Availability of locker rooms;

(4) Quality of locker rooms;

(5) Maintenance of practice and competitive facilities; and

(6) Preparation of facilities for practice and competitive events.

g. *Provision of Medical and Training Facilities and Services (§ 86.41(c)(8)).* Compliance will be assessed by examining, among other factors, the equivalence for men and women of:

(1) Availability of medical personnel and assistance;

(2) Health, accident and injury insurance coverage;

(3) Availability and quality of weight and training facilities;

(4) Availability and quality of conditioning facilities; and

(5) Availability and qualifications of athletic trainers.

h. *Provision of Housing and Dining Facilities and Services (§ 86.41(c)(9)).* Compliance will be assessed by examining, among other factors, the equivalence for men and women of:

(1) Housing provided;

(2) Special services as part of housing arrangements (e.g., laundry facilities, parking space, maid service).

i. *Publicity (§ 86.41(c)(10)).* Compliance will be assessed by examining, among other factors, the equivalence for men and women of:

(1) Availability and quality of sports information personnel;

(2) Access to other publicity resources

---

[6] The Department's jurisdiction over the employment practices of recipients under Subpart E, §§ 86.51–86.61 of the Title IX regulation has been successfully challenged in several court cases. Accordingly, the Department has suspended enforcement of Subpart E. Section 86.41(c)(6) of the regulation, however, authorizes the Department to consider the compensation of coaches of men and women in the determination of the equality of athletic opportunity provided to male and female athletes. It is on this section of the regulation that this Policy Interpretation is based.

for men's and women's programs; and

(3) Quantity and quality of publications and other promotional devices featuring men's and women's programs.

4. *Application of the Policy—Other Factors (§ 86.41(c)).* a. *Recruitment of Student Athletes.*[7] The athletic recruitment practices of institutions often affect the overall provision of opportunity to male and female athletes. Accordingly, where equal athletic opportunities are not present for male and female students, compliance will be assessed by examining the recruitment practices of the athletic programs for both sexes to determine whether the provision of equal opportunity will require modification of those practices.

Such examinations will review the following factors:

(1) Whether coaches or other professional athletic personnel in the programs serving male and female athletes are provided with substantially equal opportunities to recruit;

(2) Whether the financial and other resources made available for recruitment in male and female athletic programs are equivalently adequate to meet the needs of each program; and

(3) Whether the differences in benefits, opportunities, and treatment afforded prospective student athletes of each sex have a disproportionately limiting effect upon the recruitment of students of either sex.

b. *Provision of Support Services.* The administrative and clerical support provided to an athletic program can affect the overall provision of opportunity to male and female athletes, particularly to the extent that the provided services enable coaches to perform better their coaching functions.

In the provision of support services, compliance will be assessed by examining, among other factors, the equivalence of:

(1) The amount of administrative assistance provided to men's and women's programs;

(2) The amount of secretarial and clerical assistance provided to men's

[7] Public undergraduate institutions are also subject to the general anti-discrimination provision at § 86.23 of the regulation, which reads in part:

"A recipient * * * shall not discriminate on the basis of sex in the recruitment and admission of students. A recipient may be required to undertake additional recruitment efforts for one sex as remedial action * * * and may choose to undertake such efforts as affirmative action * * *"

Accordingly, institutions subject to § 86.23 are required in all cases to maintain equivalently effective recruitment programs for both sexes and, under § 86.41(c), to provide equivalent benefits, opportunities, and treatment to student athletes of both sexes.

and women's programs.

5. *Overall Determination of Compliance.* The Department will base its compliance determination under § 86.41(c) of the regulation upon an examination of the following:

a. Whether the policies of an institution are discriminatory in language or effect; or

b. Whether disparities of a substantial and unjustified nature exist in the benefits, treatment, services, or opportunities afforded male and female athletes in the institution's program as a whole; or

c. Whether disparities in benefits, treatment, services, or opportunities in individual segments of the program are substantial enough in and of themselves to deny equality of athletic opportunity.

C. Effective Accommodation of Student Interests and Abilities.

1. *The Regulation.* The regulation requires institutions to accommodate effectively the interests and abilities of students to the extent necessary to provide equal opportunity in the selection of sports and levels of competition available to members of both sexes.

Specifically, the regulation, at § 86.41(c)(1), requires the Director to consider, when determining whether equal opportunities are available—

Whether the selection of sports and levels of competition effectively accommodate the interests and abilities of members of both sexes.

Section 86.41(c) also permits the Director of the Office for Civil Rights to consider other factors in the determination of equal opportunity. Accordingly, this section also addresses competitive opportunities in terms of the competitive team schedules available to athletes of both sexes.

2. *The Policy.* The Department will assess compliance with the interests and abilities section of the regulation by examining the following factors:

a. The determination of athletic interests and abilities of students;

b. The selection of sports offered; and

c. The levels of competition available including the opportunity for team competition.

3. *Application of the Policy— Determination of Athletic Interests and Abilities.*

Institutions may determine the athletic interests and abilities of students by nondiscriminatory methods of their choosing provided:

a. The processes take into account the nationally increasing levels of women's interests and abilities;

b. The methods of determining interest and ability do not disadvantage the members of an underrepresented sex;

c. The methods of determining ability take into account team performance records; and

d. The methods are responsive to the expressed interests of students capable of intercollegiate competition who are members of an underrepresented sex.

4. *Application of the Policy—Selection of Sports.*

In the selection of sports, the regulation does not require institutions to integrate their teams nor to provide exactly the same choice of sports to men and women. However, where an institution sponsors a team in a particular sport for members of one sex, it may be required either to permit the excluded sex to try out for the team or to sponsor a separate team for the previously excluded sex.

a. Contact Sports—Effective accommodation means that if an institution sponsors a team for members of one sex in a contact sport, it must do so for members of the other sex under the following circumstances:

(1) The opportunities for members of the excluded sex have historically been limited; and

(2) There is sufficient interest and ability among the members of the excluded sex to sustain a viable team and a reasonable expectation of intercollegiate competition for that team.

b. Non-Contact Sports—Effective accommodation means that if an institution sponsors a team for members of one sex in a non-contact sport, it must do so for members of the other sex under the following circumstances:

(1) The opportunities for members of the excluded sex have historically been limited;

(2) There is sufficient interest and ability among the members of the excluded sex to sustain a viable team and a reasonable expectation of intercollegiate competition for that team; and

(3) Members of the excluded sex do not possess sufficient skill to be selected for a single integrated team, or to compete actively on such a team if selected.

5. *Application of the Policy—Levels of Competition.*

In effectively accommodating the interests and abilities of male and female athletes, institutions must provide both the opportunity for individuals of each sex to participate in intercollegiate competition, and for athletes of each sex to have competitive team schedules which equally reflect their abilities.

a. Compliance will be assessed in any one of the following ways:

(1) Whether intercollegiate level participation opportunities for male and female students are provided in numbers substantially proportionate to their respective enrollments; or

(2) Where the members of one sex have been and are underrepresented among intercollegiate athletes, whether the institution can show a history and continuing practice of program expansion which is demonstrably responsive to the developing interest and abilities of the members of that sex; or

(3) Where the members of one sex are underrepresented among intercollegiate athletes, and the institution cannot show a continuing practice of program expansion such as that cited above, whether it can be demonstrated that the interests and abilities of the members of that sex have been fully and effectively accommodated by the present program.

b. Compliance with this provision of the regulation will also be assessed by examining the following:

(1) Whether the competitive schedules for men's and women's teams, on a program-wide basis, afford proportionally similar numbers of male and female athletes equivalently advanced competitive opportunities; or

(2) Whether the institution can demonstrate a history and continuing practice of upgrading the competitive opportunities available to the historically disadvantaged sex as warranted by developing abilities among the athletes of that sex.

c. Institutions are not required to upgrade teams to intercollegiate status or otherwise develop intercollegiate sports absent a reasonable expectation that intercollegiate competition in that sport will be available within the institution's normal competitive regions. Institutions may be required by the Title IX regulation to actively encourage the development of such competition, however, when overall athletic opportunities within that region have been historically limited for the members of one sex.

6. *Overall Determination of Compliance.*

The Department will base its compliance determination under § 86.41(c) of the regulation upon a determination of the following:

a. Whether the policies of an institution are discriminatory in language or effect; or

b. Whether disparities of a substantial and unjustified nature in the benefits, treatment, services, or opportunities afforded male and female athletes exist in the institution's program as a whole;

or

c. Whether disparities in individual segments of the program with respect to benefits, treatment, services, or opportunities are substantial enough in and of themselves to deny equality of athletic opportunity.

VIII. The Enforcement Process

The process of Title IX enforcement is set forth in § 86.71 of the Title IX regulation, which incorporates by reference the enforcement procedures applicable to Title VI of the Civil Rights Act of 1964.[8] The enforcement process prescribed by the regulation is supplemented by an order of the Federal District Court, District of Columbia, which establishes time frames for each of the enforcement steps.[9]

According to the regulation, there are two ways in which enforcement is initiated:

• *Compliance Reviews*—Periodically the Department must select a number of recipients (in this case, colleges and universities which operate intercollegiate athletic programs) and conduct investigations to determine whether recipients are complying with Title IX. (45 CFR 80.7(a))

• *Complaints*—The Department must investigate all valid (written and timely) complaints alleging discrimination on the basis of sex in a recipient's programs. (45 CFR 80.7(b))

The Department must inform the recipient (and the complainant, if applicable) of the results of its investigation. If the investigation indicates that a recipient is in compliance, the Department states this, and the case is closed. If the investigation indicates noncompliance, the Department outlines the violations found.

The Department has 90 days to conduct an investigation and inform the recipient of its findings, and an additional 90 days to resolve violations by obtaining a voluntary compliance agreement from the recipient. This is done through negotiations between the Department and the recipient, the goal of which is agreement on steps the recipient will take to achieve compliance. Sometimes the violation is relatively minor and can be corrected immediately. At other times, however, the negotiations result in a plan that will correct the violations within a specified period of time. To be acceptable, a plan must describe the manner in which institutional resources will be used to correct the violation. It also must state

acceptable time tables for reaching interim goals and full compliance. When agreement is reached, the Department notifies the institution that its plan is acceptable. The Department then is obligated to review periodically the implementation of the plan.

An institution that is in violation of Title IX may already be implementing a corrective plan. In this case, prior to informing the recipient about the results of its investigation, the Department will determine whether the plan is adequate. If the plan is not adequate to correct the violations (or to correct them within a reasonable period of time) the recipient will be found in noncompliance and voluntary negotiations will begin. However, if the institutional plan is acceptable, the Department will inform the institution that although the institution has violations, it is found to be in compliance because it is implementing a corrective plan. The Department, in this instance also, would monitor the progress of the institutional plan. If the institution subsequently does not completely implement its plan, it will be found in noncompliance.

When a recipient is found in noncompliance and voluntary compliance attempts are unsuccessful, the formal process leading to termination of Federal assistance will be begun. These procedures, which include the opportunity for a hearing before an administrative law judge, are set forth at 45 CFR 80.8–80.11 and 45 CFR Part 81.

IX. Authority

(Secs. 901, 902, Education Amendments of 1972, 86 Stat. 373, 374, 20 U.S.C. 1681, 1682; sec. 844, Education Amendments of 1974, Pub. L. 93–380, 88 Stat. 612; and 45 CFR Part 86)

Dated: December 3, 1979.

Roma Stewart,

Director, Office for Civil Rights, Department of Health, Education, and Welfare.

Dated: December 4, 1979.

Patricia Roberts Harris,

Secretary, Department of Health, Education, and Welfare.

Appendix A—Historic Patterns of Intercollegiate Athletics Program Development

1. Participation in intercollegiate sports has historically been emphasized for men but not women. Partially as a consequence of this, participation rates of women are far below those of men. During the 1977–78 academic year women students accounted for 48 percent of the national undergraduate enrollment (5,496,000 of 11,267,000

---

[8] Those procedures may be found at 45 CFR 80.6–80.11 and 45 CFR Part 81.

[9] *WEAL v. Harris,* Civil Action No. 74–1720 (D. D.C., December 29, 1977).

students).[1] Yet, only 30 percent of the intercollegiate athletes are women.[2]

The historic emphasis on men's intercollegiate athletic programs has also contributed to existing differences in the number of sports and scope of competition offered men and women. One source indicates that, on the average, colleges and universities are providing twice the number of sports for men as they are for women.[3]

2. Participation by women in sports is growing rapidly. During the period from 1971–1978, for example, the number of female participants in organized high school sports increased from 294,000 to 2,083,000—an increase of over 600 percent.[4] In contrast, between Fall 1971 and Fall 1977, the enrollment of females in high school decreased from approximately 7,600,000 to approximately 7,150,000 a decrease of over 5 percent.[5]

The growth in athletic participation by high school women has been reflected on the campuses of the nation's colleges and universities. During the period from 1971 to 1976 the enrollment of women in the nation's institutions of higher education rose 52 percent, from 3,400,000 to 5,201,000.[6] During this same period, the number of women participating in intramural sports increased 108 percent from 276,167 to 576,167. In club sports, the number of women participants increased from 16,386 to 25,541 or 55 percent. In intercollegiate sports, women's participation increased 102 percent from 31,852 to 64,375.[7] These developments reflect the growing interest of women in competitive athletics, as well as the efforts of colleges and universities to accommodate those interests.

3. The overall growth of women's intercollegiate programs has not been at the expense of men's programs. During the past decade of rapid growth in women's programs, the number of intercollegiate sports available for men has remained stable, and the number of male athletes has increased slightly. Funding for men's programs has increased from $1.2 to $2.2 million between 1970–1977 alone.[8]

4. On most campuses, the primary problem confronting women athletes is the absence of a fair and adequate level of resources, services, and benefits. For example, disproportionately more financial aid has been made available for male athletes than for female athletes. Presently, in institutions that are members of both the National Collegiate Athletic Association (NCAA) and the Association for Intercollegiate Athletics for Women (AIAW), the average annual scholarship budget is $39,000. Male athletes receive $32,000 or 78 percent of this amount, and female athletes receive $7,000 or 22 percent, although women are 30 percent of all the athletes eligible for scholarships.[9]

Likewise, substantial amounts have been provided for the recruitment of male athletes, but little funding has been made available for recruitment of female athletes.

Congressional testimony on Title IX and subsequent surveys indicates that discrepancies also exist in the opportunity to receive coaching and in other benefits and opportunities, such as the quality and amount of equipment, access to facilities and practice times, publicity, medical and training facilities, and housing and dining facilities.[10]

5. At several institutions, intercollegiate football is unique among sports. The size of the teams, the expense of the operation, and the revenue produced distinguish football from other sports, both men's and women's. Title IX requires that "an institution of higher education must comply with the prohibition against sex discrimination imposed by that title and its implementing regulations in the administration of any revenue producing

[1] *The Condition of Education 1979*, National Center for Education Statistics, p. 112.

[2] Figure obtained from Association for Intercollegiate Athletics for Women (AIAW) member survey, *AIAW Structure Implementation Survey Data Summary*, October 1978, p. 11.

[3] U.S. Commission on Civil Rights, Comments to DHEW on proposed Policy Interpretation; Analysis of data supplied by the National Association of Directors of Collegiate Athletics.

[4] Figures obtained from National Federation of High School Associations (NFHSA) data.

[5] *Digest of Education Statistics 1977–78*, National Center for Education Statistics (1978), Table 40, at 44. Data, by sex, are unavailable for the period from 1971 to 1977; consequently, these figures represent 50 percent of total enrollment for that period. This is the best comparison that could be made based on available data.

[6] Ibid. p. 112.

[7] These figures, which are not precisely comparable to those cited at footnote 2, were obtained from *Sports and Recreational Programs of the Nation's Universities and Colleges*, NCAA Report No. 5, March 1978. It includes figures only from the 722 NCAA member institutions because comparable data was not available from other associations.

[8] Compiled from NCAA *Revenues and Expenses for Intercollegiate Athletic Programs*, 1978.

[9] Figures obtained from *AIAW Structure Implementation Survey Data Summary*, October, 1978, p. 11.

[10] 121 Cong. REc. 29791–95 (1975) (remarks of Senator Williams); Comments by Senator Bayh, Hearings on S. 2106 Before the Subcommittee on Education of the Senate Committee on Labor and Public Welfare, 94th Congress, 1st Session 48 (1975) "Survey of Women's Athletic Directors," AIAW Workshop (January 1978).

intercollegiate athletic activity."[11] However, the unique size and cost of football programs have been taken into account in developing this Policy Interpretation.

Appendix B—Comments and Responses

The Office for Civil Rights (OCR) received over 700 comments and recommendations in response to the December 11, 1978 publication of the proposed Policy Interpretation. After the formal comment period, representatives of the Department met for additional discussions with many individuals and groups including college and university officials, athletic associations, athletic directors, women's rights organizations and other interested parties. HEW representatives also visited eight universities in order to assess the potential of the proposed Policy Interpretation and of suggested alternative approaches for effective enforcement of Title IX.

The Department carefully considered all information before preparing the final policy. Some changes in the structure and substance of the Policy Interpretation have been made as a result of concerns that were identified in the comment and consultation process.

Persons who responded to the request for public comment were asked to comment generally and also to respond specifically to eight questions that focused on different aspects of the proposed Policy Interpretation.

Question No. 1: Is the description of the current status and development of intercollegiate athletics for men and women accurate? What other factors should be considered?

Comment A: Some commentors noted that the description implied the presence of intent on the part of all universities to discriminate against women. Many of these same commentors noted an absence of concern in the proposed Policy Interpretation for those universities that have in good faith attempted to meet what they felt to be a vague compliance standard in the regulation.

Response: The description of the current status and development of intercollegiate athletics for men and women was designed to be a factual, historical overview. There was no intent to imply the universal presence of discrimination. The Department recognizes that there are many colleges and universities that have been and are making good faith efforts, in the midst of

---

[11] See April 18, 1979, Opinion of General Counsel, Department of Health, Education, and Welfare, page 1.

increasing financial pressures, to provide equal athletic opportunities to their male and female athletes.

Comment B: Commentors stated that the statistics used were outdated in some areas, incomplete in some areas, and inaccurate in some areas.

Response: Comment accepted. The statistics have been updated and corrected where necessary.

Question No. 2: Is the proposed two-stage approach to compliance practical? Should it be modified? Are there other approaches to be considered?

Comment: Some commentors stated that Part II of the proposed Policy Interpretation "Equally Accommodating the Interests and Abilities of Women" represented an extension of the July 1978, compliance deadline established in § 86.41(d) of the Title IX regulation.

Response: Part II of the proposed Policy Interpretation was not intended to extend the compliance deadline. The format of the two stage approach, however, seems to have encouraged that perception; therefore, the elements of both stages have been unified in this Policy Interpretation.

Question No. 3: Is the equal average per capita standard based on participation rates practical? Are there alternatives or modifications that should be considered?

Comment A: Some commentors stated it was unfair or illegal to find noncompliance solely on the basis of a financial test when more valid indicators of equality of opportunity exist.

Response: The equal average per capita standard was not a standard by which noncompliance could be found. It was offered as a standard of presumptive compliance. In order to prove noncompliance, HEW would have been required to show that the unexplained disparities in expenditures were discriminatory in effect. The standard, in part, was offered as a means of simplifying proof of compliance for universities. The widespread confusion concerning the significance of failure to satisfy the equal average per capita expenditure standard, however, is one of the reasons it was withdrawn.

Comment B: Many commentors stated that the equal average per capita standard penalizes those institutions that have increased participation opportunities for women and rewards institutions that have limited women's participation.

Response: Since equality of average per capita expenditures has been dropped as a standard of presumptive compliance, the question of its effect is no longer relevant. However, the Department agrees that universities that had increased participation opportunities for women and wished to take advantage of the presumptive compliance standard, would have had a bigger financial burden than universities that had done little to increase participation opportunities for women.

Question No. 4: Is there a basis for treating part of the expenses of a particular revenue producing sport differently because the sport produces income used by the university for non-athletic operating expenses on a non-discriminatory basis? If, so, how should such funds be identified and treated?

Comment: Commentors stated that this question was largely irrelevant because there were so few universities at which revenue from the athletic program was used in the university operating budget.

Response: Since equality of average per capita expenditures has been dropped as a standard of presumed compliance, a decision is no longer necessary on this issue.

Question No. 5: Is the grouping of financially measurable benefits into three categories practical? Are there alternatives that should be considered? Specifically, should recruiting expenses be considered together with all other financially measurable benefits?

Comment A: Most commentors stated that, if measured solely on a financial standard, recruiting should be grouped with the other financially measurable items. Some of these commentors held that at the current stage of development of women's intercollegiate athletics, the amount of money that would flow into the women's recruitment budget as a result of separate application of the equal average per capita standard to recruiting expenses, would make recruitment a disproportionately large percentage of the entire women's budget. Women's athletic directors, particularly, wanted the flexibility to have the money available for other uses, and they generally agreed on including recruitment expenses with the other financially measurable items.

Comment B: Some commentors stated that it was particularly inappropriate to base any measure of compliance in recruitment solely on financial expenditures. They stated that even if proportionate amounts of money were allocated to recruitment, major inequities could remain in the benefits to athletes. For instance, universities could maintain a policy of subsidizing visits to their campuses of prospective students of one sex but not the other. Commentors suggested that including an examination of differences in benefits to prospective athletes that result from recruiting methods would be appropriate.

Response: In the final Policy Interpretation, recruitment has been moved to the group of program areas to be examined under § 86.41(c) to determine whether overall equal athletic opportunity exists. The Department accepts the comment that a financial measure is not sufficient to determine whether equal opportunity is being provided. Therefore, in examining athletic recruitment, the Department will primarily review the opportunity to recruit, the resources provided for recruiting, and methods of recruiting.

Question No. 6: Are the factors used to justify differences in equal average per capita expenditures for financially measurable benefits and opportunities fair? Are there other factors that should be considered?

Comment: Most commentors indicated that the factors named in the proposed Policy Interpretation (the "scope of competition" and the "nature of the sport") as justifications for differences in equal average per capita expenditures were so vague and ambiguous as to be meaningless. Some stated that it would be impossible to define the phrase "scope of competition", given the greatly differing competitive structure of men's and women's programs. Other commentors were concerned that the "scope of competition" factor that may currently be designated as "non-discriminatory" was, in reality, the result of many years of inequitable treatment of women's athletic programs.

Response: The Department agrees that it would have been difficult to define clearly and then to quantify the "scope of competition" factor. Since equal average per capita expenditures has been dropped as a standard of presumed compliance, such financial justifications are no longer necessary. Under the equivalency standard, however, the "nature of the sport" remains an important concept. As explained within the Policy Interpretation, the unique nature of a sport may account for perceived inequities in some program areas.

Question No 7: Is the comparability standard for benefits and opportunities that are not financially measurably fair and realistic? Should other factors controlling comparability be included? Should the comparability standard be revised? Is there a different standard which should be considered?

Comment: Many commentors stated that the comparability standard was fair and realistic. Some commentors were concerned, however, that the standard was vague and subjective and could lead to uneven enforcement.

Response: The concept of comparing the non-financially measurable benefits and opportunities provided to male and female athletes has been preserved and expanded in the final Policy Interpretation to include all areas of examination except scholarships and accommodation of the interests and abilities of both sexes. The standard is that equivalent benefits and opportunities must be provided. To avoid vagueness and subjectivity, further guidance is given about what elements will be considered in each program area to determine the equivalency of benefits and opportunities.

Question No. 8: Is the proposal for increasing the opportunity for women to participate in competitive athletics appropriate and effective? Are there other procedures that should be considered? Is there a more effective way to ensure that the interest and abilities of both men and women are equally accommodated?

Comment: Several commentors indicated that the proposal to allow a university to gain the status of presumed compliance by having policies and procedures to encourage the growth of women's athletics was appropriate and effective for future students, but ignored students presently enrolled. They indicated that nowhere in the proposed Policy Interpretation was concern shown that the current selection of sports and levels of competition effectively accommodate the interests and abilities of women as well as men.

Response: Comment accepted. The requirement that universities equally accommodate the interests and abilities of their male and female athletes (Part II of the proposed Policy Interpretation) has been directly addressed and is now a part of the unified final Policy Interpretation.

Additional Comments

The following comments were not responses to questions raised in the proposed Policy Interpretation. They represent additional concerns expressed by a large number of commentors.

(1) *Comment:* Football and other "revenue producing" sports should be totally exempted or should receive special treatment under Title IX.

Response: The April 18, 1978, opinion of the General Counsel, HEW, concludes that "an institution of higher education must comply with the prohibition against sex discrimination imposed by that title and its implementing regulation in the administration of any revenue producing activity". Therefore, football or other "revenue producing" sports cannot be exempted from coverage of Title IX.

In developing the proposed Policy Interpretation the Department concluded that although the fact of revenue production could not justify disparity in average per capita expenditure between men and women, there were characteristics common to most revenue producing sports that could result in legitimate non-discriminatory differences in per capita expenditures. For instance, some "revenue producing" sports require expensive protective equipment and most require high expenditures for the management of events attended by large numbers of people. These characteristics and others described in the proposed Policy Interpretation were considered acceptable, non-discriminatory reasons for differences in per capita average expenditures.

In the final Policy Interpretation, under the equivalent benefits and opportunities standard of compliance, some of these non-discriminatory factors are still relevant and applicable.

(2) *Comment:* Commentors stated that since the equal average per capita standard of presumed compliance was based on participation rates, the word should be explicitly defined.

Response: Although the final Policy Interpretation does not use the equal average per capita standard of presumed compliance, a clear understanding of the word "participant" is still necessary, particularly in the determination of compliance where scholarships are involved. The word "participant" is defined in the final Policy Interpretation.

(3) *Comment:* Many commentors were concerned that the proposed Policy Interpretation neglected the rights of individuals.

Response: The proposed Policy Interpretation was intended to further clarify what colleges and universities must do within their intercollegiate athletic programs to avoid discrimination against individuals on the basis of sex. The Interpretation, therefore, spoke to institutions in terms of their male and female athletes. It spoke specifically in terms of equal, average per capita expenditures and in terms of comparability of other opportunities and benefits for male and female participating athletes.

The Department believes that under this approach the rights of individuals were protected. If women athletes, as a class, are receiving opportunities and benefits equal to those of male athletes, individuals within the class should be protected thereby. Under the proposed Policy Interpretation, for example, if female athletes as a whole were receiving their proportional share of athletic financial assistance, a university would have been presumed in compliance with that section of the regulation. The Department does not want and does not have the authority to force universities to offer identical programs to men and women. Therefore, to allow flexibility within women's programs and within men's programs, the proposed Policy Interpretation stated that an institution would be presumed in compliance if the average per capita expenditures on athletic scholarships for men and women, were equal. This same flexibility (in scholarships and in other areas) remains in the final Policy Interpretation.

(4) *Comment:* Several commentors stated that the provision of a separate dormitory to athletes of only one sex, even where no other special benefits were involved, is inherently discriminatory. They felt such separation indicated the different degrees of importance attached to athletes on the basis of sex.

Response: Comment accepted. The provision of a separate dormitory to athletes of one sex but not the other will be considered a failure to provide equivalent benefits as required by the regulation.

(5) *Comment:* Commentors, particularly colleges and universities, expressed concern that the differences in the rules of intercollegiate athletic associations could result in unequal distribution of benefits and opportunities to men's and women's athletic programs, thus placing the institutions in a posture of noncompliance with Title IX.

Response: Commentors made this point with regard to § 86.6(c) of the Title IX regulation, which reads in part:

"The obligation to comply with (Title IX) is not obviated or alleviated by any rule or regulation of any * * * athletic or other * * * association * * *"

Since the penalties for violation of intercollegiate athletic association rules can have a severe effect on the athletic opportunities within an affected program, the Department has re-examined this regulatory requirement to determine whether it should be modified. Our conclusion is that modification would not have a beneficial effect, and that the present requirement will stand.

Several factors enter into this decision. First, the differences between rules affecting men's and women's programs are numerous and change constantly. Despite this, the Department has been unable to discover a single case in which those differences require members to act in a discriminatory manner. Second, some rule differences may permit decisions resulting in discriminatory distribution of benefits and opportunities to men's and women's programs. The fact that institutions respond to differences in rules by choosing to deny equal opportunities, however, does not mean that the rules themselves are at fault; the rules do not prohibit choices that would result in compliance with Title IX. Finally, the rules in 'question are all established and subject to change by the membership of the association. Since all (or virtually all) association member institutions are subject to Title IX, the opportunity exists for these institutions to resolve collectively any wide-spread Title IX compliance problems resulting from association rules. To the extent that this has not taken place, Federal intervention on behalf of statutory beneficiaries is both warranted and required by the law. Consequently, the Department can follow no course other than to continue to disallow any defenses against findings of noncompliance with Title IX that are based on intercollegiate athletic association rules.

(6) *Comment:* Some commentors suggested that the equal average per capita test was unfairly skewed by the high cost of some "major" men's sports, particularly football, that have no equivalently expensive counterpart among women's sports. They suggested that a certain percentage of those costs (e.g., 50% of football scholarships) should be excluded from the expenditures on male athletes prior to application of the equal average per capita test.

Response: Since equality of average per capita expenditures has been eliminated as a standard of presumed compliance, the suggestion is no longer relevant. However, it was possible under that standard to exclude expenditures that were due to the nature of the sport, or the scope of competition and thus were not discriminatory in effect. Given the diversity of intercollegiate athletic programs, determinations as to whether disparities in expenditures were nondiscriminatory would have been made on a case-by-case basis. There was no legal support for the proposition that an arbitrary percentage of expenditures should be excluded from the calculations.

(7) *Comment:* Some commentors urged the Department to adopt various forms of team-based comparisons in assessing equality of opportunity between men's and women's athletic programs. They stated that well-developed men's programs are frequently characterized by a few "major" teams that have the greatest spectator appeal, earn the greatest income, cost the most to operate, and dominate the program in other ways. They suggested that women's programs should be similarly constructed and that comparability should then be required only between "men's major" and "women's major" teams, and between "men's minor" and "women's minor" teams. The men's teams most often cited as appropriate for "major" designation have been football and basketball, with women's basketball and volleyball being frequently selected as the counterparts.

Response: There are two problems with this approach to assessing equal opportunity. First, neither the statute nor the regulation calls for identical programs for male and female athletes. Absent such a requirement, the Department cannot base noncompliance upon a failure to provide arbitrarily identical programs, either in whole or in part.

Second, no subgrouping of male or female students (such as a team) may be used in such a way as to diminish the protection of the larger class of males and females in their rights to equal participation in educational benefits or opportunities. Use of the "major/minor" classification does not meet this test where large participation sports (e.g., football) are compared to smaller ones (e.g., women's volleyball) in such a manner as to have the effect of disproportionately providing benefits or opportunities to the members of one sex.

(8) *Comment:* Some commenters suggest that equality of opportunity should be measured by a "sport-specific" comparison. Under this approach, institutions offering the same sports to men and women would have an obligation to provide equal opportunity within each of those sports. For example, the men's basketball team and the women's basketball team would have to receive equal opportunities and benefits.

Response: As noted above, there is no provision for the requirement of identical programs for men and women, and no such requirement will be made by the Department. Moreover, a sport-specific comparison could actually create unequal opportunity. For example, the sports available for men at an institution might include most or all of those available for women; but the men's program might concentrate resources on sports not available to women (e.g., football, ice hockey). In addition, the sport-specific concept overlooks two key elements of the Title IX regulation.

First, the regulation states that the selection of sports is to be representative of student interests and abilities (86.41(c)(1)). A requirement that sports for the members of one sex be available or developed solely on the basis of their existence or development in the program for members of the other sex could conflict with the regulation where the interests and abilities of male and female students diverge.

Second, the regulation frames the general compliance obligations of recipients in terms of program-wide benefits and opportunities (86.41(c)). As implied above, Title IX protects the individual as a student-athlete, not as a basketball player, or swimmer.

(9) *Comment:* A coalition of many colleges and universities urged that there are no objective standards against which compliance with Title IX in intecollegiate athletics could be measured. They felt that diversity is so great among colleges and universities that no single standard or set of standards could practicably apply to all affected institutions. They concluded that it would be best for individual institutions to determine the policies and procedures by which to ensure nondiscrimination in intercollegiate athletic programs.

Specifically, this coalition suggested that each institution should create a group representative of all affected parties on campus.

This group would then assess existing athletic opportunities for men and women, and, on the basis of the assessment, develop a plan to ensure nondiscrimination. This plan would then be recommended to the Board of Trustees or other appropriate governing body.

The role foreseen for the Department under this concept is:

(a) The Department would use the plan as a framework for evaluating complaints and assessing compliance;

(b) The Department would determine whether the plan satisfies the interests of the involved parties; and

(c) The Department would determine whether the institution is adhering to the plan.

These commenters felt that this approach to Title IX enforcement would ensure an environment of equal opportunity.

Response: Title IX is an anti-discrimination law. It prohibits discrimination based on sex in educational institutions that are recipients of Federal assistance. The legislative history of Title IX clearly shows that it was enacted because of discrimination that currently was being practiced against women in educational institutions. The Department accepts that colleges and universities are sincere in their intention to ensure equal opportunity in intercollegiate athletics to their male and female students. It cannot, however, turn over its reponsibility for interpreting and enforcing the law. In this case, its responsibility includes articulating the standards by which compliance with the Title IX statute will be evaluated.

The Department agrees with this group of commenters that the proposed self-assessment and institutional plan is an excellent idea. Any institution that engages in the assessment/planning process, particularly with the full participation of interested parties as envisioned in the proposal, would clearly reach or move well toward compliance. In addition, as explained in Section VIII of this Policy Interpretation, any college or university that has compliance problems but is implementing a plan that the Department determines will correct those problems within a reasonable period of time, will be found in compliance.

[FR Doc. 79-37965 Filed 12-10-79; 8:45 am]

BILLING CODE 4110-12-M

Appendix M

Protective Strategies for Change-Makers

Dr. Billye Ann Cheatum

It's about as safe for a college staff member to work for sex equity in athletics as it would be for a spectator to lurch onto a football field and stumble into the path of a defensive tackle.

When women employed by colleges and universities challenge long-standing practices and policies of male-dominated administrative and athletic systems, the women (and their supporters) often suffer irreparable political and career damage.

But women who want to work toward sex equity and still keep their jobs can address their dilemma by developing a system of protective strategies.

Before developing strategies, however, would-be changemakers have to scout and map the territory. Generally, the school Title IX or Affirmative Action Officer will be the focus of carefully considered actions.

Therefore, questions worth considering when devising strategy and then reconsidering before taking any specific action, include:

- To whom is the institution's Title IX or Affirmative Action Officer responsible?

- Is the Title IX or Affirmative Action Officer in a position to effectively change discriminatory practices or procedures?

- What political recourse is available when there seems to be inaction on the part of the Title IX or Affirmative Action Officer?

- What was the disposition of past grievances filed against the institution? Was there a difference in the disposition of past grievances filed with or without legal assistance?

- Are policies, practices and procedures for administration, faculty and staff the same?

To avoid having careers used as hockey pucks, two kinds of strategies are needed: (1) strategies for effecting the change, and (2) strategies for protecting employees and students working for the change. Sometimes these strategies overlap.

Formation of a Central Committee

Basic to both change and protection of changemakers is the formation of a "Title IX Advisory Committee." This is a vehicle for developing a network of informed supporters who can provide genuine service to an overburdened Affirmative Action Officer and/or official Affirmative Action Coordinating Committee, while protecting network members from the political repercussions that often are the result of working to bring about non-sexist education.

The duties of the Title IX Advisory Committee should not duplicate those of an already existing Affirmative Action Coordinating Committee or an Affirmative Action Officer. The following suggested activities can be proposed to an Affirmative Action Office for approval:

- Help establish time lines for implementation of Title IX and oversee compliance with the guidelines.

- Inform staff, faculty, and students of their rights under Title IX as groups and individuals.

- Advise the Title IX Officer on grievance procedures.

- Support individual grievants.

Protective Strategies for the Title IX Advisory Committee - As a Whole

The next step by the Title IX Advisory Committee is to initiate strategy to protect the committee as a whole by touching all political bases, developing broad support, and setting up procedures to thoroughly educate the committee about regulations that have an impact on sex equity matters.

- Request a letter from the Affirmative Action Officer confirming formation of the Title IX Advisory Committee and setting forth the objectives of the committee.

- Meet with the Affirmative Action Coordinating Committee to assure them that the Title IX Advisory Committee has no intention of usurping their role, but plans to concentrate on concerns of women and to relay information on problems and violations to the Affirmative Action Officer who chairs their committee.

- Solicit committee members from all levels of the university including students, faculty, staff, and administration, as well as from each college within the university and organizations which support equity for women.

- Divide the tasks governing equity for women such as Title IX, Title VII, Title VI, AIAW rules, NCAA rules and grievance procedures (both on campus and those involving federal laws) among committee members.

- Avoid negative reactions to criticisms made by the committee by carefully documenting each area of noncompliance. The committee must:

  - have accurate knowledge of federal regulations;

  - interpret regulations correctly (calling Washington and/or the state Title IX officer when necessary);

  - avoid supporting unfounded grievances or making judgements that could be used to discredit any future action of the committee.

- Make an effort in the second year of operation to enlarge the basic committee and gain additional campus-wide influence by:

  - obtaining male supporters as members of the committee;

  - selecting new personnel based upon specific talents such as research techniques, computer skills and writing ability for publications, newsletters and news articles;

- gaining membership and support from influential organizations on campus such as: AAUP, Faculty Senate, Women's Commission, Athletic Board, athletic sub-committees, and Affirmative Action Coordinating Committee;

- joining other organizations on campus and sharing mutual concerns.

Protective Strategies for the Title IX Advisory Committee - As Individuals

In order to minimize career risk for faculty and staff members of the Title IX Advisory Committee, certain precautions should be built into the committee procedures. The committee should be able to take the initiative and to react to sex discrimination without individual committee members being subjected to career risk. The following procedures are suggested:

- Omit from the membership list, names of faculty members who do not yet have tenure.

- Avoid designating one person as Chair of the Advisory Committee so that no one individual is held accountable for activities of the total committee.

- Approve all communications at weekly meetings or in the case of an emergency by a consensus of several members.

- Designate two committee members with political savvy and letter writing ability to compose most of the official letters.

- Sign official letters as "Title IX Advisory Committee" so that specific individuals are not pressured by the administration.

- Send xerox copies of all communications to each member of the Title IX Advisory Committee as soon as or before letters are mailed to the recipient.

- Keep Title IX Committee members who serve on other committees informed of any action that affects their committee. (For example, if a member of the Title IX Committee serves on the Athletic Board and a coaching position is filled without posting requirements, the action can be questioned at the next Athletic Board meeting. If immediate action is essential, the political route then involves contacting the Affirmative Action Coordinating Committee or Officer, who makes official inquiry.)

Protection of Communication

In order to make certain that correspondence reaches its intended audience and is not misinterpreted, a system of dating, xeroxing, sending carbon copies and filing letters should be set up. In addition, in order to be able to document telephone conversations, a system of logging phone calls and following telephone communication with written confirmation should be devised. The committee needs to:

- Forward letters to each member of specific committees to assure that the full committee and not just the Chair is reached.

- Make certain each letter is dated, and note whether the letter was sent to the committee Chair or to each committee member and to whom carbon copies have been sent.

- Forward carbon copies of responses to those administrative officials who have received copies of any letter sent to the Title IX Committee.

- Refer to dates of previous communications when seeking information from persons who fail to respond to letters requesting data.

- Notify people concerned, such as the Women's Athletic Director, when letters of inquiry are sent to federal agencies.

- Keep a log of telephone calls and information received.

- Follow verbal agreements made on the telephone or in private conferences with written confirmation.

- Prevent distortion of letters written by the Title IX Committee by requesting copies of the letters for each member of any committee scheduled to discuss the communication.

- Prevent distortion of actions and rules within other states, institutions and organizations by calling the organization or institution and requesting written information, or clarification of the data.

- Maintain two central notebooks which include all minutes, letters and documents received or sent, actions taken and/or recommendations made by the committee, organized chronologically. For the purpose of annual reports and follow-up letters, a second notebook should be organized by issue or topic.

- Xerox copies of all significant material for each member of the committee.

Protection by External Support

External support systems are an excellent way to protect the work of the entire committee and its members.

- Cooperate with your state Title IX Coordinator in the development of a state-wide post-secondary organization to review processes for the elimination of discrimination under Title IX and Affirmative Action.

- Obtain support from other state organizations by attending meetings or working with members of organizations such as the committee on the status of women of AAUP, women's commissions, WEAL, NOW, and coalition groups.

- Maintain contact with attorneys within the state who have successfully represented girls and women in discrimination cases.

- Make certain that all news items referring to Title IX are accurate. (One committee member should work with news reporters keeping them informed of various actions within the committee and the University as a whole.)

Meeting Place and Time

Seek additional protection by exercising care in choosing a meeting time and place, and by promptly delivering minutes of meetings to all involved.

- Select sites for meetings and workshops based not only upon the support provided by the particular department or unit, but also by the vulnerability of the faculty and the administrative personnel of that unit (be it a church, women's center or department) to pressures from other administrators or sources within the university.

- Experiment with meetings scheduled twice a month and weekly. Short weekly meetings can serve to keep each other informed of campus-wide activities.

- Type, xerox, and mail minutes to committee members the day of the meeting.

There is no way to guarantee results of safety for those who are involved in working toward sex equity in education. But there is no need to "go it alone" either, or to venture into the fray un-protected. No running back heads toward a goal line without the rest of the team helping, nor does a hockey goalie guard the nets without protective equipment. When you score, you want to survive to enjoy the victory.

Appendix N

Sample Letter for Filing a Title IX Complaint

_____, Director

Office for Civil Rights, Region _____

U.S. Department of Health, Education and Welfare

Address for your region

Dear _____:

   I am/We are filing a complaint of sex discrimination under Title IX of the Education Amendments of 1972 against *name and address of school district, college or other institution receiving federal education aid.*

   The next paragraph should explain what person or group of people you believe is being discriminated against. You need only identify them generally—"the girls in sixth grade gym classes," for example—unless it's just one or two people who have been victims of specific acts of discrimination. In that case it would be helpful to give HEW their names and addresses, though it is not required.

   Follow this with as complete a description of the sex discrimination as you can. Make sure to tell what happened, when it happened and if the discrimination is still going on. Attach any evidence you may have which supports the complaint, such as letters, student handbooks, and so on. Name any people you think were responsible for the discrimination and their position in the school.

   The following people have agreed to provide further information to your staff. *Here, list the people willing to talk to HEW. Explain how they can provide valuable information relating to your complaint, and tell HEW where they can be reached. If their names must be kept confidential, note this as well.*

   I/We ask that you investigate this complaint immediately and notify me/us when the investigation will begin. Please keep me/us advised of the status of the investigation. And please send me/us a copy of your findings as soon as they are sent to *name of school district or college.* In addition, please send me/us copies of all correspondence with *name of institution.*

                    Sincerely,

                    Name

                    Address

                    *Daytime phone number, unless you prefer not to
                    receive calls about the complaint at work.*

If you are sending copies of your complaint to other persons, list them below. For example:

cc: *School Board*
     Senators
     Members of Congress
     Governor
     State Legislators
     Local Organizations
     National Organizations
     Newspapers
     PEER

                                        Anyone's Guide to Filing a Title IX Complaint

Filing a Title IX Complaint

REGION I: Connecticut, Maine, Massachusetts, New Hampshire, Rhode Island, Vermont
John G. Bynoe, Director
Office for Civil Rights, DHEW
140 Federal St., 14th Floor
Boston, Mass. 02110
(617) 223-6397

REGION II: New Jersey, New York, Puerto Rico, Virgin Islands
William R. Valentine, Acting Director
Office for Civil Rights, DHEW
Room 33-130
26 Federal Plaza
New York, N.Y. 10007
(212) 264-4633

REGION III: Delaware, Maryland, Pennsylvania, Virginia, Washington, D.C., West Virginia
Dewey Dodds, Director
Office for Civil Rights, DHEW
3535 Market St., P.O. Box 13716
Philadelphia, Pa. 19101
(215) 596-6771

REGION IV: Alabama, Florida, Georgia, Kentucky, Mississippi, North Carolina, South Carolina, Tennessee
William Thomas, Director
Office for Civil Rights, DHEW
101 Marietta St., N.W.
Atlanta, Ga. 30323
(404) 221-2954

REGION V:
Illinois, Minnesota, Wisconsin
Kenneth A. Mines, Director
Office for Civil Rights, DHEW
300 South Wacker Dr., 8th Floor
Chicago, Ill. 60606
(312) 353-2520

Michigan, Ohio, Indiana
Ortha Barr, Chief, Elementary and Secondary Education*
Office for Civil Rights, DHEW
55 Erieview Plaza, Room 222
Cleveland, Ohio 44114
(216) 522-4970

REGION VI: Arkansas, Louisiana, New Mexico, Oklahoma, Texas
Dorothy Stuck, Director
Office for Civil Rights, DHEW
1200 Main Tower Building, 19th Floor
Dallas, Texas 75202
(214) 767-3951

REGION VII: Iowa, Kansas, Missouri, Nebraska
Taylor D. August, Director
Office for Civil Rights, DHEW
1150 Grand Ave., 7th Floor
Kansas City, Mo. 64106
(816) 374-2474

REGION VIII: Colorado, Montana, North Dakota, South Dakota, Utah, Wyoming
Gilbert D. Roman, Director
Office for Civil Rights, DHEW
1961 Stout St.
Denver, Co. 80294
(303) 837-2025

REGION IX: Arizona, California, Hawaii, Nevada
Floyd L. Pierce, Director
Office for Civil Rights, DHEW
100 Van Ness Ave., 14th Floor
San Francisco, Ca. 94102
(415) 556-8586

REGION X: Alaska, Idaho, Oregon, Washington
Marlaina Kiner, Director
Office for Civil Rights, DHEW
1321 Second Ave.
M/S 508
Seattle, Washington 98101
(206) 442-0473

*Please note: The Cleveland office handles complaints against elementary and secondary schools only. Complaints against colleges and universities anywhere in Region V should be addressed to Kenneth Mines in the Chicago office.

Index

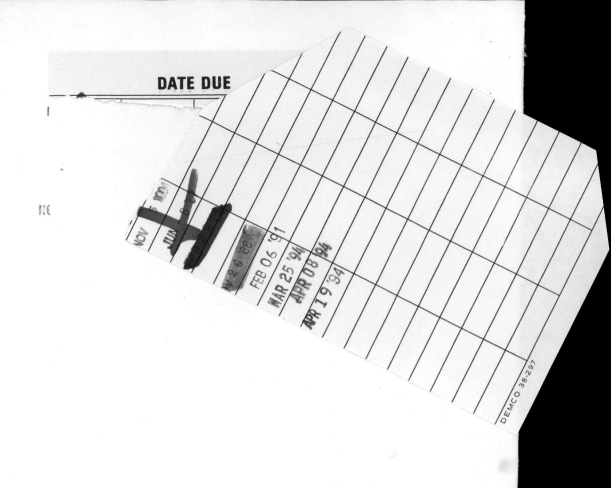